THE LAW

OF

EVIDENCE

First Edition

This casebook is intended for use as part of an Evidence course in an American law school. It integrates case excerpts, scholarly commentary, and problems to encourage an interactive approach to both doctrine and theory.

© 2020 Jeffrey Bellin

THE LAW OF EVIDENCE

by Jeffrey Bellin

A trial reconstructs a narrative of past events for a neutral factfinder under the scrutiny of keenly interested parties. The Law of Evidence is a rough shorthand for the rules that govern the flow of information about the case -- "evidence" -- to the factfinder during this proceeding. The primary sources of this law are evidence codes promulgated by the various legal jurisdictions.

Evidence rules apply in the civil and criminal context, to trials before judges and juries. The rules can also apply in less formal proceedings, although proceedings like preliminary hearings or sentencings typically employ more permissive and ad hoc rules than those governing trials.

Constitutions are another source of evidence law. The United States Supreme Court interprets various provisions of the federal Constitution to prohibit certain evidence and require the admission of other evidence. These constitutional provisions apply in state as well as federal proceedings, making them an important component of the Law of Evidence.

This book explores the Law of Evidence in the United States, focusing on the most difficult and important admissibility questions. The overarching goals are to (1) explain what evidence can be properly introduced (or excluded), and (2) offer a methodology for finding these answers in the wide variety of scenarios that arise in litigation. For the most part, the book does not delve into tactics or the precise mechanics of introducing and objecting to evidence. As a former litigator, I can attest that the best way to learn those topics is through experience. By contrast, the substance of the law of evidence can be learned in law school -- and that knowledge, which is not as widespread as it should be, provides a distinct real-world advantage. The Law of Evidence determines what the jury hears at trial and it is evidence, more than anything else, that changes outcomes.

A note on the format. The book is designed to maximize readability. There is much to cover, but time is a precious commodity and no one's eyesight improves from reading. I ruthlessly edit court opinions and other excerpts to keep the focus on key evidentiary points. I leave out the clunky internal citations that clutter legal writing, sparsely employing a skeletal citation format.

Curious readers will still be able to find the referenced sources, but the book is designed to be read not cite checked. Citations that include only a case name and year refer to opinions of the Supreme Court. The book relies heavily on problems, particularly for the most difficult concepts. It also leaves space for instructors to supplement the book with their own unique perspectives, alongside interactive exercises, clips, and vignettes.

An exciting journey lies ahead. Welcome to #TeamEvidence!

© 2020 Jeffrey Bellin
Professor, William & Mary Law School
Williamsburg, Virginia

ISBN: 979-8-65295-807-7
LCCN: 2020910886

Table of Contents

Chapter 1

Chapter 2

Chapter 3

Chapter 4

Table of Contents

Chapter 5

Chapter 6

Table of Contents

Chapter 7

Chapter 8

Chapter 9

Table of Contents

Chapter 10

INTRODUCTION

THE INFLUENCE OF THE FEDERAL RULES

Like virtually all Evidence casebooks used in American law schools, this book is organized around the Federal Rules of Evidence. As a technical matter, the federal rules were written to govern proceedings in federal court. By happy coincidence, "the influence of the Federal Rules of Evidence was much wider; forty-five states and Puerto Rico have all adopted or modeled their own rules on the Federal Rules of Evidence."[1]

Even in the few states that have not adopted the federal model, the evidence rules generally parallel the Federal Rules of Evidence. There are three reasons for this.

(1) State and federal evidence rules are based on the same common law heritage.

(2) The few states (like California) that codified their evidence rules prior to the creation of the federal rules influenced the drafters of the federal rules.

(3) The runaway success of the federal rules in law schools, case law, and commentary, influences the rules even in jurisdictions that continue to resist adoption. As those (dwindling) jurisdictions amend and interpret their rules, they increasingly conform to the federal model.

The success of the federal rules in standardizing American evidence law makes those rules the ideal backbone for an Evidence course. The federal rules offer a framework for exploring the concepts and theories underlying evidence law, while also providing important practical lessons that students can take with them into legal practice in any jurisdiction. All of that said, it is important to remember that there is variation among jurisdictions, both in the rules themselves and the case law interpreting those rules. The book will identify some of that variation to highlight the important policy choices available to

---

[1] Bennett Capers, Evidence Without Rules, 94 Notre Dame L. Rev. 867 (2018).

evidence policymakers. But these examples are meant to illustrate not catalogue the variation.

The Origins of the Federal Rules of Evidence

At the outset, it is helpful to understand how the Federal Rules of Evidence came into being. The Reporter to the Advisory Committee that drafted the rules, Professor Edward Cleary, provided the following description of American evidence law prior to the federal rules:

> The legal background against which the Rules were drafted and enacted was a vast collection of common law precedents. True, occasional jurisdictions had enacted codes, and some parts of evidence law, e.g., privilege and competency of witnesses, were largely statutory almost everywhere, but in the main the generalization held. This rather formless body of case law attracted much faithful and perhaps uncritical adherence from among the legal profession, partly because it had been evolved by the internal processes of the legal profession itself, and partly because it comprised one of its familiar basic tools.[1]

How did practitioners work with this "formless body of case law"? Some of the most prominent scholars of the pre-Rules era, such as John Henry Wigmore, published treatises on the law of evidence that chronicled the rules worked out by the courts. A lawyer arguing an evidence point in an American court referred not to any code of evidence, but to treatise authors like Wigmore as persuasive authority.

The Federal Rules of Evidence sought to replace this unsatisfying state of affairs by setting forth clear and considered evidence rules that could be swiftly consulted and consistently applied. An Advisory Committee of prominent practitioners, judges, and scholars drafted the rules, and sent them to the Supreme Court. The Court then transmitted the rules to Congress. Both the House of Representatives and the Senate grappled extensively with the rules, amending some and rejecting others. At the conclusion of that deliberation, Congress enacted the rules as amended. The project is generally considered a success.

---

[1] Preliminary Notes on Reading the Rules of Evidence, 57 Neb. L. Rev. 908 (1978).

The rules themselves provide most of the answers to evidentiary questions, and almost always offer the best starting point for the inquiry. For example, the rules provide a precise answer to the question alluded to in the preface, about the proceedings to which the rules apply. Federal Rule of Evidence 1101(b) and (d) states:

> These rules apply in:
>
> > · civil cases and proceedings, including bankruptcy, admiralty, and maritime cases;
> >
> > · criminal cases and proceedings; and
> >
> > · contempt proceedings, except those in which the court may act summarily.
>
> These rules — except for those on privilege — do not apply to the following:
>
> > (1) the court's determination, under Rule 104(a), on a preliminary question of fact governing admissibility;
> >
> > (2) grand-jury proceedings; and
> >
> > (3) miscellaneous proceedings such as:
> >
> > > · extradition or rendition;
> > >
> > > · issuing an arrest warrant, criminal summons, or search warrant;
> > >
> > > · a preliminary examination in a criminal case;
> > >
> > > · sentencing;
> > >
> > > · granting or revoking probation or supervised release; and
> > >
> > > · considering whether to release on bail or otherwise.

ARE THE RULES REALLY RULES?

Yes. But it is important to see why this is a question worth asking. The enactment of the Federal Rules of Evidence in 1975 was a radical change. In the absence of codified evidence rules, judges had great freedom to apply and mold amorphous common law evidence principles to the circumstances of each case and ruling. As the next excerpt from a prominent treatise explains, the federal rules greatly circumscribed that freedom:

Soon after Congress enacted the Federal Rules of Evidence, Edward Cleary, the Reporter and principal drafter of the rules, received an inquiry from a federal appeals court judge asking about the degree to which the seemingly concrete rules might actually have "some play in the joints."

Federal judges were, after all, used to a common law of evidence that permitted great flexibility, particularly for appellate judges whose rulings were rarely reviewed. Under the pre-Rules, common law approach, each application of evidentiary principles could be adopted and melded to the then-presented scenario…. It is little wonder, then, that Cleary's correspondent incredulously pondered how the slim pamphlet of rules could ever replace his "ten volumes of Wigmore" on the common law of evidence. The common law evidence rules, in short, allowed enterprising judges a great deal of play in the joints and many judges were, no doubt, reluctant to say goodbye to such wonderfully flexible rules.

In response to the inquiring judge, Cleary published an essay explaining that judging under the federal rules would be a different experience from the one judges had grown used to. The Rules did not, Cleary responded, have "play in the joints" and no longer encouraged "creativity on the part of judges." Cleary explained that Congress would never have approved an evidence system as flexible as the common law. Instead, under the new system, answers to evidentiary questions would be found in the rules themselves, interpreted according to "general principles of statutory construction." In another publication, Cleary similarly explained that the rules are, "in the final analysis legislative in nature, and problems of their effect are problems of statutory interpretation." Cleary's point made logical sense. The Federal Rules of Evidence were drafted by a committee of eminent practitioners, judges, and scholars under the auspices of the Supreme Court. The Court forwarded the proposed rules to Congress. After careful study, Congress enacted the rules, often in amended form. President Ford signed them into law. The rules looked a lot like statutes. Cleary thought they should be treated as such.

Cleary's view of the proper interpretation of the rules has largely won the day. As one prominent commentator explains:

> The Federal Rules of Evidence became law as a result of a process that concluded with legislation, and perhaps not surprisingly, the Supreme Court has treated the Rules as a statute subject to an analysis which commences with the stated objective of discerning legislative intent.[1]

Further, there is no suggestion in the pertinent authorities that after the passage of the rules, the federal common law of evidence survives in any form. Rather, as the Supreme Court repeatedly demonstrates through its words and actions, the Federal Rules of Evidence "now govern the treatment of evidentiary questions in federal courts."

The rigid codification of evidence rules articulated by Cleary may seem harsh, but it is easily defended. The codification fosters consistency and predictability in evidentiary rulings. This is particularly important in a system that overwhelmingly depends on pretrial resolution, even for the most serious civil or criminal matters....

Courts should view the federal evidence rules as indistinguishable from statutes and treat them as equally binding. For the most part courts do just that.... True, trial judges enjoy a considerable amount of discretion in their evidence rulings. But the discretion is never in deciding whether to apply a rule according to its intended meaning. Rather, the trial court's discretion in this context involves the application of an evidence rule to a murky factual scenario. A court has no authority, for example, to deem evidence "hearsay" if it is not "hearsay" and vice versa.... In short, the "district court's construction of the rules of evidence is reviewed de novo" and "basing an evidentiary ruling on an erroneous view of the law constitutes an abuse of discretion per se."[2]

---

[1] Glen Weissenberger, The Supreme Court and the Interpretation of the Federal Rules of Evidence, 53 Ohio St. L.J. 1307 (1992).

[2] Charles A. Wright & Jeffrey Bellin, 30B Fed. Prac. & Proc. Evid. § 6702 (2020 ed.). The author of this casebook authored the Federal Practice & Procedure treatise Volume on Hearsay. Excerpts of that volume appear throughout, cited as "Wright & Bellin."

INTERPRETING THE RULES OF EVIDENCE

Recognizing that the federal rules of evidence are equivalent to federal statutes, largely answers the question of how courts should go about the process of interpreting and applying those rules. As the Supreme Court states, "We interpret the legislatively enacted Federal Rules of Evidence as we would any statute." The broad contours of the process are fairly well accepted:

> The rules are generally well drafted. But like any legislative provision they can be ambiguous....

> The good news is that courts encounter ambiguity and unclear language with regularity in the related context of statutory interpretation. This is the business of courts. The Supreme Court has repeatedly stressed that the same process used in interpreting statutory language applies to application of the Federal Rules of Evidence....

> In the context of the Federal Rules of Evidence, it is clear that the goal of interpretation should be to effectuate the rules' drafters and enactors' intent. The evidence rules had a known, specialized audience: judges and litigators. They were crafted with this audience in mind and include guidance in a form tailor-made for judges and litigators. The Advisory Committee Note for each rule includes specialized legal discussion of the rule geared toward practitioners and judges, complete with citations to leading evidence treatises and familiar court decisions. The rules also include a provision, Rule 102, that signals the drafters' recognition that they would need judges' help to effectuate the rules' intent in the many circumstances when application would be unclear. Federal Rule of Evidence 102 states:

> > These rules should be construed so as to administer every proceeding fairly, eliminate unjustifiable expense and delay, and promote the development of evidence law, to the end of ascertaining the truth and securing a just determination.

The proper interpretation of each evidence rule, then, is one that is faithful to the intent of that rule as expressed first and foremost in the rule's text, and secondarily in the rule's legislative history.[1]

There is some question about the weight that courts should give to the Advisory Committee Notes that accompanied each of the rules transmitted to the Supreme Court and Congress. It is important to emphasize, however, that agreement in this context far outweighs disagreement:

> [E]veryone agrees: courts should look to the Notes to interpret ambiguous provisions of the rules, or when applying clear provisions in unusual circumstances…. The practice of routinely looking at the legislative history of a rule, and particularly its Advisory Committee Note, should not be mistaken for a disregard of the rule's text. Quite the opposite is true. As with statutory interpretation generally, courts must "begin with the language of the Rule itself." As Cleary himself explained, courts should seek to discern Congress' intent as to the meaning of the rule, viewing the text of the rule as "the prime source of meaning." The legislative history fills out the generally sparse text of the rules, giving meaning to the "statutory reference points" set forth by the rules' drafters….
>
> [T]he courts must begin with the text of the rule. Then, they should look to the Advisory Committee Notes that accompanied each rule and, where applicable, the reports of the Congressional bodies that considered and amended the rules. These sources, along with the common law context in which the rules were first drafted, generally suffice to give meaning to ambiguous or poorly phrased evidence-rule text. Then, once the intent of a federal rule of evidence is identified it must be followed unless the rule is overridden by more powerful authority, such as a constitutional provision.[2]

As the foregoing suggests, any sophisticated understanding of the law of evidence begins with the rules of evidence. This means that every time you encounter a Federal Rule of Evidence in the text below, you should look up

---

[1] Wright & Bellin § 6703.
[2] Wright & Bellin § 6703.

the rule and carefully read its text. Then, just as a court or litigator would do, review the accompanying Advisory Committee Note.

RULE REVISIONS AND AMENDMENTS

The Advisory Committee on the Federal Rules of Evidence continues to operate and periodically recommends amendments to the rules to Congress. Those amendments frequently become law. One of the most sweeping changes to the rules of evidence occurred with the 2011 restyling project. The "restylers" provided an explanation of that project as a note to Federal Rule of Evidence 101. The critical point is that: "These changes are intended to be stylistic only. There is no intent to change any result in any ruling on evidence admissibility." Nevertheless, it is important to be aware of the restyling because pre-restyled rules frequently appear in older federal court opinions and in States that have not (yet) adopted the restyled versions of the federal rules. Here is an excerpt from the restyling note, which appears in most compendiums as a note to the first rule of evidence:

The Style Project

... 4. Rule Numbers

The restyled rules keep the same numbers to minimize the effect on research. Subdivisions have been rearranged within some rules to achieve greater clarity and simplicity.

5. No Substantive Change

The Committee made special efforts to reject any purported style improvement that might result in a substantive change in the application of a rule. The Committee considered a change to be "substantive" if any of the following conditions were met:

a. Under the existing practice in any circuit, the change could lead to a different result on a question of admissibility (e.g., a change that requires a court to provide either a less or more stringent standard in evaluating the admissibility of particular evidence);

b. Under the existing practice in any circuit, it could lead to a change in the procedure by which an admissibility decision is made (e.g., a change in the time in which an objection must be made, or a change in whether a court must hold a hearing on an admissibility question);

c. It alters the structure of a rule in a way that may alter the approach that courts and litigants have used to think about, and argue about, questions of admissibility (e.g., merging Rules 104(a) and 104(b) into a single subdivision); or

d. It changes a "sacred phrase" — phrases that have become so familiar in practice that to alter them would be unduly disruptive. Examples in the Evidence Rules include "unfair prejudice" and "truth of the matter asserted."

There are three different kinds of evidence rules you can expect to encounter as you study the Law of Evidence: (1) Federal rules that are currently in force; (2) Unrestyled rules floating around in various sources; and (3) State rules of evidence that typically track but may not be identical to their federal analogues. To illustrate, the next page presents a collection of various versions of one of the first substantive rule of evidence we will study: relevance. Notice that, at least in this case, the similarities overwhelm any superficial distinctions.

Federal Rules of Evidence (pre-2011)

Rule 401. DEFINITION OF "RELEVANT EVIDENCE"

"Relevant evidence" means evidence having any tendency to make the existence of any fact that is of consequence to the determination of the action more probable or less probable than it would be without the evidence.

Federal Rules of Evidence (current)

Rule 401. Test for Relevant Evidence

Evidence is relevant if:

(a) it has any tendency to make a fact more or less probable than it would be without the evidence; and

(b) the fact is of consequence in determining the action.

Virginia Rule of Evidence

Rule 2:401 DEFINITION OF "RELEVANT EVIDENCE"

"Relevant evidence" means evidence having any tendency to make the existence of any fact in issue more probable or less probable than it would be without the evidence.

California Evidence Code

Evidence Code Section 220

"Relevant evidence" means evidence, including evidence relevant to the credibility of a witness or hearsay declarant, having any tendency in reason to prove or disprove any disputed fact that is of consequence to the determination of the action.

Texas Rule of Evidence

Rule 401: Test For Relevant Evidence

Evidence is relevant if:

(a) it has any tendency to make a fact more or less probable than it would be without the evidence; and

(b) the fact is of consequence in determining the action.

Chapter 1

STIPULATIONS AND JUDICIAL NOTICE

In American trials, not every fact must be supported by evidence. Sometimes the parties stipulate to certain evidence -- that is, they agree that a certain fact is established. This agreement can then be presented to the jury, either through a judicial instruction or in some other form, like a written statement. The key to a stipulation is that both parties must agree. Stipulations typically occur when there is no real dispute about a fact, and the party that benefits from proving the fact could prove the fact conclusively if it had to. In that circumstance, the opposing party may stipulate. There may be tactical advantages that both sides perceive to doing so. Above all, this practice allows witnesses to avoid the trouble of having to come to court and speeds up the glacial pace of courtroom proceedings.

RULE 201

There is one category of facts that are relied on by decisionmakers but need not be supported by evidence or stipulation. These are sometimes called "legislative facts." The Advisory Committee Note to Rule 201 explains: "Legislative facts ... are those which have relevance to legal reasoning and the lawmaking process, whether in the formulation of a legal principle or ruling by a judge or court or in the enactment of a legislative body." The Note offers as an example, the Supreme Court's observation in a 1958 case that "Adverse testimony given in criminal proceedings would, we think, be likely to destroy almost any marriage." The Court heard no evidence on that question, but nonetheless the rule drafters thought this kind of intuitive reasoning was better left outside the formal processes of the rules of evidence.

By contrast, the Note explains that "adjudicative facts" are "the facts of the particular case"; "facts that normally go to the jury"; "[t]hey relate to the parties, their activities, their properties, their businesses." These facts must be proven by evidence or stipulation. Or, in rare circumstances, they can be introduced through "judicial notice." Rule 201 provides two categories of facts that can be judicially noticed, Rule 201(b)(1) & (2). There is little case law interpreting the rule, perhaps because judges use it sparingly. Here is a brief excerpt from an Eleventh Circuit case illustrating the rule's limited applicability.

SHAHAR v. BOWERS
120 F.3d 211 (11th Cir. 1997)

Robin Shahar's petition for rehearing relies, in part, on two recent newspaper articles reporting that former Attorney General Michael J. Bowers has admitted to having an adulterous affair in the past with a woman employed in the [Georgia] Department of Law. She requests that this information become part of the record in this case by judicial notice....

[T]he taking of judicial notice of facts is, as a matter of evidence law, a highly limited process. The reason for this caution is that the taking of judicial notice bypasses the safeguards which are involved with the usual process of proving facts by competent evidence in district court. Courts can take notice of certain facts without formal proof but only where the fact in question is "one not subject to reasonable dispute in that it is either (1) generally known within the territorial jurisdiction of the trial court or (2) capable of accurate and ready determination by resort to sources whose accuracy cannot reasonably be questioned."

For example, the kinds of things about which courts ordinarily take judicial notice are (1) scientific facts: for instance, when does the sun rise or set; (2) matters of geography: for instance, what are the boundaries of a state; or (3) matters of political history: for instance, who was president in 1958. Shahar asks us to take judicial notice of the conduct of one person, Michael J. Bowers; and she asks us to take judicial notice of conduct which is not his official conduct (an example of his official conduct which might be judicially noticed would be that he issued a particular official opinion on a certain date). She has shown us no case—and we have found none—where a federal court of appeals took judicial notice of the unofficial conduct of one person based upon newspaper accounts (or the person's campaign committee's press release) about that conduct.

> [Footnote] We stress that we are not asked merely to take judicial notice of the fact that the media has reported "X" or the fact that a press release says "X." We are asked to know "X."

We are not inclined to extend the doctrine of judicial notice as far as Plaintiff asks us to take it.

***

Next consider this excerpt from a law review article[1] that summarizes the rationale for judicial notice and intriguing prospects for the practice created by the accumulation of information on the Internet.

> The concept of judicial notice emerged from a judge-centered, common-law tradition in order to make fact-finding more efficient and accurate. As John Henry Wigmore summarized:

>> The object of this rule is to save time, labor, and expense in securing and introducing evidence on matters which are not ordinarily capable of dispute and are actually not bona fide disputed, and the tenor of which can safely be assumed from the tribunal's general knowledge or from slight research on its part. . . . It thus becomes a useful expedient for speeding trials and curing informalities. Initially arising as a means to soften strict pleading rules, in which the omission of a fact could result in the dismissal of a complaint, judicial notice became a useful shortcut in the ordinary course of trial.

> Central to the legitimacy of the shortcut, however, was the correctness of the judicially noticed fact. Judicially noticed facts were either "notorious" (meaning obvious) or verifiable. As Wigmore wrote,

>> A fact may be judicially noticed which, in view of the state of commerce, industry, history, language, science, or other human activity, is so notorious in the community that the introduction of evidence would be unnecessary.... Illustrations. That July 4 is the anniversary of the Declaration of Independence; that extreme cold is apt to be experienced in railway transportation in January but not in June; that the distance between Chicago and New York is nearly 1000 miles....

---

[1] Jeffrey Bellin & Andrew Ferguson, Trial by Google, 108 Nw. U. L. Rev. 1137 (2014).

The sources of these judicially noticed facts came from traditional forms of collected knowledge including almanacs, government documents, dictionaries, encyclopedias, maps, and judicial records. Judges did not need to know the information personally, as long as they could reasonably rely on these traditional sources. Judges expressly were not to rely on private experience or personal observation, but only on shared common knowledge. The result was a patchwork of judicial notice rulings that covered the scope of human existence (and litigation needs)....

The boundless avenues for fact-finding presented by the novel combination of an expansive judicial notice rule and the Internet's vast repository of information are already on display in American courts. The ubiquitous practices of "Googling" unfamiliar people and things, checking weather and geography online, and seeking supplemental information on any topic through a click of a mouse are predictably moving from our personal lives onto the pages of judicial reports. The importance of judicial notice to this phenomenon is its ability to sweep away a series of evidentiary hurdles that might otherwise frustrate efforts to bring information obtained on the Internet into the courtroom.

As lawyers well know, finding information is not the same as being able to introduce that information in court. Though the Internet is breaking down barriers to counsel's access to information, a wholly separate set of barriers restricts the flow of online information to judges and jurors. These barriers consist primarily of evidentiary rules--rules that sometimes make little sense when applied to facts gleaned online....

Several factors make the prospect of more widespread and rational judicial notice of online sources attractive. Most obviously, the exercise can bring reliable information into the decision-making process, leading to more accurate determinations. In addition, online information is available to everyone and easy to access. Counsel need not worry about whether the Internet will cooperate, assert a Fifth Amendment privilege, or slant its story when approached by one party or the other to litigation. Google Maps cooperates with all on equal terms--it does not change its story based on the inquirer. Further, using the Internet is largely free of charge (or, more precisely, free of incremental costs). Even websites that do assess a fee are generally less expensive than analogous sources of information, such as experts. An overburdened, under-motivated, resource-strapped public defender can review, and seek judicial notice of, the same websites as the most high-powered, well-funded white-collar defender. Finally, by removing unnecessary evidentiary obstacles, judicial notice preserves court time and resources, while also decreasing the burden on witnesses who might otherwise have to testify on uncontroversial points, such as the authenticity of a printout from Google Maps or the owner of the website, "www.mcdonalds.com."

The Article suggests that some online sources provide fertile ground for judicial notice under Rule 201, while others - like the one discussed in the next case - do not.

IN MATTER OF ROKOWSKI
168 N.H. 57 (2015)

DALIANIS, C.J.

The respondent, Shane Rokowski, appeals the final decree in his divorce from the petitioner, Tammy Rokowski. On appeal, he argues that the Circuit Court erred by ... conducting its own internet research to ascertain the value of the marital home ....

We first consider the respondent's arguments regarding the court's internet research, property distribution, and alimony award. The parties' primary assets were the marital home in Connecticut and the respondent's businesses. Neither party provided the trial court with formal appraisals of the home or the businesses.

The court valued the marital home at $150,000 as of the date of the 2014 final divorce decree and awarded it to the respondent; however, the court ordered him to pay the petitioner $75,000 and mandated that the debt be secured by a mortgage....

To determine the value of the marital home and to choose a valuation date, the court relied upon … [the] "on-line service" … "Zillow," a website that "offers free residential real-estate estimates along with other tools for real-estate buyers and sellers." Zillow provides an estimated value for a home called a "Zestimate." "[T]he Zestimate is not calculated using individual home appraisals by Zillow employees, but is calculated from public and user submitted data." "Realtors, homeowners, and others submit data to the website and to local government agencies, and Zillow collects the data and runs it through a secret algorithm to estimate the value of properties." "Zillow does not itself obtain the data [upon which it relies to estimate property values] or test it for accuracy."

The trial court relied upon its internet research to evaluate the respondent's comparable sales data, which consisted of the tax records for homes on the same street as the marital home. For instance, the tax record for one home demonstrated that, although it was assessed at $160,000, it sold in 2011 for $76,862. The trial court observed that "[a]ccording to [the] Zillow web site, … this same property sold [in 2013] for $116,472[,] [s]uggesting the property may have been a short-sale to avoid foreclosure." Similarly, the tax record for another home showed that it was assessed at $146,000 and sold in 2011 for $82,000. The trial court noted that Zillow estimated the property's value to be $103,222 and indicated that the property was again for sale. The tax record for a third potential comparable sale demonstrated that the home was assessed at $126,000, although it sold in 2012 for $40,000. The court stated that Zillow estimated the property's resale value as $112,649.

The trial court also relied upon its internet research to choose a valuation date, finding that the area where the home is located "is experiencing a recovery with sales or projected sales prices reflecting other than foreclosure or short-sale pricing," and, thus, choosing to value the home as of 2014 (when the decree was issued) instead of 2011 (when the petition was filed).

The respondent argues that the trial court erred when it relied upon its own internet research to ascertain the home's value and to choose a valuation date. We agree.

16

It is axiomatic that a trial court "cannot go outside of the [evidentiary] record except as to matters judicially noticed." Doing so is "inconsistent with the established role of the trial court in adversary litigation."

Under New Hampshire Rule of Evidence 201, the circumstances under which a judge may judicially notice a fact are limited.... Under Rule 201, "[a] judicially noticed fact must be one not subject to reasonable dispute in that it is either (1) generally known within the territorial jurisdiction of the trial court or (2) capable of accurate and ready determination by resort to sources whose accuracy cannot reasonably be questioned." Here, we conclude that Zillow's "Zestimate" is not "capable of accurate and ready determination by resort to sources whose accuracy cannot reasonably be questioned."

Appellate courts in other jurisdictions have found reversible error when a trial court relies upon internet information from outside of the evidentiary record that fails to meet the standard for judicial notice. See Tribbitt v. Tribbitt (Del. 2008) (concluding that trial court could not reject unrefuted expert testimony about wife's earning capacity based, in part, upon trial court's outside-of-the-record computer search of potential jobs available to wife). We reach the same conclusion here and hold that, because the trial court relied, in part, upon Zillow's "Zestimates" to ascertain the home's value and choose a valuation date, the court erred. Because the marital home was one of the parties' most significant assets, we [reverse]....

PROBLEM 1-1: DISTANCE TO SCHOOL

A person is charged with selling heroin in Washington, D.C. The relevant law doubles the permissible penalty if the jury finds that the sale occurred within 1000 feet of an elementary school. D.C. Code Ann. § 48-904.07a. Police officer testimony establishes the precise location where the sale is alleged to have occurred (dot). The prosecutor then asks the judge to take judicial notice, using Google Maps that (i) the alleged drug deal took place about a street width away from an elementary school, and (ii) that D.C. streets are less than 1000 feet wide. The defense attorney objects. *How should the trial court rule?*

too vague

Chapter 2

RELEVANCE

RULE 401 & 402

Rule 402 says that evidence must be relevant to be admissible. How do we know what evidence is relevant? The answer can be found in Rule 401.

Rule 401's definition of "relevant" should track your intuition. "Relevant" is a term used in everyday conversations. It is important to know the definition in Rule 401, and to be able to speak to courts using the rule's jargon. But don't lose track of your existing intuitions about what counts as relevant. Before you looked at Rule 401, you could explain why the defendant's confession is relevant evidence in a murder trial, while the defense attorney's grocery list is not. Rule 401 provides structure and precision to the intuitions that drive that conclusion.

Rule 401 sets out a two-part test. To be relevant, (a) evidence must make a fact more or less probable, and (b) that fact must be a "fact of consequence." The second point can be stated another way: the fact you are proving with the evidence must matter to the legal proceeding. Reading through this definition, you can see why the Advisory Committee Note states that relevance is not an "inherent characteristic of any item." An item's relevance will always depend on the factual and legal context.

The best way to understand the rule is to apply it.

PROBLEM 2-1: BARRY BONDS

In the Spring of 2011, the government prosecuted a famous baseball player, Barry Bonds, for lying to federal investigators. Prosecutors claimed Bonds lied when he denied having used performance enhancing drugs (steroids). Among the many items of evidence offered by the prosecution in the case were:

- Testimony by Bonds' trainer that the trainer gave *other players* steroids during the time that he was working with Bonds.

- Testimony from an equipment manager that during the period when Bonds was alleged to have been using steroids, Bonds requested a bigger baseball hat + Testimony from a doctor, who studies steroid use, that head growth is a side effect of steroids.

Is this evidence relevant? How should a court analyze these items of evidence under Rule 401?

PROBLEM 2-2: FAINTING

In 2014, the United States prosecuted Wall Street trader Mathew Martoma in federal court in New York City for insider trading. The prosecution alleged that Martoma received a tip from two doctors about the success of a new Alzheimer's drug in clinical trials and advised his firm, SAC Capital, to purchase stock in the drug producers (Elan and Wyeth), resulting in $276 million in profits for SAC Capital in 2008.

Prior to trial, Martoma moved to exclude certain evidence as irrelevant. The court described the evidence as follows:

> "Martoma . . . moved to exclude evidence that he fainted when approached by FBI agents outside his home on November 8, 2011, approximately a year before his arrest. Martoma fainted after agents told him that they wanted to talk with him about his insider trading in Elan and Wyeth stock while at SAC Capital. Martoma was quickly revived, and suffered no lasting effects. The Government argues that evidence of Martoma's fainting should be admitted as evidence of consciousness of guilt."

In considering the government's argument the court referenced analogous evidence that courts routinely admit as relevant:

> "… Courts have admitted -- as consciousness of guilt evidence -- proof that a defendant had made arrangements to flee the country the day after a crime was committed, bribed a witness to provide a false statement to investigators, made false exculpatory statements to the police, or attempted to intimidate a prosecution witness. Such evidence is admitted on the theory that it is probative of the defendant's state of mind."

How should the court rule on the defense motion to exclude the above-described fainting evidence as irrelevant? Is it similar to the other "consciousness of guilt evidence" referenced by the court?

KNAPP v. STATE
168 Ind. 153 (1907)

GILLETT, J.

Appellant appeals from a judgment in the above-entitled cause, under which he stands convicted of murder in the first degree....

Appellant, as a witness in his own behalf, offered testimony tending to show a killing in self-defense. He afterwards testified, presumably for the purpose of showing that he had reason to fear the deceased, that before the killing he had heard that the deceased, who was the marshal of Hagerstown, had clubbed and seriously injured an old man in arresting him, and that he died a short time afterwards. On appellant being asked, on cross-examination, who told him this, he answered: "Some people around Hagerstown there. I can't say as to who it was now." The state was permitted, on rebuttal, to prove by a physician, over the objection and exception of the defense, that the old man died of senility and alcoholism, and that there were no bruises or marks on his person.

Counsel for appellant contend that it was error to admit this testimony; that the question was as to whether he had, in fact, heard the story, and not as to its truth or falsity. While it is laid down in the books that there must be an open and visible connection between the fact under inquiry and the evidence by which it is sought to be established, yet the connection thus required is in the logical processes only, for to require an actual connection between the two facts would be to exclude all presumptive evidence. Within settled rules, the competency of testimony depends largely upon its tendency to persuade the judgment. As said by Wharton: "Relevancy is that which conduces to the proof of a pertinent hypothesis." In Stevenson v. Stuart, it was said: "The competency of a collateral fact to be used as the basis of legitimate argument is not to be determined by the conclusiveness of the inferences it may afford in reference to the litigated fact. It is enough if these may tend in a slight degree to elucidate the inquiry, or to assist, though remotely, to a determination probably founded in truth."

We are of opinion that the testimony referred to was competent. While appellant's counsel are correct in their assertion that the question was whether appellant had heard a story to the effect that the deceased had offered serious violence to the old man, yet it does not follow that the testimony complained of did not tend to negative the claim of appellant as to what he had heard. One of the first principles of human nature is the impulse to speak the truth. "This principle," says Dr. Reid, whom Professor Greenleaf quotes at length in his work on Evidence, "has a powerful operation, even in the greatest liars; for where they lie once they speak truth 100 times." Truth speaking preponderating, it follows that to show that there was no basis in fact for the statement appellant claims to have heard had a tendency to make it less probable that his testimony on this point was true…. The fact proved by the state tended to discredit appellant, since it showed that somewhere between the fact and the testimony there was a person who was not a truth speaker, and, appellant being unable to point to his informant, it must at least be said that the testimony complained of had a tendency to render his claim as to what he had heard less probable….

Judgment affirmed.

CASE STUDY: "MERCY KILLING"

Whether a fact is "of consequence" in determining the action, under Rule 401(b), depends on the legal questions being tried. That, in turn, depends on the underlying law. For the next case from Michigan, here are the critical underlying laws:

§752.1027. Criminal assistance to suicide

> Sec. 7. (1) A person who has knowledge that another person intends to commit or attempt to commit suicide and who intentionally does either of the following is guilty of criminal assistance to suicide…:
>
> > (a) Provides the physical means by which the other person attempts or commits suicide.
>
> > (b) Participates in a physical act by which the other person attempts or commits suicide.

... (3) Subsection (1) does not apply to prescribing, dispensing, or administering medications or procedures if the intent is to relieve pain or discomfort and not to cause death, even if the medication or procedure may hasten or increase the risk of death....

Murder

"In Michigan, murder is not statutorily defined. This Court [has] defined the term as follows:

> Murder is where a person of sound memory and discretion unlawfully kills any reasonable creature in being, in the peace of the state, with malice prepense or aforethought, either express or implied.

> [A]s 'malice aforethought' is now defined, a killing may be murder even though the actor harbored no hatred or ill will against the victim."[1]

People v. Kevorkian
248 Mich. App. 373 (2001)

A jury convicted defendant [Dr. Jack Kevorkian - "the medical pathologist who willfully helped dozens of terminally ill people end their lives, becoming the central figure in a national drama surrounding assisted suicide"][2] of second-degree murder.... The trial court sentenced him to ... prison [for] ten to twenty-five years.... Defendant appeals as of right and we affirm.

This case is about death; in particular, the death of former racecar driver Thomas Youk in September 1998. Youk was fifty-two years old and had amyotrophic lateral sclerosis (ALS), also known as Lou Gehrig's disease....

[Among other claims on appeal,] defendant claims that the trial court erred in excluding the testimony of Terrence and Melody Youk, Thomas' brother and sister-in-law. However, defendant ... fails entirely to demonstrate how the proposed testimony would have been relevant. Thus, ..., defendant's arguments have no merit....

.... Before trial, the prosecutor moved to preclude defendant from asserting the defenses of consent and euthanasia and from introducing any irrelevant

---

[1] People v. Aaron, 409 Mich. 672 (1980); *People v. Morrin*, 31 Mich. App. 301 (1971).
[2] https://www.nytimes.com/2011/06/04/us/04kevorkian.html

testimony regarding Youk's medical condition, pain and suffering, and quality of life, and to prevent a jury nullification argument. In its opinion and order, the trial court granted the prosecutor's motions, but allowed evidence of Youk's pain and suffering and quality of life where such evidence related to the assisted suicide charge that was still pending at that time. When the prosecutor decided not to pursue the assisted suicide charge, defendant asked the trial court to reconsider its decision to exclude evidence of Youk's pain and suffering, among other things. The trial court denied this motion.

When defendant submitted his witness list, however, it included Melody and Terrence Youk. The trial court instructed defendant that he needed to make an offer of proof concerning the two witnesses....

The trial court made a special record regarding defendant's offer of proof. Melody Youk testified that when she met with defendant, she explained Youk's condition, and she indicated that they understood that defendant may be able to "assist [them] in relieving his pain and suffering." According to Melody Youk, in a subsequent conversation, she, Terrence Youk, and defendant discussed what defendant could do "to bring an end to this situation."

Following arguments of the parties, the trial court ruled that Melody Youk's testimony was not appropriate. The trial court stated that defendant was attempting to introduce evidence of a mercy killing, which is not cognizable under state laws, and that his proffered evidence related to the law and a legal argument or debate, which do not go before a jury.... The trial court reiterated that any consent to defendant's action was irrelevant.

With regard to Terrence Youk's testimony, ... the trial court again ruled that the offer of proofs indicated that the witnesses would only testify concerning euthanasia and consent, which were not legally cognizable defenses.

Defendant now argues that the trial court erred in barring him from calling Terrence and Melody Youk to testify at trial. Defendant ... asserts, Terrence and Melody Youk could have testified about Youk's death, the effect of his disease, his daily life conditions, and his consent, as well as rebutting the prosecutor's argument that defendant's purpose was to seek publicity and to advance his own agenda.

[W]e review the trial court's decision to exclude this evidence for an abuse of that discretion….

…. As the trial court noted repeatedly, the two witnesses simply had no relevant testimony to offer to the jury. "'Relevant evidence' means evidence having any tendency to make the existence of any fact that is of consequence to the determination of the action more probable or less probable than it would be without the evidence." Mich. R. Ev. 401. A variety of factors, including the elements of the charged crimes, the theories of admissibility, and the defenses asserted all help determine whether any particular piece of evidence is relevant.

The testimony Terrence and Melody Youk would have provided to the jury concerned Youk's medical condition, pain, suffering, and the conditions of his daily life, as well as his consent. By proffering such evidence, defendant sought to justify killing Youk. In fact, although defendant claims that he proffered their testimony for other reasons, the crux of his claims consistently relate to consent and euthanasia. Simply put, consent and euthanasia are not recognized defenses to murder. As the trial court noted, "[a] trial court may exclude from the jury testimony concerning a defense that has not been recognized by the Legislature as a defense to the charged crime." Thus, Terrence and Melody Youk's testimony was inconsequential to the determination of this case.

…. Accordingly, we conclude that the trial court did not abuse its discretion in precluding Terrence and Melody Youk from testifying.

PROBLEM 2-3: THREE STRIKES

The following problem is drawn from People v. Taylor (Cal. 1999):[1]

Facts: Two security guards apprehended a homeless man, Gregory Taylor, in the alcove of St. Joseph's Church at 4:30 a.m. The guards observed Taylor using a piece of wood in an apparent effort to pry open the church's kitchen door. Taylor frequently received free food from a priest living in the church's friary, which was located near the kitchen door. In addition to the food, the friary provided access to the rest of the church where there were items of value such as crucifixes, chalices and alms boxes.

---

[1] Cf. Jeffrey Bellin, *Is Punishment Relevant After All?* 90 B.U. L. Rev. 2223 (2010).

Taylor is charged with burglary – entering a building with intent to steal. According to the testimony, Taylor stuck a wooden tool into the door jamb, which is legally sufficient under California law to establish "entry." The sole question at trial is Taylor's intent.

Theory of Defense: Taylor claims that he (mistakenly) believed he had permission to enter the friary to obtain food if needed. If credited, this defense establishes that Taylor lacked the intent to steal and so would not be guilty of burglary.

Evidence at issue: In a pretrial conference, defense counsel moves to admit the following evidence: Taylor has previously been convicted of two offenses that count as "strikes" under California law. This means that if convicted of burglary, it will be his "third strike" and Taylor will automatically be sentenced to life in prison.

Question: Why might defense counsel seek to introduce this evidence? Can the prosecution object to defense counsel's offer of evidence on relevance grounds? What might defense counsel argue in response? How should a trial court rule?

NOTE: RELEVANCE IN PRACTICE

Most relevance questions do not lead to extensive legal disputes for two reasons:

(1) The standard for relevance ("any tendency") is extremely permissive and non-technical;

(2) The standard overlaps with common intuitions about the kind of evidence that will be persuasive.

Attorneys seek to introduce evidence that will persuade the trier of fact. Most evidence that is not relevant is not persuasive, and consequently neither party tries to introduce it.

As the examples we have already covered illustrate, the second point loses force in one important scenario. Sometimes persuasive evidence, i.e., information that might sway the factfinder, is made off limits by applicable legal standards. A juror might care, for example, that a charged murder is a "mercy killing" even if the law does not.

One of the best examples of this disconnect is evidence of severe punishments that will apply in certain contexts if a defendant is convicted of a crime. In rejecting a contention that a defendant should have been permitted to inform the jury of so-called "punishment evidence," the Supreme Court stated the following:

> It is well established that when a jury has no sentencing function, it should be admonished to "reach its verdict without regard to what sentence might be imposed." The principle that juries are not to consider the consequences of their verdicts is a reflection of the basic division of labor in our legal system between judge and jury. The jury's function is to find the facts and to decide whether, on those facts, the defendant is guilty of the crime charged. The judge, by contrast, imposes sentence on the defendant after the jury has arrived at a guilty verdict. Information regarding the consequences of a verdict is therefore irrelevant to the jury's task.[1]

While evidence of the sentence that would follow from a conviction answers an important question that many jurors care about (whether the system's treatment of the defendant upon a conviction will be proportionate and fair), the law takes that questions away from the jury. As a result, courts typically treat sentencing information as not relevant. Since many jurors might not agree with the "division of labor" proposed by the Supreme Court, relevance rulings -- which try to make it impossible for jurors to consider information like sentence length that courts deem off limits -- can have far-reaching consequences.

CONDITIONAL RELEVANCE

RULE 104(b)

As the preceding discussion reveals, relevance determinations are typically free-wheeling explorations of logical inference and common sense. One type of relevance, however, has more technical rules: "conditional relevance." Rule 104(b) governs "[w]hen the relevance of evidence depends on whether a fact

---

[1] Shannon v. United States, 512 U.S. 573 (1994).

exists." In that circumstance, the trial court must condition admission on the presentation (or promise) of other evidence "sufficient to support a finding that the fact does exist."

To see how this works, consider a murder case where the defendant claims to have acted in self-defense. The defense seeks to introduce the autopsy report's finding that there was methamphetamine in the victim's bloodstream. Here is the theory of relevance that the defense offers to support its request:

Meth in Blood → Meth Causes Aggressive Behavior → Victim Was Acting Aggressively

To support this chain of reasoning, the defendant could offer expert testimony about the effects of methamphetamine use. That testimony could directly connect the autopsy results to the defendant's claim that the victim was behaving aggressively at the time of the killing. But what if the defense did not present expert testimony? Would evidence of the autopsy finding still be relevant? That question can be analyzed as one of *conditional* relevance. The relevance of the meth in the victim's blood depends on whether a fact exists -- namely whether meth causes aggressive behavior. Here is how the Tenth Circuit considered that question in evaluating a trial court's exclusion of such evidence.

> The necessity of expert testimony involves the principle of conditional relevance. Under this principle, a district court may exclude evidence if the jury could not reasonably find the existence of a preliminary fact essential to make the evidence relevant.... Methamphetamine had been found on [the victim-]Mr. Garcia's body and in his bloodstream. Together, this evidence supported an inference that Mr. Garcia was on methamphetamine, and lay witnesses may have been able to testify that he was high. So Mr. Tony might not have needed expert testimony to show that methamphetamine causes erratic, violent behavior.[1]

The underlying issue is the logical leap necessary to make the drug evidence relevant, the middle link in the logical chain diagrammed above.

In the case quoted above, the appeals court concluded that a jury could reasonably make the leap (find the missing fact) even without expert testimony

---

[1] United States v. Tony (10th Cir. 2020).

that explicitly filled out the inferential chain. Applying Rule 104(b), the court thought the missing link could be established through common sense and testimony from a witness (like the defendant) that the victim appeared high.

There are three points worth emphasizing about conditional relevance.

(1) Practitioners rarely invoke the "conditional relevance" rule, relying instead on more familiar, and easily argued, relevance principles under Rule 401. Comments like the following in appellate opinions are common:

- "The admissibility of Puckett's testimony is governed by Indiana Evidence Rule 104(b), 'Relevancy Conditioned on Fact,' although neither party cites this rule."[1]
- "Despite the Government's apparent failure to confront the Rule 104(b) analysis on appeal, we are persuaded that Taylor's testimony was admissible…."[2]
- "Though the parties do not explicitly frame it this way, this case raises the 'abstruse' concept of conditional relevance."[3]

(2) If you look hard enough, virtually every chain of reasoning "depends on whether a fact exists." This means that there is no bright line between matters of relevance that must be analyzed solely under Rule 401, and those labeled "conditional relevance" that must be analyzed under Rule 104(b).

(3) Not much turns on the distinction. Part of the reason for the odd state of affairs described above is that the ability to distinguish "conditional relevance" from "regular" relevance matters little in the rough and tumble of human inference and common sense -- or as *Knapp* states, in the mysterious "logical processes" that allow humans to draw conclusions.

---

[1] Cox v. State, 696 N.E.2d 853 (Ind. 1998).
[2] United States v. Coplan, 703 F.3d 46 (2d Cir. 2012).
[3] United States v. Snyder, 789 F. App'x 501 (6th Cir. 2019).

APPLYING RULE 104(B)

The technical difference between relevance inquiries under Rule 401 and 104(b) can best be illustrated with another example.

GUIDED PROBLEM 2-4: NO NOTICE?

A defendant is accused of the criminal offense of knowingly violating a judicial "stay away" order -- a formal order that the defendant stay away from a specific address. After the defendant was arrested at the prohibited location, the defense claims that the defendant did not know about the order and so cannot be punished for violating it. The prosecution concedes that the defendant was not in the courtroom at the time that the judge pronounced the order. And the prosecution does not have any conclusive evidence to show that the court's mailed notice reached the defendant. However, the prosecution would like to offer, as part of its case, evidence that the defendant's mother was present in the courtroom when the judge issued the stay away order.

The defense objects that the evidence is "not relevant, because it is the defendant, not the defendant's mother who is on trial!"

How should the court rule on this evidence under Rule 401?

> Under Rule 401, the trial court would determine whether the offered evidence (testimony about the mother's presence in the courtroom at the time the order was pronounced) has any tendency to make a fact of consequence more likely.

> The prosecution would claim that its evidence supports a conclusion that the defendant knew of the court order. *Why?* The prosecutor would argue, based on logic and common-sense, that if the defendant's mother was present at the hearing where the judge imposed the order, then it is more likely that the defendant knew of the order. *How do you think a judge would rule on that relevance question?*

Now imagine that the defense instead framed the relevance objection as a conditional relevance objection under Rule 104(b). *How should a court analyze the question now?*

The defense argument is that the relevance of the defendant's mother's presence in the courtroom "depends on whether a fact exists." *What fact?* That the defendant's mother communicated with the defendant after the hearing.

If the trial court accepted this framing, as it seemingly should, then the court would have to apply a slightly different analysis. The court, under Rule 104(b), would have to determine whether there is sufficient proof "to support a finding that the fact does exist."

Note that here, the trial judge is not determining whether the judge thinks the fact exists. Rather, the judge is asked to determine whether the factfinder (e.g., a jury) could find it.

The Supreme Court in Huddleston v. United States (1988) weighed in on precisely how the trial court should go about this:

> "In determining whether the Government has introduced sufficient evidence to meet Rule 104(b), the trial court neither weighs credibility nor makes a finding that the Government has proved the conditional fact by a preponderance of the evidence. The court simply examines all the evidence in the case and decides whether the jury could reasonably find the conditional fact —… — by a preponderance of the evidence."[1]

Why preponderance of evidence? As we will see, the courts have identified the permissive "preponderance of the evidence" (i.e., more likely than not) standard as the default for preliminary questions of admissibility that must be resolved by a judge under the rules of evidence.

The ellipses in the *Huddleston* quote represent the fact in question. In our example, something like: "did the defendant's mother communicate with him after the hearing."

How would the prosecution convince the judge that its evidence survives the Rule 104(b) objection? That depends on the case. The prosecution might offer evidence about the relationship between the mother and the defendant, for example:

---

[1] Huddleston v. United States, 485 U.S. 681 (1988).

evidence that they live together. Perhaps the prosecutor could call the mother to testify. Or the prosecutor might simply argue that logic and common sense support a finding that the defendant's mother would promptly tell her son about an important court order that directed him to stay away from a specific address -- putting us right back into the free flowing analysis of Rule 401.

These alternatives help to explain why the distinction between relevance and conditional relevance can be both recognized in the rules of evidence, and rarely fought about in practice. While the conditional relevance inquiry adds a level of technical formality, it eventually boils down to the same set of reasoning based on intuition and inference that characterizes Rule 401.

For another illustration, think back to our Barry Bonds example about steroid use and head growth (Problem 2-1). The equipment manager's testimony that the defendant needed a bigger baseball hat fits neatly into a conditional relevance analysis. The relevance of that evidence depends on whether a fact exists ("that steroid use causes head growth"). *How did the prosecutor in that case overcome the Rule 104(b) problem?* By offering an expert's testimony that, in fact, head growth is a symptom of steroid use. Clearly, with that testimony, Rule 104(b) is satisfied. The factfinder could reasonably find the preliminary fact established by a preponderance of the evidence. *Is this an example of the utility of Rule 104(b)? Or does even this example suggest that all relevance questions would be better resolved through Rule 401 alone?*

Chapter 3

UNFAIR PREJUDICE

RULE 403

Rule 401 defines relevance. Rule 402 says that only relevant evidence is admissible. But just because evidence is relevant does not make it admissible. Rule 402 adds that "Relevant evidence is admissible unless any of the following provides otherwise … these rules." One of the rules frequently invoked to exclude relevant evidence is Rule 403.

APPLYING RULE 403

Remember the fainting example in Problem 2-2. Here is District Court Judge Gardephe's actual ruling in the case:

> "Under these circumstances, it would not be reasonable for a jury to infer that Martoma fainted because he knew that he was guilty of insider trading…. It is just as likely that he fainted simply from shock, surprise, or alarm at being accused of such a serious crime, which could have such a damaging effect on his professional and personal life…. I further conclude, under Fed. R. Evid. 403, that whatever limited probative value this evidence has is "substantially outweighed by a danger of … unfair prejudice." In other words, there is a significant risk that the jury will give this evidence more weight than it deserves."[1]

Notice that Judge Gardephe makes two rulings on this evidence: (1) the fainting evidence is not relevant, Rule 401; and (2) even if it is relevant, it must be excluded under Rule 403.

This second ruling is common. Often evidence only slightly influences the probability of a material fact, or strongly influences the probability of a fact that is only slightly material. In Rule 403 parlance, such evidence has little "probative value." With respect to Rule 401, slight is enough. But evidence

---

[1] United States v. Martoma (S.D.N.Y. 2014).

with only slight probative value is vulnerable to exclusion under Rule 403. *Why?* Because it is easily outweighed by the dangers listed under that rule. As the Ninth Circuit explains: "Where the evidence is of very slight (if any) probative value, it's an abuse of discretion to admit it if there's even a modest likelihood of unfair prejudice or a small risk of misleading the jury."[1]

Substantially Outweighs

Rule 403 sets out a series of factors that can warrant exclusion:

- Unfair Prejudice
- Confusing the Issues
- Misleading the Jury
- Undue Delay
- Wasting Time
- Needlessly Presenting Cumulative Evidence

But it is important to see that Rule 403 does not set up a fair fight. It is weighted in favor of the admission of evidence. The dangers listed in the rule must **substantially outweigh** the probative value of the challenged evidence for exclusion to be warranted. When evidence has significant probative value, Rule 403 typically will not exclude it.

Unfair Prejudice

By far the most important of the Rule 403 considerations is "unfair prejudice." At least with respect to evidence that has significant probative value, the other factors are rarely dispositive. One reason for this is that, to the extent they are used correctly, factors like "confusing the issues" and "misleading the jury" can fit comfortably within the concept of "unfair prejudice." As the Advisory Committee Note to Rule 403 states: "'Unfair prejudice' within its context means an undue tendency to suggest decision on an improper basis, commonly, though not necessarily, an emotional one." A verdict arising out of confusion or directed toward the wrong issues, would be an improper basis for decision, and thus a kind of "unfair prejudice" to the aggrieved party. And the other three factors, essentially "the evidence takes too much time to

---

[1] United States v. Hitt, 981 F.2d 422 (9th Cir. 1992).

present," will *substantially* outweigh only the most insignificant or duplicative evidence.

Importantly, Rule 403 is unconcerned with "prejudice" in the sense of damage to the objecting party's case. As courts like to say, all relevant evidence will be prejudicial to one degree or another. The key to exclusion under Rule 403 is **unfair** prejudice.

- "The damage done to the defense is not a basis for exclusion; the question under Rule 403 is one of 'unfair' prejudice—not of prejudice alone."[1]
- "Of course, 'unfair prejudice' as used in Rule 403 is not to be equated with testimony simply adverse to the opposing party. Virtually all evidence is prejudicial or it isn't material. The prejudice must be 'unfair.'"[2]
- "Unfair prejudice under rule 403 is not merely damaging evidence, even severely damaging evidence; rather, unfair prejudice is evidence that persuades by illegitimate means, giving one party an unfair advantage."[3]

CASE STUDY: DRUGS IN THE VICTIM'S BLOOD

A California jury convicted Edward Pitzer of second-degree murder, rejecting his claim of self-defense. Pitzer made one argument on appeal. He challenged a trial court ruling that excluded evidence that the victim had methamphetamine in his blood. The trial court excluded the evidence as irrelevant and outweighed by the dangers listed in California's equivalent of Rule 403, Evidence Code § 352.[4]

Consider these facts from the (unpublished!) opinion in the case:

---

[1] United States v. Munoz, 36 F.3d 1229 (1st Cir. 1994).
[2] Dollar v. Long Mfg., 561 F.2d 613 (5th Cir. 1977).
[3] State v. Schulz, 691 N.W.2d 474 (Minn. 2005).
[4] People v. Pitzer (Cal. Ct. App. 2006). Evidence Code § 352 states: "The court in its discretion may exclude evidence if its probative value is substantially outweighed by the probability that its admission will (a) necessitate undue consumption of time or (b) create substantial danger of undue prejudice, of confusing the issues, or of misleading the jury."

Early in the morning on June 16, 2003, Pitzer was drinking coffee on the patio of a Jack in the Box restaurant. Benjamin Schmid approached Pitzer and the two appeared to have an argument. Schmid walked away from the restaurant in the direction of his truck, and Pitzer, after a short delay, followed. When Pitzer caught up to Schmid, Schmid turned to face Pitzer. Pitzer then stabbed Schmid once with a pocketknife…. Schmid then returned to his truck, started the engine and attempted to run over Pitzer. When Pitzer hid behind a tree, Schmid drove away. Schmid continued to drive erratically, crashed into another vehicle, and finally veered off the road. Schmid's truck rolled over, causing him to suffer additional injuries. Rescue workers arrived at the scene but were unable to revive Schmid, and he died.

The medical examiner determined that the cause of death was a three-inch stab wound in Schmid's right underarm. The wound damaged an artery, and Schmid bled to death.

Pitzer testified in his own defense, providing the only context for a crime that was witnessed from a distance and/or with little interest by the prosecution witnesses. Pitzer had never met Schmid before the stabbing. He testified that on the day of the incident, he had been speaking with an acquaintance named "Chris" outside of the San Diego Health Alliance Methadone Clinic when Schmid approached them, seeking to buy heroin. Pitzer stated that he did not have any heroin and walked away from the two men in the direction of the Jack in the Box restaurant….

Once Pitzer reached the Jack in the Box restaurant, he purchased coffee and sat down to drink it on the outdoor patio. He next saw Schmid, driving by in a pickup truck, "glaring" at him. Schmid "had a look of anger in his eyes." Schmid stopped the truck, got out and walked to the patio area; he got within three feet of Pitzer and yelled, "Fuck your fat friend and fuck you. You better watch your back." Pitzer believed that Chris had "burned" Schmid—i.e., taken his money and not given him any heroin in return. Pitzer and Schmid continued yelling at each other; Pitzer yelled that he was 52 years old, did not want to fight, and had not done anything to Schmid. Pitzer testified that he was "no match for [Schmid] whatsoever" as he was in poor health, and Schmid was almost 30 years younger than him....

After the initial confrontation, Schmid walked back in the direction of his truck. Because of Schmid's "full-on rage," Pitzer believed that Schmid "wasn't done with the argument whatsoever" but rather was going to get a weapon from the truck. Pitzer followed Schmid in what he claimed was an attempt to defuse the situation. As Pitzer caught up with Schmid, he perceived a weapon in Schmid's hand. Schmid "spun around" to face Pitzer "real fast," raising his arm. Pitzer, interpreting Schmid's sudden action as a prelude to an assault, attempted to "back [Schmid] up" so he "could get away" by jabbing his pocketknife at Schmid's arm. In so doing, he stabbed Schmid....

The trial court held a hearing to learn about the evidence Pitzer sought to offer.

At the hearing, Dr. Alan Abrams, a psychiatrist, first summarized the findings of the medical examiner's toxicology report which had been prepared as part of Schmid's autopsy. The report established the presence of an opiate drug (either heroin or morphine), methamphetamine, and methadone in Schmid's blood at the time of his death, demonstrating Schmid's "recent use" of those substances. Dr. Abrams next explained the effects these drugs would have on a typical user: "Methamphetamine reproduces in an exaggerated way what caffeine or adrenalin produce in people. It makes people look more alert. Their eyes dilate, so their eyes are bigger. They have more muscle tension." People coming down from a methamphetamine high become "depressed and angry," or in more extreme cases, "paranoid and violent," with their irritability increasing as time passes from their last dose. The methamphetamine high is short lived, "and the irritability, the over stimulated, hyper excitability is what remains for most of the trajectory."...

Dr. Abrams opined that the toxicology report prepared by the medical examiner "indicates that ... Mr. Schmid was probably at the bottom of his opiate trajectory and was probably withdrawing also from methamphetamine."…. Dr. Abrams concluded that the "toxicology report [is] very consistent with somebody who might be perceived as belligerent, irritable, aggressive, perhaps even paranoid."

After hearing the testimony and argument of counsel, the trial court excluded the testimony of Dr. Abrams in its entirety. Citing Evidence Code Section 352, the court ruled that to the extent the testimony and underlying evidence of Schmid's recent drug use was relevant, its probative value was outweighed by the likelihood it would confuse the issues....

Before reading any further, what is your assessment of the trial court's ruling?

Here is what the California Court of Appeal (Irion, J.) ruled:

> The trial court's rulings excluded a wide range of proffered defense evidence, including: (i) all evidence that Schmid recently used drugs and had drugs in his system when he encountered Pitzer; (ii) all of Dr. Abrams's testimony about the general effects of those drugs; and (iii) Dr. Abrams's opinion about where Schmid was in the drug trajectory, i.e., that Schmid was probably at the end of the trajectory and therefore suffering withdrawal effects.

> The trial court's decision to exclude the proffered evidence was driven by its determination that this evidence was only marginally, if at all, relevant. As the trial court correctly noted, "the only relevant issue" in the case was "what was going on in the mind of Mr. Pitzer at the time of the attack: What he observed, what he heard, [and] what he saw." The trial court, however, was incorrect in its implied assumption that, in his efforts to prove this disputed issue, Pitzer could not rely on the proffered evidence of Schmid's drug use. The excluded evidence corroborated Pitzer's account of what he observed....; Pitzer was therefore entitled to introduce that evidence to persuade the jury that his account was credible.

> The excluded evidence was especially significant given the sole, narrow issue in the case. To obtain a murder conviction, the prosecution was required to show that Pitzer acted out of malice, rather than out of a fear of imminent harm, as Pitzer claimed. Pitzer's defense, conversely, had only one goal—to establish reasonable doubt as to Pitzer's state

of mind when he stabbed Schmid. If the defense could do so, the jury was required to find Pitzer not guilty of murder.

In light of the inability of the prosecution witnesses to testify as to the specific interaction between Pitzer and Schmid prior to the stabbing, Pitzer's own testimony provided virtually the sole evidence on the crucial question of his state of mind. Consequently, the case came down to Pitzer's credibility, and the verdict depended on whether the jury credited his claim that Schmid's behavior caused him to fear for his life.

Pitzer testified that it was the startling severity of Schmid's unprovoked rage that caused him to fear an imminent attack, and to believe that even after Schmid turned back towards his truck, Schmid "wasn't done with the argument," but was instead returning to his truck to get a weapon. According to Pitzer, Schmid, without any real provocation, came within a few feet of Pitzer, wide-eyed and "in a full-on rage," shouting threats and "yelling and screaming." In light of this behavior, Pitzer believed Schmid was "going through withdrawals" and was "a time bomb waiting to blow up" who had "snapped in his head."

As it formed the sole basis for his asserted fear, Pitzer's testimony that Schmid was in an irrational, apparently drug-induced, "full-on rage" was the cornerstone of the defense case. Yet this testimony was highly suspect absent some evidence suggesting an explanation for why Schmid was behaving as Pitzer claimed. The defense explanation was that Schmid had injected heroin and methamphetamine and was experiencing the effects of withdrawal from those drugs. The jury, however, was not permitted to hear the evidence on which this explanation was based and was left solely with the defendant's uncorroborated assertions....

Given the probative value of the excluded evidence, exclusion of that evidence under § 352 was only proper if a countervailing consideration listed in that section "substantially outweighed" that probative value. Here, the trial court cited the likelihood of confusing the issues as the basis for exclusion. On appeal, however, the Attorney General makes no attempt to argue that the excluded evidence would have "confus[ed] the issues," an implicit concession that we believe is warranted.....

In the instant case, the excluded evidence was relevant to an issue that was already before the jury, namely, the plausibility of the defense claim that Schmid acted in a manner that caused Pitzer to fear for his life. Thus, the trial court could not properly exclude evidence relevant to that issue as "confusing the issues" under Section 352.

Having concluded that the proffered evidence was of significant probative value, and its exclusion was not authorized on the ground relied on by the trial court, we consequently determine that the trial court's evidentiary ruling constituted an abuse of its discretion....

Is there another Rule 403 ground the prosecution could have cited in arguing for exclusion? On appeal, the California Attorney General argued that the California courts should uphold the ruling not on the grounds of misleading the jury, but "undue prejudice" (the California equivalent of Rule 403's "unfair prejudice"). Here is how Justice Irion responded to that point:

> The Attorney General ... suggests that we should uphold the trial court's ruling on the ground that the probative value of the excluded evidence was substantially outweighed by undue prejudice. Citing People v. Kelly (1992), the Attorney General argues that "[a] trial court is not required to admit evidence, such as a murder victim's drug use, 'that merely makes the victim of a crime look bad.'" The Attorney General's reliance on Kelly is misplaced. Pitzer did not offer the evidence of the victim's drug use merely to make the victim "look bad." Instead, he offered evidence of the victim's drug use, in addition to expert testimony explaining the effects of that use, to prove a key issue in the case—the effect that Schmid's allegedly drug-induced behavior had on Pitzer's state of mind. Therefore, Kelly is inapposite, and the alternate ground suggested by the Attorney General for exclusion is untenable.

OLD CHIEF v. UNITED STATES
519 U.S. 172 (1997)

Justice SOUTER delivered the opinion of the Court.

…. In 1993, petitioner, Old Chief, was arrested after a fracas involving at least one gunshot. The ensuing federal charges included not only assault with a dangerous weapon and using a firearm in relation to a crime of violence but violation of 18 U.S.C. § 922(g)(1). This statute makes it unlawful for anyone "who has been convicted in any court of, a crime punishable by imprisonment for a term exceeding one year" to "possess in or affecting commerce, any firearm…." ….

The earlier crime charged in the indictment against Old Chief was assault causing serious bodily injury. Before trial, he moved for an order requiring the Government "to refrain from mentioning—by reading the Indictment, during jury selection, in opening statement, or closing argument—and to refrain from offering into evidence or soliciting any testimony from any witness regarding the prior criminal convictions of the Defendant, except to state that the Defendant has been convicted of a crime punishable by imprisonment exceeding one (1) year." He said that revealing the name and nature of his prior assault conviction would unfairly tax the jury's capacity to hold the Government to its burden of proof beyond a reasonable doubt on current charges of assault, possession, and violence with a firearm, and he offered to "solve the problem here by stipulating, agreeing and requesting the Court to instruct the jury that he has been convicted of a crime punishable by imprisonment exceeding one (1) yea[r]." He argued that the offer to stipulate to the fact of the prior conviction rendered evidence of the name and nature of the offense inadmissible under Rule 403 of the Federal Rules of Evidence, the danger being that unfair prejudice from that evidence would substantially outweigh its probative value. He also proposed this jury instruction:

> "The phrase 'crime punishable by imprisonment for a term exceeding one year' generally means a crime which is a felony. The phrase does not include any state offense classified by the laws of that state as a misdemeanor and punishable by a term of imprisonment of two years or less and certain crimes concerning the regulation of business practices.

"[I] hereby instruct you that Defendant JOHNNY LYNN OLD CHIEF has been convicted of a crime punishable by imprisonment for a term exceeding one year."

The Assistant United States Attorney refused to join in a stipulation, insisting on his right to prove his case his own way, and the District Court agreed, ruling orally that, "If he doesn't want to stipulate, he doesn't have to." At trial, over renewed objection, the Government introduced the order of judgment and commitment for Old Chief's prior conviction. This document disclosed that on December 18, 1988, he "did knowingly and unlawfully assault Rory Dean Fenner, said assault resulting in serious bodily injury," for which Old Chief was sentenced to five years' imprisonment. The jury found Old Chief guilty on all counts, and he appealed.

…. We granted Old Chief's petition for writ of certiorari because the Courts of Appeals have divided sharply in their treatment of defendants' efforts to exclude evidence of the names and natures of prior offenses in cases like this. We now reverse the judgment ….

II

A

As a threshold matter, there is Old Chief's erroneous argument that the name of his prior offense as contained in the record of conviction is irrelevant to the prior-conviction element, and for that reason inadmissible under Rule 402. Rule 401 defines relevant evidence as having "any tendency to make the existence of any fact that is of consequence to the determination of the action more probable or less probable than it would be without the evidence." To be sure, the fact that Old Chief's prior conviction was for assault resulting in serious bodily injury rather than, say, for theft was not itself an ultimate fact, as if the statute had specifically required proof of injurious assault. But its demonstration was a step on one evidentiary route to the ultimate fact, since it served to place Old Chief within a particular sub-class of offenders for whom firearms possession is outlawed by § 922(g)(1). A documentary record of the conviction for that named offense was thus relevant evidence in making Old Chief's § 922(g)(1) status more probable than it would have been without the evidence.

Nor was its evidentiary relevance under Rule 401 affected by the availability of alternative proofs of the element to which it went, such as an admission by Old Chief that he had been convicted of a crime "punishable by imprisonment for a term exceeding one year" within the meaning of the statute. The 1972 Advisory Committee Notes to Rule 401 make this point directly:

> "The fact to which the evidence is directed need not be in dispute. While situations will arise which call for the exclusion of evidence offered to prove a point conceded by the opponent, the ruling should be made on the basis of such considerations as waste of time and undue prejudice (see Rule 403), rather than under any general requirement that evidence is admissible only if directed to matters in dispute.".....

B

The principal issue is the scope of a trial judge's discretion under Rule 403, which authorizes exclusion of relevant evidence when its "probative value is substantially outweighed by the danger of unfair prejudice, confusion of the issues, or misleading the jury, or by considerations of undue delay, waste of time, or needless presentation of cumulative evidence." Old Chief relies on the danger of unfair prejudice.

1

The term "unfair prejudice," as to a criminal defendant, speaks to the capacity of some concededly relevant evidence to lure the factfinder into declaring guilt on a ground different from proof specific to the offense charged. So, the Committee Notes to Rule 403 explain, "'Unfair prejudice' within its context means an undue tendency to suggest decision on an improper basis, commonly, though not necessarily, an emotional one."

Such improper grounds certainly include the one that Old Chief points to here: generalizing a defendant's earlier bad act into bad character and taking that as raising the odds that he did the later bad act now charged.... Rule of Evidence 404(b) reflects this common-law tradition by addressing propensity reasoning directly: "Evidence of other crimes, wrongs, or acts is not admissible to prove the character of a person in order to show action in conformity therewith." Fed. Rule Evid. 404(b). There is, accordingly, no question that propensity would be an "improper basis" for conviction and that evidence of a prior conviction is subject to analysis under Rule 403 for relative probative value and for prejudicial risk of misuse as propensity evidence.

.... [A] reading of the companions to Rule 403, and of the commentaries that went with them to Congress, makes it clear that what counts as the Rule 403 "probative value" of an item of evidence, as distinct from its Rule 401 "relevance," may be calculated by comparing evidentiary alternatives. The Committee Notes to Rule 401 explicitly say that a party's concession is pertinent to the court's discretion to exclude evidence on the point conceded. Such a concession, according to the Notes, will sometimes "call for the exclusion of evidence offered to prove [the] point conceded by the opponent...." As already mentioned, the Notes make it clear that such rulings should be made not on the basis of Rule 401 relevance but on "such considerations as waste of time and undue prejudice (see Rule 403)...." The Notes to Rule 403 then take up the point by stating that when a court considers "whether to exclude on grounds of unfair prejudice," the "availability of other means of proof may ... be an appropriate factor." The point gets a reprise in the Notes to Rule 404(b), dealing with admissibility when a given evidentiary item has the dual nature of legitimate evidence of an element and illegitimate evidence of character: "No mechanical solution is offered. The determination must be made whether the danger of undue prejudice outweighs the probative value of the evidence in view of the availability of other means of proof and other facts appropriate for making decision of this kind under 403." Thus the notes leave no question that when Rule 403 confers discretion by providing that evidence "may" be excluded, the discretionary judgment may be informed not only by assessing an evidentiary item's twin tendencies, but by placing the result of that assessment alongside similar assessments of evidentiary alternatives.

2

In dealing with the specific problem raised by § 922(g)(1) and its prior-conviction element, there can be no question that evidence of the name or nature of the prior offense generally carries a risk of unfair prejudice to the defendant. That risk will vary from case to case, for the reasons already given, but will be substantial whenever the official record offered by the Government would be arresting enough to lure a juror into a sequence of bad character reasoning. Where a prior conviction was for a gun crime or one similar to other charges in a pending case the risk of unfair prejudice would be especially obvious, and Old Chief sensibly worried that the prejudicial effect of his prior assault conviction, significant enough with respect to the current gun charges alone, would take on added weight from the related assault charge against him.

The District Court was also presented with alternative, relevant, admissible evidence of the prior conviction by Old Chief's offer to stipulate, evidence necessarily subject to the District Court's consideration on the motion to exclude the record offered by the Government. Although Old Chief's formal offer to stipulate was, strictly, to enter a formal agreement with the Government to be given to the jury, even without the Government's acceptance his proposal amounted to an offer to admit that the prior-conviction element was satisfied, and a defendant's admission is, of course, good evidence.

Old Chief's proffered admission would, in fact, have been not merely relevant but seemingly conclusive evidence of the element. The statutory language in which the prior-conviction requirement is couched shows no congressional concern with the specific name or nature of the prior offense beyond what is necessary to place it within the broad category of qualifying felonies, and Old Chief clearly meant to admit that his felony did qualify, by stipulating "that the Government has proven one of the essential elements of the offense." As a consequence, although the name of the prior offense may have been technically relevant, it addressed no detail in the definition of the prior-conviction element that would not have been covered by the stipulation or admission. Logic, then, seems to side with Old Chief.

3

There is, however, one more question to be considered before deciding whether Old Chief's offer was to supply evidentiary value at least equivalent to what the Government's own evidence carried. In arguing that the stipulation or admission would not have carried equivalent value, the Government invokes the familiar, standard rule that the prosecution is entitled to prove its case by evidence of its own choice, or, more exactly, that a criminal defendant may not stipulate or admit his way out of the full evidentiary force of the case as the Government chooses to present it. The authority usually cited for this rule is Parr v. United States (1958), in which the Fifth Circuit explained that the "reason for the rule is to permit a party 'to present to the jury a picture of the events relied upon. To substitute for such a picture a naked admission might have the effect to rob the evidence of much of its fair and legitimate weight.'"

This is unquestionably true as a general matter. The "fair and legitimate weight" of conventional evidence showing individual thoughts and acts amounting to a crime reflects the fact that making a case with testimony and tangible things not only satisfies the formal definition of an offense, but tells a colorful story with descriptive richness. Unlike an abstract premise, whose force depends on going precisely to a particular step in a course of reasoning, a piece of evidence may address any number of separate elements, striking hard just because it shows so much at once; the account of a shooting that establishes capacity and causation may tell just as much about the triggerman's motive and intent. Evidence thus has force beyond any linear scheme of reasoning, and as its pieces come together a narrative gains momentum, with power not only to support conclusions but to sustain the willingness of jurors to draw the inferences, whatever they may be, necessary to reach an honest verdict. This persuasive power of the concrete and particular is often essential to the capacity of jurors to satisfy the obligations that the law places on them. Jury duty is usually unsought and sometimes resisted, and it may be as difficult for one juror suddenly to face the findings that can send another human being to prison, as it is for another to hold out conscientiously for acquittal. When a juror's duty does seem hard, the evidentiary account of what a defendant has thought and done can accomplish what no set of abstract statements ever could, not just to prove a fact but to establish its human significance, and so to implicate the law's moral underpinnings and a juror's obligation to sit in judgment. Thus, the prosecution may fairly seek to place its evidence before the jurors, as much to tell a story of guiltiness as to support an inference of guilt, to convince the jurors that a guilty verdict would be morally reasonable as much as to point to the discrete elements of a defendant's legal fault.

But there is something even more to the prosecution's interest in resisting efforts to replace the evidence of its choice with admissions and stipulations, for beyond the power of conventional evidence to support allegations and give life to the moral underpinnings of law's claims, there lies the need for evidence in all its particularity to satisfy the jurors' expectations about what proper proof should be. Some such demands they bring with them to the courthouse, assuming, for example, that a charge of using a firearm to commit an offense will be proven by introducing a gun in evidence. A prosecutor who fails to produce one, or some good reason for his failure, has something to be concerned about. "If [jurors'] expectations are not satisfied, triers of fact may penalize the party who disappoints them by drawing a negative inference against that party." Expectations may also arise in jurors' minds simply from the experience of a trial itself. The use of witnesses to describe a train of events naturally related can raise the prospect of learning about every ingredient of that natural sequence the same way. If suddenly the prosecution presents some occurrence in the series differently, as by announcing a stipulation or admission, the effect may be like saying, "never mind what's behind the door," and jurors may well wonder what they are being kept from knowing. A party seemingly responsible for cloaking something has reason for apprehension, and the prosecution with its burden of proof may prudently demur at a defense request to interrupt the flow of evidence telling the story in the usual way.

In sum, the accepted rule that the prosecution is entitled to prove its case free from any defendant's option to stipulate the evidence away rests on good sense. A syllogism is not a story, and a naked proposition in a courtroom may be no match for the robust evidence that would be used to prove it. People who hear a story interrupted by gaps of abstraction may be puzzled at the missing chapters, and jurors asked to rest a momentous decision on the story's truth can feel put upon at being asked to take responsibility knowing that more could be said than they have heard. A convincing tale can be told with economy, but when economy becomes a break in the natural sequence of narrative evidence, an assurance that the missing link is really there is never more than second best.

4

This recognition that the prosecution with its burden of persuasion needs evidentiary depth to tell a continuous story has, however, virtually no application when the point at issue is a defendant's legal status, dependent on some judgment rendered wholly independently of the concrete events of later criminal behavior charged against him. As in this case, the choice of evidence for such an element is usually not between eventful narrative and abstract proposition, but between propositions of slightly varying abstraction, either a record saying that conviction for some crime occurred at a certain time or a statement admitting the same thing without naming the particular offense.... Congress ... has made it plain that distinctions among generic felonies do not count for this purpose; the fact of the qualifying conviction is alone what matters under the statute. "A defendant falls within the category simply by virtue of past conviction for any [qualifying] crime ranging from possession of short lobsters, see 16 U.S.C. § 3372, to the most aggravated murder." The most the jury needs to know is that the conviction admitted by the defendant falls within the class of crimes that Congress thought should bar a convict from possessing a gun, and this point may be made readily in a defendant's admission and underscored in the court's jury instructions. Finally, the most obvious reason that the general presumption that the prosecution may choose its evidence is so remote from application here is that proof of the defendant's status goes to an element entirely outside the natural sequence of what the defendant is charged with thinking and doing to commit the current offense. Proving status without telling exactly why that status was imposed leaves no gap in the story of a defendant's subsequent criminality, and its demonstration by stipulation or admission neither displaces a chapter from a continuous sequence of conventional evidence nor comes across as an officious substitution, to confuse or offend or provoke reproach.

Given these peculiarities of the element of felony-convict status and of admissions and the like when used to prove it, there is no cognizable difference between the evidentiary significance of an admission and of the legitimately probative component of the official record the prosecution would prefer to place in evidence. For purposes of the Rule 403 weighing of the probative against the prejudicial, the functions of the competing evidence are distinguishable only by the risk inherent in the one and wholly absent from the other. In this case, as in any other in which the prior conviction is for an offense likely to support conviction on some improper ground, the only reasonable conclusion was that the risk of unfair prejudice did substantially outweigh the discounted probative value of the record of conviction, and it was an abuse of discretion to admit the record when an admission was available. What we have said shows why this will be the general rule when proof of convict status is at issue, just as the prosecutor's choice will generally survive a Rule 403 analysis when a defendant seeks to force the substitution of an admission for evidence creating a coherent narrative of his thoughts and actions in perpetrating the offense for which he is being tried.

The judgment is reversed.

O'Connor, J. Dissenting

…. Rule 403 does not permit the court to exclude the Government's evidence simply because it may hurt the defendant. As a threshold matter, evidence is excludable only if it is "unfairly" prejudicial, in that it has "an undue tendency to suggest decision on an improper basis." Advisory Committee's Notes on Fed. Rule Evid. 403…. Perhaps petitioner's case was damaged when the jury discovered that he previously had committed a felony and heard the name of his crime. But I cannot agree with the Court that it was unfairly prejudicial for the Government to establish an essential element of its case against petitioner with direct proof of his prior conviction….

[I]n our system of justice, a person is not simply convicted of "a crime" or "a felony." Rather, he is found guilty of a specified offense, almost always because he violated a specific statutory prohibition. For example, in the words of the order that the Government offered to prove petitioner's prior conviction in this case, petitioner "did knowingly and unlawfully assault Rory Dean Fenner, said assault resulting in serious bodily injury, in violation of Title 18 U.S.C. §§ 1153 and 113(f)." That a variety of crimes would have satisfied the prior conviction element of the § 922(g)(1) offense does not detract from the fact that petitioner committed a specific offense. The name and basic nature of petitioner's crime are inseparable from the fact of his earlier conviction and were therefore admissible to prove petitioner's guilt….

The Court never explains precisely why it constitutes "unfair" prejudice for the Government to directly prove an essential element of the § 922(g)(1) offense with evidence that reveals the name or basic nature of the defendant's prior conviction. It simply notes that such evidence may lead a jury to conclude that the defendant has a propensity to commit crime, thereby raising the odds that the jury would find that he committed the crime with which he is currently charged….

Yes, to be sure, Rule 404(b) provides that "[e]vidence of other crimes, wrongs, or acts is not admissible to prove the character of a person in order to show action in conformity therewith." But Rule 404(b) does not end there. It expressly contemplates the admission of evidence of prior crimes for other purposes, "such as proof of motive, opportunity, intent, preparation, plan, knowledge, identity, or absence of mistake or accident." The list is plainly not exhaustive, and where, as here, a prior conviction is an element of the charged offense, neither Rule 404(b) nor Rule 403 can bar its admission. The reason is simple: In a prosecution brought under § 922(g)(1), the Government does not submit evidence of a past crime to prove the defendant's bad character or to "show action in conformity therewith." It tenders the evidence as direct proof of a necessary element of the offense with which it has charged the defendant....

Any incremental harm resulting from proving the name or basic nature of the prior felony can be properly mitigated by limiting jury instructions. Federal Rule of Evidence 105 provides that when evidence is admissible for one purpose, but not another, "the court, upon request, shall restrict the evidence to its proper scope and instruct the jury accordingly." Indeed, on petitioner's own motion in this case, the District Court instructed the jury that it was not to "'consider a prior conviction as evidence of guilt of the crime for which the defendant is now on trial.'" The jury is presumed to have followed this cautionary instruction, and the instruction offset whatever prejudice might have arisen from the introduction of petitioner's prior conviction.... I respectfully dissent.

LIMITING INSTRUCTIONS

RULE 105

Justice O'Connor dissenting in *Old Chief* raises a possible solution to the danger of unfair prejudice. The trial judge could instruct the jury not to consider the nature of Old Chief's past conviction in the unfairly prejudicial manner. *Take a moment to think about what an instruction like that would say.*

"Limiting instructions" are specifically authorized in Rule 105. The Advisory Committee Note to that rule states:

> "A close relationship exists between this rule and Rule 403 which requires exclusion when 'probative value is substantially outweighed

by the danger of unfair prejudice, confusion of the issues, or misleading the jury.' The present rule recognizes the practice of admitting evidence for a limited purpose and instructing the jury accordingly. The availability and effectiveness of this practice must be taken into consideration in reaching a decision whether to exclude for unfair prejudice under Rule 403."

As the Note recognizes, the degree to which a limiting instruction solves the Rule 403 problem depends on its "effectiveness." The effectiveness of limiting instructions varies by context. For the most part, however, courts will presume that jurors follow the instructions that judges give them even if the empirical basis for that assumption is uncertain.

Here is a representative excerpt from a Supreme Court case summarizing this concept:

> This accords with the almost invariable assumption of the law that jurors follow their instructions, which we have applied in many varying contexts. For example, in Harris v. New York (1971), we held that statements elicited from a defendant in violation of Miranda v. Arizona (1966) can be introduced to impeach that defendant's credibility, even though they are inadmissible as evidence of his guilt, so long as the jury is instructed accordingly. Similarly, in Spencer v. Texas (1967), we held that evidence of the defendant's prior criminal convictions could be introduced for the purpose of sentence enhancement, so long as the jury was instructed it could not be used for purposes of determining guilt. See also Tennessee v. Street (1985) (instruction to consider accomplice's incriminating confession only for purpose of assessing truthfulness of defendant's claim that his own confession was coerced); Watkins v. Sowders (1981) (instruction not to consider erroneously admitted eyewitness identification evidence); Walder v. United States (1954) (instruction to consider unlawfully seized physical evidence only in assessing defendant's credibility).[1]

In that same case, the Supreme Court also candidly noted that: "The rule that juries are presumed to follow their instructions is a pragmatic one, rooted less

---

[1] Richardson v. Marsh, 481 U.S. 200 (1987).

in the absolute certitude that the presumption is true than in the belief that it represents a reasonable practical accommodation of the interests of the state and the defendant in the criminal justice process."

The presumption does not apply in all circumstances. As the Supreme Court itself has recognized:

> "[T]here are some contexts in which the risk that the jury will not, or cannot, follow instructions is so great, and the consequences of failure so vital to the defendant, that the practical and human limitations of the jury system cannot be ignored."[1]

Any time a court or practitioner doubts the efficacy of an instruction, one will typically find the famous quote of Justice Jackson: "The naive assumption that prejudicial effects can be overcome by instructions to the jury, all practicing lawyers know to be unmitigated fiction."[2]

The Advisory Committee Note to Rule 403, similarly states: "In reaching a decision whether to exclude on grounds of unfair prejudice, consideration should be given to the probable effectiveness or lack of effectiveness of a limiting instruction."

AN ILLUSTRATIVE EXAMPLE: PHOTOS

A common Rule 403 scenario involves gruesome photographs of crime scenes and injuries. Here is a representative discussion of the issue from State v. Bondy,[3] an Arizona case involving a horrific car crash that resulted in murder charges for the driver who caused it:

> "Whether the trial court abused its discretion in admitting a photograph turns on (1) the photograph's relevance, (2) its tendency to inflame the jury, and (3) its probative value compared to its potential to cause unfair prejudice." "Photographs of the deceased are relevant in a murder case 'because the fact and cause of death are always relevant in a murder prosecution.'" And, photographs of deceased victims are admissible in murder prosecutions "to show the nature and

---

[1] Bruton v. United States, 391 U.S. 123 (1968).
[2] Krulewitch v. United States (1949) (concurring opinion).
[3] Ariz. Ct. App. 2019.

location of the fatal injury, to help determine the degree or atrociousness of the crime, to corroborate state witnesses, to illustrate or explain testimony, and to corroborate the state's theory of how and why the homicide was committed."

Relevant photographs may be admitted even though they "also have a tendency to prejudice the jury against the person who committed the offense." "When a relevant photograph is inflammatory, however, the court should not admit it without first determining whether the danger of unfair prejudice substantially outweighs the photograph's probative value."

Warning: the following excerpt includes a short description of extremely disturbing photographs; if you think it will disturb you, feel free to skip over the balance of this excerpt to the next italicized text.

Bondy concedes Exhibit 108 was relevant to illustrating how the accident occurred but contends that ... the photograph was inflammatory because M.C.'s decapitated body is "deeply disturbing" and asserts the redactions made the photograph "only slightly less gruesome," as "[t]he absence of a head is still troubling" and the presence of brain matter on the backseat and J.C.'s "flattened head" were still visible. Bondy also argues the trial court erred in finding J.C.'s head did not need to be redacted. Finally, Bondy contends that a "black bar could have been placed so as to cover [M.C.]'s body above the tire marks, as the defense suggested, and [J.C.]'s flattened head and the brain matter" in order to "remove[ ] the horror and [make] it less likely for the jury to make a decision based on emotion." Therefore, Bondy argues, the court erred by not ordering further redaction of Exhibit 108. We disagree.

First, although Bondy did not dispute the manner of the accident or cause of death, the photograph was relevant to show how the accident occurred and to explain the cause of death. And, because Bondy was charged with second-degree murder, the issue was whether he acted recklessly "[u]nder circumstances manifesting extreme indifference to human life" when he caused the accident. Exhibit 108 depicts the car with its roof shorn off by the impact and tire marks on M.C.'s shirt.

Thus, the photograph reveals the extreme nature of the accident and resulting injuries. Exhibit 108 could help the jury determine the degree of the crime, corroborate the state's witnesses and explain their testimony, and support the state's theory that the accident was caused by Bondy acting recklessly. It was relevant.

Second, although Exhibit 108 was disturbing, it was not inflammatory. Contrary to Bondy's assertion that M.C.'s vertebrae were merely "blurred" and that "it is still clear that her head is absent," the state placed a gray circle over M.C.'s body from below the headrest to the tire marks on her chest, thereby obscuring the area where M.C.'s head would have been. The state also redacted the piece of skull and brain matter in the backseat. Together, these redactions eliminated the chief elements that made the photograph gruesome, thus making it unlikely to inflame the jury. Further, the trial court was within its discretion when it determined J.C.'s head was not gruesome and did not require redaction. The court did not abuse its discretion in implicitly finding the photograph's probative value was not outweighed by the potential for unfair prejudice. See State v. Rienhardt, 190 Ariz. 579 (1997) ("There is nothing sanitary about murder, and there is nothing in Rule 403 that requires a trial judge to make it so.")

If it makes you uncomfortable to read about the photographs, what does that say about their likely impact on the jurors? Does the Arizona court disagree? If not, why are the photograph admissible?

Rule 104(c)

One last point on this topic. If a court excludes evidence on the ground that it would improperly influence the jury, logic dictates that the court should rule in a manner that prevents the jury from becoming aware of the excluded evidence. Rule 104(c) captures this insight. It states: "The court must conduct any hearing on a preliminary question so that the jury cannot hear it if … justice so requires." Notice that this is an important distinction between a jury trial and a "bench trial," where the judge acts as factfinder.

PROBLEM 3-1 LITIGATION ETHICS

Imagine an attorney seeks to introduce evidence that is likely to influence jurors in an advantageous but legally improper way. The attorney comes up with a permissible purpose for the evidence and the trial court rules that the evidence is admissible over the opponent's Rule 403 objection. Has the successful attorney done something unethical by introducing the evidence if the attorney's true motive is a desire that the jurors rely on the evidence for the (legally) improper purpose? Here is one answer from an experienced lawyer and law professor in one of the most explosive contexts:

> "There is nothing unethical about using racial, gender, ethnic, or sexual stereotypes in criminal defense. It is simply an aspect of zealous advocacy. Prejudice exists in the community and in the courthouse, and criminal defense lawyers would be foolhardy not to recognize this as a fact of life."[1]

Do you agree? Does your answer depend on the attorney role involved (civil, criminal, prosecution, defense)? Does it depend on the type of improper purpose or the type of case? How should lawyers answer these questions?

---

[1] Abbe Smith, Defending Defending, 28 Hofstra L. Rev. 925 (2000).

Chapter 4

CHARACTER EVIDENCE

American evidence law draws on its common law heritage for one of its defining features: the complex regulation of character evidence.

PROHIBITION OF CHARACTER EVIDENCE

We first encountered character evidence in the *Old Chief* case in the preceding section. Recall that in *Old Chief*, the defendant faced two charges: (1) possessing a firearm unlawfully because of a prior felony conviction, and (2) "assault with a dangerous weapon." The second charge enhanced the prospect that the introduction of the name of Old Chief's prior conviction -- "assault resulting in serious bodily injury" -- would be *unfairly* prejudicial. The jury might have considered the past conviction not solely as proof of an element of the firearm offense, but also as evidence that Old Chief was a violent person. As Justice Souter explained more fully in a portion of the opinion omitted from the earlier excerpt, the reason this constitutes *unfair* prejudice stemmed from Rule 404's prohibition of character evidence:

> Such improper grounds [for the use of the name of the prior conviction] certainly include the one that Old Chief points to here: generalizing a defendant's earlier bad act into bad character and taking that as raising the odds that he did the later bad act now charged (or, worse, as calling for preventive conviction even if he should happen to be innocent momentarily). "Although ... 'propensity evidence' is relevant, the risk that a jury will convict for crimes other than those charged—or that, uncertain of guilt, it will convict anyway because a bad person deserves punishment—creates a prejudicial effect that outweighs ordinary relevance." Justice Jackson described how the law has handled this risk:
>
> > "Courts that follow the common-law tradition almost unanimously have come to disallow resort by the prosecution to any kind of evidence of a defendant's evil character to establish a probability of his guilt. Not that the law invests the

defendant with a presumption of good character, but it simply closes the whole matter of character, disposition and reputation on the prosecution's case-in-chief. The state may not show defendant's prior trouble with the law, specific criminal acts, or ill name among his neighbors, even though such facts might logically be persuasive that he is by propensity a probable perpetrator of the crime. The inquiry is not rejected because character is irrelevant; on the contrary, it is said to weigh too much with the jury and to so overpersuade them as to prejudge one with a bad general record and deny him a fair opportunity to defend against a particular charge. The overriding policy of excluding such evidence, despite its admitted probative value, is the practical experience that its disallowance tends to prevent confusion of issues, unfair surprise and undue prejudice." Michelson v. United States (1948).

Rule of Evidence 404(b) reflects this common-law tradition....[1]

Another summary of the law's prohibition of character evidence comes from then-Judge Cardozo in People v. Zackowitz, 254 N.Y. 192 (1930).

[C]haracter is never an issue in a criminal prosecution unless the defendant chooses to make it one. In a very real sense a defendant starts his life afresh when he stands before a jury, a prisoner at the bar. There has been a homicide in a public place. The killer admits the killing, but urges self-defense and sudden impulse. Inflexibly the law has set its face against the endeavor to fasten guilt upon him by proof of character or experience predisposing to an act of crime. The endeavor has been often made, but always it has failed. At times, when the issue has been self-defense, testimony has been admitted as to the murderous propensity of the deceased, the victim of the homicide, but never of such a propensity on the part of the killer. The principle back of the exclusion is one, not of logic, but of policy. There may be cogency in the argument that a quarrelsome defendant is more likely to start a quarrel than one of milder type, a man of dangerous mode of

---

[1] Old Chief v. United States (1997).

life more likely than a shy recluse. The law is not blind to this, but equally it is not blind to the peril to the innocent if character is accepted as probative of crime. 'The natural and inevitable tendency of the tribunal -- whether judge or jury -- is to give excessive weight to the vicious record of crime thus exhibited, and either to allow it to bear too strongly on the present charge, or to take the proof of it as justifying a condemnation irrespective of guilt of the present charge.'

RULE 404(a)(1) & (b)(1)

As Justice Souter points out in *Old Chief*, the common law tradition barring character evidence is now captured in Rule 404. The Rule states the prohibition in its first sentence, Rule 404(a)(1):

> "Evidence of a person's character or character trait is not admissible to prove that on a particular occasion the person acted in accordance with the character trait."

The paradigmatic effect of this prohibition is that the prosecution cannot try to establish that a defendant is a "bad person" (character) or a "violent person" (character trait) to suggest that the defendant, therefore, is more likely to have committed a charged crime.

Rule 404(b)(1) restates the principle already stated in Rule 404(a)(1), addressing the most obvious means of violating Rule 404(a)(1) -- through the introduction of a past "crime, wrong or other act." Rule 404(b)(1) makes clear, for example, that the prosecution in *Old Chief* could not offer the testimony of the victim of Old Chief's 1988 assault (or a paper record of that past crime) to suggest that Old Chief is the kind of person who would have committed the 1993 assault with which he was charged.

Here is one last explanation for the prohibition of character evidence from the Supreme Court of New Jersey:

> It has oft been recognized that "[t]he underlying danger of admitting other-crime [or bad-act] evidence is that the jury may convict the defendant because he is 'a "bad" person in general.'" For that reason, any evidence that is in the nature of prior bad acts, wrongs, or, worse, crimes by a defendant is examined cautiously because it "'has a unique

tendency'" to prejudice a jury. Put simply, a defendant must be convicted on the basis of his acts in connection with the offense for which he is charged…. Because N.J.R.E. 404(b) guards against the wholly unacceptable prospect that a jury might become prejudiced against a defendant based on earlier reprehensible conduct, the rule "is often described as [one] of exclusion."[1]

ADMISSIBILITY FOR ANOTHER PURPOSE

Rule 404 does not preclude evidence of uncharged (bad) acts entirely. It only bars use of those acts for a particular purpose, "propensity reasoning." We can think of propensity reasoning as a type of logic:

Past Violent Act → Defendant is Violent Person → Defendant Committed Charged Violent Crime

or

Past Careless Act → Plaintiff is Careless Person → Plaintiff Acted Negligently in Incurring Injury

Under the common law tradition, the jury is simply not permitted to engage in that kind of reasoning. Consequently, Rule 404 excludes evidence offered to support such reasoning.

RULE 404(b)(2)

Sometimes, a past act can be offered to support a different line of reasoning. If so, Rule 404 does not prohibit that evidence (as Rule 404(b)(2) makes clear). This is one of the most important areas of Evidence law to get right. Courts and litigants often struggle with these concepts and they can be important to case outcomes. But don't take my word for it:

- "Rule 404(b) has generated more published opinions than any other subsection of the Federal Rules. In many jurisdictions, alleged errors

---

[1] State v. Skinner, 218 N.J. 496, 514 (2014).

in the admission of uncharged misconduct evidence are the most common ground for appeal in criminal cases."[1]

- "No other evidentiary rule comes close to this rule as a breeder of issues for appeals."[2]

- "Rule 404(b) has become the most cited evidentiary rule on appeal."[3]

- "This case is another in the ever-increasing number of cases interpreting the rule excluding other crimes evidence, the most litigated rule of evidence."[4]

- "Rule 404(b) has emerged as one of the most cited rules in the Rules of Evidence."[5]

Given its prominence in the evidentiary landscape, Rule 404(b) takes up the balance of this Chapter.

CASE STUDIES: OTHER PURPOSES

Consider the following excerpts where courts allowed the government to introduce evidence of acts other than those charged in the case. *Carefully assess why this was permissible under Rule 404.*

• *United States v. Pindell* concerned multiple robberies of men soliciting prostitutes in Washington, D.C.[6] The government's case against Warren Pindell was based, in part, on identifications by the prostitutes. "Prior to trial, the government sought and received the district court's permission to introduce testimony from two prostitutes — each of whom witnessed a robbery charged in the indictment — that Pindell had previously paid them to engage in sexual acts."

The D.C. Circuit rejected Pindell's argument on appeal that this evidence violated Rule 404(b):

---

[1] Edward Imwinkelried, *The Use of Evidence of an Accused's Uncharged Misconduct to Prove Mens Rea*, 51 OHIO ST. L.J. 575 (1990).
[2] Thomas Reed, *Admitting the Accused's Criminal History: The Trouble with Rule 404(b)*, 78 TEMP. L. REV. 201 (2005).
[3] United States v. Davis, 726 F.3d 434 (3d Cir. 2013).
[4] State v. Rutchik, 116 Wis. 2d 61 (1984) (Abrahamson, J. dissenting).
[5] FED. R. EV. 404, Advisory Committee Note to 1991 Amendment.
[6] 336 F.3d 1049 (D.C. Cir. 2003).

The government offered this evidence because it showed the prostitutes' familiarity with Pindell, and hence "their ability to identify" him. Pindell's identity as the uniformed robber was plainly at issue in the trial, and particularly so because Pindell proffered defense witnesses who testified that a man named "Boo" Farrow had been robbing prostitutes' customers during the relevant period — implying that the prosecution witnesses had mistaken Farrow for Pindell. Since Rule 404(b) expressly permits the admission of "other crimes" evidence to prove identity, the district court did not err in admitting the testimony.

• In *United States v. Early*,[1] the government sought to prove that Glen Early was the driver of a car that flipped over during a police chase. A police officer identified Early as the driver and described Early, during his escape from the flipped car, holding his arm as if it was injured. About a week later, police arrested Early who now had a cast on his arm. At the time of his arrest, Early had "a Kaiser Permanente health card in the name of Marcus Williams." In their case against Early, the government offered this evidence to prove another act (i.e., an act other than that for which he was charged), specifically Early's possession of the health card and evidence that "the day after the car chase, someone used this health card to receive treatment for an injury to his left arm, and that person was not Marcus Williams."

The D.C. Circuit rejected Early's argument that this violated Rule 404, explaining:

> Rule 404(b) bars only the introduction of evidence offered solely to show a defendant's character, and the testimony pertaining to the use of the Kaiser Permanente health card was offered for a different and proper purpose of proving Early's identity as the driver of the car.... The testimony revealing that Early used his cousin's Kaiser Permanente health insurance card to obtain medical treatment ... helped establish his identity as the driver of the Mazda—Officer Jewell had observed that after the car overturned, its driver was holding his

---

[1] 12 F.3d 1128 (D.C. Cir. 1994).

left arm as if it were injured, and Early was treated for an injured left arm.

• In *United States v. Morris*,[1] the government sought to prove that Murl Morris resisted arrest by assaulting a federal officer with a handgun. Prior to trial, Morris "filed a motion in limine to prevent the submission of evidence that [at the time of the alleged assault,] the FBI was looking for him in regard to a murder in the State of Texas." The Tenth Circuit rejected Morris' argument that informing the jury of the alleged Texas murder violated Rule 404:

> [T]he district court took precautions to limit the prejudicial nature of the evidence. References to the outstanding murder warrant were limited, no details of the murder were given to the jury, and the jury was warned that Mr. Morris was presumed innocent of the murder charge. Because the evidence was highly probative of Mr. Morris' motive to flee arrest and possibly use deadly force in order to avoid arrest, the district court correctly allowed its admission.

***

These three cases illustrate the principle set out in Rule 404(b)(2). Evidence of acts other than those that constitute the charged crime cannot be admitted to show propensity, but can be admitted for "another purpose." The rule then sets forth a list of other purposes drawn from pre-rules case law: "proving motive, opportunity, intent, preparation, plan, knowledge, identity, absence of mistake, or lack of accident."

The distinction between past acts prohibited and permitted under Rule 404 is a critical one in the law of evidence. Here are three key points to consider in this context:

(1) Rule 404(b)(2) does not create an exception to the bar on propensity reasoning. Rather, Rule 404(b)(2) illustrates the limited restriction of Rule 404(a)(1) and (b)(1). This is why the Advisory Committee Note to the rule characterizes Rule 404(b) as an *application* of the prohibition on propensity reasoning:

---

[1] 287 F.3d 985 (10th Cir. 2002).

"Subdivision (b) deals with a specialized but important application of the general rule excluding circumstantial use of character evidence. Consistently with that rule, evidence of other crimes, wrongs, or acts is not admissible to prove character as a basis for suggesting the inference that conduct on a particular occasion was in conformity with it. However, the evidence may be offered for another purpose, such as proof of motive, opportunity, and so on, which does not fall within the prohibition."

The key conceptual point is that other act evidence can be used for "another purpose" -- i.e., a purpose other than the forbidden propensity reasoning. It is that showing -- that the evidence is being used for a purpose other than to support propensity reasoning -- that enables admission under Rule 404(b)(2). As we will see, it is not a proper interpretation of the rule to allow evidence of other acts to prove "motive," "identity," etc., through propensity reasoning.

(2) "This prohibition [on using other acts as propensity evidence] remains even when the court has admitted the Rule 404(b) evidence for some permissible non-propensity purpose—the government cannot later argue that the evidence shows the defendant's propensity to engage in criminal behavior."[1]

For example, in the *Morris* case, even after the court admitted the evidence of the outstanding warrant, the prosecution could not argue to the jury that this evidence supported an inference that Morris was a violent or dangerous person -- the kind of person who might be expected to assault a police officer.

(3) Rule 404 is a rule of exclusion not admission. That means that even if evidence makes it through Rule 404's restrictions, there are other rules, like Rule 403, that may still require exclusion. In applying Rule 403, the danger that the evidence, even if admissible for a non-propensity purpose, will nevertheless be used to support propensity reasoning, will often be a powerful factor counseling against admission.

PROBLEM 4-1: ARSON UNDER DURESS?

In considering this problem, keep in mind that Rule 404's prohibition on character reasoning applies to any type of propensity reasoning. The rule bars

---

[1] United States v. Richards, 719 F.3d 746 (7th Cir. 2013).

the jury from using propensity reasoning about anyone in a case, the defendant, victim, a witness, anyone.

In *United States v. Jones*,[1] "Calvin Jones was convicted … for participating in an arson with Samson Wright. The issue at trial was whether Wright coerced Jones into participating" -- i.e., duress. At trial, Jones sought to introduce evidence about past violent actions engaged in by Wright.

> "Jones wanted to establish prior assaults by Wright, Wright's reputation for violence, and Wright's tendency to carry a gun to inform the jury about why Jones has a well-founded fear of Wright the night of the arson. Jones proffered that he would testify that in 2010, Wright pulled a gun on him and demanded payment of a $30 debt, which Jones then paid, and that on another occasion Wright put Jones in a headlock and touched a bullet that is lodged in Jones's neck against his spine and then laughed about it after releasing Jones. Jones would also testify that he knew the following: 'Wright shot Clifford Ellis in the rear end, and on another occasion Samson Wright hit Clifford Ellis over the head with a baseball bat to collect a claimed debt'; 'Wright made a man strip naked, put a dog leash around his neck, made him bark, and paraded him down to E. Jefferson'; 'Wright regularly carried a gun and a switchblade'; …. Jones sought to introduce this evidence via his own testimony, cross-examination of Wright, and the testimony of seven witnesses who said they had witnessed one or more of these events and would corroborate Jones's testimony. These witnesses would also testify to Wright's reputation for violence and other specific violent acts that Wright carried out."

To establish the defense of duress, Jones needs to convince the jury that he "was under an unlawful and present, imminent, and impending threat of such a nature as to induce a well-grounded apprehension of death or serious bodily injury."

Should the trial court have admitted the evidence offered by Jones? If so, for what purpose?

---

[1] *United States v. Jones*, 554 F. App'x 460 (6th Cir. 2014).

PROBLEM 4-2: ONLINE CRIME

Jimmy Chill is charged with unlawfully accessing the James Hill High School computer system in October 2015 and redirecting funds from the school to a charity, Rehabilitating Sex Offenders (RSO). The charity provides persons convicted of sex offenses with housing and employment opportunities to try to help prevent recidivism.

Citing Rule 404(b), the prosecution seeks at trial to introduce testimony from the high school principal that in May 2013, Chill, then a high school senior, admitted to hacking into the high school's computers to alter his grades. The principal will also testify that Chill repeatedly got in trouble at school for fighting with other students. Finally, the government seeks to introduce evidence that Chill was convicted in 2014 of a felony sex offense.

Evaluate the potential admissibility of the three types of evidence that the government seeks to offer:

    (1) evidence of the May 2013 computer hacking;

    (2) evidence of the defendant's school disciplinary problems;

    (3) evidence of the defendant's sex offense conviction.

UNITED STATES v. MILLER
673 F.3d 688 (7th Cir. 2012)

HAMILTON, Circuit Judge.

In April 2008, acting on a tip from a confidential informant, police obtained a search warrant and then raided a home where defendant Shariff Miller and several other people were staying. After apprehending Miller on his way out the side door, police searched the house and found several guns and a quantity of crack cocaine. The cocaine and a pistol were found close to some of Miller's personal effects in a room where he was alleged to be staying. Miller was tried and convicted of … possessing more than five grams of crack cocaine with intent to distribute, [and] possession of a firearm in furtherance of a drug crime…. He was sentenced to a total of twenty years in prison….

Miller objects to the introduction at trial of evidence of [1] his possession, two months earlier, of the same pistol the police found in the search.... [2] evidence that Miller had been convicted in 2000 of felony possession of cocaine with intent to distribute it....

II. Evidence of Prior Possession of the Pistol

Police found three guns while searching the house. One semi-automatic pistol was found, cocked and loaded, under the mattress in the bedroom where the crack cocaine was found and where Miller was alleged to be staying. Two rifles were located in a closet in another room. The government charged Miller with possessing all three guns "on or about April 21, 2008," the day of the search and his arrest. The jury ultimately convicted Miller of possessing the pistol and one of the rifles as a felon, and of possessing the pistol in furtherance of drug trafficking. At the trial, a witness testified that she had seen Miller take the same pistol out of his pants and place it on a table in February, some two months before his arrest....

Miller argued at trial and on appeal that this testimony was inadmissible under Federal Rule of Evidence 404(b), which prohibits the use of prior bad acts to suggest a propensity to have committed such an act on a particular occasion. According to Miller, the government used the testimony that he unlawfully possessed a gun in February to suggest to the jury that he is the sort of person who unlawfully possesses guns, and so likely possessed a gun in April when charged. The government counters, and we agree, that the testimony was in fact circumstantial evidence of the charged crime. It concerned the same gun, and the prior observed possession was relatively recent. In the language of Rule 404(b), the government used the evidence for "another purpose" permitted by the rule. Miller's prior possession and display of the rusty grey pistol suggest that he owned or at least had the ability to exercise control over that rusty grey pistol....

III. Evidence of Prior Intent to Distribute Cocaine

The government's use of Miller's eight-year-old conviction for possession of cocaine with intent to distribute was far more problematic, and the admission of that evidence here requires reversal of his conviction on the two drug-related charges. Miller was caught in 2000 with crack cocaine and pled guilty to felony possession with intent to distribute. At that time, the cocaine was also packaged in small plastic bags inside larger plastic bags—though Miller was of course not unusual in packaging drugs for sale in this way. When officers searched the house on April 21, 2008, they found crack cocaine packaged in plastic bags on the bed in Miller's alleged room. They also found a scale and similarly packaged cocaine in shoe boxes that also contained some of Miller's personal papers. Miller has never argued that the bags of drugs— some of which had price tags attached—were not intended for distribution. His defense at trial was instead that, despite the proximity to his personal effects, the drugs were not in fact his and he was not staying in the room where the drugs and pistol were found....

The arguments presented in this case suggest that admission of prior drug crimes to prove intent to commit present drug crimes has become too routine. Closer attention needs to be paid to the reasons for using prior drug convictions—to lessen the danger that defendants like Miller will be convicted because the prosecution invited, and the jury likely made, an improper assumption about propensity to commit drug crimes.

Rule 404(b) does not provide a rule of automatic admission whenever bad acts evidence can be plausibly linked to "another purpose," such as knowledge or intent, listed in the rule. The Rule 402 requirement of relevance and the unfair prejudice balancing inquiries of Rule 403 still apply with full force. This must be so because the "list of exceptions in Rule 404(b), if applied mechanically, would overwhelm the central principle. Almost *any* bad act evidence simultaneously condemns by besmirching character and by showing one or more of 'motive, opportunity, intent, preparation, plan, knowledge, identity, or absence of mistake or accident', not to mention the 'other purposes' of which this list is meant to be illustrative." Rule 404(b) requires a case-by-case determination, not a categorical one. The trial judge must balance the relevance of the proposed use of the evidence to the case—and the evidence's relevance to that proof—against the high risk that the evidence will also tend to establish bad character and propensity to commit the charged crime. When, as was true here, intent is not meaningfully disputed by the defense, and the bad acts evidence is relevant to intent only because it implies a pattern or propensity to so intend, the trial court abuses its discretion by admitting it....

It is helpful to distinguish between two aspects of the relevance inquiry. The first aspect concerns whether a Rule 404(b) exception, like intent, is "at issue"—that is, whether the issue is relevant to the case. For example, knowledge may not be at issue at all where the charge is a strict liability offense, so that knowledge is not even an element of the crime. Similarly, while intent is at least formally relevant to all specific intent crimes, intent becomes more relevant, and evidence tending to prove intent becomes more probative, when the defense actually works to deny intent, joining the issue by contesting it. When, as in this case, the drugs in question were clearly a distribution quantity, the packages had price tags, and the defendant did not deny they were intended for distribution by someone, intent was "at issue" in only the most attenuated sense.

The second aspect of relevance is not concerned with whether the government must prove intent or how difficult that proof might be. This second inquiry assumes intent is relevant to the case and asks whether the bad acts evidence offered is relevant to and probative of intent, without being too unfairly prejudicial by invoking a propensity inference. In other words, can the government fairly use this evidence to meet its burden of proof on this issue? Intent can be "automatically at issue" because it is an element of a specific intent crime, but the prior bad acts evidence offered to prove intent can still be completely irrelevant to that issue, or relevant only in an impermissible way. Here, even though the purpose of proving "intent" was invoked, the bad acts evidence was not probative of intent except through an improper propensity inference....

We recognize that many of our cases approve the admission of prior drug-dealing crimes to show intent in drug-dealing prosecutions, despite the fact that, of the Rule 404(b) other purpose exceptions, intent is the exception most likely to blend with improper propensity uses. But in each of these cases, after discussing relevance of the evidence to intent, the court balanced the asserted probative value of the evidence against its potential for unfair prejudice. We have never approved admission of bad acts evidence solely because it was formally relevant to intent and intent was "at issue."

There may be enough cases affirming such admissions, however, that in cases charging specific-intent drug crimes, the admission of prior drug convictions may have come to seem almost automatic. It is not. ...

Confusion and misuse of Rule 404(b) can be avoided by asking the prosecution exactly how the proffered evidence should work in the mind of a juror to establish the fact the government claims to be trying to prove. Here, Miller claimed that the drugs found in the shoe box and on the bed were not his, that he was in effect an innocent bystander. Witnesses told the jury about Miller's arrest and conviction for dealing drugs in 2000. The government defends use of that evidence on the ground that it showed his intent to distribute drugs in 2008. How, exactly, does Miller's prior drug dealing conviction in 2000 suggest that he intended to deal drugs in 2008? When the question is framed this way, the answer becomes obvious, even though implicit: "He intended to do it before, ladies and gentlemen, so he must have intended to do it again." That is precisely the forbidden propensity inference.

And this is where the district court erred, even as it undertook the correct Rule 402 relevance and Rule 403 prejudice analysis—and cited some of our cases mentioned above. The court focused on whether intent was at issue based on Miller's defense and on the government's obligations of proof. Having concluded that intent was at issue, the court turned to analyze prejudice and simply stated that the evidence was highly probative of intent. Had the court asked more specifically how the prior conviction tended to show intent eight years later, it would have recognized that it was dealing with propensity evidence all the way down. Unless there is a persuasive and specific answer to the question, "How does this evidence prove intent?" then the real answer is almost certainly that the evidence is probative only of propensity....

.... The relevance of the prior conviction here boils down to the prohibited "once a drug dealer, always a drug dealer" argument. A prosecutor who wants to use prior bad acts evidence must come to court prepared with a specific reason, other than propensity, why the evidence will be probative of a disputed issue that is permissible under Rule 404(b). Mere recitation that a permissible Rule 404(b) purpose is "at issue" does not suffice.

For these reasons, we conclude that the admission of the details of Miller's 2000 conviction was an abuse of the district court's discretion.

***

The Seventh Circuit's opinion in *Miller* illustrates a variety of points. First, it is helpful in emphasizing a critical theme of this Chapter -- that simply relabeling propensity reasoning as proof of "intent" or "motive" or "lack of accident" does not avoid the character evidence prohibition in Rule 404. But the case also illustrates a tension that fills Rule 404(b) case law. The courts do not strictly police the line described above.

The Seventh Circuit strives to reconcile its ruling in *Miller* with other cases where the defendant admits to possessing drugs but claims not to have intended to sell those drugs (often the difference between a misdemeanor and felony conviction). In those cases, courts are more likely to admit a prior conviction for selling drugs as relevant to the 404(b) "exception" for "intent." Here is some language from one of the cases *Miller* cites:

> "The most obvious justifiable situation in which prior convictions are admissible in drug prosecutions on the issue of intent are in those situations in which the defendant, while admitting possession of the substance, denies the intent to distribute it." United States v. Jones, 455 F.3d 800 (7th Cir.2006).

Compare that language to the reasoning *Miller* says Rule 404 prohibits. Here are *Miller*'s instructions:

> (1) "Confusion and misuse of Rule 404(b) can be avoided by asking the prosecution exactly how the proffered evidence should work in the mind of a juror to establish the fact the government claims to be trying to prove."

> (2) "A prosecutor who wants to use prior bad acts evidence must come to court prepared with a specific reason, other than propensity, why the evidence will be probative of a disputed issue that is permissible under Rule 404(b)."

Apply *Miller*'s directive to *Jones*. *How would a past conviction for selling drugs "work in the mind of a juror to establish" the defendant's intent to sell a different set of drugs he is charged with possessing today?* Is the answer, "He intended to do it before, ladies and gentlemen, so he must have intended to do it again." Isn't that "precisely the forbidden propensity inference," barred by Rule 404? If so, then *Miller* is not carving out one set of circumstances ("innocent bystander") where a prior drug conviction should not be allowed as evidence of "intent." *Miller* is actually (and without explicitly stating it) casting doubt on cases like *Jones*.

The use (and abuse) of Rule 404(b) is an ongoing source of controversy. Consider the concurring opinion by Judge Ketchum of the Supreme Court of West Virginia:[1]

> …. I feel compelled to write separately because I believe that the use of "bad acts" evidence under Rule 404(b) in criminal trials is now routinely used to convince the jury that they should convict the defendant because he or she is not a nice person….

> As early as 1872, this Court said that evidence of misconduct other than that for which a defendant was being tried could not be used at a trial. We held in Watts v. State (1872):

>> Evidence of a distinct, substantive offense cannot be admitted in support of another offense.

> …. When I first started practicing law in 1967, prosecutors rarely if ever tried to convict a defendant using evidence of "uncharged misconduct" and "other bad acts." Courts were exceptionally restrictive, and rarely allowed the use of collateral crimes to be admitted. The defendant was tried for the crime charged in the warrant or the indictment. The common-law rule of evidence on "other bad acts" in West Virginia was a clear rule of exclusion: the evidence could not be admitted, except for a few narrow exceptions….

> In 1975, Congress adopted the Federal Rules of Evidence…. Rule 404(b) of the Federal Rules of Evidence codified the "uncharged misconduct" doctrine in two sentences, but it shifted the doctrine from being exclusionary to being inclusionary. That is to say, under Rule 404(b), it became easier to admit evidence of other bad acts…. With a few variations, this Court adopted most of the Federal Rules into the West Virginia Rules of Evidence in 1985.

> Because of the potentially decisive impact of uncharged misconduct, and its countervailing prejudicial character, defense attorneys vigorously contest the use of uncharged misconduct evidence. Consequently, Rule 404(b) disputes are the most frequently litigated

---

[1] *State v. Willett*, 223 W. Va. 394 (2009).

evidentiary issue in appellate courts.... In many cases, I believe that Rule 404(b) is being applied inconsistently. It appears that prosecutors and trial courts often search for a convenient "pigeonhole" to admit proof of other bad acts, then perform a perfunctory balance of the probative value against its prejudicial effect before admitting the other bad acts evidence. Because a trial court's review of questions under Rule 404(b) are discretionary, on appeal this Court has rarely found that the trial court abused its discretion in admitting the other bad acts evidence. If the Court does find the trial court abused its discretion, then this Court will often then hold that the admission of the other bad acts evidence in a criminal case was "harmless error."

As you work through this section, consider whether you agree with Judge Ketchum and if so, who do you think bears most of the blame (prosecutors, the rule drafters, or judges)?

MODUS OPERANDI

UNITED STATES v. MYERS
550 F.2d 1036 (5th Cir. 1977)

CLARK, Circuit Judge:

Larry Allen Myers challenges the validity of his federal bank robbery conviction. He contends that the district court committed reversible error when it ... admitted evidence indicating that Myers had previously been convicted of armed bank robbery....

On June 13, 1974, at approximately two o'clock in the afternoon, a branch of the First Federal Savings and Loan Association of Largo, located in Clearwater, Florida, was robbed by a lone gunman. He escaped with an estimated $1500. After changing cars at a nearby motel, the robber disappeared. There is no dispute about how the robbery was committed; the central issue in this case, despite two eyewitnesses and hundreds of still photographs taken by an automatic camera, is by whom.

.... Myers has been tried twice. The first trial ended with the declaration of a mistrial after the jury announced its inability to reach a verdict. A fortnight later, a second jury found Myers guilty as charged. The district court sentenced him to ten years' imprisonment on February 17, 1976....

Myers ... insists that the district court erred in admitting evidence of [a July 29, 1974] bank robbery in Pennsylvania for the alleged purpose of identifying Myers as the perpetrator of the Florida robbery. We agree.

> [Footnote 10] The fact that the uncharged crime occurred after rather than before the charged crime does not affect its admissibility.... Myers was indicted in connection with the Pennsylvania robbery. He pled not guilty, but was convicted on February 10, 1975.

Evidence of crimes not charged in the indictment is not admissible for the purpose of showing that the defendant has a criminal disposition in order to generate the inference that he committed the crime with which he is charged. Fed.R.Evid. 404(b). A concomitant of the presumption of innocence is that a defendant must be tried for what he did, not for who he is....

The government asserts that the evidence of the Pennsylvania bank robbery was admissible to prove that Myers committed the Florida bank robbery because it exhibits his characteristic modus operandi. This is a proper purpose. Fed.R.Evid. 404(b). The probity of evidence of other crimes where introduced for this purpose depends upon both the uniqueness of the modus operandi and the degree of similarity between the charged crime and the uncharged crime. Of course, it is not necessary that the charged crime and the other crimes be identical in every detail. But they must possess a common feature or features that make it very likely that the unknown perpetrator of the charged crime and the known perpetrator of the uncharged crime are the same person.... The evidence of other crimes involved in this case was admitted on this theory.

.... We have consistently held that for evidence of other crimes to be admissible the inference of identity flowing from it must be extremely strong. In United States v. Goodwin, for example, we said that evidence of a prior crime was inadmissible to prove identity because the two crimes did not "bear such peculiar, unique, or bizarre similarities as to mark them as the handiwork of the same individual." The question before us is whether the evidence of other crimes introduced in this case meets that standard.

In order to support its argument that the evidence of the Pennsylvania robbery was properly admitted, the government points to the following similarities between the charged and the uncharged crime: (1) both crimes were bank robberies, (2) perpetrated by [Myers' friend Dennis] Coffie and Myers, (3) between two and three o'clock in the afternoon. In both robberies the victimized bank was (4) located on the outskirts of a town, (5) adjacent to a major highway. In both robberies the participants (6) used a revolver, (7) furnished their own bag for carrying off the proceeds, and wore (8) gloves and (9) masks crudely fashioned from nylon stockings. Finally, (10), in one of the banks, two women employees were present; in the other, five women employees were present. The government's position is that these ten common features give the evidence of the other crime sufficient probative value to outweigh the prejudice its admission must inevitably cause Myers.

There are several flaws in this analysis. To begin with, the assertion that Coffie and Myers robbed both banks begs the question which the evidence of the uncharged crime is supposed to help us to answer: whether Myers perpetrated the Florida robbery. Moreover, the number and gender of employees present could only be a circumstance controlled by the robbers if they timed the robbery to coincide with the presence of such employees. Thus the time of the robbery and the presence of only a few female employees really constitute only a single common feature. Equally significant is the fact that each of the eight remaining similarities is a common component of armed bank robberies. When they are considered as a whole, the combination still lacks distinction. The presence of a marked dissimilarity that the charged crime was perpetrated by a lone gunman, while the uncharged crime was committed by two armed men further undermines the force of the inference of identity. An early afternoon robbery of an outlying bank situated on a highway, by revolver-armed robbers wearing gloves and stocking masks, and carrying a bag for the loot, is not such an unusual crime that it tends to prove that one of the two individuals involved must have been the single bandit in a similar prior robbery. The probative value of this evidence does not outweigh its substantial prejudicial effect. It was improperly admitted [and] reversible error.

STATE v. VORHEES
248 S.W.3d 585 (Mo. 2008)

[Shane Vorhees was charged with sexually assaulting his stepdaughter, J.W., over a two-year period, starting when she was 13 years old. A jury convicted Vorhees and the judge sentenced him to sixty years in prison.]

…. The issue in this appeal is whether the trial court properly admitted evidence of other uncharged sexual conduct with another minor to help prove that Vorhees committed the offenses in this case….

There are a number of exceptions to the general ban on evidence of prior criminal acts. These exceptions "are as well established as the rule itself" and include: (1) motive; (2) intent; (3) the absence of mistake or accident; (4) a common scheme or plan embracing the commission of two or more crimes so related to each other than proof of one tends to establish the other; and (5) the identity of the person charged with the commission of the crime on trial….

In addition to these "well-established" exceptions, the signature modus operandi exception, for corroboration, has emerged in this Court's jurisprudence as an exception to the general rule banning the admission of evidence of prior criminal acts. The signature modus operandi exception was first discussed [in Missouri case law by] Judge [David] Thomas [who] provided a general description of the requirements for signature modus operandi evidence of prior crimes, stating that such evidence would be admissible "to prove other like crimes by the accused so nearly identical in method as to earmark them as the handiwork of the accused. Here much more is demanded than the mere repeated commission of crimes of the same class, such as repeated burglaries or thefts. The device used must be so unusual and distinctive as to be like a signature." Judge Thomas conceived of [another form] of the signature modus operandi exception …, which Judge Thomas called "signature modus operandi/corroboration." Since there is no issue as to Vorhees' identity, it is the signature modus operandi corroboration exception that is at issue in the present case.

The classic example of the signature modus operandi identity exception discussed by Judge Thomas is the case of Jones v. State, 460 So.2d 1384 (Ala.Cr.App.1984). In Jones, the defendant was charged with leading his victim into an empty barn, where the victim was robbed at gunpoint by a second man who used a "long-barreled pistol" and wore a Halloween mask and a black wig. The court allowed testimony from a criminal investigator who testified that two weeks after the first robbery, he and another investigator went to a farm and posed as cattle buyers. The investigator was met by the defendant, who took him to a barn where the investigator was robbed at gunpoint by a man holding a long-barreled pistol and wearing a Halloween mask and a black wig. The signature modus operandi identity exception was used to admit the evidence of the second offense in order to connect the identity of the defendant with the identity of the perpetrator of the nearly-identical charged offense. In Jones, the defendant did not dispute whether or not the crime had occurred, but rather, whether he was the person who had perpetrated the crime. Evidence of the uncharged offense was relevant to establish the defendant's identity.

The signature modus operandi identity exception is simply a more specific form of the already established identity exception. Under the signature modus operandi identity exception, evidence of the defendant's prior criminal acts is not offered to prove his propensity to commit the charged offense. Instead, the prior acts are offered to establish the identity of the defendant as the perpetrator of the charged criminal act.

This identity exception has no bearing on the case at hand because J.W.'s testimony was not offered to establish Vorhees's identity, but instead to corroborate the testimony of the alleged victim in the charged case, S.W....

In cases where the signature modus operandi corroboration exception is used, the defendant does not dispute the purported victim's identification of the alleged perpetrator, but instead disputes whether or not a crime was actually committed. Evidence of highly similar prior criminal acts perpetrated by the defendant is offered, not to establish the identity of the perpetrator, but instead to corroborate the testimony of the alleged victim in the charged case. The logic behind this exception is that if a defendant committed a very similar crime previously, it is much more likely that the subsequent victim is telling the truth regarding the defendant's conduct in the charged case. Judge Thomas's proposed signature modus operandi corroboration exception was adopted by this Court in State v. Bernard (1993)....

Under the signature modus operandi corroboration exception, this Court in State v. Gilyard, upheld the trial court's admission of testimony concerning the defendant's prior criminal acts and affirmed the defendant's conviction for forcible rape and false imprisonment. This Court found that the record showed "a remarkably consistent pattern of sexual assaults that include[d] demanding sex and enforcing those demands through the unusual and distinctive means of biting the victims on the cheek." The Gilyard defendant did not argue that the victim had misidentified him; instead, the defendant argued that the acts of sexual intercourse underlying the charged offense had been consensual. Explaining its application of the signature corroboration exception, this Court stated that "[i]n a rape case, corroborative evidence can be highly probative of victim credibility and may even be essential, such as where the victim's testimony is unconvincing or contradictory."...

Signature evidence used for corroboration is, at base, propensity evidence masquerading under the well-recognized identity exception, a category of exception in which it does not belong.

Even in his initial proposal of the corroboration exception, Judge Thomas expressed … reservations, saying "[a]lthough we have called this exception corroboration, it really involves reasoning from the signature modus operandi based upon the propensity of the defendant to commit this type of crime to the conclusion that the defendant committed the crime charged. This reasoning goes squarely against the rationale for the general rule."….

By admitting the prior act evidence, the court is reasoning that if the defendant committed a very similar crime once before, it is more likely that he committed the same crime on a subsequent occasion. This reasoning, as Judge Thomas warned, undermines the general rule banning propensity evidence. Adding in the additional analytical step of saying that because the defendant acted in a particular way once before, it makes it more likely that the current victim is telling the truth about the defendant's conduct in the current case, does not alter the logic of the underlying rationale….

…Because signature modus operandi evidence is actually just propensity evidence by another name, the legal or logical relevance of such evidence is irrelevant to its admissibility….

In invalidating the signature modus operandi corroboration exception, this Court acts in conformity with the Federal Rules of Evidence governing corroborative evidence. Professor Imwinkelried, in his treatise Uncharged Misconduct Evidence, explains that "[c]orroborating evidence is merely evidence that confirms other evidence of a fact.... Any similar uncharged act generally corroborates in the sense that the act shows the defendant's propensity toward that type of crime and thereby increases the likelihood that the defendant committed the charged act. But that is precisely the theory of logical relevance forbidden by Rule 404(b). That 'corroborative' use of uncharged misconduct would be a patent violation of Rule 404(b). If 'corroboration' were a separate 'exception' to the exclusionary rule, that exception would swallow the rule."

This Court's decision also is consistent with the law of most other states. The vast majority of states do not recognize a signature modus operandi corroboration exception. Missouri's corroboration exception was far more liberal even than that recognized by a very small minority of states. In invalidating the signature modus operandi corroboration exception, Missouri brings its law in line with the federal and majoritarian state view and with its own constitutional principles....

The judgment of the circuit court is reversed, and the cause is remanded for a new trial.

***

In the wake of the *Vorhees* case, Missouri amended its evidence rules as follows:

> Notwithstanding the provisions of sections 17 and 18(a) of this article to the contrary, in prosecutions for crimes of a sexual nature involving a victim under eighteen years of age, relevant evidence of prior criminal acts, whether charged or uncharged, is admissible for the purpose of corroborating the victim's testimony or demonstrating the defendant's propensity to commit the crime with which he or she is presently charged. The court may exclude relevant evidence of prior criminal

acts if the probative value of the evidence is substantially outweighed by the danger of unfair prejudice.[1]

UNITED STATES v. WILLIAMS
458 F.3d 312 (3d Cir. 2006)

ALDISERT, Circuit Judge.

....I.

On May 16, 2003, detectives from the East Orange Police Department ... saw a silver Audi sedan pull into the driveway of [a] house. Williams and another man, Leon Clark, exited the vehicle. A third man, Andre Urlin, was waiting in the driveway for them.... Suspecting (correctly) that the car was stolen ... the detectives converged on the scene[.] Williams fled up the driveway and into the house. As he fled, one of the detectives observed that he was clutching a "machine-pistol type weapon" against his chest. The detective cried out "Gun!" and chased Williams into the house.

The detective chased Williams through the first floor of the house, losing sight of him only as he turned the corners. He and another detective finally cornered Williams in a bedroom, where he was crouching over a bed with his back to the door. They apprehended, searched and handcuffed him. Finding no weapon, one of the detectives began searching the bedroom. She found a gun—a semi-automatic Cobray–Leinard, Model PM–11, nine-millimeter handgun loaded with a clip containing two hollow-point bullets and 18 "full metal jacket" bullets—hidden between the mattress and the box-spring of the bed over which Williams had been found crouching.... Two other individuals were also found in the home.

.... Williams was subsequently ... charged with possession of a firearm by a convicted felon, in violation of 18 U.S.C. § 922(g)(1).

Prior to trial, Williams filed a motion in limine for admission of "reverse [Rule] 404(b)" evidence that Urlin had recently been convicted for possession of a firearm by a felon. Williams contended that this evidence was admissible to

---

[1] Mo. Const. art. I, § 18(c).

show that Urlin, rather than Williams, had possessed the weapon in question. The District Court delayed a ruling on the question until the close of evidence, at which time it denied the motion without explanation. The jury returned a verdict of guilty....

III.

A.

At the center of this case is this Court's decision in United States v. Stevens, our seminal case addressing the admissibility of what is known as "reverse Rule 404(b)" evidence. "In contrast to ordinary 'other crimes' evidence [under Rule 404(b)], which is used to incriminate criminal defendants, 'reverse [Rule] 404(b)' evidence is utilized to exonerate defendants." Such evidence is most commonly introduced by a defendant to show that someone else committed a similar crime or series of crimes, implying that he or she also must have committed the crime in question.

In *Stevens*, we held that the district court erred in excluding reverse Rule 404(b) evidence of a similar robbery involving a victim who failed to identify the defendant as the assailant. The evidence was offered to show that the same person committed both robberies and that because the defendant was not identified as the perpetrator of the first robbery, he was not the perpetrator of the second. Although one of the robberies involved a sexual assault and the other did not, both crimes: (1) took place within a few hundred yards of one another; (2) were armed robberies; (3) involved a handgun; (4) occurred between 9:30 p.m. and 10:30 p.m.; (5) were perpetrated on military personnel; and (6) involved a black assailant who was described similarly by his victims. The two robberies also occurred within days of one another, and the fruits of both robberies were discovered in similar locations.

At issue in *Stevens* was what degree of similarity should be required when a defendant offers evidence of bad acts committed by a third party. The government argued that the same standard of similarity should apply regardless of who offers the evidence, and that the two robberies did not satisfy the high standard that would apply if it sought to introduce evidence of bad acts by a defendant. See, e.g., Carter v. Hewitt, 617 F.2d 961 (3d Cir.1980) (observing that the degree of similarity required to prove "identity" is extremely high when the government seeks to introduce a defendant's bad acts). Specifically, it contended that the defendant must show that there has been more than one similar crime or that the other crime was sufficiently similar to be called a "signature" crime. We disagreed, concluding that Rule 404(b) was primarily intended to protect defendants and that "a lower standard of similarity should govern 'reverse Rule 404(b)' evidence because prejudice to the defendant is not a factor." Recasting our conclusion in terms of the Federal Rules of Evidence, we stated that "a defendant may introduce 'reverse 404(b)' evidence so long as its probative value under Rule 401 is not substantially outweighed by Rule 403 considerations."

Williams reads this language in *Stevens* to mean that evidence of bad acts involving someone other than the defendant is admissible whenever its probative value is not substantially outweighed by Rule 403 considerations, regardless of the purpose for which it is admitted: propensity, identity, motive or otherwise. Williams' defense in this case is that Urlin possessed the gun, not him. He argues that Urlin's prior conviction "rationally tends to disprove his [own] guilt"—the import of the conviction being that Urlin has a propensity to possess firearms and that, therefore, the gun recovered from under the mattress was likely Urlin's.

Williams misreads *Stevens*. This Court has never held that Rule 404(b)'s prohibition against propensity evidence is inapplicable where the evidence is offered by the defendant. In *Stevens*, it was indisputable that the evidence was being offered to show identity, i.e., that the perpetrator of the second robbery was the same as the perpetrator of the first because of the similarity of the crimes. Rule 404(b) expressly permits such evidence of other similar crimes to prove identity. The evidence was not being used to show that the perpetrator of the first robbery committed the second robbery simply because he had a general propensity to commit robberies.

It was implicit in *Stevens* that we do not begin to balance the evidence's probative value under Rule 401 against Rule 403 considerations unless the evidence is offered under one of the Rule 404(b) exceptions. That the prohibition against propensity evidence applies regardless of by whom—and against whom—it is offered is evident from Rule 404(b)'s plain language, which states that "[e]vidence of other crimes, wrongs, or acts is not admissible to prove the character of *a person* in order to show action in conformity therewith." Rather than restricting itself to barring evidence that tends to prove "the character of the accused" to show conformity therewith, Rule 404(b) bars evidence that tends to prove the character of any "person" to show conformity therewith. Although, under *Stevens*, a defendant is allowed more leeway in introducing non-propensity evidence under Rule 404(b), he or she is not allowed more leeway in admitting propensity evidence in violation of Rule 404(b). We therefore reject Williams' argument, and affirm that the prohibition against the introduction of bad acts evidence to show propensity applies regardless of whether the evidence is offered against the defendant or a third party....

THE DOCTRINE OF CHANCES

The Doctrine of Chances is one of the most contested and celebrated evidence doctrines. As you read through the next case, try to pinpoint the theory of logical relevance that the Supreme Court of Michigan associates with the doctrine. Then reflect on whether that theory is, as the Court contends, "a theory of logical relevance that does not depend on a character inference."

PEOPLE v. MARDLIN
487 Mich. 609 (2010)

CORRIGAN, J.

The Court of Appeals erroneously concluded that evidence of an unusual number of prior fires—each associated with property owned or controlled by defendant—was inadmissible in this arson case in which defendant was accused of intentionally starting a fire in his home. Because the evidence was not offered to prove defendant's bad character or his propensity to act in conformity with a bad character, the trial court correctly concluded that MRE 404(b)(1) did not preclude admission of the evidence. Further, the trial court did not abuse its discretion by concluding that the evidence was sufficiently probative to outweigh any danger of unfair prejudice under MRE 403.... [T]he evidence was noncharacter evidence admissible under the theory of logical relevance known as the doctrine of chances. Accordingly, we reverse ..., reinstate defendant's convictions, and remand to the Court of Appeals for that Court to consider defendant's remaining arguments on appeal.

I. FACTS AND PROCEEDINGS

Defendant admitted that he was the only person present at his home just before it caught fire on the afternoon of November 13, 2006. He left the premises to visit his brother shortly before the fire was reported by neighbors. After the fire, defendant filed an insurance claim seeking compensation for the damage to his home. The investigating police detective and a fire investigator for defendant's insurer both concluded that the fire had been intentionally set and originated from a love seat in the living room. Accordingly, the prosecution charged defendant with arson of a dwelling house, and burning insured property. Defendant claimed that the fire was an accident likely caused by faulty electrical wiring.

At trial, the prosecution showed that defendant had fallen behind on his mortgage payments and utility bills before the fire occurred. The prosecution also showed that defendant had been associated with four previous home or vehicle fires—each of which also involved insurance claims and arguably benefitted defendant in some way—in the 12 years preceding the charged fire. Specifically, defendant's home caught fire in the spring of 2006, apparently as the result of a blanket being left on a kerosene heater. Defendant filed an insurance claim for the resulting smoke damage. In 2003, a van driven by defendant but owned by his employer caught fire. The prosecution argued that defendant had a motive to damage this van. The employer had recently transferred a newer van, previously issued to defendant, to another employee; it then issued the van that later caught fire, which was an older model, to defendant. After the older van burned, the employer was forced to replace it. In 2001, defendant's own van caught fire and the fire spread to his mobile home. Defendant received an insurance payment for that van. Finally, in 1994, defendant's truck caught fire, for which he submitted an insurance claim. Although none of these fires was established to have resulted from arson, the prosecution argued that the pattern was probative to rebut defendant's claim that he had not intentionally set the November 2006 fire.

The jury indeed concluded from all the evidence that defendant intentionally set the November 2006 fire. It convicted him, as charged, of arson of a dwelling house and burning insured property. The trial court sentenced defendant to concurrent prison terms of 3 to 20 years and 1 to 10 years.

The Court of Appeals reversed, concluding that the trial court improperly admitted the evidence of previous fires under MRE 404(b)(1) [and] remanded for a new trial.

The prosecution [appealed]…

III. MRE 404(b)(1)

…. To admit evidence under MRE 404(b), the prosecutor must first establish that the evidence is logically relevant to a material fact in the case, as required by MRE 401 and MRE 402, and is not simply evidence of the defendant's character or relevant to his propensity to act in conformance with his character. The prosecution thus bears an initial burden to show that the proffered evidence is relevant to a proper purpose under the nonexclusive list in MRE 404(b)(1) or is otherwise probative of a fact other than the defendant's character or criminal propensity. Evidence relevant to a noncharacter purpose is admissible under MRE 404(b) even if it also reflects on a defendant's character. Evidence is inadmissible under this rule only if it is relevant solely to the defendant's character or criminal propensity. Stated another way, the rule is not exclusionary, but is inclusionary, because it provides a nonexhaustive list of reasons to properly admit evidence that may nonetheless also give rise to an inference about the defendant's character. Any undue prejudice that arises because the evidence also unavoidably reflects the defendant's character is then considered under the MRE 403 balancing test, which permits the court to exclude relevant evidence if its "probative value is substantially outweighed by the danger of unfair prejudice…." MRE 403. Finally, upon request, the trial court may provide a limiting instruction to the jury under MRE 105 to specify that the jury may consider the evidence only for proper, noncharacter purposes.

IV. THE DOCTRINE OF CHANCES

The doctrine of chances—also known as the "doctrine of objective improbability"—is a " 'theory of logical relevance [that] does not depend on a character inference.'" Under this theory, as the number of incidents of an out-of-the-ordinary event increases in relation to a particular defendant, the objective probability increases that the charged act and/or the prior occurrences were not the result of natural causes. The doctrine is commonly discussed in cases addressing MRE 404(b) because the doctrine describes a logical link, based on objective probabilities, between evidence of past acts or incidents that may be connected with a defendant and proper, noncharacter inferences that may be drawn from these events on the basis of their frequency. If a type of event linked to the defendant occurs with unusual frequency, evidence of the occurrences may be probative, for example, of his criminal intent or of the absence of mistake or accident because it is objectively improbable that such events occur so often in relation to the same person due to mere happenstance. To illustrate, United States v. York provides a classic description of the doctrine when used to negate innocent intent:

> The man who wins the lottery once is envied; the one who wins it twice is investigated. It is not every day that one's wife is murdered; it is more uncommon still that the murder occurs after the wife says she wants a divorce; and more unusual still that the jilted husband collects on a life insurance policy with a double-indemnity provision. That the same individual should later collect on exactly the same sort of policy after the grisly death of a business partner who owed him money raises eyebrows; the odds of the same individual reaping the benefits, within the space of three years, of two grisly murders of people he had reason to be hostile toward seem incredibly low, certainly low enough to support an inference that the windfalls were the product of design rather than the vagaries of chance.... This inference is purely objective, and has nothing to do with a subjective assessment of [the defendant's] character.

The seminal English case employing the doctrine, Rex v. Smith, acknowledged that evidence of past alleged accidents may be admitted to show "whether the acts alleged to constitute the crime charged in the indictment were designed or accidental, or to rebut a defence which would otherwise be open to the accused." Rex v. Smith infamously involved a defendant[, George Smith,] accused of drowning his wife in the bath [in July 1912. Trial was held in 1915.] The Court of Criminal Appeal concluded that the trial court properly admitted evidence that two other wives of the defendant were each similarly found dead in their baths from apparent accidental drowning[, one in December 1913 and the other in December 1914].

Consistent with the modern rule, the court acknowledged that the prosecution generally may not adduce evidence tending to shew that the accused has been guilty of criminal acts other than those covered by the indictment, for the purpose of leading to the conclusion that the accused is a person likely, from his criminal conduct or character, to have committed the offence for which he is being tried. On the other hand, the mere fact that the evidence adduced tends to shew the commission of other crimes does not render it inadmissible if it be relevant to an issue before the jury....

Thus, the evidence that several of the defendant's wives had drowned in their baths was properly admitted "for the purpose of shewing [sic] the design of the [defendant]." The court also observed that the judge was appropriately "careful to point out to the jury the use they could properly make of the evidence."

The doctrine of chances is often similarly employed in cases alleging arson to argue that the fire at issue was not an accident, but was intentionally caused by the defendant. Indeed, arguably the doctrine is epitomized in arson cases in which apparently accidental fires befall property linked to the defendant with uncommon frequency. As explained by Professor Edward Imwinkelried:

> Based on ordinary common sense and mundane human experience it is unlikely that a large number of similar accidents will befall the same victim in a short period of time. Considered in isolation, the charged fire ... may be easily explicable as an accident. However, when all similar incidents are considered collectively or in the aggregate, they amount to an extraordinary coincidence; and the doctrine of chances can create an inference of human design. The recurrence of similar incidents incrementally reduces the possibility of accident. The improbability of a coincidence of acts creates an objective probability of an actus reus.

V. APPLICATION TO THIS CASE

The fires here were admissible precisely because they constituted a series of similar incidents—fires involving homes and vehicles owned or controlled by defendant—the frequency of which objectively suggested that one or more of the fires was not caused by accident. The Court of Appeals principally erred by incorrectly assuming that evidence of the past fires could only be admitted if the prosecutor proved that defendant intentionally set them or that they shared other special qualities or additional significant indices of similarity....

To the contrary, application of the doctrine of chances "varies with the issue for which it is offered." As with all arguments involving prior acts or events, the "method of analysis to be employed depends on the purpose of the offer and its logical relevance." The acts or events need not bear striking similarity to the offense charged if the theory of relevance does not itself center on similarity.

.... Past events—such as fires in relation to an arson case—that suggest the absence of accident are offered on the basis of a theory of logical relevance that is a subset of innocent intent theories. As such, the past events need only be of the same general category as the charged offense. Professor Imwinkelried explained, in the context of arson cases:

> Suppose that the defendant is charged with arson. The defendant claims that the fire was accidental. The cases routinely permit the prosecutor to show other acts of arson by the defendant and even nonarson fires at premises owned by the defendant. In these cases, the courts invoke the doctrine of objective chances. The courts reason that as the number of incidents increases, the objective probability of accident decreases. Simply stated, it is highly unlikely that a single person would be victimized by so many similar accidental fires....

Accordingly, here the Court of Appeals erred by basing its analysis on its conclusion that the past fires were not highly similar to the charged fire due largely to the lack of definitive proof that defendant intentionally set the past fires. Because defendant owned or controlled all the burned property, the unusual number of past fires was classically relevant to defendant's claim that the November 2006 fire was an accident; the frequency of past fires so closely associated with defendant logically suggested a lack of coincidence....

In sum, the past fires were logically relevant to the objective probability that the November 2006 fire was intentionally set. Thus, the fires were admissible to negate defendant's claim that the fire was a mere accident.

Although defendant and the dissent emphasize that he offered innocent explanations for the past fires and other evidence tending to show that he had no motive to burn particular property, his innocent explanations do not control the admissibility analysis. For example, he claimed that the fire involving his employer's van also destroyed defendant's personally owned work tools. He also established that, although he turned on the kerosene heater involved in the spring 2006 house fire, his housemate admitted leaving the fire-causing blanket on the heater. He stressed that the 2001 fire involving his insured van spread to his mobile home, which was not insured. Further, he presented evidence that, after the 1994 fire that damaged his truck, he nonetheless was required to keep making payments on the damaged truck despite obtaining the insurance proceeds. With regard to the November 2006 fire, defendant also presented an expert who opined that the fire began behind the love seat thus implying that an electrical fault might have caused it....

But these explanations do not render evidence of the past fires inadmissible. Rather, the very function of the doctrine of chances is to permit the introduction of events that might appear accidental in isolation, but that suggest human design when viewed in aggregate. Because the prosecution's noncharacter theory for admission was sound, the evidence was admissible. Further, a jury may generally decide whether a defendant's claim of innocence—here his claim that all five fires were accidental—is more credible or likely than the prosecution's claim of guilt....

The trial court [also considered whether the past crimes evidence] was more probative than unduly prejudicial under MRE 403.... As explained above, first, the prior fires were highly, objectively relevant to defendant's claim that all five fires, including the November 2006 fire, were mere accidents. Second, the amount of "unfair prejudice," MRE 403, was minimal. "Evidence is unfairly prejudicial when there exists a danger that marginally probative evidence will be given undue or preemptive weight by the jury." Thus, MRE 403 "does not prohibit prejudicial evidence; only evidence that is unfairly so." Here, there was minimal unfair prejudice—such as improper character implications—because any prejudice arose properly from the objective frequency of fires associated with property owned or controlled by defendant.

Indeed, defendant's insistence—echoed by the Court of Appeals and the dissent—that there was no proof he intentionally caused the past fires actually weighs in favor of admission because, absent proof of past criminal intent associated with the evidence, the evidence does not create the traditional intermediate inference about character or criminal propensities associated with established, past criminal acts or convictions.

…. Finally, the trial court correctly instructed the jury to consider the evidence only for proper, noncharacter purposes pursuant to MRE 105. A limiting instruction generally "suffice[s] to enable the jury to compartmentalize evidence and consider it only for its proper purpose...."

PROBLEM 4-3: THE TERMINATOR

In the movie *The Terminator,* humans and machines of the future are fighting a terrible war. The good news is that the humans have finally gained the upper hand, in large part due to their charismatic leader, John Connor. The bad news is that the machines have a clever idea to turn the tide. They send a murderous cyborg, The Terminator, back in time to kill John Connor's mother. With Sarah Connor out of the way, John will never be born and the machines will triumph.

The Terminator has a problem though. When he returns to 1984 Los Angeles to kill Sarah Connor, he discovers that there are three people named Sarah Connor living in the city at that time, and he doesn't know which one is his target. He solves the problem by trying to kill them all.

[A] Imagine that The Terminator succeeds and is later prosecuted for one of the murders. The Terminator claims the killing was an accident. At trial, can the prosecution introduce evidence of the other two (uncharged) Sarah Connor killings? What is the theory of relevance of the other killings? Does it depend on propensity reasoning?

[B] Now imagine that there is no Terminator. We are back in the real world. And in an odd twist of fate, three people with the same name die in a major city in the same month. Two are believed to be accidental deaths, but one is thought to be a murder. There is no apparent connection between them. In the trial of the one murder should the prosecution be able to introduce evidence of the two accidental deaths? If not, does that shed any light on the Doctrine of Chances -- the so-called, "doctrine of objective improbability"?

SEVERANCE

One common way for prosecutors to introduce evidence of multiple crimes is to bring multiple charges in a single trial. Jurisdictions vary in the criminal procedure rules governing so-called joint trials. For our purposes, it is important to recognize that even when multiple charges are tried in the same proceeding, Rule 404 still applies.

For example, imagine the prosecutor tries a defendant in one trial on two separate charges of bank robbery. One robbery occurred in February 2020 and the other in March 2021. The judge would have to, upon request, instruct the jury that it could not consider the evidence that the defendant committed one of the robberies as suggesting, through a propensity inference, guilt of the other. Instead, the jury must consider each count separately. Here is a representative discussion from an appellate court opinion: "The District Court appropriately told the jury to 'separately consider the evidence that relates to each offense and return a separate verdict for each offense.' It also admonished the jury that their decision as to 'one offense … should not influence their decision on the other offenses.'"[1] The trial court must consider the ability of the jury to follow these kinds of instructions in deciding whether to permit a joint trial, or require the prosecution to sever the charges -- i.e., try each count in a separate proceeding.

---

[1] United States v. Mathis, 568 F. App'x 149 (3d Cir. 2014).

RULE 404(b) SUMMARY EXERCISE

Here is a summary of common examples of each of the listed Rule 404(b) pathways to admission. Keep in mind that even though some courts accept theories like those described below, that does not mean that these rulings are correct. To cement this point, as you read, place an asterisk next to any questionable "non-character" theories of relevance.

- <u>Motive</u>   e.g., D's membership in a criminal street gang, to explain why D would have shot rival gang member, Shannon v. Artuz, 984 F.Supp. 807 (S.D.N.Y. 1997)

Prosecutor could argue:

"D's gang membership is not being introduced to show the defendant's criminal character, but rather to establish his **motive** *– protecting gang territory, etc. – for committing the alleged crime."*

- <u>Opportunity</u> e.g., D's prison release to show D was in the area and needed transportation at the time and location where the auto theft occurred

Prosecutor could argue: ✱

"The fact that D was just released from prison near the scene of a car theft is not offered to show that D is a lawbreaker (or has a criminal character), but rather to show that he had the opportunity to commit the crime."

- <u>Intent</u>   e.g., person arrested with drugs; to prove intent to sell drugs, prosecution offers prior sales, US v. Miller (above); US v. Harris, 587 F.3d 861 (7th Cir. 2009)

Prosecutor could argue: ✱

"The evidence that the D previously sold cocaine is not offered to show that he is a drug dealer or the type of person who deals drugs, but as evidence of his intent to sell the particular cocaine police found in his pocket, thus establishing guilt of the instant charge of possession with intent to distribute cocaine."

e.g., civil case to show discrimination or fraud, Manuel v. City of Chicago, 335 F.3d 592 (7th Cir. 2003)

Plaintiff could argue: ✱

"The evidence that D acted in discriminatory fashion towards other older employees is not offered to show that D has a propensity to unlawfully discriminate, but rather to show D's discriminatory intent in firing P, an elderly employee."

- Preparation/Plan

> e.g., D commits component crimes as part of criminal endeavor
> State v. Bussard (Idaho App. 1988); *Oceans' 11*

Prosecutor could argue:

"The D's (uncharged) theft of a car that was later used as a getaway car in the bank robbery is not offered to show that D is a lawbreaker/criminal/thief, but rather to show his participation in a planned course of conduct that culminated in the charged bank robbery."

- Knowledge e.g., Prob. 4-2

Prosecutor could argue:

"The D's admitted hacking of the school computer system is not offered to show that D has a propensity to hack computers, but to show that D had the specialized computer skills required to commit the charged crime."

- Identity e.g., modus operandi, see *U.S. v. Myers and State v. Vorhees*

Prosecutor could argue:

"The D's commission of the earlier (uncharged) robbery is not offered to show that he is a robber by nature. Instead, the earlier robbery is so similar to the charged robbery that both robberies must have been committed by the same person; thus it establishes the identity of the robber in the charged offense. Given the distinct similarities between the two offenses, since we know that D committed the earlier robbery, it follows, without any propensity reasoning, that he also committed the charged robbery."

- Absence of Mistake/Accident e.g., Problem 4-3

Prosecutor could argue:

"D's commission of an accidental shooting of his first wife while cleaning his rifle, suggests that he would have been much more careful when cleaning the gun on future occasions, and thus is unlikely to have 'accidentally' shot his second wife."

e.g., prior instances of child abuse, U.S. v. Lewis, 837 F.2d 415 (9th Cir. 1988)

Prosecutor could argue:

"Evidence of D's commission of an uncharged act of child abuse on a prior occasion is not offered to show that D is a bad person or child molester by nature, but rather to rebut his claim that he accidentally injured his child during the incident for which he now stands charged with child abuse."

STATE VARIATION: AN EXCEPTION FOR DOMESTIC VIOLENCE

In 1996, shortly after a jury acquitted O.J. Simpson of the murder of his wife, California amended its Evidence rules, through a law referred to by the name of the victim: the "Nicole Brown Simpson Law."[1] The Legislative Digest explained the change as follows:

> "Under existing law, evidence of a person's character or a trait of his or her character is inadmissible when offered to prove his or her conduct on a specified occasion, except as provided.
>
> This bill would provide that in a criminal action in which the defendant is accused of an offense involving domestic violence, as defined, evidence of the defendant's commission of other domestic violence is not inadmissible under the above rule...."

The law has been amended over the years to include similar provisions for elder abuse and child abuse. Here is the current version of the California Code:

> § 1109. Evidence of defendant's other acts of domestic violence
>
> [I]n a criminal action in which the defendant is accused of an offense involving domestic violence, evidence of the defendant's commission of other domestic violence is not made inadmissible by Section 1101 [California's Rule 404] if the evidence is not inadmissible pursuant to Section 352 [California's Rule 403]....

Essentially, this rule permits certain past acts to be introduced to show propensity in a subset of cases.

Do you consider the California rule change good or bad policy?

---

[1] See Tom Lininger, Evidentiary Issues in Federal Prosecutions of Violence Against Women, 36 Ind. L. Rev. 687 (2003).

EXCEPTIONS FOR SEXUAL OFFENSE CASES

STATE v. KIRSCH
139 N.H. 647 (1995)

BATCHELDER, Justice.

The defendant, David Kirsch, appeals his convictions, after a jury trial ... of aggravated felonious sexual assault. He argues that the trial court erred: ... in admitting evidence of other sexual assaults under New Hampshire Rule of Evidence 404(b).... We reverse and remand.

The defendant was tried on thirteen indictments charging sexual assaults on three young girls between 1984 and 1987. In addition to the three victims named in the indictments, three other young women testified, pursuant to Rule 404(b), about sexual abuse committed against them by the defendant from the late 1970's to the mid–1980's. With minor variations, each young woman testified to similar activity and association with the defendant. During that time period, the defendant led pre-teen church groups at the Granite State Baptist Church in Salem, occasionally driving the church bus that transported the children from their homes to the church. In addition to leading a group called Alpha–Teens that provided recreational activities, the defendant was one of several church staff members who monitored sleep-overs at the church. He also hosted church sleep-overs at his home in Salem and, later, at his home in Plaistow. Each of the victim/witnesses testified to having been approximately seven to ten years old when she met the defendant through her association with the church and to having become close to him through the church groups she attended. Each rode on the bus or in his van with the defendant and spent the night at the church or at his home. Some remembered sitting in the defendant's lap, and all remembered the defendant's inappropriate touching, from fondling of the breasts and vaginal area to digital penetration, fellatio, cunnilingus, and sexual intercourse.

Of the thirteen indictments on which the defendant was tried, seven were dismissed at the close of the State's case. The six remaining indictments all involved the same victim, Karen G., and were comprised of three counts each of aggravated felonious sexual assault and felonious sexual assault. The defendant was found guilty of all six charges.

…. The defendant … argues that the trial court erred in permitting the State to introduce evidence of other bad acts committed by the defendant. Prior to trial the State moved to introduce evidence of other uncharged sexual assaults as evidence of the defendant's motive, intent, and common plan or scheme. See N.H.R.Ev. 404(b). According to the State's proffer to the trial court, the evidence would show that the defendant "selected and seduced each victim by always choosing as his victims young girls, who lived well below the poverty line, in dysfunctional households, without any real father figure." It would further show, according to the State, that the defendant "positioned himself," through his role in the church, as a trusted father figure who occasionally fed and clothed them and "then seduced each of the little girls in the same manner." After a hearing, the trial court ruled that the evidence was relevant to prove motive, intent, and common plan or scheme, that there was clear proof the defendant committed the acts, and that the probative value of the evidence was not substantially outweighed by prejudice to the defendant. As its expressed basis for finding the evidence relevant, the trial court stated:

> The witnesses described incidents of sexual assault occurring in the basement of the church during sleep overs and during "junior church," in the defendant's van while playing "Simon Says," or while sitting in the panel seat next to the defendant who was driving, in the downstairs and upstairs bedrooms of the defendant's Plaistow home, in the hot-tub in the defendant's Plaistow home, and in the attic of the defendant's Salem home….

In ruling that the probative value of the evidence was not substantially outweighed by the prejudice, the court found that the victims all met the defendant through the church, that most of them had no father, came from broken homes, were poor, and that the defendant "offered emotional support to the victims and became a father figure to them," taking them out to eat and to amusement parks. "In this manner," the court explained in its order, "the State seeks to prove that the defendant gained the trust and confidence of the victims to lure them into his home and into his life."

…. Evidence of other bad acts is only admissible if relevant for a purpose other than to prove the defendant's character or disposition, if there is clear proof the defendant committed the other acts, and if the prejudice to the defendant does not substantially outweigh the probative value of the evidence.

…. To meet the relevancy requirement, the other bad acts evidence "must have some direct bearing on an issue actually in dispute," and there must be "a clear connection between the particular evidentiary purpose, as articulated to the trial court, and the [other bad acts]." The burden is on the State to articulate to the trial judge the precise evidentiary purpose for which it seeks to introduce the other crimes evidence and the purported connection between the evidence and the stated purpose. The State proffered, and the trial court found, three evidentiary purposes for the other bad acts evidence; namely, motive, intent, and common plan or scheme. We examine each in turn.

Motive is generally understood to refer to the "reason that nudges the will and prods the mind to indulge the criminal intent," or what prompts a defendant to engage in a particular criminal activity. The State argued below that the evidence of the uncharged assaults would show the defendant's "motive in selecting these particular victims," and argues on appeal that the evidence showed "the motive with which the defendant acted when he involved himself in the church's pre-teen program, and subsequently in the lives of each of these girls." We think the State misperceives the issue. Motive, to the extent it is at issue at all, concerns the defendant's reason for committing the charged crime, not his motivation for engaging in ancillary activities that may have been precursors to criminal conduct. The crux of the State's argument appears to be that the other incidents show the defendant's desire for sexual activity with a certain type of victim. This, however, "is proof of propensity, not motive." We are not persuaded that the State demonstrated a clear connection between motive and the uncharged assaults.

The second reason advanced by the State for admitting the other acts was that they were probative of the defendant's intent. "To be relevant to intent, evidence of other bad acts must be able to support a reliable inference, not dependent on the defendant's character or propensity, that the defendant had the same intent on the occasions of the charged and uncharged acts."

In the trial court, the State put forth essentially the same argument with respect to relevance to prove intent as it did to prove motive. Focusing on the number and similarity of the assaults and the defendant's mode of seduction, the State argued that "[t]hese actions on the part of the defendant show how he purposely selected and seduced his victims. As such this type of evidence bears directly on the defendant's intent...."

This argument is indistinguishable from one that would seek to use the evidence to show the defendant's propensity to sexually assault young girls and therefore to imply his intent to commit the charged assaults. "The only connection is the putative similarity of the activity," and to argue that evidence of the defendant's other similar assaults tends to prove his guilt of the charged offenses is to seek to show "propensity, pure and simple; calling it relevant to prove 'state of mind' does not make it so."

With respect to the State's common plan or scheme rationale for relevance, the State argued to the trial court that the defendant's "routine used in assaulting any one of the victims is similar, if not identical, to the manner in which he assaulted other victims." The common plan exception to the Rule 404(b) prohibition requires more. "A pattern or systematic course of conduct is insufficient to establish a plan." Rather, to be admissible as evidence showing the defendant's plan, other bad acts must be constituent parts of some overall scheme. "Therefore, it is not enough to show that each crime was 'planned' in the same way; rather, there must be some overall scheme of which each of the crimes is but a part." Showing that the defendant had a pre-existing "plan" to gain the trust of young girls from deprived homes in order to seduce and sexually assault them does not demonstrate a common plan or scheme.... It is merely proof of the defendant's penchant or propensity for committing the same offense repeatedly; this is "the precise purpose, under Rule 404(b), for which it may not be used."

Whether nominally labeled motive, intent or common plan, the ostensible purpose for which the prosecution sought to admit evidence of a multitude of other uncharged sexual assaults was to show the defendant's predilection for molesting young females over whom he was able to gain control through engendering trust. At most, this is evidence of the defendant's disposition to commit the offenses with which he was charged, impermissible under Rule 404(b). Because it was not relevant for a permissible purpose, the evidence should have been excluded, and its introduction was an abuse of discretion.... Reversed and remanded.

PROBLEM 4-4: PROSECUTOR ETHICS

Problem 3-1 asked about potential ethical limits on an attorney's introduction of evidence that a jury may use for a legally improper purpose. Do you think the prosecutors in *Kirsch* crossed an ethical line?

The most commonly invoked guidance on prosecutor ethics comes from a 1935 Supreme Court case Berger v. United States, which says:

> "The [prosecutor's] interest . . . in a criminal prosecution is not that it shall win a case, but that justice shall be done. [W]hile he may strike hard blows, he is not at liberty to strike foul ones. It is as much his duty to refrain from improper methods calculated to produce a wrongful conviction as it is to use every legitimate means to bring about a just one."

Does that help?

***

New Hampshire retried Kirsch on the charges described above. The second trial, conducted without the other acts evidence, resulted in a hung jury after the jurors split 8 to 4 for conviction. After trial, the jurors expressed surprise when informed by members of the media about the now-excluded other acts evidence. One juror said, "They're limiting the evidence so extensively you might as well not have a jury at all." Another said, "In my opinion, we need some reform and let people hear all of the evidence that exists.... If there is evidence, we can't allow a case to be one person's word against another."

New Hampshire legislators proposed a bill (House Bill 1549) to change New Hampshire's evidence rules to allow evidence like the evidence that was ultimately excluded in *Kirsch*. While popular with legislators, the bill did not become law. This was no doubt in large part because the New Hampshire Supreme Court, in response to a formal inquiry from the legislature, issued an advisory opinion that the proposed bill would violate the New Hampshire Constitution by jeopardizing the right to a "fair trial" and encroaching on the judiciary's prerogative to determine the rules governing procedure in the States' courts.[1]

In 1996, Kirsch was tried a third time, convicted and sentenced to over 25 years in prison.[2]

RULES 413, 414, 415

Enacted in 1994, Rules 413, 414 and 415 are relatively recent additions the Federal Rules of Evidence. Because of this, they did not become law in the States that enacted the original package of federal rules of evidence. In addition, the States have not been as quick to adopt these Rules. This is particularly important because sex crimes are typically tried in state court. Nevertheless, many States have adopted these Rules, or apply similar doctrines in the guise of applying Rule 404(b) or judicially created exceptions to the character evidence prohibition.

Unlike the rest of the federal rules of evidence, these Rules were enacted by Congress, over the objection of the typical rulemaking authorities. Here is an excerpt from the floor remarks of one of the chief sponsors of the legislation, Representative Susan Molinari.[3]

> Mr. Speaker, the revised conference bill contains a critical reform that I have long sought to protect the public from crimes of sexual violence-general rules of admissibility in sexual assault and child molestation cases for evidence that the defendant has committed offenses of the same type on other occasions. The enactment of this reform is first and foremost a triumph for the public-for the women who will not be raped and the children who will not be molested because we have strengthened the legal system's tools for bringing the perpetrators of these atrocious crimes to justice.
>
> The new rules will supersede in sex offense cases the restrictive aspects of federal rule of evidence 404(b). In contrast to rule 404(b)'s general

---

[1] https://www.courts.state.nh.us/supreme/opinions/1997/96-280.htm

[2] See Nancy West, More Facts for a Jury, New Hampshire Union Leader, March 3, 1996; Jerry Miller, Former Church Volunteer Gets 25 Years in Sex Case, New Hampshire Union Leader, October 25, 1996.

[3] 140 Cong. Rec. 23375 (1994).

prohibition of evidence of character or propensity, the new rules for sex offense cases authorize admission and consideration of evidence of an uncharged offense for its bearing "on any matter to which it is relevant." This includes the defendant's propensity to commit sexual assault or child molestation offenses, and assessment of the probability or improbability that the defendant has been falsely or mistakenly accused of such an offense.

In other respects, the general standards of the rules of evidence will continue to apply, including the restrictions on hearsay evidence and the court's authority under evidence rule 403 to exclude evidence whose probative value is substantially outweighed by its prejudicial effect. Also, the Government-or the plaintiff in a civil case will generally have to disclose to the defendant any evidence that is to be offered under the new rules … before trial.

The proposed reform is critical to the protection of the public from rapists and child molesters, and is justified by the distinctive characteristics of the cases it will affect. In child molestation cases, for example, a history of similar acts tends to be exceptionally probative because it shows an unusual disposition of the defendant-a sexual or sado-sexual interest in children that simply does not exist in ordinary people. Moreover, such cases require reliance on child victims whose credibility can readily be attacked in the absence of substantial corroboration. In such cases, there is a compelling public interest in admitting all significant evidence that will illumine the credibility of the charge and any denial by the defense.

Similarly, adult-victim sexual assault cases are distinctive, and often turn on difficult credibility determinations. Alleged consent by the victim is rarely an issue in prosecutions for other violent crimes-the accused mugger does not claim that the victim freely handed over his wallet as a gift-but the defendant in a rape case often contends that the victim engaged in consensual sex and then falsely accused him. Knowledge that the defendant has committed rapes on other occasions is frequently critical in assessing the relative plausibility of these claims and accurately deciding cases that would otherwise become unresolvable swearing matches.

other crimes can't claim consent

The practical effect of the new rules is to put evidence of uncharged offenses in sexual assault and child molestation cases on the same footing as other types of relevant evidence that are not subject to a special exclusionary rule. The presumption is in favor of admission. The underlying legislative judgment is that the evidence admissible pursuant to the proposed rules is typically relevant and probative, and that its probative value is normally not outweighed by any risk of prejudice or other adverse effects.

In line with this judgment, the rules do not impose arbitrary or artificial restrictions on the admissibility of evidence. Evidence of offenses for which the defendant has not previously been prosecuted or convicted will be admissible, as well as evidence of prior convictions. No time limit is imposed on the uncharged offenses for which evidence may be admitted; as a practical matter, evidence of other sex offenses by the defendant is often probative and properly admitted, notwithstanding very substantial lapses of time in relation to the charged offense or offenses.

Finally, the practical efficacy of these rules will depend on faithful execution by judges of the will of Congress in adopting this critical reform. To implement the legislative intent, the courts must liberally construe these rules to provide the basis for a fully informed decision of sexual assault and child molestation cases, including assessment of the defendant's propensities and questions of probability in light of the defendant's past conduct.

UNITED STATES v. DILLON
532 F.3d 379 (5th Cir. 2008)

GARWOOD, Circuit Judge:

Former Assistant City Attorney of New Orleans, Henry Dillon, appeals his jury trial conviction under 18 U.S.C. § 242 for depriving Sandy Carraby and Carolyn Carter of their right to bodily integrity under color of law. Dillon [argues] on appeal ... that the district court abused its discretion in admitting evidence of two other alleged sexual assaults by him under Federal Rule of Evidence 413....

FACTS AND PROCEEDINGS BELOW

Dillon was an attorney licensed to practice law in the state of Louisiana where he maintained a private practice. Dillon also served as an Assistant City Attorney ("ACA") for the City of New Orleans. In the latter capacity, he was assigned, on a part-time basis, to prosecute minor municipal offenses and traffic violations in the local municipal and traffic courts on behalf of the City of New Orleans. These courts operate informally with most cases resolved summarily at arraignment. Defendants often appear unrepresented and resolve their cases directly with the prosecutors, who exercise substantial discretion.

I. Carolyn Carter

Carter met Dillon after being arrested in December of 2003 for a minor traffic offense. One of her friends suggested that she talk to Dillon to see if he could help her with her tickets because he was an ACA. She followed this advice and Dillon arranged for the dismissal of some of her pending tickets. On January 15, 2004, Carter returned to traffic court to address the remaining tickets pursuant to Dillon's promise to fix them. That afternoon Carter learned that her son had been arrested on a municipal battery charge, and she sought Dillon's assistance in securing his release from jail. Dillon told Carter to come, alone, to his private law office later that day to discuss her son's situation.

Carter testified that she arrived at Dillon's office around 9:00 p.m. Dillon then asked her to give him her son's name, date of birth, and social security number. Dillon then called a state court judge to arrange for Carter's son to be "paroled." After placing the call, Dillon told Carter, "I told you I can make it happen." At that point, Carter attempted to leave, but Dillon stopped her, began kissing her, and pushed her into another room. Once in the other room, Dillon told Carter that he knew "a lot of police officers and he [could] have anybody arrested" and that if she wanted her son out of jail she should "[q]uit acting like a baby." Dillon proceeded to rape Carter….

[The facts regarding the second victim, Sandy Carraby, are similar to those set forth above.]

III. Court Proceedings

On December 2, 2005, Dillon was charged in a two-count indictment with depriving individuals of their civil rights under color of law in violation of 18 U.S.C. § 242. Count one charged Dillon with depriving Carraby of her bodily integrity by sexually assaulting her.... Count two similarly charged the defendant with depriving Carter of her bodily integrity by sexually assaulting her....

Before trial, the government timely gave notice that it was seeking to introduce evidence of four other alleged sexual assaults committed by Dillon under Federal Rule of Evidence 413. Dillon objected that this evidence was substantially more prejudicial than it was probative, and therefore, should not be admitted according to Federal Rule of Evidence 403. On April 7, 2006, the district court issued its written Order and Reasons holding that it would admit testimony relating to two of the four prior alleged sexual assaults.

The case proceeded to trial and verdict. Dillon testified, admitted sexual intercourse with Carraby and Carter on the occasions alleged, but asserted that it was entirely consensual. The jury found Dillon guilty.... The district court sentenced Dillon to life imprisonment....

DISCUSSION

.... Dillon argues that the testimony of Timika Jones and Sheena Cheneau regarding uncharged sexual assaults was improperly admitted because its probative value did not substantially outweigh its prejudicial effect.

Generally, evidence of prior bad acts is not admissible to show propensity. Fed.R.Evid. 404(b). Rule 413(a), however, allows the admission of evidence of prior sexual assaults for any relevant purpose, including to show propensity, in sexual assault cases.

To be admissible under Rule 413, the uncharged "offense of sexual assault" need not be established by a conviction.... Evidence admissible under Rule 413 is still subject to the Rule 403 balancing test, so it may be excluded if its "probative value is substantially outweighed by the danger of unfair prejudice."....

In this case, the government sought to admit testimony about four uncharged sexual assaults allegedly committed by Dillon against four different women, and gave timely notice under Rule 413(b). Dillon objected to the admission of any testimony related to the uncharged incidents on the grounds that its probative value was substantially outweighed by its danger of unfair prejudice. The district court held a hearing....

[T]he district court weighed allegations of four prior uncharged sexual assaults. It admitted the testimony of Jones and Cheneau because their alleged sexual assaults occurred within weeks of one of the charged offenses, Dillon met the women through his position as an ACA, Cheneau's assault happened in a similar manner to the charged offenses, and Dillon offered to use his power to dismiss Jones's traffic tickets in exchange for sex. This evidence was undoubtedly prejudicial to Dillon's case. "Relevant evidence is inherently prejudicial; but it is only unfair prejudice, substantially outweighing probative value, which permits exclusion of relevant matter under Rule 403." The district court clearly kept this distinction in mind because it excluded the testimony of two other alleged victims. It held that their testimony would have been unfairly prejudicial because those two alleged sexual assaults were remote in time and dissimilar in their commission to the charged offenses. The district court took great care in weighing the evidence of all these prior sexual assaults. It admitted those that it determined to be relevant, and it excluded those that it determined to be unfairly prejudicial. In making these decisions, we are unable to conclude, under the applicable standard of review, that the district court abused its discretion.

***

Rules 413 and Rule 414 undoubtedly succeeded in making it easier to convict in cases of sexual violence. One challenge that has been rejected in all of the federal courts but has never been resolved by the United States Supreme Court, is whether these rules make it *too* easy to convict certain defendants.

UNITED STATES v. MOUND (dissenting opinion)
157 F.3d 1153 (8th Cir. 1998)

MORRIS SHEPPARD ARNOLD, Circuit Judge

Because this case seems to me to involve "a question of exceptional importance," I dissent from the order denying the suggestion for rehearing en banc.

Fed. R. Evid. 413 runs counter to a centuries-old legal tradition that views propensity evidence with a particularly skeptical eye. The common law, of course, is not embodied in the Constitution, but the fact that a rule has recommended itself to generations of lawyers and judges is at least some indication that it embodies "'fundamental conceptions of justice.'" It also cannot be irrelevant that the members of two committees, consisting of 40 persons in all, and appointed by the Judicial Conference of the United States to examine Fed. R. Evid. 413 before its passage, all but unanimously urged that Congress not adopt the rule because of deep concerns about its fundamental fairness. Members of the committees worried that the new rule would displace "essential 'protections [that have] form[ed] a fundamental part of American jurisprudence and have evolved under longstanding rules and case law.'"

It seems to me that the en banc court ought to consider, as one commentator has put it, whether Fed. R. Evid. 413 "presents [so] great a risk that the jury will convict a defendant for his past conduct or unsavory character" that it violates due process. We might well conclude that the common-law rule against propensity evidence has as distinguished a legal pedigree as, say, the rule that guilt must be proved beyond a reasonable doubt. Our resolution of the relevant constitutional questions would necessarily involve us in an examination of the ultimate rationality of Fed. R. Evid. 413. There is a great deal of evidence that the prognosticative power of past sexual behavior is quite low; in fact, the recidivism rate for rape is lower than that for any major crime other than murder. While the kind of review that I think we ought to undertake would require us to consider matters that Congress has already presumably weighed, that is inevitable when fairness (a necessary component of which is rationality) is the subject of judicial inquiry.

CHARACTER EVIDENCE OFFERED BY THE DEFENSE

MICHELSON v. UNITED STATES
335 U.S. 469 (1948)

Justice JACKSON delivered the opinion of the Court.

In 1947 petitioner [Solomon] Michelson was convicted of bribing a federal revenue agent. The Government proved a large payment by accused to the agent for the purpose of influencing his official action. The defendant, as a witness on his own behalf, admitted passing the money but claimed it was done in response to the agent's demands, threats, solicitations, and inducements that amounted to entrapment. It is enough for our purposes to say that determination of the issue turned on whether the jury should believe the agent or the accused.

On direct examination of defendant, his own counsel brought out that, in 1927, he had been convicted of a misdemeanor having to do with trading in counterfeit watch dials. On cross-examination it appeared that in 1930, in executing an application for a license to deal in second-hand jewelry, he answered 'No' to the question whether he had theretofore been arrested or summoned for any offense.

Defendant called five witnesses to prove that he enjoyed a good reputation. Two of them testified that their acquaintance with him extended over a period of about thirty years and the others said they had known him at least half that long. A typical examination in chief was as follows:

'Q. Do you know the defendant Michelson? A. Yes.

'Q. How long do you know Mr. Michelson? A. About 30 years.

'Q. Do you know other people who know him? A. Yes.

'Q. Have you have occasion to discuss his reputation for honesty and truthfulness and for being a law-abiding citizen? A. It is very good.

'Q. You have talked to others? A. Yes.

'Q. And what is his reputation? A. Very good.'

These are representative of answers by three witnesses; two others replied, in substance, that they never had heard anything against Michelson.

On cross-examination, four of the witnesses were asked, in substance, this question: 'Did you ever hear that Mr. Michelson on March 4, 1927, was convicted of a violation of the trademark law in New York City in regard to watches?' This referred to the twenty-year-old conviction about which defendant himself had testified on direct examination. Two of them had heard of it and two had not.

To four of these witnesses the prosecution also addressed the question the allowance of which, over defendant's objection, is claimed to be reversible error:

> 'Did you ever hear that on October 11th, 1920, the defendant, Solomon Michelson, was arrested for receiving stolen goods?'

None of the witnesses appears to have heard of this.

The trial court asked counsel for the prosecution, out of presence of the jury, 'Is it a fact according to the best information in your possession that Michelson was arrested for receiving stolen goods?' Counsel replied that it was, and to support his good faith exhibited a paper record which defendant's counsel did not challenge.

The judge also on three occasions warned the jury, in terms that are not criticized, of the limited purpose for which this evidence was received.

> The instruction was: "'I instruct the jury that what is happening now is this: the defendant has called character witnesses, and the basis for the evidence given by those character witnesses is the reputation of the defendant in the community, and since the defendant tenders the issue of his reputation the prosecution may ask the witness if she has heard of various incidents in his career. I say to you that regardless of her answer you are not to assume that the incidents asked about actually took place. All that is happening is that this witness' standard of opinion of the reputation of the defendant is being tested. Is that clear?'"

Defendant-petitioner challenges the right of the prosecution so to cross-examine his character witnesses. The Court of Appeals held that it was permissible. The opinion, however, points out that the practice has been severely criticized and invites us, in one respect, to change the rule. Serious and responsible criticism has been aimed, however, not alone at the detail now questioned by the Court of Appeals but at common-law doctrine on the whole subject of proof of reputation or character. It would not be possible to appraise the usefulness and propriety of this cross-examination without consideration of the unique practice concerning character testimony, of which such cross-examination is a minor part.

Courts that follow the common-law tradition almost unanimously have come to disallow resort by the prosecution to any kind of evidence of a defendant's evil character to establish a probability of his guilt…. But this line of inquiry firmly denied to the State is opened to the defendant because character is relevant in resolving probabilities of guilt. He may introduce affirmative testimony that the general estimate of his character is so favorable that the jury may infer that he would not be likely to commit the offense charged….

When the defendant elects to initiate a character inquiry, another anomalous rule comes into play. Not only is he permitted to call witnesses to testify from hearsay, but indeed such a witness is not allowed to base his testimony on anything but hearsay. What commonly is called 'character evidence' is only such when 'character' is employed as a synonym for 'reputation.' The witness may not testify about defendant's specific acts or courses of conduct or his possession of a particular disposition or of benign mental and moral traits; nor can he testify that his own acquaintance, observation, and knowledge of defendant leads to his own independent opinion that defendant possesses a good general or specific character, inconsistent with commission of acts charged. The witness is, however, allowed to summarize what he has heard in the community, although much of it may have been said by persons less qualified to judge than himself. The evidence which the law permits is not as to the personality of defendant but only as to the shadow his daily life has cast in his neighborhood. This has been well described in a different connection as 'the slow growth of months and years, the resultant picture of forgotten incidents, passing events, habitual and daily conduct, presumably honest because disinterested, and safer to be trusted because prone to suspect…. It is for that reason that such general repute is permitted to be proven. It sums up a multitude of trivial details. It compacts into the brief phrase of a verdict the teaching of many incidents and the conduct of years. It is the average intelligence drawing its conclusion.'

While courts have recognized logical grounds for criticism of this type of opinion-based-on-hearsay testimony, it is said to be justified by 'overwhelming considerations of practical convenience' in avoiding innumerable collateral issues which, if it were attempted to prove character by direct testimony, would complicate and confuse the trial, distract the minds of jurymen and befog the chief issues in the litigation.

Another paradox in this branch of the law of evidence is that the delicate and responsible task of compacting reputation hearsay into the 'brief phrase of a verdict' is one of the few instances in which conclusions are accepted from a witness on a subject in which he is not an expert. However, the witness must qualify to give an opinion by showing such acquaintance with the defendant, the community in which he has lived and the circles in which he has moved, as to speak with authority of the terms in which generally he is regarded. To require affirmative knowledge of the reputation may seem inconsistent with the latitude given to the witness to testify when all he can say of the reputation is that he has 'heard nothing against defendant.' This is permitted upon assumption that, if no ill is reported of one, his reputation must be good. But this answer is accepted only from a witness whose knowledge of defendant's habitat and surroundings is intimate enough so that his failure to hear of any relevant ill repute is an assurance that no ugly rumors were about.

Thus the law extends helpful but illogical options to a defendant. Experience taught a necessity that they be counterweighted with equally illogical conditions to keep the advantage from becoming an unfair and unreasonable one. The price a defendant must pay for attempting to prove his good name is to throw open the entire subject which the law has kept closed for his benefit and to make himself vulnerable where the law otherwise shields him. The prosecution may pursue the inquiry with contradictory witnesses to show that damaging rumors, whether or not well-grounded, were afloat—for it is not the man that he is, but the name that he has which is put in issue. Another hazard is that his own witness is subject to cross-examination as to the contents and extent of the hearsay on which he bases his conclusions, and he may be required to disclose rumors and reports that are current even if they do not affect his own conclusion. It may test the sufficiency of his knowledge by asking what stories were circulating concerning events, such as one's arrest, about which people normally comment and speculate. Thus, while the law gives defendant the option to show as a fact that his reputation reflects a life and habit incompatible with commission of the offense charged, it subjects his proof to tests of credibility designed to prevent him from profiting by a mere parade of partisans.

To thus digress from evidence as to the offense to hear a contest as to the standing of the accused, at its best opens a tricky line of inquiry as to a shapeless and elusive subject matter. At its worst it opens a veritable Pandora's box of irresponsible gossip, innuendo and smear. In the frontier phase of our law's development, calling friends to vouch for defendant's good character, and its counterpart—calling the rivals and enemies of a witness to impeach him by testifying that his reputation for veracity was so bad that he was unworthy of belief on his oath—were favorite and frequent ways of converting an individual litigation into a community contest and a trial into a spectacle. Growth of urban conditions, where one may never know or hear the name of his next-door neighbor, have tended to limit the use of these techniques and to deprive them of weight with juries....

Wide discretion is accompanied by heavy responsibility on trial courts to protect the practice from any misuse. The trial judge was scrupulous to so guard it in the case before us. He took pains to ascertain, out of presence of the jury, that the target of the question was an actual event, which would probably result in some comment among acquaintances if not injury to defendant's reputation. He satisfied himself that counsel was not merely taking a random shot at a reputation imprudently exposed or asking a groundless question to waft an unwarranted innuendo into the jury box....

In this case the crime inquired about was receiving stolen goods; the trial was for bribery. The Court of Appeals thought this dissimilarity of offenses too great to sustain the inquiry in logic, though conceding that it is authorized by preponderance of authority....

The good character which the defendant had sought to establish was broader than the crime charged and included the traits of 'honesty and truthfulness' and 'being a law-abiding citizen.' Possession of these characteristics would seem as incompatible with offering a bribe to a revenue agent as with receiving stolen goods. The crimes may be unlike, but both alike proceed from the same defects of character which the witnesses said this defendant was reputed not to exhibit. It is not only by comparison with the crime on trial but by comparison with the reputation asserted that a court may judge whether the prior arrest should be made subject of inquiry. By this test the inquiry was permissible. It was proper cross-examination because reports of his arrest for receiving stolen goods, if admitted, would tend to weaken the assertion that he was known as an honest and law-abiding citizen. The cross-examination may take in as much ground as the testimony it is designed to verify. To hold otherwise would give defendant the benefit of testimony that he was honest and law-abiding in reputation when such might not be the fact; the refutation was founded on convictions equally persuasive though not for crimes exactly repeated in the present charge....

We do not overlook or minimize the consideration that 'the jury almost surely cannot comprehend the Judge's limiting instructions,' which disturbed the Court of Appeals. The refinements of the evidentiary rules on this subject are such that even lawyers and judges, after study and reflection, often are confused, and surely jurors in the hurried and unfamiliar movement of a trial must find them almost unintelligible. However, limiting instructions on this subject are no more difficult to comprehend or apply than those upon various other subjects.... [And] in cases such as the one before us, the law foreclosed this whole confounding line of inquiry, unless defendant thought the net advantage from opening it up would be with him. Given this option, we think defendants in general and this defendant in particular have no valid complaint at the latitude which existing law allows to the prosecution to meet by cross-examination an issue voluntarily tendered by the defense....

We concur in the general opinion of courts, textwriters and the profession that much of this law is archaic, paradoxical and full of compromises and compensations by which an irrational advantage to one side is offset by a poorly reasoned counter-privilege to the other. But somehow it has proved a workable even if clumsy system when moderated by discretionary controls in the hands of a wise and strong trial court. To pull one misshapen stone out of the grotesque structure is more likely simply to upset its present balance between adverse interests than to establish a rational edifice.

The present suggestion is that we adopt for all federal courts a new rule as to cross-examination about prior arrest, adhered to by the courts of only one state and rejected elsewhere. The confusion and error it would engender would seem too heavy a price to pay for an almost imperceptible logical improvement, if any, in a system which is justified, if at all, by accumulated judicial experience rather than abstract logic.

The judgment is Affirmed.

***

Michelson is a famous Evidence case, admirable both for its painstaking summary of the common law framework governing the introduction of character evidence, and for its candor in admitting that the framework makes little sense. In a footnote, the opinion adds, "law on this subject has evolved from pragmatic considerations rather than from theoretical consistency."

RULE 404(a)(2) & 405

The framework set out in *Michelson* is now distilled into the Federal Rules of Evidence. Rule 404(a)(2)(A) permits a defendant in a criminal case to offer evidence of "the defendant's pertinent [character] trait." "Once the admissibility of character evidence in some form is established under [that] rule, reference must then be made to Rule 405, which follows, in order to determine the appropriate method of proof." Advisory Committee Note to Rule 404.

Rule 405(a) requires character evidence to take the form of reputation or opinion testimony, while also allowing cross-examination into "relevant specific instances" of the defendant's conduct. What counts as a pertinent trait will depend on the issues in the case. One character trait that almost always meets the pertinent test is the generic trait of "law abiding" character.

Notice the significance of Rule 405(a)'s limitation of permissible character evidence to reputation and opinion. One particularly effective way to persuade a jury about a person's good character would be to offer specific examples of

111

upstanding conduct. The Advisory Committee Note to Rule 405 acknowledges the power of such proof but justifies its exclusion on largely practical grounds. The Note emphasizes, under Rule 405, "proof may be only by reputation and opinion."

This raises the key difference between Rule 405 and *Michelson*. The trial court in *Michelson* limited the character witnesses to testimony about the defendant's reputation only, not the witness' own personal opinion of the defendant's character. This longstanding common law restriction drew criticism from many, including Wigmore who stated:

> "The Anglo–American rules of evidence have occasionally taken some curious twistings in the course of their development; but they have never done anything so curious in the way of shutting out evidential light as when they decided to exclude the person who knows as much as humanly can be known about the character of another, and have still admitted the secondhand, irresponsible product of multiplied guesses and gossip which we term 'reputation.'"[1]

Rule 405 now permits both reputation and (personal) opinion testimony. That means that under Rule 405, the character witness can testify not just about the accused's reputation, but also about the character witness' *own opinion* as to the character of the accused. Areas like this, where the federal rules sought to change established common-law traditions, are the most likely to create variation between federal and State rules. For example, Virginia Rule of Evidence 2:405, while otherwise similar to the federal rule, continues to limit character witnesses to reputation testimony. The Federal Advisory Committee Note to Rule 405 suggests this difference will be minimal in practical terms, asserting that traditional "reputation evidence" invariably devolved into the witness' "opinion in disguise."

Rule 404(a)(2)(B) permits the accused to offer evidence about the victim's character. Again, the introduction of such evidence is controlled by Rule 405(a). Proof may only be by reputation or opinion. And specific instances can be raised only on cross-examination of the character witness. This inquiry is

---

[1] 7 J. Wigmore, Evidence § 1986.

further limited by Rule 412, the Rape Shield law (a subject for later in this Chapter).

Rules 404(a)(2)(A) and (B) also permit the prosecution to rebut defense character evidence with similar evidence of its own. This mirroring is common throughout the character evidence rules. As a general matter, the prosecution is precluded from introducing character evidence. But if the defense "opens the door" by calling its own character witnesses, the prosecution is permitted to meet those witnesses with witnesses of its own. The prosecution witnesses will similarly be restricted by Rule 405(a). One exception to this ordering principle is that, under Rule 404(a)(2)(C), the prosecution is permitted to introduce evidence of a homicide victim's peaceful character to rebut a suggestion that the victim was the "first aggressor." Again, such evidence must go through Rule 405(a).

STATE VARIATION: TEXAS RULE 405

Texas introduces an interesting restriction on character evidence. While otherwise mirroring the federal rule, Texas Rule of Evidence 405 states, "a witness may testify to the defendant's character or character trait only if, *before the day of the offense*, the witness was familiar with the defendant's reputation or the facts or information that form the basis of the witness's opinion." *Why do you think Texas includes this limitation?*

VIRGIN ISLANDS v. ROLDAN
612 F.2d 775 (3d Cir. 1979)

GARTH, Circuit Judge.

This is an appeal from a conviction for murder in the first degree. Juan A. Roldan, the convicted defendant, challenges ... the admission into evidence of his prior conviction.... Because we are satisfied that the district court did not err in its evidentiary ruling ..., we affirm.

I.

On the morning of March 23, 1978, Enrique Garcia was found dead in a yard close to Roldan's property. His body, which was covered with blood, revealed multiple stab wounds....

Roldan, who was a neighbor of the owners of the yard where the body was found … was found guilty by a jury after a two-day trial. Testimony included that of Luz Maria Cruz, the wife of Roldan's nephew. Cruz was called by the Government. Defense counsel's cross-examination began as follows:

> Q Mrs. Cruz, I am a lawyer for Mr. Roldan, I am going to ask you a few questions.
>
> Now, have you known Mr. Roldan for two or three years?
>
> A Yes. I am married to my husband since 1961, ever since I know him.
>
> Q Do you ever see people other than Mr. Roldan going to his house?
>
> A No.
>
> Q Would you say that he is a lonely unsociable fellow?
>
> A He is a man that never bother anybody.

This line of questioning was not continued.

The Government, at a sidebar conference, and in chambers during a recess, contended that Roldan's counsel, by these inquiries, had introduced evidence of Roldan's good character, thereby allowing the Government to impeach Cruz' testimony on redirect examination. The Government offered defense counsel a choice either retract the third question ("Would you say that he is a lonely unsociable fellow?"), and strike the answer given, or the Government would question Cruz about Roldan's prior murder conviction. Roldan's attorney refused to retract the question or to move to strike the answer. At the same time he also objected to the Government's proposed impeachment. The district court then made clear to defense counsel that the Government would be allowed to question Cruz about the prior conviction.

On redirect examination, Cruz was asked the following questions by the Government:

> Q Mrs. Cruz, you are aware, are you not, that the Defendant was convicted previously of murder in the 1st degree?

MR. JOHNSON: (defense counsel) I object to the question and ask that it be stricken and the jury instructed to disregard.

THE COURT: I will overrule the objection on the grounds I previously stated.

A (By the witness) Yes, I knew about that.

Q (By Mr. Schwartz (Assistant U.S. Attorney)) You knew he was convicted of murder in the 1st degree?

A Yes, sir, I have known of that.

Q And you would still say he is a man who never bothers anyone?

A Now, yes, I have to say that.

Before instructing the jury, the district court denied Roldan's motions for a mistrial based on admission of the prior conviction, ... The jury was instructed as to the elements of first and second degree murder and returned a verdict of guilty of first degree murder. Roldan was sentenced to life imprisonment.

II.

Roldan argues that it was error for the district court to have allowed the Government to inquire whether Cruz knew that Roldan had been convicted previously of first degree murder, since evidence of prior bad acts is generally inadmissible.

A.

Rule 404 of the Federal Rules of Evidence [permits the defense to introduce] [e]vidence of a pertinent trait of his character offered by an accused, or by the prosecution to rebut the same;...

Thus, if Roldan "opened the door" by putting his character in issue, it was permissible for the Government to put in evidence of Roldan's bad character through impeachment of Cruz's good character assessment, by asking her about her familiarity with Roldan's prior conviction. The permissible methods of doing so are specified in Fed.R.Evid. 405.

Cruz was closely related to Roldan and could have been expected to render a positive character evaluation. The district court determined that by asking the questions about Roldan's social habits, Roldan's counsel had put Roldan's character in issue. We agree. The last two questions which Roldan's counsel asked Cruz, are apparently directed toward establishing that Roldan had little contact with anyone and would therefore be unlikely to have reason to murder anyone. We do not think that Cruz' answer, "He is a man that never bother anybody," was a gratuitous, unsolicited remark; on the contrary, it was precisely the type of answer called for by defense counsel. The court's admission of the Government's impeachment testimony was thus proper.

B.

Any doubts we might have had concerning the question whether Roldan had intentionally put his character in issue, or was rather the unfortunate victim of an unexpected and unresponsive answer, are resolved by the Government's willingness to forgo inquiry into Roldan's bad character provided Roldan's counsel agreed to retract the third question and move to strike Cruz' answer....

There can be little question that Cruz' answer went to Roldan's character. Counsel's refusal to retract the question and to move to strike the answer based on his persistence in an erroneous belief that the Government could not impeach its own witness negates any possible claim that Roldan should not be held responsible for soliciting Cruz' character testimony. Since Roldan thereby invited the Government's damaging cross-examination, he "will not be heard to complain of matters which result from his own conduct."

C.

Roldan objects further to the form of the impeachment questions, arguing that it was improper to use the phrases, "you are aware, are you not," and "(y)ou knew," rather than the form, "have you heard."

... we find no error. Roldan's argument is predicated on Michelson v. United States (1948)

> Since the whole inquiry, as we have pointed out, is calculated to ascertain the general talk of people about defendant, rather than the

witness' own knowledge of him, the form of inquiry, "Have you heard?" has general approval, and "Do you know?" is not allowed.

Nevertheless, it has been suggested that "this language appears to represent a summary of existing authority, rather than a direct proscription by the Court of questions in such form." Moreover, the Advisory Committee Note to rule 405 implies that rule 405 overruled this aspect of Michelson:

> According to the great majority of cases, on cross-examination inquiry is allowable as to whether the reputation witness has heard of particular instances of conduct pertinent to the trait in question. The theory is that, since the reputation witness relates what he has heard, the inquiry tends to shed light on the accuracy of his hearing and reporting. Accordingly, the opinion witness would be asked whether he knew, as well as whether he had heard. The fact is, of course, that these distinctions are of slight if any practical significance, and the second sentence of subdivision (a) eliminates them as a factor in formulating questions.

There is thus no basis in the form of the impeachment questions for reversing Roldan's conviction.

***

An attorney's questions are not considered evidence. Still, allowing, for example, the prosecution to ask a character witness about specific instances of the defendant's bad conduct raises a significant prospect of abuse. *Michelson* references this problem when it emphasized in reference to the prosecution's questions that: "[The trial judge] satisfied himself that counsel was not merely taking a random shot at a reputation imprudently exposed or asking a groundless question to waft an unwarranted innuendo into the jury box."

A commonly cited D.C. Circuit case, *United States v. Lewis*, sets forth generally accepted limits on questioning in this context, including the requirement that the inquiring attorney has a "good faith" basis for any questions asked:

> "Merely to ask a character witness about his knowledge of a report is to get the facts reported before the jury; once there, notwithstanding

the judge's limiting instruction, they may influence the jury's determination on the issue of guilt....

The courts have, however, developed a series of restrictions designed to mitigate the potential hazard. The matters the witness is to be asked about should first be established to the trial judge's satisfaction as actual events. The questions put to the witness should be carefully and narrowly framed. The questions, of course, must be restricted to events affecting the character trait or traits the accused has placed in issue; their propriety is to be determined "by comparison with the reputation asserted." The process demands close supervision.... And obedient to the principle governing any use of evidence indicative of other criminality, the inquiry should be permitted only when "the probative value of the information which might be elicited outweighs the prejudice to the defendant."[1]

While *Lewis* predates the Federal Rules of Evidence, its guidance is cited by courts applying those rules. The last line in the excerpt should be understood as a reference to Rule 403.

***

Up to this point we have not had any reason to discuss Rule 405(b). Rule 405(b) only applies when "character is an essential element" of a criminal charge, civil claim, or defense. In that unusual circumstance, Rule 405(b) permits the parties to introduce whatever type of character evidence they like -- specific instances, reputation or opinion -- to prove the charge, claim, or defense (subject, of course, to the other rules of evidence). Think about how rarely character will be an **essential** element. Essential, in this context, means that the party *must* prove that a person's character was of a certain type in order to prevail. The rarity of modern examples comes through in the Advisory Committee Note's strained effort to suggest scenarios where Rule 405(b) applies. See Advisory Committee Note to Rule 404 (offering as an example, "chastity of the victim under a statute specifying her chastity as an element of the crime of seduction").

---

[1] 482 F.2d 632 (D.C. Cir. 1973).

There are modern examples where Rule 405(b) could apply: a civil case where a defendant must prove, for example, that a statement that "my neighbor is a lying cheat" is true to avoid liability for slander; a child custody dispute that turns on a parent's fitness to raise a child; a civil action seeking damages from a defendant for lending a car to a habitually negligent driver. But these examples are infrequent. Consequently, Rule 405(b)'s blessing of a character-evidence free-for-all rarely comes into play.

EXCEPTION FOR WITNESS CHARACTER EVIDENCE

RULE 404(a)(3)

Rule 404(a)(3) creates another exception to the ban on propensity evidence. It allows any party in a civil or criminal case to introduce evidence relating to the character of a trial witness. As with evidence introduced under Rule 404(a)(2), evidence offered under Rule 404(a)(3) must satisfy a series of specific requirements to be admitted. The Rule itself points to "Rules 607, 608, and 609," the source of these requirements.

RULE 607

Rule 607 may be the simplest rule in the Federal Rules of Evidence. It states that: "Any party, including the party that called the witness, may attack the witness's credibility." The key to understanding this rule is that it eliminates, rather than creates, restrictions. Here is an excerpt from a book comparing the Federal Rule to the Virginia Rule:

> "The federal rules permit impeachment of any witness, allowing those who encounter this rule to rejoice at its simplicity and move on to other matters. Virginia litigants are not so lucky."

The problem for litigants in Virginia, and other jurisdictions that do not take the federal approach, is that they must contend with the complex thicket of rules that restrict a party's ability to attack the credibility of a witness called *by that party* to testify. By the way, this was the source of the defense attorney's unfortunate confusion in the *Roldan* case. Since the federal rules do away with all of that, we get to "move on to other matters."

RULE 608

Trials often turn on efforts by one party to discredit the opposing party's witnesses. There are countless ways to go about this. For example, a party may show that a witness has made inconsistent statements, or is mistaken or confused, or is biased by a connection to the parties or a stake in the outcome. The admissibility of evidence offered to support these common arguments is governed by familiar rules: relevance, hearsay, and Rule 403.

Rule 608 governs a party's efforts to discredit a witness by impugning the witness' character. This is a rarer form of attack on a witness' credibility, but an important one. One way to attack a witness' character under the Federal Rules is to introduce the witness' record of past criminal convictions. That scenario is governed exclusively by Rule 609 (discussed separately below). Rule 608 covers other attacks on a witness' character.

Rule 608 limits permissible attacks on a witness' character to those that speak to the witness' truthfulness. Using the parlance of Rule 405, the only character trait that is "pertinent" for a trial witness is the witness' honesty, or "character for truthfulness or untruthfulness."

Further symmetry with Rule 405(a) is apparent in that:

- Rule 608(a) limits character witnesses to testifying about reputation or opinion.
- Rule 608(b) makes explicit the prohibition on proof of specific instances ("extrinsic evidence") that is implicit in Rule 405.
- Rule 608(b)(2) permits cross-examination of the character witness on specific instances probative of truthfulness.

There are also two important distinctions between Rule 608 and Rule 405(a).

- Evidence that a witness has a truthful (as opposed to untruthful) character can only be introduced "after the witness's character for truthfulness has been attacked." Rule 608(a).
- Rule 608(b)(1) permits cross-examination of "the witness" with specific instances of (that witness') untruthfulness.

PROBLEM 4-5: CLERKSHIP APPLICATIONS

Consider these facts from a court case and New York Times article.

Matthew Martoma was prosecuted for insider trading in federal court in 2014. Prior to trial, the government sought permission to introduce evidence about an unrelated past incident.

In 1999, Martoma applied for clerkships at the District of Columbia Circuit using an altered transcript with inflated grades. When the discrepancy between his actual grades and the transcripts he submitted to the judges was brought to the attention of the Harvard Law School Registrar, Martoma told the Registrar that he had made a mistake. And that since, at the time of his interviews (Jan. 26 and 27) he had planned to immediately withdraw his clerkship applications due to his lack of interest, he had decided not to inform the judges.

To support his claim, Martoma later provided the Registrar with an email he sent to another Harvard official dated Feb. 1. But investigation suggested that the email Martoma submitted had been altered. It was actually sent on Feb. 2, after the confrontation with the Registrar. Martoma also claimed that he withdrew his applications before the confrontation, providing letters dated Jan. 31, but the letters were actually postmarked Feb. 3.

Harvard expelled Martoma, concluding that he "falsified his transcript, interviewed with judges under false pretenses, and gave untruthful answers to administrators at the Law School."[1]

Assume that the government claims that Martoma altered or deleted evidence related to the now-pending insider trading allegations. The government argues that the 1999 false clerkship applications/attempted cover-up is relevant to show Martoma's knowledge, ability and intent to delete or alter electronic evidence in order to influence an investigation. *How should the court rule on the government's pretrial motion to introduce the 1999 law school incident to show this knowledge and intent?*

Assume the judge denies the government's motion. But then, at trial, Martoma testifies that he did not trade on insider information. *Is there a new argument that*

---

[1] See James B. Stewart, *Past Fictions, a Lack of Trust and No Deal in SAC Case*, N.Y. Times, February 6, 2014; United States v. Martoma (S.D.N.Y. Jan. 9, 2014)

the government can make to try to use the evidence of the 1999 incident at trial? How should the trial court rule now?

Rule 611

Rule 608 illustrates one of the ways that witnesses can face unpleasant questioning at trial. Rule 611 attempts to improve the lot of a witness somewhat by authorizing judges to intervene in witness examinations when necessary to "protect witnesses from harassment or undue embarrassment." This rule does not authorize the exclusion of evidence or relevant questioning, but it does permit some regulation of the way the examination is conducted. When a party complains that counsel is treating a witness poorly ("berating the witness"), Rule 611 authorizes the trial court to intervene.

STATE VARIATIONS: SPECIFIC INSTANCES

Different jurisdictions use slight variations on the rules governing attacks on a witness' character. For example,

Texas Rule of Evidence 608:

> **(b) Specific Instances of Conduct.** Except for a criminal conviction under Rule 609, a party may not inquire into or offer extrinsic evidence to prove specific instances of the witness's conduct in order to attack or support the witness's character for truthfulness.

Similarly, Virginia Rule of Evidence 608(b) only permits cross-examination of a *character witness* regarding specific instances of another witness' untruthfulness. It does not permit such questioning of the witness themselves, except with respect to specific instances of perjury. *Do you prefer these state rules or the federal rule as a matter of policy?*

PRIOR CONVICTIONS

Rule 404(a)(3) identifies Rule 609 as one of the permitted pathways to attack a witness' character. Rule 609 authorizes the use of certain criminal convictions to attack "a witness's character for truthfulness."

RULE 609

The best way to explain Rule 609 is through historical context.

> The roots of the practice of impeachment with prior convictions can be traced to English common law, which categorically barred witnesses previously convicted of a felony (or other "infamous crime") from testifying. Throughout the late nineteenth and early twentieth centuries, these and other disqualifications of witness classes gradually disappeared in American jurisdictions. This trend culminated in the Supreme Court's pronouncement in 1918, as "the conviction of [the] time," that "the truth is more likely to be arrived at by hearing the testimony of all persons of competent understanding who may seem to have knowledge of the facts involved in a case, leaving the credit and weight of such testimony to be determined by the jury."
>
> The statutory reforms that abolished the testimonial disqualification of felons and other classes of witnesses nevertheless retained some of the spirit of the common law tradition by permitting the credibility of previously disqualified witnesses to be impeached with the once disqualifying factors. In the case of "felons," this meant impeachment with their prior convictions. Thus, the practice of impeaching testifying witnesses with prior convictions was not, at least originally, intended to penalize defendants. Instead, it was a byproduct of a progressive reform....[1]

These reforms carried through to the Federal Rules of Evidence. Rule 601 states that: "Every person is competent to be a witness unless these rules provide otherwise." The only remaining disqualifications are narrow and understandable, like the rule that prohibits a sitting juror from testifying in the case being tried. Fed. R. Ev. 606(a). And while the Rules bar some means of impeachment with once-disqualifying factors, like religion in Rule 610, Rule 609 permits impeachment with prior convictions.

State code sections similarly reflect the historical connection between the competency rules and impeachment with prior convictions. For example, Virginia Code § 19.2-269 states:

---

[1] Jeffrey Bellin, Circumventing Congress: How the Federal Courts Opened the Door to Impeaching Criminal Defendants with Prior Convictions, 42 U.C. Davis L. Rev. 289 (2008).

"A person convicted of a felony or perjury shall not be incompetent to testify, but the fact of conviction may be shown in evidence to affect his credit."

When would a prior conviction affect a witness' "credit"? That is a question that is hotly disputed, with many scholars taking the position that the answer is rarely, if at all. But courts and policymakers generally take a different view.

Here is an emphatic defense of the practice of impeachment by prior convictions by Judge George MacKinnon:

> "[C]onvicted felons are not generally permitted to stand pristine before a jury with the same credibility as that of a Mother Superior. Fairness is not a one-way street and in the search for the truth it is a legitimate concern that one who testifies should not be allowed to appear as credible when his criminal record of major crimes suggests that he is not."[1]

The tone of that quote contrasts with recent efforts to reduce the stigma of a criminal record by rethinking official terminology. In 2016, for example, federal Department of Justice officials sought to purge words like "felon" or "criminal" from official pronouncements, stating that "no punishment is harsher than being permanently branded a 'felon' or 'offender.'"[2] This effort can be seen in Department of Justice press releases that sometimes use "justice-involved individuals" instead of derogatory terms.[3]

Whether these efforts to reduce the stigma of prior convictions succeed remains to be seen. But for now, the rules of evidence continue to assume the relevance of a witness' record of prior convictions.

Apart from the relevance question, there is also the problem of unfair prejudice. Although prior convictions admitted under Rule 609 are only relevant to witness credibility, a jury may use them to draw forbidden propensity inferences. This is particularly true when past convictions are used

---

[1] U.S. v. Lipscomb, 702 F.2d 1049 (D.C. Cir. 1983) (concurrence).
[2] https://www.washingtonpost.com/news/true-crime/wp/2016/05/04/guest-post-justice-dept-to-alter-its-terminology-for-released-convicts-to-ease-reentry/
[3] https://www.justice.gov/opa/pr/departments-justice-and-housing-and-urban-development-award-175-million-help-justice-involved

to impeach one type of witness, a criminal defendant who testifies. That dilemma generated great Congressional interest in Rule 609:

> [Rule 609 as originally drafted by the Advisory Committee] directed trial courts to admit convictions for all crimes "punishable by death or imprisonment in excess of one year" (i.e., felonies) as well as all crimes (felony or misdemeanor) involving "dishonesty or false statement regardless of the punishment" for "the purpose of attacking the credibility of a witness."….
>
> Upon receipt of the Advisory Committee's draft Rule 609, Congress prohibited the Rule from taking effect and enacted an alternative….
>
> Congress was not of one mind on the question, however. The Rule as finally enacted, and currently in force, embodies a compromise between "two diametrically opposed positions": the position of the Senate (circa 1974) that all felony convictions should be admissible to impeach testifying defendants; and that of the House of Representatives that impeachment should be limited to the narrow subset of so-called crimen falsi convictions, crimes involving "proof or admission of an act of dishonesty or false statement."
>
> The Conference Committee that drafted the final text of the Rule bridged the broad gap between the two chambers by retaining the general principle that all felonies could potentially be admissible as impeachment. It mandated, however, that [for testifying defendants] any felony outside the "narrow spectrum" of crimen falsi convictions would be admissible only if "the [trial] court determines that the probative value of admitting this evidence outweighs its prejudicial effect to the defendant."[1]

Thus, a legislative compromise led to Rule 609(a)(1)(B)'s carefully calibrated balancing test for the introduction of prior convictions of defendants who testify. The application of this test by the courts was almost immediately complicated by a five-factor framework, derived from a Seventh Circuit

---

[1] Bellin, Circumventing Congress, 42 U.C. Davis L. Rev. 289 (2008).

opinion, *United States v. Mahone*, issued shortly after the enactment of Rule 609. Here is the critical excerpt from that case:

> "Some of the factors which the judge should take into account in making his determination were articulated by then Judge Burger in Gordon v. United States (D.C. Cir. 1967):
>
> > (1) The impeachment value of the prior crime.
> >
> > (2) The point in time of the conviction and the witness' subsequent history.
> >
> > (3) The similarity between the past crime and the charged crime.
> >
> > (4) The importance of the defendant's testimony.
> >
> > (5) The centrality of the credibility issue."[1]

These factors swept the federal courts and many state courts as a means of guiding the Rule 609(a)(1)(B) analysis. The problem with the factors is twofold: (1) they appear to cloud rather than clarify the Rule 609 balance; and (2) courts differ in how these factors apply, with some courts applying the fourth factor backwards. Keep this in mind as you read the following excerpts which are intended to both illuminate the modern doctrinal landscape and highlight a powerful critique.

UNITED STATES v. CALDWELL
760 F.3d 267 (3d Cir. 2014)

SMITH, Circuit Judge.

Akeem Caldwell brings this appeal following his conviction of being a felon in possession of a firearm under 18 U.S.C. § 922(g)(1)... Because we conclude that admission of Caldwell's prior convictions was improper, we will vacate the judgment of the District Court and remand for further proceedings.

---

[1] United States v. Mahone, 537 F.2d 922 (7th Cir. 1976).

I.

On January 24, 2012, at approximately 11:45 p.m., three detectives with the Pittsburgh Police Department … observed Caldwell remove a black firearm from his waistband and hold it behind [his companion, Darby] Tigney's back…. [Caldwell then] released the firearm, letting it fall to the ground directly between Tigney's legs."…. [After being stopped,] Caldwell provided his identity to the detectives, and a records search revealed that he had a prior criminal record. After discovering that Caldwell was a convicted felon who was not permitted to possess a firearm, the detectives transported him to the Allegheny County Jail for processing….

The case against Caldwell proceeded to trial … on December 4, 2012…. Caldwell's theory at trial was that Tigney—and only Tigney—possessed the gun on the evening of his arrest. In support of this claim, Caldwell repeatedly emphasized that Tigney provided a false name to the detectives at the scene, and that this indicated a consciousness of guilt. Caldwell also sought to admit, as a statement against interest, Tigney's out-of-court admission to defense investigators that he had possessed the gun….

In addition to arguing that Tigney possessed the firearm, Caldwell sought to impeach the credibility of the testifying detectives. Caldwell theorized that the detectives targeted him rather than Tigney as the possessor of the gun because he had a prior felony conviction, thus subjecting him to federal charges, whereas Tigney, a juvenile, was subject to only an adjudication of delinquency. Caldwell also pointed out that, despite having done so in other cases, investigators never sought to obtain surveillance footage of the Northview Heights scene of his encounter with police from the Housing Authority. Such evidence, he maintained, would have shown that Tigney possessed the gun.

Caldwell testified in his defense. He claimed that, at the time he was stopped by the detectives, he was holding a cell phone in his hand—not a gun—and was talking to his girlfriend, Tiffany Dungan. Dungan corroborated this claim by testifying that she was on the phone with Caldwell when the police stopped him. She also presented phone records showing that, around the time of the arrest, she participated in a seventeen minute phone call with a number that she claimed belonged to Caldwell. Caldwell also offered the testimony of a bystander, Manly Banks, who stated that he witnessed an officer take a cell phone out of Caldwell's hand and hang up the phone.

In the course of cross-examining Caldwell, the Government sought to introduce, under both Rule 404(b) and Rule 609(a)(1)(B) of the Federal Rules of Evidence, two prior convictions for unlawful firearm possession. One of Caldwell's "priors" was a federal conviction for possession of a firearm by a convicted felon—the very offense for which he was being tried. With respect to Rule 404(b), the Government argued the evidence was admissible to show "knowledge and absence of mistake or accident." Caldwell's counsel countered that absence of mistake and knowledge were irrelevant because the only issue in the case was whether Caldwell actually possessed the gun. Indeed, he conceded that "[w]hoever possessed [the gun] knew it."

The District Court was initially skeptical of the Government's claim that the evidence was admissible [but ultimately allowed its admission]. The Court [explained]:

> I understand it's prejudicial, but when you have a situation where this is a complete credibility determination, Mr. Caldwell has testified in a manner diametrically opposed to those of the police officers and I do believe it is probative for knowledge and intent and that that probative value outweighs the prejudicial effect, which I acknowledge is prejudicial.

Defense counsel immediately objected to the Court's reference to Caldwell's "credibility," which is generally not a concern in the 404(b) inquiry. This, in turn, prompted the Court to clarify its position: "So the record is clear, I'm not saying ... it is admissible for credibility. I'm saying it's admissible for knowledge and intent...."

.... [T]he jury returned a verdict convicting Caldwell of the charged offense. The District Court sentenced Caldwell to 77 months in prison and three years of supervised release. Caldwell timely filed this appeal.

II.

[The Court rejected the government's argument that the prior convictions were admissible under Rule 404(b).]

The Government alternatively argues that the evidence of Caldwell's prior convictions was admissible for impeachment purposes under Federal Rule of Evidence 609(a)(1)(B). The Government preserved this argument by proffering Rule 609 as a basis for admission both in its pretrial filings and during trial.... Accordingly, we consider whether Rule 609 provided an alternative basis for admitting the evidence of Caldwell's prior convictions.

Rule 609 permits evidence of a prior felony conviction to be offered to impeach a testifying witness. However, when the testifying witness is also the defendant in a criminal trial, the prior conviction is admitted only "if the probative value of the evidence outweighs its prejudicial effect to that defendant." Fed.R.Evid. 609(a)(1)(B). This reflects a heightened balancing test and a reversal of the standard for admission under Rule 403. Commentators have observed that structuring the balancing in this manner creates a "predisposition toward exclusion." "An exception is made only where the prosecution shows that the evidence makes a tangible contribution to the evaluation of credibility and that the usual high risk of unfair prejudice is not present."

Our Court has recognized four factors that should be considered when weighing the probative value against the prejudicial effect under this heightened test. These factors include: "(1) the kind of crime involved; (2) when the conviction occurred; (3) the importance of the [defendant's] testimony to the case; [and] (4) the importance of the credibility of the defendant."

When evaluating the first factor—the kind of crime involved—courts consider both the impeachment value of the prior conviction as well as its similarity to the charged crime. The impeachment value relates to how probative the prior conviction is to the witness's character for truthfulness. Crimes of violence generally have lower probative value in weighing credibility, but may still be admitted after balancing the other factors. In contrast, crimes that by their nature imply some dishonesty, such as theft, have greater impeachment value and are significantly more likely to be admissible.

With respect to the similarity of the crime to the offense charged, the balance tilts further toward exclusion as the offered impeachment evidence becomes more similar to the crime for which the defendant is being tried. As the Fourth Circuit has explained:

> Admission of evidence of a similar offense often does little to impeach the credibility of a testifying defendant while undoubtedly prejudicing him. The jury, despite limiting instructions, can hardly avoid drawing the inference that the past conviction suggests some probability that defendant committed the similar offense for which he is currently charged. The generally accepted view, therefore, is that evidence of similar offenses for impeachment purposes under Rule 609 should be admitted sparingly if at all.

The second factor is the age of the prior conviction. Convictions more than ten years old are presumptively excluded and must satisfy the special balancing requirements in Rule 609(b) to overcome this presumption. But even where the conviction is not subject to the ten-year restriction, "the passage of a shorter period can still reduce [a prior conviction's] probative value." The age of a conviction may weigh particularly in favor of exclusion "where other circumstances combine with the passage of time to suggest a changed character." For example, a prior conviction may have less probative value where the defendant-witness has maintained a spotless record since the earlier conviction or where the prior conviction was a mere youthful indiscretion. Conversely, the probative value of an older conviction may remain undiminished if the defendant was recently released from confinement or has multiple intervening convictions, both of which could suggest his character has not improved.

The third factor inquires into the importance of the defendant's testimony to his defense at trial. "The tactical need for the accused to testify on his or her own behalf may militate against use of impeaching convictions. If it is apparent to the trial court that the accused must testify to refute strong prosecution evidence, then the court should consider whether, by permitting conviction impeachment, the court in effect prevents the accused from testifying." "If, on the other hand, the defense can establish the subject matter of the defendant's testimony by other means, the defendant's testimony is less necessary, so a prior conviction is more likely to be admitted."

The final factor concerns the significance of the defendant's credibility to the case. "When the defendant's credibility is a central issue, this weighs in favor of admitting a prior conviction." See United States v. Johnson (3d Cir. 2002) (affirming admission of prior conviction under Rule 609(a) because the defendant's credibility was important). Conversely, the probative value of a defendant's prior conviction may be diminished "where the witness testifies as to inconsequential matters or facts that are conclusively shown by other credible evidence."

After reviewing the record and the arguments presented on appeal, we conclude that the Government has failed to carry its burden of showing that the probative value of Caldwell's prior convictions outweighs their prejudicial effect under Rule 609(a)(1)(B). The only factor the Government identified in favor of admission is that Caldwell's credibility was a central feature of the case. We do not minimize this point. At its core, this case was a "he said, they said" battle between Caldwell's version of events and that of the detectives. But this single factor is not enough to warrant admission of the prior convictions where all others favor exclusion. Caldwell's prior state conviction was quite similar to the charged offense, and his prior federal conviction was an identical match. That made the "priors" highly prejudicial. At the opposite end, the impeachment value of the prior convictions is low because unlawful firearms convictions do not, by their nature, imply a dishonest act. The Government also failed to show that the probative value of the evidence was not diminished by the passage of more than six-and-a-half years. And finally, Caldwell's testimony was fundamentally important to his defense. As already noted, the jury was required to choose between Caldwell's version of events and that provided by the officers. Given the consistency of the officers' accounts, Caldwell would have taken a great risk by failing to testify in his defense.

When offering a prior conviction to impeach a testifying defendant, the government bears the burden of satisfying the heightened balancing test set out in Rule 609(a)(1)(B). Based on our review of the record before us, the Government failed to establish that "the probative value of the evidence outweighs its prejudicial effect." Accordingly, Rule 609 was not a proper alternative basis for admitting Caldwell's prior convictions.

***

Caldwell is one of the most thorough treatments in the appellate case law of Rule 609(a)(1)(B). In a footnote to the case, the Third Circuit cites the author of this casebook to highlight an oddity about two of the factors it considered.

> We acknowledge the tension between the related third and fourth factors. See, e.g., … Jeffrey Bellin, Circumventing Congress: How the Federal Courts Opened the Door to Impeaching Criminal Defendants with Prior Convictions, 42 U.C. Davis L.Rev. 289, 318 (2008) ("In essence, the factors cancel each other out. To the extent a defendant's testimony is 'important' (for example, if the defendant is the key defense witness), his credibility becomes 'central' in equal degree, leading to a curious equipoise…. Thus, [these] factors seem [ ] to have no practical significance at all, existing in a rough state of equipoise that prevent[s] either factor from impacting the overall impeachment calculus.")

Nevertheless, the *Caldwell* Court went on to state:

> Be that as it may, these factors have long been accepted as independent components of the Rule 609(a)(1) balancing inquiry and we conclude that they should continue to inform the district court's admissibility determination.

Unfortunately, other courts do not apply nearly as critical a lens to the long-standing factors.

UNITED STATES v. PERKINS
937 F.2d 1397 (9th Cir. 1991)

RYMER, Circuit Judge:

Ernest Perkins appeals his conviction for bank robbery under 18 U.S.C. § 2113(a)…. We affirm.

I. Facts

On November 9, 1987, at approximately 12:40 p.m., [a man robbed a bank, getting away with a total of $653]…. After a four-day trial in which the defendant testified, the jury found Perkins guilty [of the robbery]. The district court ... sentenced him to twelve years imprisonment....

Perkins ... contends that the district court erred in denying his motion to preclude introduction under Fed.R.Evid. 609 of his prior bank robbery conviction. Perkins claims that because the prior conviction is for the same crime as the charged offense, there is a strong likelihood that the jury would consider the evidence as character evidence. The district court's decision to admit this evidence is reviewed for an abuse of discretion.

Rule 609(a)(1) allows the introduction of prior felony convictions to impeach the credibility of a witness if the court determines that the probative value of admitting this evidence outweighs its prejudicial effect to the defendant. In United States v. Browne, where we considered a claim similar to Perkins's, we reiterated five factors which should be considered in performing this balancing: (1) the impeachment value of the prior crime; (2) the point in time of the conviction; (3) the similarity between the past crime and the charged offense; (4) the importance of the defendant's testimony; and (5) the centrality of the defendant's credibility. There, as here, all of the factors except the similarity of the prior to the charged offense counseled in favor of admissibility. We therefore specifically noted that if "a bank robbery conviction serves a proper impeachment purpose, it, like evidence of other crimes, may be admissible in spite of its similarity to the offense at issue." Accordingly, the admission under Rule 609 of a bank robbery conviction in a bank robbery trial is not an abuse of discretion when the conviction serves a proper impeachment purpose, such as when the defendant's testimony and credibility are central to the case.

In this case, defendant's credibility and testimony were central to the case, as Perkins took the stand and testified that he did not commit the robbery. We therefore conclude that the district court did not abuse its discretion in denying Perkins's motion to preclude the government from asking him about his recent prior conviction for bank robbery, which Perkins admitted on direct examination, and painting a complete picture of Perkins's trustworthiness as a witness....

We therefore affirm Perkins's conviction.

STATE v. SWANSON
707 N.W.2d 645 (Minn. 2006)

Clinton Swanson appeals from his convictions of first-degree felony murder, second-degree murder, kidnapping, and false imprisonment.... [W]e affirm....

Swanson argues that he should receive a new trial due to erroneous admission of his five prior felony convictions (theft of a motor vehicle, two counts of second-degree assault, criminal vehicular operation, and possession of stolen property) for impeachment. When evaluating whether prior convictions are admissible for impeachment, a court considers five factors set out in State v. Jones (Minn. 1978). Swanson alleges that the district court did not sufficiently analyze the Jones factors on the record [and] that his convictions were more prejudicial than probative, ...

Evidence that a witness has been convicted of a felony is admissible for impeachment if the court "determines that the probative value of admitting this evidence outweighs its prejudicial effect." Minn. R. Evid. 609(a)(1). To decide this, a court examines:

> (1) the impeachment value of the prior crime, (2) the date of the conviction and the defendant's subsequent history, (3) the similarity of the past crime with the charged crime (the greater the similarity, the greater the reason for not permitting use of the prior crime to impeach), (4) the importance of defendant's testimony, and (5) the centrality of the credibility issue.

... [A] district court should demonstrate on the record that it has considered and weighed the Jones factors.... Our examination of these factors includes:

A. The impeachment value of the prior crime.

Swanson argues that there is very little to no impeachment value in his prior convictions. But we have held that a prior conviction can have impeachment value by helping the jury see the "whole person" of the defendant and better evaluate his or her truthfulness. Because Swanson's convictions are admissible under this analysis, Swanson's argument is unavailing.

B. The date of the conviction and defendant's subsequent history.

134

All of Swanson's convictions occurred within 10 years of his murder trial. Swanson notes that the assault convictions occurred in 1996 when he was under 20 years of age. But even an older conviction can remain probative if later convictions demonstrate a "history of lawlessness." Because Swanson's convictions show a pattern of lawlessness and because the convictions were all less than 10 years old, the dates of the convictions do not weigh against admission of the prior convictions.

C. The similarity of the past crime to the crime charged.

The more similar the alleged offense and the crime underlying a past conviction, the more likely it is that the conviction is more prejudicial than probative. Swanson argues that the two assault convictions are very similar to the charged offense of murder. Due to the similarity between the crime charged and past convictions, this factor weighs against admission of the assault convictions.

D. The importance of defendant's testimony and the centrality of credibility.

If credibility is a central issue in the case, the fourth and fifth Jones factors weigh in favor of admission of the prior convictions. Before trial, Swanson gave notice that he intended to present an alibi defense, a defense for which his testimony was the only evidence. The jury had to determine whether to believe Swanson or [the prosecution witnesses]. Because credibility was a central issue here, the fourth and fifth Jones factors weigh in favor of admission of the prior convictions.

Because only one of the Jones factors weighs against the admission of Swanson's assault convictions and none of the Jones factors weigh against admission of his remaining prior convictions, the district court did not abuse its discretion under Minn. R. Evid. 609(a)(1)....

Affirmed.

PROBLEM 4-6: MORE ETHICS

How should we think about an attorney's, and especially a prosecutor's, ethical role in a jurisdiction where courts seem to be incorrectly interpreting controlling authority to the detriment of criminal defendants. Can prosecutors "take advantage" of such case law without violating their ethical obligations to "do justice"? Or do they have an independent obligation to enforce the law? Does the following guidance, also from Berger v. United States (1935), complicate or clarify the answer? "[The prosecutor] is in a peculiar and very definite sense the servant of the law."

Does this ABA Model Rule of Professional Conduct help?

Rule 3.3 Candor Toward the Tribunal

(a) A lawyer shall not knowingly:

(1) make a false statement of fact or law to a tribunal . . .

(2) fail to disclose to the tribunal legal authority in the controlling jurisdiction known to the lawyer to be directly adverse to the position of the client and not disclosed by opposing counsel; or

(3) offer evidence that the lawyer knows to be false.

[Comment] Legal Argument

[4] Legal argument based on a knowingly false representation of law constitutes dishonesty toward the tribunal. A lawyer is not required to make a disinterested exposition of the law, but must recognize the existence of pertinent legal authorities....

***

To try to understand how often prior convictions are admitted in federal courts, one scholar surveyed federal judges and examined published federal trial court opinions. In his examination of published opinions, he found that trial courts "admitted two-thirds of [defendants'] prior convictions [as impeachment], and the jury is told the name of the prior conviction only about half the time."[1]

---

[1] Ric Simmons, An Empirical Study of Rule 609 and Suggestions for Practical Reform, 59 B.C. L. Rev. 993 (2018).

The question is particularly important due to the prevalence of criminal records among those charged with offenses. One official study of felony defendants in large cities reported that 75% of suspects charged with a felony had a prior arrest, 60% had a prior felony arrest, 60% "had at least one prior conviction," and 43% "had at least one prior felony conviction."[1]

***

The admission of criminal defendants' prior convictions under Rule 609 presents the jury with a difficult test of its analytical abilities. Here is an example of an instruction delivered to a federal jury in Virginia:

> You have received evidence that . . . the defendant has been previously convicted of a crime. You may consider [a] prior conviction in determining a witness' credibility as a witness, because the testimony of a witness may be discredited or impeached by evidence showing that the witness has been convicted of a felony. However, you should not conclude that because the defendant may have committed a crime in the past, that he is more likely to have committed the offenses with which he is currently charged. Nor should you conclude that any prior conviction shows general bad character or a likelihood that the defendant would commit future crimes.

How likely is it that jurors will use a prior conviction for the permitted purpose, and not the impermissible purpose? One way to test that question is to compare juror responses to two kinds of convictions: a conviction for a crime that is similar to the charged offense, and a conviction for a crime of dishonesty. Since the convictions are admitted solely to shed light on the defendant's character for truthfulness, jurors who follow their instructions should convict more frequently in the latter scenario.

Below is an excerpt from a paper reporting the results of an experiment along these lines.[2] The author asked a large pool of mock jurors how they would vote in a jewelry store burglary case. All of the jurors were presented with the same facts. Only one factor varied throughout the experiment: whether the

---

[1] Brian A. Reaves, Bureau Of Justice Statistics, Felony Defendants In Large Urban Counties, 2009 - Statistical Tables 8.
[2] Jeffrey Bellin, The Silence Penalty, 103 Iowa L. Rev. 395 (2018).

defendant testified and, if so, the type of conviction (if any) used as impeachment.

The jurors were instructed to consider the prior conviction to assess the defendant's credibility not his propensity to commit crimes. When the defendant testified, "[t]he defendant's testimony was summarily described as being 'consistent with that of' a defense alibi witness whose testimony (that he and the defendant were watching a baseball game at the time of the crime) appeared in all four scenarios." The results were as follows:

> Jurors voted to convict in 73% of the cases. The following table reveals the breakdown of guilty votes by scenario, ordered by descending conviction percentage.

Defendant Testifies?	Impeachment	Number (n)	Scenario	Guilty
Yes	Robbery	100	4	82%
No	None	96	1	76%
Yes	Criminal Fraud	100	3	73%
Yes	None	97	2	62%

Approximately 100 distinct mock jurors voted in each scenario. As the above table shows, the conviction rate was highest for Scenario 4 where the defendant testified and was impeached with a prior robbery. The lowest conviction rate occurred in Scenario 2 where the defendant testified and was not impeached with any prior crimes. The other two scenarios--where the defendant did not testify, or testified and was impeached with a criminal fraud conviction--returned similar conviction rates.

The results are consistent with the social science literature …. The jury's learning of prior convictions negatively impacted the defendant's chances for acquittal. The jurors convicted most often (82%) when they learned that the defendant had a prior robbery conviction. The conviction rate was also elevated (73%) over the no record condition (62%) when the defendant was impeached with a "criminal fraud" conviction. Overall, jurors voted to convict 78% of the time in the two prior conviction conditions, but only 62% of the time when the same testifying defendant was not impeached with any prior crimes. This variance achieves statistical significance.

These findings ... support the critique ... that prior conviction impeachment does not operate in the manner that the law contemplates. If prior conviction impeachment speaks only to the defendant's character for truthfulness, crimes of dishonesty would be most damaging. Here, the fraud conviction should have been most damaging since it is a crime that, unlike robbery, speaks directly to truthful character. "Criminal fraud" is one of a handful of offenses specifically referenced in the legislative history to Federal Rule of Evidence 609 and its advisory committee notes as directly "bearing on the accused's propensity to testify truthfully." Instead, in this experiment, the robbery conviction--an offense that was likely seen by lay participants as similar to the charged jewelry store burglary--had a larger negative impact. This suggests (consistent with the prior research ...) that jurors indulged a forbidden, criminal propensity inference."

Notice that in the table above, the defendant also had a lower chance of acquittal when he did not testify even though, in that scenario, no convictions were introduced. *Why might that be?*

NOTE ON APPELLATE REVIEW OF RULE 609

The Supreme Court strictly limits the circumstances under which federal criminal defendants can appeal Rule 609 rulings. In *Luce v. United States* (1984), the Court held that "to raise and preserve for review the claim of improper impeachment with a prior conviction, a defendant must testify." In *Ohler v. United States* (2000), the Court held that "a defendant who preemptively introduces evidence of a prior conviction on direct examination may not on appeal claim that the admission of such evidence was error."

The significance of theses rulings requires some context. Often, a defendant will seek a ruling prior to trial (commonly called an *in limine* motion) on the admissibility of prior convictions under Rule 609(a)(1)(B). If the trial court rules that the defendants' conviction(s) are admissible, defendants will often decline to testify to avoid the admission of the convictions.

If the defendant does testify, sound tactics suggest that, if the convictions will be admitted anyway, the defense attorney should elicit them from the defendant. Why? The defense attorney's questioning can present the prior convictions in a more favorable light, and the defendant will appear more forthcoming.

Luce and *Ohler* remove these tactical advantages for any defendant who wants to preserve the ability to appeal the trial court's in limine ruling. Under *Luce* and *Ohler*, a defendant will not be able to appeal a trial court's Rule 609(a)(1)(B) ruling unless the defendant testifies <u>and</u> waits for the prosecutor to introduce the defendant's prior conviction(s).

STATE VARIATION: APPELLATE REVIEW

Luce and *Ohler* only bind federal courts. Some state courts follow both decisions, some follow one or the other, and some follow neither. Here is another short excerpt from *State v. Swanson* to illustrate this point:

> A threshold issue is whether Swanson has waived this issue. After the denial of his motion in limine to prevent the prosecution from using his prior felony convictions as impeachment under Minn. R. Evid. 609, Swanson testified about his previous convictions on direct examination. Relying on Ohler v. United States (2000), the state argues that when a defendant testifies about his prior convictions on direct examination after denial of a motion to exclude the convictions, the defendant has waived review of [their] admissibility.

> While instructive, Ohler is an interpretation of the Federal Rules of Evidence and is not binding on this court. The reasoning of Ohler is at odds with Minnesota precedent. In Ohler, the Court cited Luce v. United States (1984), as support for its reasoning. Luce held that a defendant must actually testify in order to preserve the issue of the admissibility of prior convictions for appeal. But, in Minnesota, a defendant need not testify to preserve this issue on appeal. The Court in Ohler also indicated that its holding is based on the idea that it is fair to hold a defendant to the consequences of tactical trial decisions. We recently rejected similar reasoning, stating that "[i]t is inconsistent with our precedent and with our notion of fairness to conclude that

once a defendant chooses to stipulate to evidence he was unsuccessful in getting excluded he has waived the opportunity to argue on appeal that the court erred in admitting the evidence." In light of our prior decisions on these issues, we hold that a defendant who testifies about his convictions on direct examination after denial of a motion in limine to exclude those convictions has not forfeited the opportunity to appeal the admissibility of those prior convictions.

STATE VARIATION: NAMING CONVICTIONS

When courts do admit prior convictions under Rule 609, they typically do not permit the introduction of details of the underlying crime. Sometimes parties will seek to exclude even the name of the conviction. Here is a federal court's rejection of the suggestion that Rule 609 requires such exclusion:

> "The overwhelming weight of authority … suggests that, while it may be proper to limit, under Rule 609(a)(1), evidence of the underlying facts or details of a crime of which a witness was convicted, inquiry into the 'essential facts' of the conviction, including the nature or statutory name of each offense … is presumptively required by the Rule, subject to balancing under Rule 403."[1]

By contrast, some States bar the introduction of the name of the conviction. For example, in Virginia:

> "[T]he Commonwealth may ask a defendant who testifies in a criminal proceeding the number of times he has been convicted of a felony, but … not the names of the felonies, other than perjury, and not the nature or details thereof."[2]

STATE VARIATION: BARRING PRIOR CONVICTION IMPEACHMENT

A few States do not allow criminal defendants to be impeached with prior convictions at all. Here is Hawaii's Rule 609:

---

[1] United States v. Estrada, 430 F.3d 606 (2d Cir. 2005)
[2] Sadoski v. Commonwealth, 219 Va. 1069 (1979).

(a) General rule. For the purpose of attacking the credibility of a witness, evidence that the witness has been convicted of a crime is inadmissible except when the crime is one involving dishonesty. However, in a criminal case where the defendant takes the stand, the defendant shall not be questioned or evidence introduced as to whether the defendant has been convicted of a crime, for the sole purpose of attacking credibility, unless the defendant has oneself introduced testimony for the purpose of establishing the defendant's credibility as a witness, in which case the defendant shall be treated as any other witness as provided in this rule.

Other jurisdictions permit broader impeachment than Rule 609. Here is the statute governing the courts of the District of Columbia (D.C. Code § 14-305):

… for the purpose of attacking the credibility of a witness, evidence that the witness has been convicted of a criminal offense shall be admitted if offered, either upon the cross-examination of the witness or by evidence aliunde, but only if the criminal offense (A) was punishable by death or imprisonment in excess of one year under the law under which he was convicted, or (B) involved dishonesty or false statement (regardless of punishment).

As the D.C. Courts recognize, "under § 14–305 the trial court has no discretion to preclude the use of prior convictions for impeachment, including reference to the nature of the crimes, even though in a particular case the prejudicial impact on the party they are used against may outweigh the probative value to the party who elicits them."[1]

***

Rule 609 includes other less-frequently litigated provisions. Rule 609(a)(2) makes a small set of dishonesty-crimes admissible without balancing. As Congress' Conference Report states, these include: "crimes such as perjury or subornation of perjury, false statement, criminal fraud, embezzlement, or false pretense, or any other offense in the nature of crimen falsi, the commission of which involves some element of deceit, untruthfulness, or falsification."

---

[1] Langley v. United States, 515 A.2d 729 (D.C. 1986).

Rule 609(b) places additional restrictions on the use of convictions "if more than 10 years have passed since the witness's conviction or release from confinement for it, whichever is later." Rule 609(c), (d) and (e) place additional restrictions on the admission of certain convictions.

REVIEW PROBLEM 4-7: POP SINGER IN TROUBLE

A popular singer, Larry Logan is charged with shooting an overly aggressive reporter in Los Angeles. The defense offers the following witnesses at trial:

- Larry testifies in his own defense that the shooting was an accident, and the gun went off while Larry was trying to make sure it was not loaded. The prosecution then moves to introduce a certified record of Larry's 5-year-old conviction for felony theft.
- Tina Foy testifies that she has known Larry for 10 years and she believes Larry has a very law-abiding character.
- Justin Barber testifies that he has known Larry for 10 years and he believes Larry is a very truthful person.

During pretrial preparation, the prosecution discovers from reliable sources that Larry:

(i) plagiarized his college admissions essay, and

(ii) was arrested for driving drunk a year before trial.

(1) Do the rules allow the introduction of a record of Logan's prior conviction?

(2) What rules, if any, permit the testimony of defense witnesses, Foy and Barber?

(3) Can the prosecutor ask any of the defense witnesses, Foy, Logan, or Barber, about the two matters (i) and (ii) described above? If so, which witnesses can be asked which questions?

In answering the questions, identify the specific portions of each rule that apply. The ability to identify the source of authority for each answer is necessary for applying these complex rules in the wide variety of circumstances in which they arise.

RAPE SHIELD LAWS

The traditional character evidence rules, memorialized in the federal rules of evidence, open two potential avenues for a criminal defendant to impugn the character of a crime victim: (1) the defendant can introduce evidence of the victim's "pertinent" character trait - see Rule 404(a)(2); and (2) assuming the victim testifies, the defendant can introduce evidence that undermines the victim-witness' character for truthfulness - see Rule 404(a)(3).

Prior to the passage of Rule 412, defendants charged with sexual assault could take advantage of these rules to "attack the victim" in an effort to win acquittal. The Rule 404(a)(2) pathway is most obvious. In fact, the Advisory Committee Note to that rule offered as one of its two examples: "an accused may introduce pertinent evidence of the character of the victim, as in support of a claim of … consent in a case of rape." This is precisely the kind of evidence that is now forbidden by Rule 412.

Defendants' problematic use of the pathway now embodied in Rule 404(a)(3) is likely less clear to a modern reader. The answer lies in the realization that it is not merely the rules of evidence that determine what evidence is permitted, but also the beliefs and prejudices of the judges applying them. Thus, the Supreme Court of Washington, writing in 1891, noted the following (bizarre) exchange that took place during a murder trial:

> "One Gabrielle Monard was called and examined as a witness for the prosecution. Upon cross–examination she testified that she was a married woman, whereupon defendant's attorney asked her a further question, as to whether she was not a prostitute."

The Washington Court went on to endorse this cross-examination -- even though it had no connection to the facts of the case -- because, in the judges' view, it spoke to the witness' character for truthfulness. The Court's opinion states:

> "If she chose to answer and admit, if such was the fact, that she had wantonly violated the restraints and passed outside the limits which religion, society, and the law have long established for woman's welfare

and protection, her testimony would have been very seriously impaired."[1]

A notorious 1895 opinion by the Supreme Court of Missouri further illustrates the role of judicial preconceptions in filling in the substance of the rules. In that case, the Missouri court reversed a conviction because the prosecution introduced evidence of the defendant's bad character for chastity "for the purpose of impeaching him as a witness." The Court ruled that the evidence rules permitted such attacks on female, but not male witnesses. Here is a quote from the court's opinion:

> "It is a matter of common knowledge that the bad character of a man for chastity does not even in the remotest degree affect his character for truth, when based upon that alone, while it does that of a woman. It is no compliment to a woman to measure her character for truth by the same standard that you do that of man's predicated upon character for chastity. What destroys the standing of the one in all the walks of life has no effect whatever on the standing for truth of the other."[2]

Rulings like this explain one facet of the legal reform efforts that followed. As Harriet Galvin notes, reformers "lacked confidence in a predominantly male judiciary to apply fairly a rule that allowed the judiciary considerable discretion."[3] This helps to explain why Rule 412, and state analogues, give precise instructions designed to override the countervailing influence of judicial bias.

RULE 412

In 1978, Congress enacted Rule 412. Remarks from the floor by two members of the House of Representatives illustrate the rule's intent:

Elizabeth Holtzman (NY):

> "Too often in this country victims of rape are humiliated and harassed when they report and prosecute the rape. Bullied and cross-examined

---

[1] State v. Coella, 3 Wash. 99 (1891).
[2] State v. Sibley, 131 Mo. 519 (1895).
[3] Shielding Rape Victims in the State and Federal Courts, 70 Minn. L. Rev. 763 (1986).

about their prior sexual experiences, many find the trial almost as degrading as the rape itself. Since rape trials become inquisitions into the victim's morality, not trials of the defendant's innocence or guilt, it is not surprising that it is the least reported crime. It is estimated that as few as one in ten rapes is ever reported.

Mr. Speaker, over 30 States have taken some action to limit the vulnerability of rape victims to such humiliating cross-examination of their past sexual experiences and intimate personal histories. In federal courts, however, it is permissible still to subject rape victims to brutal cross-examination about their past sexual histories. H.R. 4727 would rectify this problem in Federal courts and I hope, also serve as a model to suggest to the remaining states that reform of existing rape laws is important to the equity of our criminal justice system...."

James Mann (South Carolina):

"[F]or many years in this country, evidentiary rules have permitted the introduction of evidence about a rape victim's prior sexual conduct. Defense lawyers were permitted great latitude in bringing out intimate details about a rape victim's life. Such evidence quite often serves no real purpose and only results in embarrassment to the rape victim and unwarranted public intrusion into her private life....

Mr. Speaker, the principal purpose of this legislation is to protect rape victims from the degrading and embarrassing disclosure of intimate details about their private lives. It does so by narrowly circumscribing when such evidence may be admitted. It does not do so, however, by sacrificing any constitutional right possessed by the defendant. The bill before us fairly balances the interests involved—the rape victim's interest in protecting her private life from unwarranted public exposure; the defendant's interest in being able adequately to present a defense by offering relevant and probative evidence; and society's interest in a fair trial, one where unduly prejudicial evidence is not permitted to becloud the issues before the jury...."[1]

---

[1] 124 Cong. Record H. 11944 (1978).

The legislation passed. As a result, Rule 412 severely restricts efforts to undermine sexual assault victims' credibility by referencing their sexual history. Specifically, the Rule bars, in any proceeding involving alleged sexual misconduct:

> (1) evidence offered to prove that a victim engaged in other sexual behavior; or

> (2) evidence offered to prove a victim's sexual predisposition.

There are three narrow and straightforward exceptions to these prohibitions. *See* Rule 412(b)(1)(A)-(C).

Rule 412 goes a long way toward eliminating the use of sexual history as a means of attacking a victim's character in court. The effort is aided by the fact that, by the time legal reforms were enacted, the judicial and societal attitudes heightening the need for reform were (slowly) changing as well. *See, e.g.*, State ex rel. Pope v. Superior Court, 113 Ariz. 22 (1976) (declaring that there is no connection between sexual behavior and witness veracity).

Rule 412 takes pains to protect the victim even in circumstances where such evidence is not introduced. *See* Rule 412(c). This contrasts with other rules of evidence, like Rule 403, that focus only on the parties' interests. *See* State v. Baker (Iowa 2004) ("[O]utside a special law such as a rape-shield law …, courts weighing potential prejudice have shown little solicitude for the personal interests and sensibilities of nonparty witnesses.")

Rule 412 was amended in 1994 to strengthen its protections. The Advisory Committee Note to that amendment stresses that the Rule's prohibitions should be interpreted broadly to maximize the protections afforded to sexual assault victims. Barred evidence of "sexual behavior" and "sexual predisposition" includes: evidence "relating to alleged victim's mode of dress, speech, or life-style…"; "activities of the mind, such as fantasies or dreams"; and evidence that implies sexual conduct such as contraceptives use, the birth of a child outside of marriage, and the presence of venereal disease. As these examples suggest, the Rule seeks to exclude even "evidence that does not directly refer to sexual activities or thoughts but that the proponent believes may have a sexual connotation for the factfinder." 1994 Advisory Committee Note.

All 50 states now have some version of a Rape Shield law. The Seventh Circuit sums up the general appeal of the rule as follows:

> "The essential insight behind the rape shield statute is that in an age of post-Victorian sexual practice, in which most unmarried young women are sexually active, the fact that a woman has voluntarily engaged in a particular sexual activity on previous occasions does not provide appreciable support for an inference that she consented to engage in this activity with the defendant on the occasion on which she claims that she was raped. And allowing defense counsel to spread the details of a woman's sex life on the public record not only causes embarrassment to the woman but by doing so makes it less likely that victims of rape will press charges."[1]

WILLIAMS v. STATE
681 N.E.2d 195 (Ind. 1997)

BOEHM, Justice.

A jury convicted defendant Adrian Williams of attempted criminal deviate conduct, a Class A felony, and criminal confinement, a Class B felony. A majority of the Court of Appeals reversed the convictions on the grounds that the trial court erred in excluding certain evidence. Because we conclude that the evidence was properly excluded and no other reversible error occurred, we … reinstate the convictions….

Factual and Procedural History

During the early morning hours on January 9, 1993, the victim was working as a topless dancer at a nightclub in downtown Indianapolis. The following is her version of the events of that night. When she finished work at approximately 2:45 a.m., she walked out into the parking lot and asked two strangers, Williams and co-defendant Antoine Edmondson, for a ride home. The two men agreed and she got into the car. Williams did not drive the car directly to the victim's home. Instead, he told her that "they had to make a stop." He drove into an alley behind a different club where Edmondson exited the car. The victim then

---

[1] Sandoval v. Acevedo, 996 F.2d 145 (7th Cir. 1993).

attempted to run away but Edmondson grabbed her arms and pulled her into the back seat of the car. As the victim struggled with Edmondson in the car, Williams drove to a public park and stopped the car in a dark area of its parking lot.

The two then ordered the victim to engage in sexual acts with them simultaneously. Edmondson pulled a gun out of his pocket and placed it on the arm rest of the front seat. He then removed the victim's shoe and sock and pulled her right pants leg off. The victim managed to grab the gun, open the car door, and run away. As she ran, she fired the gun behind her and, although she apparently had never fired a weapon before, shot Edmondson in the jaw. Williams and Edmondson were subsequently arrested and each was charged with two counts of attempted criminal deviate conduct, criminal confinement, and carrying a handgun without a license. The two men were tried together.

Three days before trial, the State filed two motions in limine. In the first motion, the State sought to exclude evidence of the victim's sexual history pursuant to Indiana Evidence Rule 412.... In the second motion, the State sought to exclude evidence of the victim's history of drug use.... The trial court granted both motions and excluded the evidence of both the victim's sexual history and her prior drug use. However, Williams was allowed to question the victim about drug use at the time of the incident.

During the trial of the two defendants, the victim testified on cross-examination that she did not use cocaine on the day of the incident or on the day of the trial. At defense counsel's request, the court conducted a hearing outside the presence of the jury regarding the exclusion of evidence of the victim's prior drug use. Williams joined in Edmondson's argument that the victim's prior drug use was pertinent to her credibility. Williams specifically argued that she had "a poor recall of the facts because of her cocaine habit." The trial court stood by its original decision to exclude the evidence. Thereafter, defense counsel made an offer of proof and the victim testified, outside the hearing of the jury, that she was previously addicted to cocaine and had received treatment.

Later during the trial, both Williams and Edmondson testified that the victim wanted the men to locate some cocaine for her and when they could not find any, the men agreed to give her money in exchange for sex. Williams requested that the trial court lift its proscription on testimony as to prior drug use because the victim's prior drug use and alleged acts of prostitution were now at issue. The trial court denied the request. Defense counsel then made another offer of proof that a friend of the victim would testify that the victim had previously committed acts of prostitution in exchange for money or cocaine. This evidence was also excluded by the trial court. The jury found Williams [and Edmondson] guilty of one count of attempted deviate conduct and criminal confinement. [Williams was sentenced to 25 years in prison.]

I. Evidence of the Victim's Prior Drug Use

Williams argues that he is entitled to a new trial because the trial court erred by refusing to allow the defense to inquire into the victim's prior drug use. The trial court allowed defense counsel to elicit testimony regarding the victim's use of drugs on the day of the incident because it was relevant to her ability to perceive and recall the events in dispute. However, prior drug use was held irrelevant.

…. Before the adoption of the Indiana Rules of Evidence, Indiana courts consistently upheld decisions of trial courts excluding evidence of a witness' past drug use as irrelevant…. [W]e see no reason to deviate from these prior holdings.

In this case, the victim testified that she did not use drugs on the day of the incident. The defense's effort to question the victim about her prior drug use was justified solely on the basis of challenging her credibility. The jury had ample opportunity to assess the credibility of her testimony as defense counsel repeatedly challenged the accuracy of her memory. Moreover, there was no showing that the victim's consumption of drugs on prior occasions was of such a degree that it substantially affected her current ability to perceive, remember, or testify. Indeed, the trial court noted that there was no evidence presented of the victim's inability to recall the incident. Therefore, the trial court did not abuse its discretion in excluding the evidence….

II. Evidence of the Victim's Past Sexual Conduct

The trial court also properly excluded the friend's testimony that on prior occasions the victim had committed acts of prostitution in exchange for money or cocaine. Williams claims this testimony supports his defense that the victim consented and accompanied the men because they had promised to obtain drugs for her. The trial court excluded the friend's testimony regarding the victim's prior alleged acts of prostitution because evidence of a victim's past sexual conduct is not admissible except as provided in Indiana's Rape Shield Rule. Indiana Evidence Rule 412 provides that in prosecutions for a sex crime, evidence of a victim's or witness' past sexual conduct is inadmissible, except in the following circumstances: 1) evidence of the victim's or witness' past sexual conduct with the defendant; 2) evidence that shows that some person other than the defendant committed the act upon which the prosecution is founded; 3) evidence that the victim's pregnancy at the time of trial was not caused by the defendant; or 4) evidence of a conviction for a crime offered for impeachment under Rule 609. Otherwise stated, past incidents of consent, except in these limited circumstances, are not permitted to imply consent on the date in question.

None of the exceptions to Rule 412's general prohibition of inquiry into the victim's sexual history apply here. The evidence offered here was of the classic sort precluded by the Rape Shield Rule: purported incidents with other men at other times offered simply to show that the victim had consented in the past in the hope the inference will be drawn that she consented here. Rule 412 was enacted to prevent just this kind of generalized inquiry into the reputation or past sexual conduct of the victim in order to avoid embarrassing the victim and subjecting the victim to possible public denigration. The Rule reflects a policy first embodied in Indiana's Rape Shield Act that inquiry into a victim's prior sexual activity is sufficiently problematic that it should not be permitted to become a focus of the defense. Rule 412 is intended to prevent the victim from being put on trial, to protect the victim against surprise, harassment, and unnecessary invasion of privacy, and, importantly, to remove obstacles to reporting sex crimes.

Balanced against these considerations is the defendant's right to present relevant evidence. For this reason, Rule 412 permits evidence of the defendant's past experience with the victim, but does not permit a defendant to base his defense of consent on the victim's past sexual experiences with third persons. The allegation of prostitution does not affect this calculus. We agree with the Fourth Circuit's view that it is "intolerable to suggest that because the victim is a prostitute, she automatically is assumed to have consented with anyone at any time." Moreover, even when evidence does fall within one of Rule 412's exceptions and is admissible, it is still subject to Evidence Rules 401 and 403. In this case, the evidence would shift the jury's attention away from the defendants' actions to the past acts of the victim. Any probative value is "substantially outweighed by the danger of unfair prejudice." Evid.R. 403. Thus, the trial court properly excluded the evidence.

Williams contends that the trial court's application of Indiana's Rape Shield Rule violates his Sixth Amendment right to present witnesses. Indiana's Rape Shield Rule has repeatedly been held facially constitutional. However, "the constitutionality of such a law as applied to preclude particular exculpatory evidence remains subject to examination on a case by case basis." Many jurisdictions acknowledge that a rape shield statute or rule serves to emphasize the general irrelevance of a victim's sexual history. Although there are instances where the application of the Rape Shield Rule may violate a defendant's Sixth Amendment right, this is not one of them. For example, admission of such evidence may be constitutionally required where the evidence is offered not to show the victim's consent but to establish some other point such as that an injury could have been inflicted by someone other than the defendant. It may also be required when the trial court restricts a defendant from giving his own account of the events at issue....

In this case, there was no restriction on the ability of the defense to present evidence of the incident. The trial court allowed both defendants to testify that the victim agreed to perform sex acts in exchange for money. The jury was informed through testimony of the defendants and the victim that the victim voluntarily entered a car with two strange men at 2 a.m. in the parking lot of a topless club. Whatever her initial motive, at some point, according to her, she clearly communicated her lack of consent to proceeding as the men directed. Whatever her sexual past, if the jury accepted that story, conviction was proper. As noted above, the excluded evidence did not serve to explain any physical evidence. Under these facts, exclusion of the victim's past sexual experiences with third persons is not unconstitutional....

... The reasoning of the Court of Appeals would permit evidence of the victim's past sexual conduct to support the theory that the victim consented to the sex acts on the night in question for the same reason as she had allegedly consented in the past. Similar reasoning would subject any complaining victim with an allegedly promiscuous past to unfettered examination of sexual history. That is precisely what Evidence Rule 412 prevents. Where a specific rule—Evidence Rule 412—makes the past sexual conduct of a victim or witness inadmissible, except under specified circumstances, a party cannot circumvent the requirements of Rule 412(b) by relying on the general doctrines of Rule 404(b). We conclude that the trial court properly excluded evidence of the victim's prior drug history and past sexual conduct pursuant to Indiana's Evidence Rules.

STATE VARIATION: "DISTINCTIVE" BEHAVIOR

Tennessee's Rule 412 tracks the federal rule but adds the following exception:

> (4) If the sexual behavior was with persons other than the accused,...

> (iii) to prove consent if the evidence is of a pattern of sexual behavior so distinctive and so closely resembling the accused's version of the alleged encounter with the victim that it tends to prove that the victim consented to the act charged or behaved in such a manner as to lead the defendant reasonably to believe that the victim consented.

Do you think the Williams court would have allowed the disputed evidence if it had been applying the Tennessee Rule?

***

Rule 412(b)(1)(C) provides an exception for "evidence whose exclusion would violate the defendant's constitutional rights." The exception is curious in that the Constitution always trumps the evidence rules whether or not the rules offer their blessing. Rule 412(b)(1)(C)'s main function, therefore, is signaling. It acknowledges the legislative drafters' understanding that in certain circumstances, Rule 412's broad sweep could threaten the defendant's constitutional right to a fair trial. Indeed, this concern is one of the leading critiques of the rule. And, as we will see, the judicial discretion that Rule 412 sought to limit reemerges in the evaluation of these constitutional claims.

The occasional clash between a criminal defendant's Constitutional rights and the evidence rules is an important and complicated aspect of the law of Evidence. We will address it separately in Chapter 7. For now, it suffices to recognize that when Rule 412 precludes evidence, a criminal defendant can argue, as in *Williams*, that the Rule as applied violates the Constitution. And, as in *Williams*, the likelihood of success on such a claim is typically low.

***

The Advisory Committee Notes to the 1994 Amendment also highlight (and resolve) an important issue that has arisen in the case law: "Evidence offered to prove allegedly false prior claims by the victim is not barred by Rule 412. However, the evidence is subject to the requirements of Rule 404." This is consistent with the general trend. In 2004, the Iowa Supreme Court stated: "Virtually all cases considering the issue have found that false claims of prior sexual conduct do not fall within the coverage of rape-shield laws."[1] Take a look at Rule 412. *Do you see why the courts have reached this conclusion?*

The Advisory Committee's reference to Rule 404 in the above quote is cryptic, but important. *What do you think the Advisory Committee has in mind?* Think back to the character evidence rules discussed in the preceding sections. *How, if at all, can a defendant offer evidence of a witness' prior false claim under those rules?*

PROBLEM 4-8: CHARACTER EVIDENCE POLICY

The beginning of this Chapter referenced the treatment of character evidence as a distinctive feature of American evidence law. Now that we have come to the end of the Chapter, what are your impressions of that feature? Specifically, do the federal rules prohibit too much character evidence, allow too much character evidence, or get the balance about right? The common law tradition is often contrasted with practice in Continental Europe. For example,

> "The French do not share American concerns about character evidence and poisoning the well, reflected in the United States' elaborate rules of evidence. Rather, they want to get as full an understanding as possible of the person on trial."[2]

---

[1] State v. Baker, 679 N.W.2d 7 (Iowa 2004).
[2] Renée Lettow Lerner, The Intersection of Two Systems: An American on Trial for an American Murder in the French Cour D'assises, 2001 U. Ill. L. Rev. 791 (2001).

Chapter 5

LAY AND EXPERT OPINION

Rule 602 limits (non-expert) witnesses to testifying based on "personal knowledge of the matter." This longstanding requirement could be read to require witnesses to testify only to facts and not to opinions or inferences based on those facts. This was the approach of the common law but, as Judge Learned Hand observed, "[t]he line between opinion and fact is at best only one of degree."[1]

LAY WITNESS OPINION

RULE 701

Rule 701 is an effort to more easily resolve questions about whether a witness, who is not testifying as an expert, can express an opinion or inference. As the following excerpt from an influential Third Circuit case authored by Judge Becker explains,[2] the rule is best understood as a reaction to the common law that preceded it:

> …. Rule 701 represents a movement away from the courts' historically skeptical view of lay opinion evidence. At common law, witnesses not qualifying as experts were not permitted to draw conclusions which could be characterized as opinion testimony, but rather were required to limit their testimony to facts, those things "they had seen, heard, felt, smelled, tasted, or done."
>
> This rigid distinction between fact and opinion led to numerous appeals and pervasive criticism by commentators. Wigmore declared, in the first edition of his treatise, that this distinction "has done more than any one rule of procedure to reduce our litigation towards a sense of legalized gambling."

---

[1] Cent. R. Co. v. Monahan, 11 F.2d 212 (2d Cir. 1926).
[2] Asplundh Mfg. v. Benton Harbor Eng'g, 57 F.3d 1190 (3d Cir. 1995).

Characteristically, however, the most eloquent criticism of this common-law restriction on lay testimony was made by Judge Learned Hand:

> Every judge of experience in the trial of causes has again and again seen the whole story garbled, because of insistence upon a form with which the witness cannot comply, since, like most men, he is unaware of the extent to which inference enters into his perceptions. He is telling the "facts" in the only way that he knows how, and the result of nagging and checking him is often to choke him altogether, which is, indeed, usually its purpose.

Judge Hand also stated:

> The truth is, as Mr. Wigmore has observed at length, that the exclusion of opinion evidence has been carried beyond reason in this country, and that it would be a large advance if courts were to admit it with freedom. The line between opinion and fact is at best only one of degree, and ought to depend solely upon practical considerations, as, for example, the saving of time and the mentality of the witness.

These concerns about the restrictions on lay opinion testimony ... led to the adoption of Rule 701. The Advisory Committee Note to the rule reflects the fact that Rule 701's liberalization of the admissibility of opinion evidence is rooted in the modern trend away from fine distinctions between fact and opinion and toward greater admissibility, tempered with an understanding that the adversary process, and more specifically, cross-examination will correct any problems....

The prototypical example of the type of evidence contemplated by the adoption of Rule 701 relates to the appearance of persons or things, identity, the manner of conduct, competency of a person, degrees of light or darkness, sound, size, weight, distance, and an endless number of items that cannot be described factually in words apart from inferences. The more liberal approach to lay opinion testimony of this type gained acceptance as a rule of "convenience," which allowed for "'shorthand renditions' of a total situation, or [for] statements of collective facts."

As recognized by Professor Saltzburg, testimony that a person was "excited" or "angry" is more evocative and understandable than a long physical description of the person's outward manifestations. For example, a witness who testifies that an individual whom he saw staggering or lurching along the way was drunk is spared the difficulty of describing, with the precision of an orthopedist or choreographer, the person's gait, angle of walk, etc. See, e.g., United States v. Mastberg (9th Cir. 1974) (permitting under Rule 701 the testimony of a customs inspector that the defendant appeared nervous); State v. Hall (S.D. 1984) (permitting police officers to give lay opinion concerning defendant's intoxicated state); Kerry Coal Co. v. United Mine Workers (3d Cir.) (allowing the admission of testimony that plaintiff's employees were "nervous and afraid" as a shorthand report of witnesses' observations of employee reactions).

Perhaps the best judicial description of this type of testimony under Rule 701 is found in United States v. Yazzie (9th Cir.1992). Yazzie was charged with statutory rape under a federal statute that permitted a defense of reasonable mistake as to the age of the minor. At trial, Yazzie asserted that he reasonably believed that the minor, age fifteen-and-a-half, was over the statutory age of sixteen. In support of this contention, Yazzie called several witnesses who offered to testify that, as of the date of the incident, their observations caused them to believe the minor to be between the age of sixteen and twenty. The trial court excluded this testimony as impermissible lay "opinion" and limited the witnesses' testimony to "facts," such as that the minor smoked cigarettes, wore make-up, and drove a car. The Court of Appeals reversed, stating:

> We understand Rule 701 to mean that opinions of non-experts may be admitted where the facts could not otherwise be adequately presented or described to the jury in such a way as to enable the jury to form an opinion or reach an intelligent conclusion. If it is impossible or difficult to reproduce the data observed by the witnesses, or the facts are difficult of

explanation, or complex, or are of a combination of circumstances and appearances which cannot be adequately described and presented with the force and clearness as they appeared to the witness, the witness may state his impressions and opinions based upon what he observed. It is a means of conveying to the jury what the witness has seen or heard.

The court concluded that the testimony of the witnesses satisfied Rule 701's requirements:

> .... The testimony helps in the understanding of the witnesses' descriptive testimony and in determining a critical fact at issue—whether it was reasonable for Yazzie to believe that the minor was sixteen or older.

> In the case before us, the jurors could not themselves assess how old the minor looked at the time of the incident: by the time of the trial, the minor was almost seventeen years old, and her appearance was undoubtedly substantially different than it had been on the night in question, a year and a half earlier. Thus, the jurors were wholly dependent on the testimony of witnesses. Yet the witnesses were permitted to testify only to the minor's describable features and behavior. Their testimony was no substitute for a clear and unequivocal statement of their opinions. It did not tell the jury that these witnesses believed the minor to be at least sixteen years old at the time of the incident.

Other examples of this type of quintessential Rule 701 opinion testimony include identification of an individual, the speed of a vehicle, the mental state or responsibility of another, whether another was healthy, the value of one's property, and other situations in which the differences between fact and opinion blur and it is difficult or cumbersome for the examiner to elicit an answer from the witness that will not be expressed in the form of an opinion. These cases, it is important to add, all meet the core definitional terms of Rule 701— the opinion is based upon personal knowledge, is rationally based thereon, and is helpful to the trier of fact....

***

The enactment of Rule 701 swung the pendulum in the other direction. As one court explained with alarm:

> "The liberalization of Rule 701 has blurred any rigid distinctions that may have existed between lay witnesses and expert witnesses. No longer is lay opinion testimony limited to areas within the common knowledge of ordinary persons. Rather, the individual experience and knowledge of a lay witness may establish his or her competence, without qualification as an expert, to express an opinion on a particular subject outside the realm of common knowledge."[1]

The Advisory Committee agreed that parties were taking advantage of the freedom provided by Rule 701 to introduce testimony from "expert[s] in lay witness clothing." The Committee responded by adding what is now subsection (c) to Rule 701.

UNITED STATES v. PEOPLES
250 F.3d 630 (8th Cir. 2001)

WOLLMAN, Chief Judge.

Cornelius Peoples and Xavier Lightfoot were convicted of aiding and abetting the murder of a federal government witness. The district court sentenced each of them to life imprisonment without the possibility of parole. Both defendants appeal their convictions. We reverse and remand for a new trial.

I.

In December of 1997, Lightfoot was arrested and charged with the robbery of a federally insured credit union in Omaha, Nebraska, based on information supplied by Jovan Ross, who shared a house with Lightfoot.... Lightfoot was held at a private pretrial detention facility operated by the Corrections Corporation of America (CCA facility), where he remained at all times relevant to this case. Through the discovery process in the robbery case, Lightfoot learned of Ross's cooperation with law enforcement. Shortly before Lightfoot's trial was scheduled to begin, Ross was murdered.

---

[1] United States v. Paiva (1st Cir. 1989).

The government's theory at trial was that Lightfoot and Peoples entered into a contract to pay unknown persons to kill Ross because he was providing information about Lightfoot's criminal activity to law enforcement. Although Ross had no substantial information implicating Peoples in criminal activity, the government argued that Peoples believed that his involvement would be discovered if Ross continued to cooperate with law enforcement. The government further argued that Peoples and others had robbed a jewelry store in St. Joseph, Missouri, to obtain funds to pay the killers. At trial, the government offered into evidence recordings of conversations between Lightfoot and Peoples that occurred while Lightfoot was incarcerated at the CCA facility.

On appeal, the defendants contend that the district court erred … in admitting certain testimony….

5. Special Agent Neal's Testimony

Special Agent Joan Neal, the FBI case agent in charge of the investigation of Ross's murder, testified in connection with the recorded telephone and visitation conversations between Peoples and Lightfoot. Drawing on her investigation, Agent Neal gave her opinion regarding the meaning of words and phrases used by the defendants during those conversations. Her testimony was not limited to coded, oblique language, but included plain English words and phrases. She did not personally observe the events and activities discussed in the recordings, nor did she hear or observe the conversations as they occurred. Agent Neal's testimony included her opinions about what the defendants were thinking during the conversations, phrased as contentions supporting her conclusion, repeated throughout her testimony, that the defendants were responsible for Ross's murder.

At various points during her testimony, Agent Neal asserted that Peoples went to Ross's house to murder Ross, that he had paid "the killers to do the job," that Peoples's various comments about being in need of money revolved around his debt to hit men, and that both defendants had sought confirmation of Ross's death. She asserted that during the course of her investigation she had uncovered hidden meanings for apparently neutral words; for example, she testified that when one of the defendants referred to buying a plane ticket

160

for Ross, he in fact meant killing Ross. In short, as the recordings of the Peoples/Lightfoot conversations were played for the jury, Agent Neal was allowed to offer a narrative gloss that consisted almost entirely of her personal opinions of what the conversations meant....

The following excerpts are examples of Agent Neal's testimony. After a recording of Lightfoot requesting a loan was played, Agent Neal stated, "I contend [Lightfoot] is needing a loan to pay the hit man to actually murder Ross." Peoples made repeated references in the taped conversations to "lost and found situations." Agent Neal stated, "When he discusses lost and found, I believe he is talking about no one had found the body yet. It's just a lost situation until somebody finds the body." After the jury heard a recording of Peoples saying, "I done already gave my loot," Agent Neal stated, "I contend that he has already paid the killers to do the job." In response to conversations that related to the burglary of Ross's house, Agent Neal testified, "I believe [Peoples] was there to actually murder Ross at the time."

Both before and during trial, the defendants objected to the admission of Agent Neal's testimony. The government responded by arguing that Agent Neal's contentions constituted lay opinions admissible under Rule 701 of the Federal Rules of Evidence....

Federal Rule of Evidence 602 requires that a witness have personal knowledge of the matters about which she testifies, except in the case of expert opinions. Rule 701 adds that testimony in the form of lay opinions must be rationally based on the perception of the witness.... Lay opinion testimony is admissible only to help the jury or the court to understand the facts about which the witness is testifying and not to provide specialized explanations or interpretations that an untrained layman could not make if perceiving the same acts or events.

> [Footnote 3] Although not in effect at the time of trial, the 2000 revisions to Rules 701 and 702 emphasize this distinction between lay and expert opinion testimony.

Law enforcement officers are often qualified as experts to interpret intercepted conversations using slang, street language, and the jargon of the illegal drug trade. See, e.g., United States v. Delpit (8th Cir.1996) (police officer gave expert testimony interpreting slang and drug codes in connection with recorded telephone calls). What is essentially expert testimony, however, may not be admitted under the guise of lay opinions. Such a substitution subverts the disclosure and discovery requirements of Federal Rules of Criminal Procedure 26 and 16 and the reliability requirements for expert testimony as set forth in Daubert v. Merrell Dow Pharmaceuticals (1993) and Kumho Tire Co. v. Carmichael (1999).

Agent Neal lacked first-hand knowledge of the matters about which she testified. Her opinions were based on her investigation after the fact, not on her perception of the facts. Accordingly, the district court erred in admitting Agent Neal's opinions about the recorded conversations....

***

As *Peoples* illustrates, no matter where the line is placed, gray areas will remain at the intersection of permissible and impermissible non-expert opinion.

PROBLEM 5-1: IDENTIFICATION OF NARCOTICS

Consider these facts drawn from United States v. Paiva (1st Cir. 1989):

> "During the trial, Christina Christo, the 21-year-old daughter of [defendant] Paiva's ex-wife, Delores (Christo) Paiva, testified for the government. Ms. Christo testified that in 1983, while she resided with her mother and Paiva in a condominium in Florida, she discovered inside one of Paiva's shoes a plastic bag containing a white powder. Ms. Christo testified that prior to 1983 she had used and tasted cocaine on many occasions and had developed a cocaine problem at age fourteen. Ms. Christo described the substance she found inside Paiva's shoe as a white powder with little bits of rocks in it. She stated that she tasted this white powder and that it tasted like cocaine. Ms. Christo testified that based upon looking at the substance and tasting it, the substance, in her opinion, was cocaine."

Was Christina Christo's testimony that the white powder was cocaine admissible under Rule 701?

If the answer is yes, could the government rely on Christina Christo to identify substances as cocaine in other cases?

***

Importantly, Rule 701(c) does not prohibit specialized opinion testimony, it simply requires it to be introduced through Rule 702. In fact, the possibility that the party could have, but did not, introduce the same evidence through a qualified expert often looms in the background of Rule 701(c) analysis.

PROBLEM 5-2: IDENTIFICATION OF GUNS

Consider these facts from United States v. Conn (7th Cir. 2002):

Federal agents found 165 firearms and 10,000 rounds of ammunition in the Indiana home of Bill Conn. Conn argued that he was a firearms collector not, as the government alleged, an unlicensed dealer of firearms. At trial:

> [ATF Agent Scott McCart] narrated the presentation of a videotape made during the search and seizure, which the jury viewed during his testimony…. [T]he Government asked Agent McCart "whether or not the firearms recovered in the search warrant … are generally considered collector's items?"
>
> …. Mr. Conn objected. Mr. Conn's attorney stated that "I don't believe this witness is qualified to answer the question…."
>
> The Government then engaged in the following colloquy with Agent McCart:
>
> Q. …. [A]s a part of your training and experience … have you been trained and have you dealt with the type of firearms that are collector's items based on their rarity and/or their value?
>
> A. Yes, I have.
>
> Q. And also as part of your training and experience, do you also receive information about firearms that are commonly used other than as collector's items, that is, used for other purposes?….
>
> A. Yes, I have.
>
> Q. And based upon that training and experience that you've had, do you believe that you can tell the jury whether or not the firearms that

are before the jury now … are collector's items, or are they firearms used for other purposes?

A. Yes….

After the voir dire, the district court overruled Mr. Conn's objection based on Agent McCart's qualifications and lack of a proper foundation. Agent McCart testified that he did "not believe that these firearms are collector's items. There are a couple that would have value to them, but the majority of them, no, are not collector's items."

…. On appeal, the Government argues that Agent McCart did not need to be qualified as an expert because his testimony was not offered as expert testimony under Rule 702, but as lay opinion testimony permitted by Rule 701….

Is Agent McCart's testimony permissible under Rule 701?

EXPERT TESTIMONY

Rule 702 permits specialized expert testimony but subjects that testimony to extra scrutiny. In addition, some pretrial disclosure requirements apply to expert, but not lay, testimony.

The primary battleground for the admissibility of expert testimony is reliability, now encapsulated in Rule 702(b)-(d). But before we get to those requirements, we must cover the initial requirements of the rule, that the witness be qualified as an expert, and that the testimony be helpful to the jury. This analysis will also require a detour into Rule 704.

RULE 702(A) - QUALIFICATION

PROBLEM 5-3: DRUG SMOKING EXPERT?

Consider the following facts from United States v. Johnson (5th Cir. 1978):

Six defendants were convicted of various crimes including importing marijuana from South America on various occasions by boat to a variety of locations in the United States.

.... At trial the principal government witness was John de Pianelli....
[On appeal, the defendants argue]... that it was improper to permit de
Pianelli to testify as an expert concerning the origin of the marijuana.
Appellants concede that the substance with which they were dealing
was marijuana. They contend, however, that there was no objective
evidence showing that the marijuana was imported from outside the
customs territory of the United States. Since no marijuana was ever
seized, the only nonhearsay evidence concerning the origin of this
marijuana came from de Pianelli. When de Pianelli was first asked to
state whether the marijuana had come from Colombia, counsel for
defendants objected. The jury was then excused and de Pianelli was
examined on voir dire and cross-examined by defense counsel. During
voir dire, he admitted that he had smoked marijuana over a thousand
times and that he had dealt in marijuana as many as twenty times. He
also said that he had been asked to identify marijuana over a hundred
times and had done so without making a mistake. He based his
identification upon the plant's appearance, its leaf, buds, stems, and
other physical characteristics, as well as upon the smell and the effect
of smoking it. On cross-examination he stated that he had been called
upon to identify the source of various types of marijuana. He explained
that characteristics such as the packaging, the physical appearance, the
smell, the taste, and the effect could all be used in identifying the source
of the marijuana. It was stipulated that he had no special training or
education for such identification. Instead, his qualifications came
entirely from "the experience of being around a great deal and smoking
it." He also said that he had compared Colombian marijuana with
marijuana from other places as many as twenty times. Moreover, he
had seen Colombian marijuana that had been grown in the United
States and had found that it was different from marijuana grown in
Colombia.

After the voir dire examination, the defendants objected to de Pianelli's
expertise for lack of authentication that he had actually smoked it,
touched it, or correctly identified it. Despite the objection, the trial
court permitted de Pianelli to give opinion evidence. Before the jury
he related his experiences with marijuana and explained that he had

tested a sample of marijuana from each [charged] importation and had verified that it came from Colombia.

[The defendants contend] … that it was an error to qualify de Pianelli as an expert because he had never been to South America and, of course, had never smoked marijuana there or seen it growing in South America. Finally, [they contend] that de Pianelli's testimony was conclusively rebutted by [the testimony of] an associate professor of biological science at Florida State University, Loren C. Anderson.

Was de Pianelli "qualified as an expert by knowledge, skill, experience, training, or education" as required under Rule 702?

***

Among the most common expert witnesses in criminal trials are police officers offered to explain various activities of the narcotics business to jurors, such as drug jargon or standard drug dealing practices. Here is one court's explanation of qualification in this context:[1]

> Expertise is not necessarily synonymous with a string of academic degrees or multiple memberships in learned societies. [Stephen] Assarian was a veteran DEA agent who had worked in law enforcement for some twelve years, much of it as a narcotics agent. He had participated in hundreds of investigations. He had specialized police training and extensive practical experience in the field. To be sure, he had written no texts and had no formal schooling in the cocaine trade. But, hard-core drug trafficking scarcely lends itself to ivied halls. In a rough-and-ready field such as this, experience is likely the best teacher. Cf. Grain Dealers Mutual Insurance Co. v. Farmers Union Cooperative Elevator and Shipping Ass'n (10th Cir.1967) (construction man familiar with grain elevators allowed to testify as to cause of damage to elevator; court stated that "[p]ractical experience may be the basis of qualification"). Under these circumstances, permitting a street-wise savant such as Assarian to voice his opinions did not amount to an abuse of discretion.

---

[1] United States v. Hoffman (1st Cir. 1987).

This language parallels the Advisory Committee's note to Rule 704 that: "The basic approach to opinions, lay and expert, in these rules is to admit them when helpful to the trier of fact."

HELPFUL TO THE JURY AND "ULTIMATE ISSUE"

Rule 702(a) limits experts to testimony that will "help the trier of fact." As a general matter, this inquiry is intuitive and intended to allow a broad spectrum of expert testimony. Expert testimony "helps" the jury if it (1) relates to specialized, technical or scientific areas unfamiliar to layperson, or (2) supplements or reveals counterintuitive aspects of a familiar topic.

Expert testimony is not helpful if it adds nothing that a layperson could not already determine from the facts presented. Additionally, an expert will typically not be permitted to offer an "opinion" about the law (the judge's role) or merely tell jury which witness to believe or what result to reach (the jury's role) -- one way to understand these limits is that such opinions are not helpful to the jury.

Consider the following brief excerpts from court opinions that deem expert testimony inadmissible because it was not helpful to the jury:

UNITED STATES v. FREEMAN
730 F.3d 590 (6th Cir. 2013)

…. A witness, lay or expert, may not form conclusions for a jury that they are competent to reach on their own. Agent Lucas's testimony falls into these very traps. His testimony consisted of many opinions and conclusions the jury was well equipped to draw on their own. He effectively spoon-fed his interpretations of the phone calls and the government's theory of the case to the jury, interpreting even ordinary English language.

Take, for example, Agent Lucas's testimony as to the phone call between Freeman, Scott, and West three minutes after the first 911 call after Day had been shot:

    WEST: What's good?

FREEMAN: Everything good, man. Except for, you know ... you know what I'm talkin' about ... just that one little thing. We ain't get the bonus, dog. But, you know what I'm sayin', the situation is over with.

When asked what "situation" Freeman had referred to, Agent Lucas testified, "The situation discussed was regarding Leonard Day and his having stolen jewelry from Roy West, Roy West having put a hit on Leonard Day and Leonard Day ultimately being killed." Somehow, when passed through Agent Lucas's interpretive lens, this cryptic exchange becomes crystal clear, and his explanation fits perfectly with the prosecution's view of the case. That is not to say a juror could not have reached the same conclusions as Agent Lucas. It is rather to say that it is not for an agent to divine what vague, plain English language means as Agent Lucas did repeatedly here. These types of conclusions are the province of a jury.

SUMMERS v. A.L. GILBERT CO.
69 Cal. App. 4th 1155 (1999)

WISEMAN, J.

On March 12, 1993, a tragedy occurred which forever altered the lives of the Summers family. Jerry Summers was driving his pickup truck and became involved in an accident with a truck pulling two trailers filled with corn. Based on a series of events, the two trailers became detached and one tipped over onto Jerry's truck, burying it in corn. In a few short moments, a husband and father of two children was gone forever.

A wrongful death action was filed against multiple defendants alleging theories of liability based on nondelegable duty, negligent hiring and retention of an incompetent contractor, and under the doctrine of respondeat superior. By the time of trial, two of the three remaining defendants included Cotton, owner of the truck and trailers, and Gilbert, owner of the corn.

On January 22, 1996, a legal tragedy occurred which, unfortunately, will also alter the lives of the Summers family. The Summerses' counsel called as an expert witness Ellis Anderson, a lawyer who specializes in the field of transportation and practices primarily before the Public Utilities Commission.

Anderson had an opinion on almost every imaginable subject related to the case. And he was allowed to testify to these opinions to the jury over one entire trial day. Anderson opined that Gilbert had a nondelegable duty; Cotton was hauling illegally; Gilbert's contracts with Cotton were illegal; Gilbert was legally required to be registered as a contract carrier rather than a private carrier; and Gilbert was liable for Cotton's acts under the doctrine of nondelegable duty, respondeat superior and negligent hiring of an incompetent contractor. Anderson even pulled out his proverbial crystal ball and predicted what future courts of appeal would do with respect to the current regulation of transportation in California.

So why is this a problem? Simply put, Anderson, under the direction of the Summerses' counsel, completely overstepped his legal bounds. He was a witness, not the judge. Both state and federal courts have held that expert testimony on issues of law are not admissible since it the judge's responsibility to instruct the jurors on the law—not that of the witness. The reason is that the lawyer-expert who expounds on the law usurps the role of the trial court.

.... California is not alone in excluding expert opinions on issues of law. The Federal Rules of Evidence also permit the admission of expert testimony which is helpful to the trier of fact and which embrace an ultimate issue in the case. [Yet,] "[i]t is black-letter law that '[i]t is not for witnesses to instruct the jury as to applicable principles of law, but for the judge.' At least seven circuit courts have held that the Federal Rules of Evidence prohibit such testimony, and we now join them as to the general rule."

.... The judgment is reversed.[1]

RULE 704(a)

Rule 704 originally consisted solely of Rule 704(a). Its purpose was to eliminate "the so-called 'ultimate issue' rule." One of the most important aspects of the Rule is found in the Advisory Committee Note, which elaborates on the limits previously discussed:

---

[1] See also Burkhart v. Washington Metro. Area Transit Auth. (D.C. Cir. 1997) ("Each courtroom comes equipped with a 'legal expert,' called a judge, and it is his or her province alone to instruct the jury on the relevant legal standards.").

"The abolition of the ultimate issue rule does not lower the bars so as to admit all opinions. Under Rules 701 and 702, opinions must be helpful to the trier of fact, and Rule 403 provides for exclusion of evidence which wastes time. These provisions afford ample assurances against the admission of opinions which would merely tell the jury what result to reach, somewhat in the manner of the oath-helpers of an earlier day."

PEOPLE v. MCDONALD
37 Cal. 3d 351 (1984)

MOSK, J.

.... Defendant was [convicted of] the murder of Jose Esparza [and sentenced to death].

At trial it was established without dispute that August 20, 1979, was payday for Esparza, a restaurant worker. At 4 p.m. he took a break from his job to cash his paycheck. Shortly after 5 p.m. he was shot and killed by a black man at the intersection of Pine and Seventh Streets in downtown Long Beach. The principal issue was the identity of the perpetrator. The prosecution presented seven eyewitnesses who identified defendant as that person with varying degrees of certainty, and one eyewitness who categorically testified that defendant was not the gunman; the defense presented six witnesses who testified that defendant was in another state on the day of the crime....

I. Expert Testimony on Eyewitness Identification

Defendant contends the court abused its discretion in excluding the testimony of an expert witness on the psychological factors that may affect the accuracy of eyewitness identification. Prior to trial the defense moved for an order admitting the testimony of Dr. Robert Shomer. Dr. Shomer is a practicing psychologist and professor of psychology of almost 20 years' experience. He has taught numerous courses on the psychology of perception, memory, and recall, and has spoken and written frequently on such topics in both medical and legal settings. He is conversant with the scientific literature on the psychology of eyewitness identification, has done experimental research on the subject himself, and has published articles on that research. He has qualified as an expert psychological witness in more than two dozen state and federal trials. The People do not question the witness' qualifications.

At the hearing on the motion Dr. Shomer explained that he proposed to inform the jury of various psychological factors that may affect the reliability of eyewitness identification, and to "help to counter some common misconceptions" about the process....

Dr. Shomer made it clear that he did not propose to offer an opinion that any particular witness at this trial was or was not mistaken in his or her identification of defendant. But he did intend to point out various psychological factors that could have affected that identification in the present case. Thus he emphasized that from the viewpoint of the witnesses the shooting of Esparza on a busy streetcorner was a sudden and unexpected event, occurring some distance away, and that because of parked and passing cars their observations were largely discontinuous. He also referred to the youth of certain of the witnesses, the words used in making the pretrial photographic identifications of defendant, and the ambiguity of those identifications. Dr. Shomer particularly noted the effect of the "cross-racial factor" in this case, emphasizing that the one witness who was certain that defendant... was not the black man at the scene was herself ... black; by contrast, two of the witnesses who positively identified defendant at trial as the assailant were of the same ethnic origin (Hispanic) as the victim.

Finally, Dr. Shomer intended to explain to the jury that empirical research has undermined a number of widespread lay beliefs about the psychology of eyewitness identification, e.g., that the accuracy of a witness's recollection increases with his certainty, that accuracy is also improved by stress, that cross-racial factors are not significant, and that the reliability of an identification is unaffected by the presence of a weapon or violence at the scene.

.... The trial court .... ruled the testimony inadmissible, [concluding] that to allow Dr. Shomer to testify "would be invading the province of the jury" [and] "cause confusion in the jurors' minds" ....

B

A traditional way of bringing scientific information to the attention of the judicial system, of course, is by the testimony of expert witnesses. But when that testimony relates to psychological factors affecting the accuracy of eyewitness identification, the courts have shown reluctance to admit it.... We inquire whether that reluctance remains justified....

[California's Evidence Code] limits [expert] testimony to such subjects "sufficiently beyond common experience that the opinion of an expert would assist the trier of fact." Th[is] make it clear that the admissibility of expert opinion is a question of degree. The jury need not be wholly ignorant of the subject matter of the opinion in order to justify its admission; if that were the test, little expert opinion testimony would ever be heard. Instead, the [Code] declares that even if the jury has some knowledge of the matter, expert opinion may be admitted whenever it would "assist" the jury. It will be excluded only when it would add nothing at all to the jury's common fund of information, i.e., when "the subject of inquiry is one of such common knowledge that men of ordinary education could reach a conclusion as intelligently as the witness."

.... It is doubtless true that from personal experience and intuition all jurors know that an eyewitness identification can be mistaken, and also know the more obvious factors that can affect its accuracy, such as lighting, distance, and duration. It appears from the professional literature, however, that other factors bearing on eyewitness identification may be known only to some jurors, or may be imperfectly understood by many, or may be contrary to the intuitive beliefs of most. For example, in the case at bar Dr. Shomer would have testified to the results of studies of relevant factors that appear to be either not widely known to laypersons or not fully appreciated by them, such as the effects on perception of an eyewitness' personal or cultural expectations or beliefs, the effects on memory of the witness' exposure to subsequent information or suggestions, and the effects on recall of bias or cues in identification procedures or methods of questioning.

Dr. Shomer would also have explained to the jury the pitfalls of cross-racial identification, evidently an important factor on the record in this case. To be sure, many jurors are likely to have some awareness of the fact that an eyewitness is more accurate in identifying a person of his own race than one of another race. But it appears that few jurors realize the pervasive and even paradoxical nature of this "own-race effect," information that has emerged from numerous empirical studies of the question....

172

In addition to the foregoing counterintuitive aspects of the own-race effect, other psychological factors have been examined in the literature that appear to contradict the expectations of the average juror. Perhaps the foremost among these is the lack of correlation between the degree of confidence an eyewitness expresses in his identification and the accuracy of that identification....

We conclude that although jurors may not be totally unaware of the foregoing psychological factors bearing on eyewitness identification, the body of information now available on these matters is "sufficiently beyond common experience" that in appropriate cases expert opinion thereon could at least "assist the trier of fact."

[Courts often reject eyewitness experts on] the ground that to admit expert psychological evidence on eyewitness identification would "take over the jury's task of determining the weight and credibility of the witness' testimony" - or, to put it in the more colorful language of legal cliché used by many courts, would "invade the province" or "usurp the function" of the jury, because such evidence "embraces the ultimate issue." As Dean Wigmore has said, however, such language "is so misleading, as well as so unsound, that it should be entirely repudiated. It is a mere bit of empty rhetoric," and "remains simply one of those impracticable and misconceived utterances which lack any justification in principle."

.... The expert testimony in question does not seek to take over the jury's task of judging credibility: as explained above, it does not tell the jury that any particular witness is or is not truthful or accurate in his identification of the defendant. Rather, it informs the jury of certain factors that may affect such an identification in a typical case; and to the extent that it may refer to the particular circumstances of the identification before the jury, such testimony is limited to explaining the potential effects of those circumstances on the powers of observation and recollection of a typical eyewitness. The jurors retain both the power and the duty to judge the credibility and weight of all testimony in the case, as they are told by a standard instruction.

Nor could such testimony in fact usurp the jury's function. As is true of all expert testimony, the jury remains free to reject it entirely after considering the expert's opinion, reasons, qualifications, and credibility....

Finally, California has abandoned the "ultimate issue" rule....: "in this state we have followed the modern tendency and have refused to hold that expert opinion is inadmissible merely because it coincides with an ultimate issue of fact." [The California] Evidence Code ... codifies this case law, declaring that "Testimony in the form of an opinion that is otherwise admissible is not objectionable because it embraces the ultimate issue to be decided by the trier of fact." ...

When an eyewitness identification of the defendant is a key element of the prosecution's case but is not substantially corroborated by evidence giving it independent reliability, and the defendant offers qualified expert testimony on specific psychological factors shown by the record that could have affected the accuracy of the identification but are not likely to be fully known to or understood by the jury, it will ordinarily be error to exclude that testimony.

.... the judgment must be reversed.

RULE 704(b)

In 1984, Congress added rule 704(b) "following the assassination attempt on the life of President Reagan" as part of a package of reforms designed "to restrict the definition of insanity, to place the burden of proving the defense of insanity on the defendant, to heighten the standard to clear and convincing, and to limit the scope of expert testimony."[1]

UNITED STATES v. MORALES
108 F.3d 1031 (9th Cir. 1997)

DAVID THOMPSON, Circuit Judge:

Federal Rule of Evidence 704(b) precludes an expert ... from stating "an opinion or inference as to whether the defendant did or did not have the mental state or condition constituting an element of the crime charged or of a defense thereto." There is a conflict in our circuit concerning the admissibility of expert testimony under this rule when an expert is asked to give an opinion

---

[1] United States v. Sanchez-Ramirez, 432 F. Supp. 2d 145 (D. Me. 2006).

on a predicate matter from which a jury might infer the defendant's required mens rea.

.... In the present case, Gloria Ann Morales, a bookkeeper, was convicted of two misdemeanor counts of willfully making false entries in a union ledger. She appeals the district court's exclusion of expert testimony that she had a weak grasp of bookkeeping principles. She proffered this testimony to establish a predicate from which the jury could infer she lacked the necessary mens rea....

We hold that the district court erred .... The error in excluding the testimony was not harmless, and we reverse Morales's conviction....

Generally, experts may testify as to their opinions on ultimate issues to be decided by the trier of fact. However, Rule 704(b) makes a limited exception to this general rule in criminal cases....

The first issue we decide is whether Rule 704(b) applies to all expert witnesses who are asked to state an opinion or inference as to a defendant's mental state or condition, or whether the rule applies only to psychiatrists or other mental health experts. Morales's proffered expert was not a psychiatrist or mental health expert. She was an accountant. If Rule 704(b) does not apply to her, it could not provide the source for the exclusion of her testimony.

Several circuits have suggested that Rule 704(b) may ... apply only to psychiatrists and other mental health experts. The circuits which support this restricted view have found support in the rule's legislative history. This legislative history suggests that Congress intended to limit the reach of Rule 704(b) to psychiatrists and other mental health experts. The 1984 Senate Report introducing Rule 704(b) explains the rule's purpose as follows:

> .... The purpose of this amendment is to eliminate the confusing spectacle of competing expert witnesses testifying to directly contradictory conclusions as to the ultimate legal issue to be found by the trier of fact. Under this proposal, expert psychiatric testimony would be limited to presenting and explaining their diagnoses, such as whether the defendant had a severe mental disease or defect and what the characteristics of such a disease or defect, if any, may have been.

Similarly, the report of the House Judiciary Committee states:

> While the medical and psychological knowledge of expert witnesses may well provide data that will assist the jury in determining the existence of the [insanity] defense, no person can be said to have expertise regarding the legal and moral decision involved. Thus, with regard to the ultimate issue, the psychiatrist, psychologist or other similar expert is no more qualified than a lay person.

…. [But b]efore looking at any legislative history, we first look at the rule itself. If the meaning of the rule is perfectly plain from its language, that ends the inquiry.

The language of Rule 704(b) is perfectly plain. It does not limit its reach to psychiatrists and other mental health experts. Its reach extends to all expert witnesses.

The introductory clause of the rule does not limit this reach. This clause provides: "No expert witness testifying with respect to the mental state or condition of a defendant …." The "mental state or condition" refers to that "of a defendant in a criminal case." If that mental state or condition is an element of the crime charged or a defense thereto, "no expert witness" may testify to it, regardless of whether the witness testifying is a psychiatrist or other mental health expert.

Because Rule 704(b) applies to the accounting expert Morales presented as a witness, the next question is whether this rule precluded the proffered testimony. We hold it did not.

To convict Morales, the government had to prove that she willfully made false bookkeeping entries.

The statute provides:

> Any person who willfully makes a false entry in … any books, records, reports, or statements required to be kept by any provision of this subchapter shall be fined not more than $10,000 or imprisoned for not more than one year, or both.

Willfulness requires that an act be done knowingly and intentionally, not through ignorance, mistake or accident. Morales had to know that her entries were false.

To exclude Crosby's expert testimony under Rule 704(b), the district court would have had to conclude that Crosby would have stated an opinion or drawn an inference which would necessarily compel the conclusion that Morales did not make the false entries willfully. This was not the content of the proposed testimony.

Crosby was not going to state an opinion or draw an inference that Morales did not intend to make false entries. Rather, she was going to state her opinion as to a predicate matter—that Morales had a weak grasp of bookkeeping principles. Morales's counsel advised the court that Crosby would testify as to Morales's "understanding of bookkeeping principles," and Morales's "level of understanding of bookkeeping concepts."

Even if the jury believed Crosby's expert testimony that Morales had a weak grasp of bookkeeping knowledge (and there was evidence to the contrary), the jury would still have had to draw its own inference from that predicate testimony to answer the ultimate factual question—whether Morales willfully made false entries. Morales could have had a weak grasp of bookkeeping principles and still knowingly made false entries as charged. Thus, Crosby was not going to testify to an opinion or draw an inference as to the ultimate issue of Morales's mens rea within the meaning of Rule 704(b).

…. In … recent cases we have adopted an interpretation of Rule 704(b) that allows testimony supporting an inference or conclusion that the defendant did or did not have the requisite mens rea, so long as the expert does not draw the ultimate inference or conclusion for the jury and the ultimate inference or conclusion does not necessarily follow from the testimony….

PROBLEM 5-4: INTENT TO DISTRIBUTE?

In United States v. Gomez-Norena (9th Cir. 1990), police apprehended the defendant at the Los Angeles International Airport carrying a suitcase containing cocaine. Consider the following testimony from the case offered to prove that the defendant possessed the cocaine "with intent to distribute":

"The government introduced Special Agent Pace as an expert witness, based on his four years' experience involving over 200 narcotics arrests. Gomez challenges the following exchange:

> Prosecutor: Now, in your opinion, Special Agent Pace, would an individual in possession of approximately $200,000 worth of cocaine, would that be an amount consistent with personal use or use for possession for distribution?
>
> Pace: Possession with intent to distribute.
>
> Prosecutor: Now, taking into consideration, Special Agent Pace, the items that were seized from [Gomez's suitcase] and the other factors that you've discussed, did you form an opinion as to whether the cocaine that was in [the suitcase] was cocaine that was possessed for personal use or possessed for distribution purposes?
>
> Pace: Possession with intent to distribute.
>
> Prosecutor: And what is the basis of that opinion?
>
> Pace: The large amount [of cocaine], the way it was concealed, and where it was coming from.

Gomez argues that Special Agent Pace testified to his mental state in violation of Federal Rule of Evidence 704(b)."

Should the testimony have been excluded?

STATE VARIATION: INDIANA RULE 704(B)

Indiana Rule of Evidence 704(a) is the same as the federal rule. Indiana Rule 704(b) is different, stating:

> "Witnesses may not testify to opinions concerning intent, guilt, or innocence in a criminal case; the truth or falsity of allegations; whether a witness has testified truthfully; or legal conclusions."

Notice that much of the Indiana rule parallels the federal and state case law prohibiting certain opinions as not helpful to the jury under Rule 702(a).

Beyond that, the rule likely serves only to prohibit certain forms of opinions, rather than the opinions themselves. For example, here is an Indiana case explaining why an arson investigator's testimony did not violate the rule:

> "[C]ontrary to Julian's assertions, Murray merely testified that the fire was set intentionally, not that Julian intended to set the fire. Therefore, Murray did not violate Evid. R. 704(b) by testifying as to the intent, guilt, or innocence of Julian."[1]

RELIABILITY

RULE 702(b)-(d)

Rule 702(b)-(d) is the main ground upon which parties fight over the admissibility of expert testimony.

Prior to the adoption of the federal rules, the primary case on expert witnesses was Frye v. United States (D.C. Cir. 1923). There, the defense sought to introduce an expert's testimony that the defendant's claim of innocence was true. The expert's opinion would be based on the application of a "systolic blood pressure deception test," a kind of early lie detector. The trial court excluded the expert's proposed testimony and the appeals court affirmed that ruling in a short opinion that included the following guidance:

> "Just when a scientific principle or discovery crosses the line between the experimental and demonstrable stages is difficult to define. Somewhere in this twilight zone the evidential force of the principle must be recognized, and while courts will go a long way in admitting expert testimony deduced from a well-recognized scientific principle or discovery, the thing from which the deduction is made must be sufficiently established to have gained **general acceptance** in the particular field in which it belongs."

Frye's "general acceptance" test proved influential in the federal and state courts until the adoption of the federal rules of evidence, which did not

---

[1] Julian v. State, 811 N.E.2d 392 (Ind. Ct. App. 2004).

reference the case or its "general acceptance" standard. Prior to a 2000 amendment, Federal Rule 702 stated only:

> If scientific, technical, or other specialized knowledge will assist the trier of fact to understand the evidence or to determine a fact in issue, a witness qualified as an expert by knowledge, skill, experience, training, or education, may testify thereto in the form of an opinion or otherwise.

The question of *Frye*'s continuing application after the adoption of the Federal Rules led to one of the most influential Supreme Court cases on Evidence.

DAUBERT v. MERRELL DOW PHARM.
509 U.S. 579 (1993)

Justice BLACKMUN delivered the opinion of the Court.

In this case we are called upon to determine the standard for admitting expert scientific testimony in a federal trial.

I

Petitioners Jason Daubert and Eric Schuller are minor children born with serious birth defects. They and their parents sued respondent in California state court, alleging that the birth defects had been caused by the mothers' ingestion of Bendectin, a prescription antinausea drug marketed by respondent. Respondent removed the suits to federal court on diversity grounds.

After extensive discovery, respondent moved for summary judgment, contending that Bendectin does not cause birth defects in humans and that petitioners would be unable to come forward with any admissible evidence that it does. In support of its motion, respondent submitted an affidavit of Steven H. Lamm, physician and epidemiologist, who is a well-credentialed expert on the risks from exposure to various chemical substances. Doctor Lamm stated that he had reviewed all the literature on Bendectin and human birth defects—more than 30 published studies involving over 130,000 patients. No study had found Bendectin to be a human teratogen (i.e., a substance capable of causing malformations in fetuses). On the basis of this review,

Doctor Lamm concluded that maternal use of Bendectin during the first trimester of pregnancy has not been shown to be a risk factor for human birth defects.

Petitioners did not (and do not) contest this characterization of the published record regarding Bendectin. Instead, they responded to respondent's motion with the testimony of eight experts of their own, each of whom also possessed impressive credentials. These experts had concluded that Bendectin can cause birth defects. Their conclusions were based upon "in vitro" (test tube) and "in vivo" (live) animal studies that found a link between Bendectin and malformations; pharmacological studies of the chemical structure of Bendectin that purported to show similarities between the structure of the drug and that of other substances known to cause birth defects; and the "reanalysis" of previously published epidemiological (human statistical) studies.

The District Court granted respondent's motion for summary judgment. The court stated that scientific evidence is admissible only if the principle upon which it is based is "'sufficiently established to have general acceptance in the field to which it belongs.'" The court concluded that petitioners' evidence did not meet this standard.... The United States Court of Appeals for the Ninth Circuit affirmed, [c]iting Frye v. United States (1923)....

II

A

In the 70 years since its formulation in the Frye case, the "general acceptance" test has been the dominant standard for determining the admissibility of novel scientific evidence at trial. Although under increasing attack of late, the rule continues to be followed by a majority of courts, including the Ninth Circuit.

The Frye test has its origin in a short and citation-free 1923 decision concerning the admissibility of evidence derived from a systolic blood pressure deception test, a crude precursor to the polygraph machine.... Because the deception test had "not yet gained such standing and scientific recognition among physiological and psychological authorities as would justify the courts in admitting expert testimony deduced from the discovery, development, and experiments thus far made," evidence of its results was ruled inadmissible.

181

The merits of the Frye test have been much debated, and scholarship on its proper scope and application is legion. Petitioners' primary attack, however, is not on the content but on the continuing authority of the rule. They contend that the Frye test was superseded by the adoption of the Federal Rules of Evidence. We agree.

We interpret the legislatively enacted Federal Rules of Evidence as we would any statute…. The drafting history [of Rule 702] makes no mention of Frye, and a rigid "general acceptance" requirement would be at odds with the "liberal thrust" of the Federal Rules and their "general approach of relaxing the traditional barriers to 'opinion' testimony." Given the Rules' permissive backdrop and their inclusion of a specific rule on expert testimony that does not mention "'general acceptance,'" the assertion that the Rules somehow assimilated Frye is unconvincing. Frye made "general acceptance" the exclusive test for admitting expert scientific testimony. That austere standard, absent from, and incompatible with, the Federal Rules of Evidence, should not be applied in federal trials.

B

That the Frye test was displaced by the Rules of Evidence does not mean, however, that the Rules themselves place no limits on the admissibility of purportedly scientific evidence. Nor is the trial judge disabled from screening such evidence. To the contrary, under the Rules the trial judge must ensure that any and all scientific testimony or evidence admitted is not only relevant, but reliable.

The primary locus of this obligation is Rule 702, which clearly contemplates some degree of regulation of the subjects and theories about which an expert may testify…. The subject of an expert's testimony must be "scientific … knowledge." The adjective "scientific" implies a grounding in the methods and procedures of science. Similarly, the word "knowledge" connotes more than subjective belief or unsupported speculation…. In short, the requirement that an expert's testimony pertain to "scientific knowledge" establishes a standard of evidentiary reliability….

Faced with a proffer of expert scientific testimony, then, the trial judge must determine at the outset, pursuant to Rule 104(a), whether the expert is proposing to testify to (1) scientific knowledge that (2) will assist the trier of fact to understand or determine a fact in issue. This entails a preliminary assessment of whether the reasoning or methodology underlying the testimony is scientifically valid and of whether that reasoning or methodology properly can be applied to the facts in issue. We are confident that federal judges possess the capacity to undertake this review. Many factors will bear on the inquiry, and we do not presume to set out a definitive checklist or test. But some general observations are appropriate.

Ordinarily, a key question to be answered in determining whether a theory or technique is scientific knowledge that will assist the trier of fact will be whether it can be (and has been) tested. "Scientific methodology today is based on generating hypotheses and testing them to see if they can be falsified; indeed, this methodology is what distinguishes science from other fields of human inquiry."

Another pertinent consideration is whether the theory or technique has been subjected to peer review and publication.... The fact of publication (or lack thereof) in a peer reviewed journal thus will be a relevant, though not dispositive, consideration in assessing the scientific validity of a particular technique or methodology on which an opinion is premised.

Additionally, in the case of a particular scientific technique, the court ordinarily should consider the known or potential rate of error, and the existence and maintenance of standards controlling the technique's operation.

Finally, "general acceptance" can yet have a bearing on the inquiry. A "reliability assessment does not require, although it does permit, explicit identification of a relevant scientific community and an express determination of a particular degree of acceptance within that community." Widespread acceptance can be an important factor in ruling particular evidence admissible, and "a known technique which has been able to attract only minimal support within the community," may properly be viewed with skepticism.

The inquiry envisioned by Rule 702 is, we emphasize, a flexible one. Its overarching subject is the scientific validity and thus the evidentiary relevance and reliability—of the principles that underlie a proposed submission. The focus, of course, must be solely on principles and methodology, not on the conclusions that they generate.

Throughout, a judge assessing a proffer of expert scientific testimony under Rule 702 should also be mindful of other applicable rules. Rule 703 provides that expert opinions based on otherwise inadmissible hearsay are to be admitted only if the facts or data are "of a type reasonably relied upon by experts in the particular field in forming opinions or inferences upon the subject." Rule 706 allows the court at its discretion to procure the assistance of an expert of its own choosing. Finally, Rule 403 permits the exclusion of relevant evidence "if its probative value is substantially outweighed by the danger of unfair prejudice, confusion of the issues, or misleading the jury...." Judge Weinstein has explained: "Expert evidence can be both powerful and quite misleading because of the difficulty in evaluating it. Because of this risk, the judge in weighing possible prejudice against probative force under Rule 403 of the present rules exercises more control over experts than over lay witnesses."

III

We conclude by briefly addressing what appear to be two underlying concerns of the parties and amici in this case. Respondent expresses apprehension that abandonment of "general acceptance" as the exclusive requirement for admission will result in a "free-for-all" in which befuddled juries are confounded by absurd and irrational pseudoscientific assertions. In this regard respondent seems to us to be overly pessimistic about the capabilities of the jury and of the adversary system generally. Vigorous cross-examination, presentation of contrary evidence, and careful instruction on the burden of proof are the traditional and appropriate means of attacking shaky but admissible evidence. Additionally, in the event the trial court concludes that the scintilla of evidence presented supporting a position is insufficient to allow a reasonable juror to conclude that the position more likely than not is true, the court remains free to direct a judgment, and likewise to grant summary judgment. These conventional devices, rather than wholesale exclusion under an uncompromising "general acceptance" test, are the appropriate safeguards where the basis of scientific testimony meets the standards of Rule 702.

Petitioners and, to a greater extent, their amici exhibit a different concern. They suggest that recognition of a screening role for the judge that allows for the exclusion of "invalid" evidence will sanction a stifling and repressive scientific orthodoxy and will be inimical to the search for truth. It is true that open debate is an essential part of both legal and scientific analyses. Yet there are important differences between the quest for truth in the courtroom and the quest for truth in the laboratory. Scientific conclusions are subject to perpetual revision. Law, on the other hand, must resolve disputes finally and quickly. The scientific project is advanced by broad and wide-ranging consideration of a multitude of hypotheses, for those that are incorrect will eventually be shown to be so, and that in itself is an advance. Conjectures that are probably wrong are of little use, however, in the project of reaching a quick, final, and binding legal judgment—often of great consequence—about a particular set of events in the past. We recognize that, in practice, a gatekeeping role for the judge, no matter how flexible, inevitably on occasion will prevent the jury from learning of authentic insights and innovations. That, nevertheless, is the balance that is struck by Rules of Evidence designed not for the exhaustive search for cosmic understanding but for the particularized resolution of legal disputes.

IV

To summarize: "General acceptance" is not a necessary precondition to the admissibility of scientific evidence under the Federal Rules of Evidence, but the Rules of Evidence—especially Rule 702—do assign to the trial judge the task of ensuring that an expert's testimony both rests on a reliable foundation and is relevant to the task at hand. Pertinent evidence based on scientifically valid principles will satisfy those demands.

The inquiries of the District Court and the Court of Appeals focused almost exclusively on "general acceptance," as gauged by publication and the decisions of other courts. Accordingly, the judgment of the Court of Appeals is vacated, and the case is remanded for further proceedings consistent with this opinion.

***

Daubert instructed courts to act as gatekeepers for "scientific" expert testimony, tying much of its reasoning to the term "scientific." In a footnote, the Court recognized that "Rule 702 also applies to 'technical, or other specialized knowledge'" but explained that "[o]ur discussion is limited to the scientific context because that is the nature of the expertise offered here." In the next case, *Kumbo Tire*, the Court took up this thread:

185

"This case requires us to decide how Daubert applies to the testimony of engineers and other experts who are not scientists. We conclude that Daubert's general holding—setting forth the trial judge's general "gatekeeping" obligation—applies not only to testimony based on "scientific" knowledge, but also to testimony based on "technical" and "other specialized" knowledge. We also conclude that a trial court may consider one or more of the more specific factors that Daubert mentioned when doing so will help determine that testimony's reliability. But, as the Court stated in Daubert, the test of reliability is "flexible," and Daubert's list of specific factors neither necessarily nor exclusively applies to all experts or in every case. Rather, the law grants a district court the same broad latitude when it decides how to determine reliability as it enjoys in respect to its ultimate reliability determination."

Equally important, the Justices in *Kumho Tire* signaled to trial courts the degree of their gatekeeping function by themselves engaging in an exhaustive reliability inquiry.

KUMHO TIRE v. CARMICHAEL
526 U.S. 137 (1999)

Justice BREYER delivered the opinion of the Court.

.... I

On July 6, 1993, the right rear tire of a minivan driven by Patrick Carmichael blew out. In the accident that followed, one of the passengers died, and others were severely injured. In October 1993, the Carmichaels brought this diversity suit against the tire's maker and its distributor, whom we refer to collectively as Kumho Tire, claiming that the tire was defective. The plaintiffs rested their case in significant part upon deposition testimony provided by an expert in tire failure analysis, Dennis Carlson, Jr., who intended to testify in support of their conclusion.

[Justice Breyer's opinion provides a detailed description of Carlson's proposed testimony.]

Kumho Tire moved the District Court to exclude Carlson's testimony on the ground that his methodology failed Rule 702's reliability requirement. The court agreed with Kumho that it should act as a Daubert-type reliability "gatekeeper," even though one might consider Carlson's testimony as "technical," rather than "scientific." The court then examined Carlson's methodology in light of the reliability-related factors that Daubert mentioned.... The District Court found that all those factors argued against the reliability of Carlson's methods, and it granted the motion to exclude the testimony (as well as the defendants' accompanying motion for summary judgment).... The Eleventh Circuit reversed....

II
A

In Daubert, this Court held that Federal Rule of Evidence 702 imposes a special obligation upon a trial judge to "ensure that any and all scientific testimony ... is not only relevant, but reliable." The initial question before us is whether this basic gatekeeping obligation applies only to "scientific" testimony or to all expert testimony. We, like the parties, believe that it applies to all expert testimony....

B

Petitioners ask more specifically whether a trial judge determining the "admissibility of an engineering expert's testimony" may consider several more specific factors that Daubert said might "bear on" a judge's gatekeeping determination…. Emphasizing the word "may" in the question, we answer that question yes.

[T]here are many different kinds of experts, and many different kinds of expertise. Our emphasis on the word "may" thus reflects Daubert's description of the Rule 702 inquiry as "a flexible one." Daubert makes clear that the factors it mentions do not constitute a "definitive checklist or test." And Daubert adds that the gatekeeping inquiry must be " 'tied to the facts'" of a particular "case." We agree with the Solicitor General that "[t]he factors identified in Daubert may or may not be pertinent in assessing reliability, depending on the nature of the issue, the expert's particular expertise, and the subject of his testimony." The conclusion, in our view, is that we can neither rule out, nor rule in, for all cases and for all time the applicability of the factors mentioned in Daubert, nor can we now do so for subsets of cases categorized by category of expert or by kind of evidence. Too much depends upon the particular circumstances of the particular case at issue.

Daubert itself is not to the contrary. It made clear that its list of factors was meant to be helpful, not definitive. Indeed, those factors do not all necessarily apply even in every instance in which the reliability of scientific testimony is challenged. It might not be surprising in a particular case, for example, that a claim made by a scientific witness has never been the subject of peer review, for the particular application at issue may never previously have interested any scientist. Nor, on the other hand, does the presence of Daubert's general acceptance factor help show that an expert's testimony is reliable where the discipline itself lacks reliability, as, for example, do theories grounded in any so-called generally accepted principles of astrology or necromancy….

To say this is not to deny the importance of Daubert's gatekeeping requirement. The objective of that requirement is to ensure the reliability and relevancy of expert testimony. It is to make certain that an expert, whether basing testimony upon professional studies or personal experience, employs in the courtroom the same level of intellectual rigor that characterizes the practice of an expert in the relevant field. Nor do we deny that, as stated in Daubert, the particular questions that it mentioned will often be appropriate for use in determining the reliability of challenged expert testimony. Rather, we conclude that the trial judge must have considerable leeway in deciding in a particular case how to go about determining whether particular expert testimony is reliable. That is to say, a trial court should consider the specific factors identified in Daubert where they are reasonable measures of the reliability of expert testimony.

The trial court must have the same kind of latitude in deciding how to test an expert's reliability, and to decide whether or when special briefing or other proceedings are needed to investigate reliability, as it enjoys when it decides whether or not that expert's relevant testimony is reliable. [A] court of appeals is to apply an abuse-of-discretion standard when it "review[s] a trial court's decision to admit or exclude expert testimony." That standard applies as much to the trial court's decisions about how to determine reliability as to its ultimate conclusion. Otherwise, the trial judge would lack the discretionary authority needed both to avoid unnecessary "reliability" proceedings in ordinary cases where the reliability of an expert's methods is properly taken for granted, and to require appropriate proceedings in the less usual or more complex cases where cause for questioning the expert's reliability arises. Indeed, the Rules seek to avoid "unjustifiable expense and delay" as part of their search for "truth" and the "jus[t] determin[ation]" of proceedings. Fed. Rule Evid. 102. Thus, whether Daubert's specific factors are, or are not, reasonable measures of reliability in a particular case is a matter that the law grants the trial judge broad latitude to determine....

III

We further explain the way in which a trial judge "may" consider Daubert's factors by applying these considerations to the case at hand, a matter that has been briefed exhaustively by the parties and their 19 amici. The District Court did not doubt Carlson's qualifications, which included a masters degree in mechanical engineering, 10 years' work at Michelin America, Inc., and testimony as a tire failure consultant in other tort cases. Rather, it excluded the testimony because, despite those qualifications, it initially doubted, and then found unreliable, "the methodology employed by the expert in analyzing the data obtained in the visual inspection, and the scientific basis, if any, for such an analysis." After examining the transcript in "some detail," and after considering respondents' defense of Carlson's methodology, the District Court determined that Carlson's testimony was not reliable. It fell outside the range where experts might reasonably differ, and where the jury must decide among the conflicting views of different experts, even though the evidence is "shaky." In our view, the doubts that triggered the District Court's initial inquiry here were reasonable, as was the court's ultimate conclusion.

For one thing, and contrary to respondents' suggestion, the specific issue before the court was not the reasonableness in general of a tire expert's use of a visual and tactile inspection to determine whether overdeflection had caused the tire's tread to separate from its steel-belted carcass. Rather, it was the reasonableness of using such an approach, along with Carlson's particular method of analyzing the data thereby obtained, to draw a conclusion regarding the particular matter to which the expert testimony was directly relevant. That matter concerned the likelihood that a defect in the tire at issue caused its tread to separate from its carcass. The tire in question, the expert conceded, had traveled far enough so that some of the tread had been worn bald; it should have been taken out of service; it had been repaired (inadequately) for punctures; and it bore some of the very marks that the expert said indicated, not a defect, but abuse through overdeflection. The relevant issue was whether the expert could reliably determine the cause of this tire's separation.

Nor was the basis for Carlson's conclusion simply the general theory that, in the absence of evidence of abuse, a defect will normally have caused a tire's separation. Rather, the expert employed a more specific theory to establish the existence (or absence) of such abuse. Carlson testified precisely that in the absence of at least two of four signs of abuse (proportionately greater tread wear on the shoulder; signs of grooves caused by the beads; discolored sidewalls; marks on the rim flange), he concludes that a defect caused the separation. And his analysis depended upon acceptance of a further implicit proposition, namely, that his visual and tactile inspection could determine that the tire before him had not been abused despite some evidence of the presence of the very signs for which he looked (and two punctures).

For another thing, the transcripts of Carlson's depositions support both the trial court's initial uncertainty and its final conclusion. Those transcripts cast considerable doubt upon the reliability of both the explicit theory (about the need for two signs of abuse) and the implicit proposition (about the significance of visual inspection in this case). Among other things, the expert could not say whether the tire had traveled more than 10, or 20, or 30, or 40, or 50 thousand miles, adding that 6,000 miles was "about how far" he could "say with any certainty." The court could reasonably have wondered about the reliability of a method of visual and tactile inspection sufficiently precise to ascertain with some certainty the abuse-related significance of minute shoulder/center relative tread wear differences, but insufficiently precise to tell "with any certainty" from the tread wear whether a tire had traveled less than 10,000 or more than 50,000 miles. And these concerns might have been augmented by Carlson's repeated reliance on the "subjective[ness]" of his mode of analysis in response to questions seeking specific information regarding how he could differentiate between a tire that actually had been overdeflected and a tire that merely looked as though it had been. They would have been further augmented by the fact that Carlson said he had inspected the tire itself for the first time the morning of his first deposition, and then only for a few hours. (His initial conclusions were based on photographs.)

Moreover, prior to his first deposition, Carlson had issued a signed report in which he concluded that the tire had "not been ... overloaded or underinflated," not because of the absence of "two of four" signs of abuse, but simply because "the rim flange impressions ... were normal." That report also said that the "tread depth remaining was 3/32 inch," though the opposing expert's (apparently undisputed) measurements indicate that the tread depth taken at various positions around the tire actually ranged from .5/32 of an inch to 4/32 of an inch, with the tire apparently showing greater wear along both shoulders than along the center.

Further, in respect to one sign of abuse, bead grooving, the expert seemed to deny the sufficiency of his own simple visual-inspection methodology. He testified that most tires have some bead groove pattern, that where there is reason to suspect an abnormal bead groove he would ideally "look at a lot of [similar] tires" to know the grooving's significance, and that he had not looked at many tires similar to the one at issue.

Finally, the court, after looking for a defense of Carlson's methodology as applied in these circumstances, found no convincing defense. Rather, it found (1) that "none" of the Daubert factors, including that of "general acceptance"

191

in the relevant expert community, indicated that Carlson's testimony was reliable, (2) that its own analysis "revealed no countervailing factors operating in favor of admissibility which could outweigh those identified in Daubert," and (3) that the "parties identified no such factors in their briefs." For these three reasons taken together, it concluded that Carlson's testimony was unreliable.

Respondents now argue to us, as they did to the District Court, that a method of tire failure analysis that employs a visual/tactile inspection is a reliable method, and they point both to its use by other experts and to Carlson's long experience working for Michelin as sufficient indication that that is so. But no one denies that an expert might draw a conclusion from a set of observations based on extensive and specialized experience. Nor does anyone deny that, as a general matter, tire abuse may often be identified by qualified experts through visual or tactile inspection of the tire. As we said before, the question before the trial court was specific, not general. The trial court had to decide whether this particular expert had sufficient specialized knowledge to assist the jurors "in deciding the particular issues in the case."

The particular issue in this case concerned the use of Carlson's two-factor test and his related use of visual/tactile inspection to draw conclusions on the basis of what seemed small observational differences. We have found no indication in the record that other experts in the industry use Carlson's two-factor test or that tire experts such as Carlson normally make the very fine distinctions about, say, the symmetry of comparatively greater shoulder tread wear that were necessary, on Carlson's own theory, to support his conclusions. Nor, despite the prevalence of tire testing, does anyone refer to any articles or papers that validate Carlson's approach. Indeed, no one has argued that Carlson himself, were he still working for Michelin, would have concluded in a report to his employer that a similar tire was similarly defective on grounds identical to those upon which he rested his conclusion here. Of course, Carlson himself claimed that his method was accurate, but, as we pointed out in Joiner, "nothing in either Daubert or the Federal Rules of Evidence requires a district court to admit opinion evidence that is connected to existing data only by the ipse dixit of the expert."

.... In sum, Rule 702 grants the district judge the discretionary authority, reviewable for its abuse, to determine reliability in light of the particular facts and circumstances of the particular case. The District Court did not abuse its discretionary authority in this case. Hence, the judgment of the Court of Appeals is reversed.

***

The Advisory Committee was not as sure as the Supreme Court that the principles set forth in *Daubert* "are embodied in Rule 702." Consequently, it amended the Rule, adding Rule 702(b), (c), and (d) "in response to" *Daubert* and *Kumho Tire*. The Advisory Committee explained that "[t]he standards set forth in the amendment are broad enough to require consideration of any or all of the specific *Daubert* factors where appropriate." The Advisory Committee Note to the 2000 amendment provides a comprehensive treatment of the reliability requirements set out in *Daubert* and, now, Rule 702.

BASIS OF EXPERT TESTIMONY

RULE 703

Rule 602's requirement that a witness testify from "personal knowledge" contains an exception for expert witnesses. See Rule 602 ("This rule does not apply to a witness's expert testimony under Rule 703.") For expert testimony, Rule 703 governs.

An excerpt from a report by the California Law Review Commission, cited but not quoted in the Advisory Committee Note to Rule 703, explains the difficulty of crafting a rule to govern this scenario:

> "The variation in the permissible bases of expert opinion is unavoidable in light of the wide variety of subjects upon which such opinion can be offered. In regard to some matters of expert opinion, an expert must ... rely on reports, statements, and other information that might not be admissible evidence. A physician in many instances cannot make a diagnosis without relying on the case history recited by the patient or on reports from various technicians or other physicians. Similarly, an appraiser must rely on reports of sales and other market data ... to give an opinion that will be of value to the jury. In the usual case where a physician's or an appraiser's opinion is required, the

adverse party also will have its expert who will be able to check the data relied upon by the adverse expert. On the other hand, a police officer can analyze skid marks, debris, and the condition of vehicles that have been involved in an accident without relying on the statements of bystanders; and it seems likely that the jury would be as able to evaluate the statements of others in the light of the physical facts, as interpreted by the officer, as would the officer himself. It is apparent that the extent to which an expert may base [an] opinion upon the statements of others is far from clear. It is at least clear, however, that it is permitted in a number of instances."

Rule 703 offers such a rule, allowing an expert to base an opinion on hearsay or, more precisely, facts or data that are not themselves admissible so long as "experts in the particular field would reasonably rely on those kinds of facts or data in forming an opinion on the subject."

Here is a brief excerpt from a Second Circuit case exploring the rule's application in rejecting a challenge to the testimony of an FBI agent in an organized crime case:

> At trial, Special Agent Schiliro testified at great length on the nature and function of organized crime families, imparting the structure of such families and disclosing the "rules" of the La Cosa Nostra. For example, Schiliro testified that a "boss" must approve all illegal activity and especially all murders, and that the functions of the "consigliere" and "underboss" are only "advisory" to the "boss." In addition, as part of his testimony, he interpreted the numerous surreptitiously taped conversations introduced into evidence, and identified the individuals speaking by their voices. Schiliro specifically named John Gotti as the boss of the alleged Gambino Family. Additionally, he identified, together with their titles, ranks, and functions, numerous members and associates of the Gambino Family and other criminal organizations. When pressed about his sources for individuals' titles, ranks, and functions, Schiliro admitted that his sources of information were not necessarily before the court....
>
> According to Rule 703, the facts that form the basis for an expert's opinions or inferences need not be admissible in evidence "[i]f of a

type reasonably relied upon by experts in the particular field." Thus, expert witnesses can testify to opinions based on hearsay or other inadmissible evidence if experts in the field reasonably rely on such evidence in forming their opinions. Therefore, Schiliro was entitled to rely upon hearsay as to such matters as the structure and operating rules of organized crime families and the identification of specific voices heard on tape in forming his opinion, since there is little question that law enforcement agents routinely and reasonably rely upon such hearsay in the course of their duties. An expert who meets the test of Rule 702, as Schiliro does, is assumed "to have the skill to properly evaluate the hearsay, giving it probative force appropriate to the circumstances." The fact that Schiliro relied upon inadmissible evidence is therefore less an issue of admissibility for the court than an issue of credibility for the jury.[1]

In a later case, the Second Circuit concluded that the government pushed the boundaries of Rule 703 too far in offering the testimony of a New York State police officer, Hector Alicea, in another organized crime case.

Under Rule 703, experts can testify to opinions based on inadmissible evidence, including hearsay, if "experts in the field reasonably rely on such evidence in forming their opinions." Alicea unquestionably relied on hearsay evidence in forming his opinions. This hearsay evidence took the form of statements by MS–13 members given in interviews, both custodial and noncustodial, as well as statements made by other law enforcement officers, statements from intercepted telephone conversations among MS–13 members…. Alicea's reliance on such materials was consistent with the ordinary practices of law enforcement officers, who "routinely and reasonably rely upon hearsay in reaching their conclusions."

The expert may not, however, simply transmit that hearsay to the jury. Instead, the expert must form his own opinions by "applying his extensive experience and a reliable methodology" to the inadmissible materials. Otherwise, the expert is simply "repeating hearsay evidence

---

[1] United States v. Locascio, 6 F.3d 924 (2d Cir. 1993).

without applying any expertise whatsoever," a practice that allows the Government "to circumvent the rules prohibiting hearsay."

…. On cross-examination, Alicea identified hearsay as the source of much of his information. For example, his testimony that the Freeport clique initially funded itself through drug sales was based on "some of the articles that [he] had researched" and "[r]eports from law enforcement personnel." His testimony about MS–13's taxation of drug sales by non-members was based on a gang member having told him so during a custodial interrogation in this case. Alicea had learned about MS–13 treasury funds from about a dozen MS–13 members both in and out of custody. Additionally, Alicea discovered his information about MS–13's involvement in Mexican immigrant smuggling through "research on the Internet," and more specifically from a website containing a media report and an interview with a law enforcement official….

Not all of Alicea's testimony was flawed, and some of the information that he provided to the jury resulted from his synthesis of various source materials. As a review of his testimony shows, however, at least some of his testimony involved merely repeating information he had read or heard…. When asked how he learned particular facts, Alicea did not explain how he had pieced together bits of information from different sources and reached a studied conclusion that he then gave to the jury. Instead, he testified that he had read an article, or had talked to gang members in custody (including, on at least one occasion, a gang member arrested as part of this investigation), or listened to a recording (evidence that could have been played to the jury in its original form, notwithstanding that some informants may have been identified in the process). This testimony strongly suggests that Alicea was acting not as an expert but instead as a case agent, thereby implicating our warning in [an earlier case]—a warning the Government appears not to have heard or heeded. Alicea did not analyze his source materials so much as repeat their contents…. These statements therefore violated Rule 703.[1]

---

[1] United States v. Mejia, 545 F.3d 179 (2d Cir. 2008).

***

As the previous excerpt shows, even when Rule 703 permits an expert to rely on inadmissible information, that does not make the information relied on admissible. The expert can weave the inadmissible information into the fabric of an expert opinion, but the expert cannot launder inadmissible information into admissible evidence. In fact, in many cases inadmissible information properly relied on by an expert will not become known to the jury. As a 2000 amendment to Rule 703 clarified, the party offering an expert can only ask the expert to reveal the inadmissible facts or data relied upon "if their probative value in helping the jury evaluate the opinion substantially outweighs their prejudicial effect."

CASE NOTE: WILLIAMS v. ILLINOIS

To appreciate the significance and difficulties of applying Rule 703, consider the facts of a 2012 Confrontation Clause case, Williams v. Illinois, which caused the Supreme Court Justices to splinter without any majority opinion.

After a woman described as L.J. was raped in Chicago in February 2000, police sent a sample of the unknown perpetrator's semen to a Cellmark lab in Maryland for analysis. Cellmark produced a DNA profile from the sample and submitted a report to the Illinois State Police (ISP). "Sandra Lambatos, a forensic specialist at the ISP lab, conducted a computer search to see if the Cellmark profile matched any of the entries in the state DNA database. The computer showed a match to a profile produced by the lab from a sample of [Sandy Williams'] blood that had been taken after he was arrested on unrelated charges on August 3, 2000." Police arrested Williams and he was tried for the rape.

The ISP specialist who produced the DNA profile of Williams' blood in August testified at the trial. In addition,

> [T]he State called Lambatos as an expert witness and had her testify [as follows]:

>> Q Was there a computer match generated of the male DNA profile found in semen from the vaginal swabs of [L.J.] to a

male DNA profile that had been identified as having originated from Sandy Williams?

A Yes, there was.

Q Did you compare the semen ... from the vaginal swabs of [L.J.] to the male DNA profile ... from the blood of Sandy Williams?

A Yes, I did....

Q [I]s the semen identified in the vaginal swabs of [L.J.] consistent with having originated from Sandy Williams?

A Yes.

The controversial evidentiary fact in question was embedded in that testimony. It was that the DNA profile that Lambatos ran through the computer database was derived from the rapist's semen. But that fact was inadmissible because it was hearsay -- it was information Lambatos learned from someone else (a Cellmark employee) who did not testify at the trial. As we will learn later, introducing this kind of hearsay against a criminal defendant normally violates the Sixth Amendment Confrontation Clause. But the prosecutor in *Williams* saw a distinction. "Invoking Illinois Rule of Evidence 703, the prosecutor argued that an expert is allowed to disclose the facts on which the expert's opinion is based even if the expert is not competent to testify to those underlying facts."

In an opinion by Justice Alito, a plurality of the Court ruled that disclosing this hearsay evidence (Cellmark's assertion that the DNA profile it sent to the ISP came from the rapist's semen) through Lambatos did not violate the Confrontation Clause. The plurality explained this was because the hearsay was not actually introduced as evidence, it only came in to illustrate the basis of the expert (Lambastos') testimony:

> The dissent is ... mistaken in its contention that the Cellmark report "was offered for its truth because that is all such 'basis evidence' can be offered for." This view is directly contrary to ... Rule 703 of the Federal Rules of Evidence.... Under that Rule, "basis evidence" that is not admissible for its truth may be disclosed even in a jury trial under

appropriate circumstances. The purpose for allowing this disclosure is that it may "assis[t] the jury to evaluate the expert's opinion." The Rule 703 approach, which was controversial when adopted, is based on the idea that the disclosure of basis evidence can help the factfinder understand the expert's thought process and determine what weight to give to the expert's opinion. For example, if the factfinder were to suspect that the expert relied on factual premises with no support in the record, or that the expert drew an unwarranted inference from the premises on which the expert relied, then the probativeness or credibility of the expert's opinion would be seriously undermined. The purpose of disclosing the facts on which the expert relied is to allay these fears—to show that the expert's reasoning was not illogical, and that the weight of the expert's opinion does not depend on factual premises unsupported by other evidence in the record—not to prove the truth of the underlying facts.

Justice Kagan wrote for the dissenting Justices:

> The plurality's primary argument ... tries to exploit a limit to the Confrontation Clause recognized in *Crawford*. "The Clause," we cautioned there, "does not bar the use of testimonial statements for purposes other than establishing the truth of the matter asserted." The Illinois Supreme Court relied on that statement in concluding that Lambatos's testimony was permissible. On that court's view, "Lambatos disclosed the underlying facts from Cellmark's report" not for their truth, but "for the limited purpose of explaining the basis for her [expert] opinion," so that the factfinder could assess that opinion's value. The plurality wraps itself in that holding, similarly asserting that Lambatos's recitation of Cellmark's findings, when viewed through the prism of state evidence law, was not introduced to establish "the truth of any ... matter concerning [the] Cellmark" report. But five Justices agree, in two opinions reciting the same reasons, that this argument has no merit: Lambatos's statements about Cellmark's report went to its truth, and the State could not rely on her status as an expert to circumvent the Confrontation Clause's requirements....

> Consider a prosaic example not involving scientific experts. An eyewitness tells a police officer investigating an assault that the

199

perpetrator had an unusual, star-shaped birthmark over his left eye. The officer arrests a person bearing that birthmark (let's call him Starr) for committing the offense. And at trial, the officer takes the stand and recounts just what the eyewitness told him. Presumably the plurality would agree that such testimony violates the Confrontation Clause.... Now ask whether anything changes if the officer couches his testimony in the following way: "I concluded that Starr was the assailant because a reliable eyewitness told me that the assailant had a star-shaped birthmark and, look, Starr has one just like that." Surely that framing would make no constitutional difference, even though the eyewitness's statement now explains the basis for the officer's conclusion. It remains the case that the prosecution is attempting to introduce a testimonial statement that has no relevance to the proceedings apart from its truth—and that the defendant cannot cross-examine the person who made it. Allowing the admission of this evidence would end-run the Confrontation Clause, and make a parody of its strictures.

And that example, when dressed in scientific clothing, is no different from this case. The Cellmark report identified the rapist as having a particular DNA profile (think of it as the quintessential birthmark). The Confrontation Clause prevented the State from introducing that report into evidence except by calling to the stand the person who prepared it. So the State tried another route—introducing the substance of the report as part and parcel of an expert witness's conclusion....

The Justices' disagreement about the Confrontation Clause issue rested on the trial court's application of Illinois Rule 703. A proper application of that rule would allow Lambatos to inform the jury of the inadmissible Cellmark profile only to the extent necessary to help the jury understand Lambatos' opinion. An improper application would allow Lambatos to become a conduit to the jury for inadmissible facts and data. Justice Kagan viewed the case as an example of the latter. Justice Alito did not necessarily disagree, but he viewed any misinterpretation of Rule 703 as a matter of state evidence law.

Chapter 6

HEARSAY

RULE 802

Rule 802 commands that "[h]earsay is not admissible" unless some other rule or statute provides otherwise. But what constitutes "hearsay"? A rough shorthand is anything a testifying witness heard from someone else. Yet, as we will see, there is much more to it than that.

RULE 801

The complex treatment of hearsay is one of the most prominent and puzzling features of the American evidence landscape. The key to unlocking this puzzle for modern practitioners lies in the precise definition of "hearsay" contained in Federal Rule of Evidence 801(a)-(c). If evidence falls within this definition, a litigant offering the evidence must invoke an exception to the hearsay prohibition or, if none apply, forego the evidence.

The hearsay definition itself is contained in Rule 801(c). That subsection defines "hearsay" as:

- an out-of-court "statement"
- offered "to prove the truth of the matter asserted" by the out-of-court speaker

Rule 801(a) defines the term "statement." Rule 801(b) defines a "declarant" to be "the person who made the statement."

Justice Kagan offered a straightforward example in *Williams*: a police officer testifies in a murder trial that an eyewitness told the officer that, "The killer had a star shaped birthmark." The officer's testimony includes an out-of-court statement and that statement appears to be offered to prove the same fact that the out-of-court speaker was trying to communicate -- the appearance of the killer. Thus, Rule 802 prevents the officer from testifying as described above.

There is, again, much more to it than that. The rest of this Chapter explores the complex concept of hearsay.

STATEMENTS

"Hearsay," as defined in Rule 801(c), requires a "statement" as that term is defined in Rule 801(a). If an out-of-court utterance, writing, conduct, etc., is not a "statement," it cannot constitute hearsay. Thus, the first challenge is determining what Rule 801(a) means by "statement."

Rule 801(a) defines "statement" to be an "oral assertion, written assertion, or nonverbal conduct, if the person intended it as an assertion." The Advisory Committee Note explains: "The effect of the definition of 'statement' is to exclude from the operation of the hearsay rule all evidence of conduct, verbal or nonverbal, not intended as an assertion." As further explained below, this is an important and tricky component of the hearsay definition. The rules drafters' emphasis on intent reverberates throughout federal hearsay analysis.

Rule 801(a) identifies three forms of potential "statements": (1) oral assertions, (2) written assertions and (3) nonverbal conduct intended as an assertion. The first two forms are the easiest to identify. By assertion, the rule means an effort to communicate information. When people write words or express themselves orally, they almost always do so with the intent to communicate. As a result, most oral utterances and virtually all writings constitute "statements" under Rule 801(a). But that doesn't mean oral and written utterances are always statements.

As the Advisory Committee Note stresses, whether something constitutes a "statement" depends on the declarant's intent. An involuntary cough or a startled exclamation ("ouch!") while oral would not qualify as a "statement" under Rule 801(a). Why? These utterances are not *intended* to assert or communicate anything. Illustrating the significance of intent to the analysis, however, a child who coughs in an effort to convince her parents to let her stay home from school, or a pedestrian's loud "ouch!" to inform a passerby that the passerby stepped on her foot, would both be "statements" under Rule 801(a). These oral utterances are intended to communicate. They are assertive and therefore constitute "statements" under Rule 801(a).

The third category of potential statements identified in Rule 801(a), "nonverbal conduct," presents more challenging questions. The federal rules drafters' decision to extend the hearsay prohibition to assertive, nonverbal conduct—while complicating the hearsay definition—makes good sense. If assertive nonverbal conduct were not covered, the hearsay prohibition would contain a loophole allowing precise parallels of oral and written hearsay to be introduced. Only a flawed hearsay definition would permit the admission of an affirmative nod of the head but prohibit the word "yes" uttered in parallel with the nod.

The hearsay definition's extension to conduct recognizes the complexity of human communication. If conduct is intended as an assertion, the declarant's use of nonverbal as opposed to oral or written alternatives to communicate should not alter the hearsay treatment. For example, an out-of-court declarant's pointing out a suspect as someone who committed an earlier crime is hearsay if offered as evidence of the suspect's guilt; similarly, a shake of the head offered as either a "yes" or a "no" constitutes a "statement" and thus potentially hearsay.

Don't get carried away examining nonverbal conduct for hearsay. As a general matter, testimony or other evidence describing nonverbal conduct does not raise hearsay concerns. For example, there is no hearsay problem when, in a trial about a car accident, a witness testifies that "the defendant drove through a red light." The driving occurred out of court, but, like most action, it is nonverbal conduct that was <u>not</u> intended as an assertion.

PROBLEM 6-1: UMBRELLAS

A car skids off a city street damaging a Hot Pretzel stand. In a later lawsuit, the driver wants to prove that it was raining. Could the driver introduce the testimony of an office worker who, at the time of the accident, looked out the window of a nearby skyscraper and saw that people in the street were holding open umbrellas? The defendant explains that the testimony would show the umbrella bearers' belief that it was raining, and thus a high likelihood that it was raining. In essence, the jury would peer into the minds of the pedestrians and perceive their belief that it was raining. But there would be no chance to question the pedestrians or require them to swear to tell the truth. *Does the testimony described above include an out-of-court "statement" under Rule 801(a)? Is it hearsay?*[1]

GUIDED PROBLEM 6-2: THE CAPTAIN

This problem is based on a famous hypothetical offered in an 1838 English case, Wright v. Tatham. A shipwreck leads to a lawsuit against the ship's owners for failing to keep the ship seaworthy. The captain and all aboard perished in the wreck. The ship owners offer the following testimony:

> A dockworker, Sam, will testify that, just before the ship departed, Sam casually observed from a nearby dock as the captain inspected every area of the ship. Then, apparently satisfied, the captain got on board and headed out to sea. The ship's owners offer Sam's in-court testimony to prove that the experienced captain believed that the ship was seaworthy at the time of departure.

Does Sam's testimony present an out-of-court "statement" to the jury? After you answer the question, continue to the analysis below.

Absent any evidence that the captain is acting for some audience when he sets out to sea, the evidence is not hearsay under the federal rules. As far as we can tell, the captain did not intend to assert anything by inspecting his ship and subsequently setting out to sea. Consequently, evidence of the captain's nonverbal conduct does not include any "statement" and thus cannot be hearsay under the federal rules.

Note that cross-examination of the captain would still be helpful. Perhaps we would learn that he was drunk at the time of his inspection or suicidal. Maybe he noticed numerous deficiencies in the ship's seaworthiness but has an unreasonably high risk tolerance. The federal rules accept these dangers of unreliability, reasoning that on balance the absence of an intent to communicate renders the evidence sufficiently reliable to be presented to the factfinder.

---

[1] See Judson F. Falknor, The "Hear-Say" Rule as a "See-Do" Rule: Evidence of Conduct, 33 U. Colo. L. Rev. 133 (1961) (illustrating hearsay conundrum with umbrella example).

Why? The rules consider this type of evidence more reliable than the bulk of out-of-court statements intended as assertions. The rationale is that people who are not acting for an audience are essentially "speaking" only to themselves. And people are less likely to lie to themselves.

PROBLEM 6-3: DELICIOUS SEAFOOD

In 2010, an explosion at a BP oil drilling rig off the coast of Louisiana led to a disastrous oil spill in the Gulf of Mexico. The spill hurt tourism in the region, due to worries about the safety of usually popular seafood. In June, President Barack Obama traveled to the city. Here is an excerpt from a news account of the trip:

> The president made a point of eating local seafood for a lunch in Gulfport [Mississippi], where he chatted with a hotel owner who told him that her business was down 40 percent, and then again for dinner in Orange Beach, Ala., where he ordered crab claws, crawfish tails, ribs and nachos.
>
> "Seafood from the gulf today is safe to eat," he said earlier in Theodore [Mississippi], where he said government agencies were increasing their monitoring of seafood processors and of fish caught outside of areas where fishing has already been banned because of the spill. "But we need to make sure it stays that way."[1]

In later litigation about the damages BP had to pay for the spill, can BP offer the President's verbal expression and/or his actions in sitting down and eating the local seafood as evidence of its safety? Is the nonverbal conduct described in the story above a "statement" under Rule 801(a)?

PROBLEM 6-4: DEMEANOR

The following problem is based on United States v. Rodriguez-Berrios (1st Cir. 2009). In a prosecution of Eddie Samir Rodríguez–Berríos for the death of his wife Yesenia Ortiz–Acosta, the government sought to illustrate a pattern of abuse by Rodríguez–Berríos. Part of that evidence included the testimony of a friend of the victim who testified to an incident where "she observed appellant

---

[1] https://www.nytimes.com/2010/06/15/us/15spill.html

pass the victim in a hallway and nudge her with his elbow, a seemingly minor incident that nonetheless caused the victim to become upset and to 'los[e] control.'" On appeal, Rodríguez–Berríos contended that "[the friend,] Ramos's testimony that the victim lost control and started crying after appellant elbowed her in the hallway was a hearsay statement." *Was it?*

PROBLEM 6-5: ABSENCE OF COMPLAINTS

In litigation about whether a restaurant meal caused a diner's food poisoning, the restaurant owner seeks to offer testimony about the lack of complaints regarding food poisoning during the week when the diner ate at the restaurant and fell ill. *Does the testimony contain out-of-court "statements" of the restaurant's other diners?*

Contrast that example with the clichéd example of a wedding, where the officiant asks the crowd, "if anyone can show just cause why this couple cannot lawfully be joined together in matrimony, let them speak now or forever hold their peace." *If no one says anything during the pause that follows, is the crowd's silence a "statement" under Rule 801(a)?*

***

In the foregoing examples, the analysis for purposes of the federal hearsay definition, and more precisely Rule 801(a)'s definition of "statement," centers on the declarant's intent. The Advisory Committee makes this crystal clear. Under Rule 801(a), only an "assertion" can be a "statement." The Advisory Committee Notes then explain that: "The key to the definition is that nothing is an assertion unless intended to be one."

Legal clarity does not mean answers will be obvious. This is because there is often factual ambiguity. In many cases judges can only guess at the true intent of an absent declarant.

For example, testimony about a person's driving route, i.e., a description of out-of-court nonverbal conduct, would normally not be hearsay. It could constitute hearsay only if, as the First Circuit noted, the driver "was engaging in a kind of charade, deliberately seeking to mislead an observer."[1] How can

---

[1] U.S. v. Butler, 763 F.2d 11 (1st Cir. 1985).

we tell? The declarant's intent must be assessed from context. Additional guidance comes from the Advisory Committee Note to Rule 801, which places a thumb on the scale in favor of admission. The Notes state that "ambiguous and doubtful cases will be resolved ... in favor of admissibility" because the "rule places the burden upon the party claiming that the intention [to assert] existed."

NON-HUMAN DECLARANTS

Rule 801(b) defines the term "declarant." The definition is sparse and largely superfluous but hints at an important limitation of hearsay to assertions by persons. Rule 801(a) reiterates this limitation with stronger force, defining a statement as "a person's" assertion. Together these definitions make clear that when information is communicated out of court by something other than a person, that out-of-court communication is not hearsay. Precisely stated, an assertion by a non-person cannot satisfy the definition of "statement" in Rule 801(a) and so cannot constitute hearsay under the federal rules.

The most common and intuitively satisfying example of the hearsay definition's limitation to statements by "persons" is found in the broad spectrum of devices that humans rely on to tell time. Witnesses can testify about the time of an event—i.e., what a clock "told" them—without drawing a valid hearsay objection. As a formal matter this is because the clock is not a "person" and so its out-of-court communication of the time was not a "statement" under Rule 801(a) and thus cannot be "hearsay" under Rule 801(c). Similarly, readouts of radar detectors, thermometers, scales, speedometers and the like are not hearsay under the federal rules because the information conveyed does not come from a human source.

The exclusion makes sense. It would be odd to object to testimony about the time on a clock or the readout of a thermometer on the ground that the device must be brought to court so that it can be placed under oath and cross-examined. There may be evidentiary concerns about the reliability of out-of-court mechanical or electronic displays, but these concerns are addressed outside of the hearsay framework through rules governing relevance (Chapter 2), confusion and unfair prejudice (Chapter 3), expert testimony (Chapter 5), and authentication (Chapter 9).

PROBLEM 6-6: POLICE DOGS

Consider the following excerpt from a Supreme Court case, Florida v. Harris (2013):

> William Wheetley is a K–9 Officer in the Liberty County, Florida Sheriff's Office. On June 24, 2006, he was on a routine patrol with Aldo, a German shepherd trained to detect certain narcotics. Wheetley pulled over respondent Clayton Harris's truck because it had an expired license plate.... Wheetley asked Harris for consent to search the truck, but Harris refused. At that point, Wheetley retrieved Aldo from the patrol car and walked him around Harris's truck for a "free air sniff." Aldo alerted at the driver's-side door handle—signaling, through a distinctive set of behaviors, that he smelled drugs there.

Does the police officer's testimony about Aldo's drug "alert" include an out-of-court statement under Rule 801(a)?

***

Don't get carried away with the limitation of hearsay to statements by persons. Many electronic, mechanical or even animal outputs simply reflect a person's earlier inputs. As a result, it is often necessary to step back from the most immediate source of the information and determine a communication's true source or author. This ensures that a party cannot launder a communication through an animal or (more likely) electronic medium to avoid the hearsay bar. The tally on an electronic scoreboard that reflects the score of a basketball game constitutes a "statement" and thus (potentially) hearsay since the true author of the display is typically a human scorekeeper, not the electronic scoreboard itself. Context matters. The answer can change as a scoring system becomes more automated and the human author's contribution recedes.

Computer or smartphone displays of text messages or email are captured in the hearsay definition despite the electronic medium from which they arise. The true authors of such communications are human and thus "persons" under Rule 801(a) and (b) even if the immediate readout comes from a machine.

The analysis becomes more complicated when the out-of-court statement falls between the extremes of a thermometer and an electronic basketball scoreboard.

UNITED STATES v. LIZARRAGA-TIRADO
789 F.3d 1107 (9th Cir. 2015)

Plotting coordinates on a map used to require a sextant, a compass and quite a bit of skill. Today, anyone can do it with a few clicks of the mouse. This appeal raises a question born of that newfound technological prowess: Are a Google Earth satellite image and a digital "tack" labeled with GPS coordinates hearsay?

I

On January 17, 2003, defendant was arrested near the United States–Mexico border. He was charged with illegal reentry under 8 U.S.C. § 1326 as a previously removed alien who "entered and was found in the United States." At trial, defendant disputed that he had entered the United States before his arrest. He testified that he was still on the Mexico side of the border, waiting for instructions from a smuggler when he was arrested. Because he was arrested on a dark night in a remote location, he insisted that the arresting Border Patrol agents must have accidentally crossed the border before arresting him.

The arresting agents, Garcia and Nunez, testified that they were very familiar with the area where they arrested defendant and were certain they arrested him north of the border. Agent Garcia also testified that she contemporaneously recorded the coordinates of defendant's arrest using a handheld GPS device. To illustrate the location of those coordinates, the government introduced a Google Earth satellite image, attached as Appendix A.

Google Earth is a computer program that allows users to pull up a bird's eye view of any place in the world. It displays satellite images taken from far above the earth's surface with high-resolution cameras. Google Earth superimposes certain markers and labels onto the images, such as names of towns and locations of borders. Relevant here, it also offers two ways for users to add markers of their own. A user can type GPS coordinates into Google Earth, which automatically produces a digital "tack" at the appropriate spot on the map, labeled with the coordinates. A user can also manually add a marker by clicking any spot on the map, which results in a tack that can be labeled by the user.

The satellite image introduced at trial depicts the region where defendant was arrested. It includes a few default labels, such as a nearby highway, a small town and the United States–Mexico border. It also includes a digital tack labeled with a set of GPS coordinates. Agent Garcia testified that the GPS coordinates next to the tack matched the coordinates she recorded the night she arrested defendant. On that basis, she surmised that the tack marked "approximately where [she was] responding to" on the night of defendant's arrest. Because the tack is clearly north of the border, the exhibit corroborated the agents' testimony that defendant was arrested in the United States. Defendant's lawyer cross-examined Agent Garcia about whether she had recorded the GPS coordinates accurately. But he couldn't cross-examine her about the generation of the satellite image or the tack because Agent Garcia hadn't generated them. Indeed, there was no testimony regarding the origin of the satellite image or the tack, and the record doesn't reflect whether the tack was automatically generated or manually placed and labeled. Defense counsel objected to the satellite image on hearsay grounds. The district court overruled that objection and admitted the image.

II

Defendant claims that both the satellite image on its own and the digitally added tack and coordinates were impermissible hearsay. The rule against hearsay bars admission of out-of-court statements to prove the truth of the matters asserted. Fed.R.Evid. 801(c)(2), 802. For hearsay purposes, a statement is defined as "a person's oral assertion, written assertion, or nonverbal conduct, if the person intended it as an assertion." Fed.R.Evid. 801(a). In defendant's view, the satellite image is hearsay because it asserts that it "accurately represented the desert area where the agents worked," and the tack and coordinates are hearsay because they assert "where the agents responded and its proximity to the border."

We first consider whether the satellite image, absent any labels or markers, is hearsay. While we've never faced that precise question, we've held that a photograph isn't hearsay because it makes no "assertion." Rather, a photograph merely depicts a scene as it existed at a particular time. The same is true of a Google Earth satellite image. Such images are produced by high-resolution imaging satellites, and though the cameras are more powerful, the result is the same: a snapshot of the world as it existed when the satellite passed overhead. Because a satellite image, like a photograph, makes no assertion, it isn't hearsay.

The tack and coordinates present a more difficult question. Unlike a satellite image itself, labeled markers added to a satellite image do make clear assertions. Indeed, this is what makes them useful. For example, a dot labeled with the name of a town asserts that there's a town where you see the dot. The label "Starbucks" next to a building asserts that you'll be able to get a Frappuccino there. In short, labeled markers on a satellite image assert that the labeled item exists at the location of the marker.

If the tack is placed manually and then labeled (with a name or GPS coordinates), it's classic hearsay, akin to Aronson v. McDonald (9th Cir. 1957), where we held that hand-drawn additions to a map—there, topography lines—were hearsay. Google Earth allows for the functional equivalent of hand-drawn additions, as a user can place a tack manually and then label it however he chooses. This is like drawing an X on a paper map and labeling it "hidden treasure." That would be an assertion by the person drawing the X that treasure can be found at that location. Similarly, a user could place a tack, label it with incorrect GPS coordinates, and thereby misstate the true location of the tack.

Because there was no evidence at trial as to how the tack and its label were put on the satellite image, we must determine, if we can, whether the tack was computer-generated or placed manually. Fortunately, we can take judicial notice of the fact that the tack was automatically generated by the Google Earth program. By looking to "sources whose accuracy cannot reasonably be questioned"—here, the program—we can "accurately and readily determine[]" that the tack was placed automatically. See Fed.R.Evid. 201(b). Specifically, we can access Google Earth and type in the GPS coordinates, and have done so, which results in an identical tack to the one shown on the satellite image admitted at trial.

A tack placed by the Google Earth program and automatically labeled with GPS coordinates isn't hearsay. The hearsay rule applies only to out-of-court statements, and it defines a statement as "a *person's* oral assertion, written assertion, or nonverbal conduct." Fed.R.Evid. 801(a). Here, the relevant assertion isn't made by a person; it's made by the Google Earth program. Though a person types in the GPS coordinates, he has no role in figuring out where the tack will be placed. The real work is done by the computer program itself. The program analyzes the GPS coordinates and, without any human intervention, places a labeled tack on the satellite image. Because the program makes the relevant assertion—that the tack is accurately placed at the labeled GPS coordinates—there's no statement as defined by the hearsay rule. In reaching that conclusion, we join other circuits that have held that machine statements aren't hearsay.

That's not to say machine statements don't present evidentiary concerns. A machine might malfunction, produce inconsistent results or have been tampered with. But such concerns are addressed by the rules of authentication, not hearsay. Authentication requires the proponent of evidence to show that the evidence "is what the proponent claims it is." Fed.R.Evid. 901(a). A proponent must show that a machine is reliable and correctly calibrated, and that the data put into the machine (here, the GPS coordinates) is accurate. A specific subsection of the authentication rule allows for authentication of "a process or system" with evidence "describing [the] process or system and showing that it produces an accurate result." Fed.R.Evid. 901(b)(9). So when faced with an authentication objection, the proponent of Google–Earth–generated evidence would have to establish Google Earth's reliability and accuracy. That burden could be met, for example, with testimony from a Google Earth programmer or a witness who frequently works with and relies on the program. It could also be met through judicial notice of the program's reliability, as the Advisory Committee Notes specifically contemplate.

But defendant didn't raise an authentication objection at trial, nor does he raise one on appeal. He raised only a hearsay objection, and that objection was properly overruled. Because the satellite image and tack-coordinates pair weren't hearsay, their admission also didn't violate the Confrontation Clause.

Affirmed.

***

In the easier part of its opinion, the Ninth Circuit in *Lizarraga-Tirado* concluded that a satellite image is not hearsay because it is not an assertion. The same conclusion could be reached more clearly by noting that even if an image constitutes an assertion, a machine-generated image, like a photograph, is not authored by a "person."

With respect to the tack-coordinates, note the Ninth Circuit's painstaking (and necessary) effort to isolate the "relevant assertion." Here, the "assertion" was that the tack on the image corresponded to the coordinates shown. The author of *that* assertion was a computer not a person. When the true author of an out-of-court communication offered into evidence is a machine, no hearsay problem exists. Only assertions by "persons" can be "statements" under Rule 801(a).

The most difficult questions in this context come down to a matter of degree. When the court identifies any non-trivial human authorship in the out-of-court communication, the communication can properly be deemed a "statement."

"OUT-OF-COURT"

The hearsay definition in Federal Rule of Evidence 801(c)(1) exempts one kind of "statement" from its reach: statements that the testifying witness makes "at the current trial or hearing." This makes perfect sense. An assertion of fact made by a live witness testifying at trial is precisely the goal the hearsay prohibition seeks to achieve.

Leaving live witness' accounts of facts they perceived out of the hearsay definition in Rule 801(c) is uninteresting. The noteworthy aspect of this portion of the hearsay definition is what is not carved out: a testifying witness's *own* out-of-court statements. Conscious of the weight of scholarly opinion against the Committee's choice, the Advisory Committee Note to Rule 801(c) candidly recognizes that there are good reasons not to include a testifying witness' prior statements in the hearsay definition. And, as we will see, a good number of testifying witness's own statements are either allowed through explicit carve outs from the hearsay prohibition, or admissible when offered as impeachment or (less commonly) corroboration. But evidentiary analysis is required in those circumstances because under Rule 801, even a witness' own prior statements can qualify as "hearsay."

Rule 801(c)(1) is typically summarized as prohibiting parties from introducing certain "out-of-court" statements to the factfinder. As a technical matter "out-of-court" is an imprecise shorthand. A statement uttered in court, but at a prior proceeding, can constitute "hearsay." Such a statement was not made, in the language of Rule 801(c)(1), at the *current* trial or hearing. Nevertheless, the "out-of-court" shorthand is ubiquitous and, in almost all cases, clarifying. Consequently, it is employed without future caveating throughout this chapter as a shorthand for statements not made "at the current trial or hearing."

TRUTH OF THE MATTER ASSERTED

Under Rule 801(c)(2), an out-of-court statement is only hearsay if it is offered to prove "the truth of the matter asserted" by the out-of-court declarant. Whether an out-of-court statement is being offered to prove the truth of the matter asserted is the most analytically demanding component of the hearsay definition.

It is important to recognize that when the rules talk about "the matter asserted," they are referring to the substance of what the out-of-court speaker was trying to communicate -- not necessarily the literal words uttered. Thus, if a defendant said sarcastically to a detective, "Yeah right, I am the killer - you got me," the matter asserted would be something like - "I am <u>not</u> the killer." If the defense offered the statement to suggest that the defendant was innocent, it would be hearsay. Similarly, an out-of-court speaker may impart information through a question (1) "Do you see the light is red?" or command (2) "Get out of the road!" Depending on the context, these utterances are likely assertions that (1) the light is red and (2) the person is standing in the road. The point is that substantial context is often needed to determine what an out-of-court speaker intended to communicate or assert. The answer to that question is the "matter asserted."

Once we identify the matter asserted, we can figure out if the statement is being offered to prove the "truth of the matter asserted." Rule 801(c)(2). If it is, the statement is hearsay.

There is a clear rationale for why the hearsay prohibition only applies to statements offered to prove the truth of the matter asserted. When a statement is offered to prove the truth of the matter asserted, the declarant's credibility is critical. Consequently, the evidence rules can demand that the opposing party be provided with an opportunity to employ the traditional tools for testing that credibility. The declarant should swear to tell the truth, testify in the presence of the factfinder, and endure cross-examination. If application of these credibility-testing tools is not possible, the statement can reasonably be excluded from evidence.

By contrast, when an out-of-court statement's importance does not depend on an assessment of its truth, the declarant's credibility becomes less important. The factfinder only needs to determine that the statement was uttered. This can be assessed through application of the traditional tools (the oath and cross-examination) to the in-court witness who testifies about the statement.

EFFECT ON THE LISTENER

Many successful non-hearsay (not-for-the-truth-of-the-matter-asserted) pathways of admission fit into familiar categories. For example, out-of-court statements are often relevant for the effect they had on someone who heard them. The party offering the statement can use this theory of relevance—that the statement provoked some relevant reaction, knowledge, or belief on the part of a person who heard it—to overcome a hearsay objection.

Perhaps the most straightforward illustration of the effect-on-the-listener purpose for offering an out-of-court statement is to show notice. A statement can be offered to demonstrate that a person who heard it was placed on notice of a pertinent matter. For example, in litigation over whether a hospital should bear responsibility for a doctor's alleged sexual harassment, the plaintiffs could introduce evidence of out-of-court complaints of harassment, not "for the truth of the matter asserted, that [the doctor] harassed other women, but to prove that [the hospital] was on notice that [he] might have been sexually harassing women."[1]

---

[1] Green v. Administrators of Tulane Educational Fund, 284 F.3d 642 (5th Cir. 2002).

The specific non-hearsay purposes in the effect-on-the-listener vein are limitless. Out-of-court statements are commonly offered to explain why an actor in the drama depicted for the jury acted a certain way. For example, a medical-malpractice defendant could offer out-of-court statements solicited from other doctors to suggest that the defendant sought expert advice and followed that advice during a disputed course of treatment.

PROBLEM 6-7: WHAT'S IN THE BAG?

A defendant is stopped getting off a train from Toronto, Canada to New York City after a police dog smells heroin in his luggage. Later, when on trial for knowingly possessing heroin, the defendant testifies that he was carrying the bag as a favor to a friend. The defendants testifies, "My friend Sammy told me that 'the bag is full of Canadian maple syrup for [Sammy's] uncle.'"

If the prosecution objects that the defendant's testimony is hearsay, how should a court rule?

UNITED STATES v. FELIZ
794 F.3d 123 (1st Cir. 2015)

On February 3, 2012, at 5:45 a.m., Puerto Rico police executed a search warrant at a home in Dorado, Puerto Rico. Five officers arrived at the house, where they found Feliz's mother, stepfather, minor sisters, and infant brother. Feliz himself, an eighteen-year-old with no criminal record, was not present. Feliz's stepfather Luis Rivera, the owner of the house, identified the bedroom in which Feliz had last stayed. The officers testified that they found a loaded pistol, more ammunition, eighty-seven capsules of cocaine base, and $1,384 in cash in the bedroom. They arrested Rivera, Feliz's stepfather, for possessing a firearm without a license. They then transported Rivera and the rest of the family, including the two-year-old infant, to the police station.

... According to the police officers, as the officers got into their patrol cars, Feliz appeared and approached the house. One of the officers, Agent José Vélez ... drove him to the police station. At the station, Agent Vélez ... gave Feliz ... Miranda warnings, ... verbally and in writing. Feliz signed that he understood his Miranda rights, and then, around 7:30 a.m., the police say he wrote a confession on the reverse side of the Miranda form. The confession

216

stated that Feliz owned the gun, drugs, and money, and that his family did not know of them.…

Feliz and his mother, Hortencia Feliz, recounted a different tale. According to them, [before Feliz confessed, they overheard] the officers [tell] him that if he failed to confess, his mother, a Dominican national, would be deported … and sisters removed to the custody of the state.

[Editor Note: The testimony from Feliz's family members came out during a hearing before a magistrate on whether the confession should be excluded as involuntary in violation of the Constitution. At a pretrial hearing on this same question, the District Court judge deemed the family members' testimony about what the agents said to Feliz to be inadmissible hearsay. The judge told Feliz's lawyer, "if you want that proof to come in, you have to Subpoena the police."

Feliz objected to this ruling on appeal. *Before you read on, think about how you would articulate an argument that the district court judge erred.*]

The district court curtailed the record before it when it excluded as hearsay Hortencia's testimony that she heard a police officer threaten Feliz with the deportation of his mother and state custody for his siblings. The court never evaluated the two competing accounts, because it ruled that only one account was before it.

This was plain error. Hearsay is a statement "the declarant does not make while testifying at the current trial or hearing," and "a party offers in evidence to prove the truth of the matter asserted in the statement." Fed.R.Evid. 801(c). Feliz did not attempt to introduce testimony of the officers' threats for the truth of the matter asserted. Hortencia testified, for example, that the officer said "your siblings are all going to the Department of Family." Before the magistrate judge, Hortencia testified that an officer said to Feliz, "We are going to deport your mother." She also testified there that the officers told Feliz that if he did not turn himself in, "they were going to deport me and they were going to call the Department of the Family to take the boy and girls." That testimony would not show that Feliz's siblings would truly be sent to the Department of the Family if he did not turn himself into police custody, or that she would have been deported. Rather, the testimony, if credible, would show the fact that the police officer made the threat to Feliz, a fact within

Hortencia's personal knowledge. See Fed.R.Evid. 801(c) advisory committee's note ("If the significance of an offered statement lies solely in the fact that it was made, no issue is raised as to the truth of anything asserted, and the statement is not hearsay."); United States v. Bellomo (2d Cir. 1999) ("Statements offered as evidence of ... threats ..., rather than for the truth of the matter asserted therein, are not hearsay.").

The government falls back to its misunderstanding of the hornbook rule of evidence that an out-of-court statement may be offered to "show the effect of the words spoken on the listener." Since Hortencia was not the intended recipient of the threat, the argument goes, she could not testify to it.

That is incorrect. The testimony here was offered to show the effect of the words spoken on the listener, Feliz. Even though Hortencia was not the target of the threat, she could still testify that the officer made the threatening statement and it was heard by Feliz. The factfinder can then infer the effect on Feliz from that testimony.... [T]he formulation "effect of the words on the listener" is not a rigid hearsay exception, but an example of a "more common type[ ] of nonhearsay utterance[ ]." As we have already explained, this statement is a nonhearsay utterance because it is not being used to prove the truth of the matter asserted.

> [Footnote] There is no safe harbor for the government in the fact that the Federal Rules of Evidence do not generally apply in suppression hearings. If anything, the inapplicability of the Federal Rules of Evidence provide further support for why Hortencia should have been permitted to testify about what she heard, because the evidence was clearly relevant.

We vacate the order denying the motion to suppress, vacate the judgment of conviction, and remand for further proceedings consistent with this opinion. Upon remand, the case shall be assigned to a different judge for a new proceeding.

***

The familiar non-hearsay categories can be useful shorthand for communicating with courts. But, as the preceding opinion demonstrates, it is a common mistake to view these categories as having independent analytical power. The analysis is never whether an out-of-court statement can be labeled with a category name, such as "verbal act," "independent legal effect," or "effect on the listener." These categories are imprecisely defined and never dispositive. The decisive legal question is always whether the statement is being offered for the truth of the matter asserted. As one court explains:

> So long as out-of-court statements are not offered for their truth, they are not hearsay, it is unnecessary to fit such statements into one particular category, like verbal act, although this is often done, primarily as a short-hand way of explaining the non-hearsay purpose for which the statement is offered.[1]

VERBAL ACTS

Sometimes the mere utterance of certain words constitutes a relevant fact. The best example of this is a criminal threat. In many jurisdictions it is a criminal offense to place someone in fear of physical harm through words. A federal law, 18 U.S.C. § 871, makes it a criminal offense to "knowingly and willfully" make "any threat ... to inflict bodily harm upon the President of the United States." If a prosecutor introduced a suspect's threat against the President, that threat would be relevant to prove the charge irrespective of the truth of the matter asserted.

PROBLEM 6-8: "HE'S NOT HERE"

The following example comes from the case of Foreman v. United States (D.C. 2002).

> "The Detective responsible for executing the arrest warrant for [George] Foreman was questioned by the government concerning the events that occurred that evening at Ms. Nicholas' home. He testified that it was 2:30 a.m. on September 26, when the police officers arrived at Ms. Nicholas' apartment. Ms. Nicholas answered the door and was informed that they had an arrest warrant for Foreman. Nicholas told the police that Foreman was not there but that her boyfriend was upstairs. The officers entered the apartment and soon located an

---

[1] U.S. v. Murphy, 193 F.3d 1 (1st Cir. 1999).

individual upstairs. The detective, who had become familiar with Foreman's face, recognized the man as appellant. Ms. Nicholas, however, produced a false identification card for Foreman, one that had his photograph and another name. Defense counsel objected generally to the questions concerning Ms. Nicholas' attempt to produce the false identification card without stating a basis for the objection."

The evidence described above was offered to suggest Foreman's consciousness of guilt of the murder that police were seeking to arrest him for, and his efforts to avoid capture. The D.C. Court of Appeals ultimately ruled that it was inadmissible hearsay. Is the Detective's testimony about: (1) Nicholas' statement that "Foreman was not there"; and (2) her offering false identification for Foreman hearsay?

"IMPLIED" ASSERTIONS[1]

The next excerpt from a treatise illustrates one of the most conceptually difficult and controversial aspects of the federal hearsay definition:

> The hearsay prohibition seeks to limit the admission of statements that communicate an out-of-court declarant's beliefs. The inability to cross-examine the declarant in such circumstances generates understandable concerns about relying on these beliefs in formal trial proceedings....
>
> Statements communicating an out-of-court speaker's beliefs virtually always fell within the broad common law conception of hearsay. But many such statements do not fall within the modern hearsay definition employed by the federal rules. That is because the federal rules' definition of hearsay is narrower than the common law definition, even if many outside the legal academy fail to fully appreciate this fact.
>
> > [Footnote] See U.S. v. Zenni, 492 F. Supp. 464 (E.D. Ky. 1980) ("many members of the bar are unfamiliar with the marked departure from the common law the Federal Rules have effected on this issue").

---

[1] Wright & Bellin § 6724 ("Implied Assertions and the Great Hearsay Definition Controversy").

This evolution of the hearsay definition confuses commentators, courts and attorneys who sometimes view hearsay through a simpler, broader perspective analogous to that of the English common law.

A helpful illustration of the English-common-law-to-federal-rules evolution of the hearsay definition comes from the classic English case of Wright v. Tatham. There, a plaintiff seeking to establish the competency of a testator offered letters written to the testator, including one by a new arrival to the Virginia colonies. The letter included the declarant's depressing, and archaically-spelled, view of conditions in colonial Virginia:

> When I arivd. I was no little consirned to find the Town in a Most Shocking Condition the People Dieing from 5 to 10 per day & scarsely a Single House in Town cleare of Descease which proves to be the Putrid Fevour.

These statements were not offered to prove the truth of the matter asserted (the ghastly conditions in Alexandria, Virginia). Instead, the letters were offered as evidence of the letter writers' belief in the testator's sound mental capacity. Even so, the relevance of the letters depended on the out-of-court declarants' beliefs (here, an apparent belief in the mental lucidity of the letters' intended recipient). Applying the common law's broad conception of the hearsay concept, the English court in Wright v. Tatham condemned the letters as hearsay.

Yet the letters considered in Wright v. Tatham would not constitute hearsay under the definition adopted by the Federal Rules of Evidence. The federal rules' drafters exempted such out-of-court statements from the hearsay definition because the drafters viewed statements reflecting a declarant's belief as sufficiently reliable for admission if that belief was not intended to be communicated by the declarant.... [S]incerity is one of the most important hearsay concerns. If the letter writers were not trying to communicate anything about the testator's competence, the theory underlying the federal hearsay definition goes, we would not expect them to be deceitful on that point....

[I]n assessing whether an out-of-court statement is hearsay, courts applying the federal hearsay definition must apply a narrow hearsay definition that focuses on the intent of the out-of-court declarant. Information communicated by out-of-court speakers or actors does not qualify as hearsay under the federal hearsay definition, "in the absence of an intent to assert." This is because "nothing is an assertion unless intended to be one." Thus, when identifying whether a statement is offered for the "truth of the matter asserted" under Rule 801(c), even assertive conduct (whether nonverbal or verbal) will not be hearsay if it is offered as a basis for inferring something other than what the out-of-court declarant intended to assert. Or, in the words of the Advisory Committee, out-of-court conduct and words will not constitute hearsay, "if offered as a basis for inferring something other than the matter asserted" by the out-of-court declarant. [quotes in above paragraph are from Advisory Committee Note to Fed. R. Evid. 801(a)]

.... Similar analysis applies to the ... hearsay treatment of statements of alleged accomplices who try to protect or reassure hapless defendants by informing them of pending danger or its absence. Perhaps the most prominent example comes from United States v. Reynolds. There, a suspect who had just been placed under arrest (Reynolds) informed an accomplice (Parran), "I didn't tell them anything about you." The Fifth Circuit determined that Reynolds' statement was hearsay. Its opinion includes this flawed passage:

> [T]he statement's relevance goes well beyond the fact that it was uttered. It is not merely intended to prove that Reynolds could speak, or that he could speak in English, or even that he directed a statement toward Parran. Instead, the government offers it to prove the truth of the assumed fact of defendant's guilt implied by its content.

The Fifth Circuit's analysis would be unobjectionable if it were applying the common law. And, in fact, Reynolds cites pre-rules cases to support its analysis. But the 1983 opinion purports to be applying the federal rules, and under Rule 801(a)-(c) the proper analysis of even oral communications is what was intended to be asserted. If the declarant intended to assert that he knew of Parran's wrongdoing or was Parran's accomplice, his out-of-court statement offered to prove that fact would be hearsay. Perhaps such an intent could be inferred from the police-officer-audience around Reynolds during his arrest. But if Reynolds did not intend to assert that he was Parran's accomplice (or some more-subtle variant of that sentiment), the statement was not offered for the truth of the matter intended to be asserted by Reynolds and was not hearsay under Rule 801(c).

[N]on-hearsay treatment of Reynolds' statement respects the consistency in the federal hearsay definition's treatment of oral, written and nonverbal assertions. If Parran or Reynolds had attempted to take incriminating evidence from each other for disposal during Reynolds' arrest, or assaulted the police in an effort to free the other accomplice, that nonverbal conduct would not be hearsay. Similarly, when one accomplice attempts to assist another through words, those words ("verbal conduct which is assertive") are not hearsay as long as they are not offered to prove the truth of the matter intended to be asserted. Stated another way, Reynolds' apparent attempt to reassure or assist Parran avoid capture is relevant, irrespective of the truth of Reynolds' assertion. Consequently, those attempts whether consisting of an oral assertion, a written assertion or nonverbal conduct are not captured within the federal definition of hearsay.

PROBLEM 6-9: THE ILLEGAL LIBRARY

Imagine that the Police Chief wants to prove that a particular location is acting as a book lending library. The Chief sends an undercover police officer to lurk near the suspected check-out desk to surreptitiously watch and report what occurs.

Later, the officer seeks to testify about a patron's interaction with a librarian. The officer testifies that the patron approached the checkout desk holding a book and stated, "I would like to check out this book." *Is that out-of-court statement hearsay?*

Consider next the related context where police arrest someone for drug dealing and then observe incoming text messages or calls requesting drugs on the suspect's phone. *Can the officer testify that the drug dealer's phone lit up with a text message from an unknown person, "Are you carrying? I need a refill."* Consider this quote from a Second Circuit case: "An assumption has a fair claim to be treated as non-hearsay since the attendant risks are not as intensively implicated as when the idea is directly enunciated in a statement."[1] *Can you translate the "fair claim" notion into an application of the federal hearsay definition?*

STATE VARIATION: TEXAS HEARSAY

Professor Oliver Wellborn of the University of Texas strongly criticized the intent-focused federal hearsay definition when it was first adopted. His influence resulted in Texas adopting a different hearsay definition. Texas Rule of Evidence 801 largely tracks the federal definition, but includes this additional provision:

> (c) "Matter asserted" means:
>
> > (1) any matter a declarant explicitly asserts; and
> >
> > (2) any matter implied by a statement, if the probative value of the statement as offered flows from the declarant's belief about the matter.

Would your answers to the previous problem change under the Texas Rules of Evidence?

GUIDED PROBLEM 6-10: THE SAFE COMBINATION

Here is an analytically challenging example offered by the Ninth Circuit:

> After a safe is opened illegally, police search the defendant and find a piece of paper in his pocket reading '26–32–7,' which the parties stipulate is the combination to the safe. At trial, the government offers the piece of paper as evidence that the defendant had the combination and, therefore, was in a position to open the safe. A hearsay objection is made—and overruled. After all, the words on the paper are not being offered for their truth; what the combination is is not an issue at trial. Rather, they are offered as circumstantial evidence that the defendant had the wherewithal to open the safe.[2]

---

[1] Headley v. Tilghman, 53 F.3d 472 (2d Cir. 1995).
[2] United States v. Arteaga, 117 F.3d 388 (9th Cir. 1997).

Do you see a problem with the court's explanation? Here is a critique of the court's reasoning:

> The court is right that the paper with the safe combination is not hearsay. But its explanation is flawed,…. Contrary to the court's claim, "what the combination is" is most definitely "an issue at trial." If the defendant had a piece of paper with numbers that did not constitute the safe combination, the paper would have no relevance at all. The reason the piece of paper is not hearsay is that the paper itself is not being offered to prove the combination of the safe. The court acknowledges this critical fact in its example, stating "the parties stipulate" that the numbers constitute "the combination to the safe." Thus, the safe combination is very much an issue in the case, but it is established through other evidence: here a stipulation. The paper is then introduced not to establish the safe combination, but to show that the defendant possessed the combination. Sure, the paper is "circumstantial evidence," but that could not be further from the point. The paper is not hearsay, because it is not being offered to prove what it asserts—the safe combination. And only out-of-court statements that are offered to prove the truth of the matter asserted are hearsay.[1]

***

Just because a party claims there is a non-hearsay purpose does not mean that there is one. The next case illustrates a common, problematic use of out-of-court statements in court.

UNITED STATES v. SILVA
380 F.3d 1018 (7th Cir. 2004)

EASTERBROOK, Circuit Judge.

Juan Silva was the subject of an extensive undercover operation that included a confidential informant, ground and aerial surveillance, and tape-recorded conversations. A jury convicted Silva of conspiracy and possession with intent

---

[1] Wright & Bellin § 6725.

to distribute methamphetamine. Sentenced to 121 months' imprisonment, he argues on appeal that he was convicted on the basis of hearsay and is entitled to a new trial.

A few examples of the evidence to which he objected will suffice. Agent Zamora, who coordinated the operation for the Drug Enforcement Administration, testified at trial to conversations conducted between the DEA's confidential informant (whose identity remained secret and who therefore did not testify) and an alleged supplier, regarding a future sale of methamphetamine. Zamora testified that he heard the supplier (who likewise did not testify) use the name "Juan" several times during the conversations and that the informant spoke on several occasions of "this individual named Juan [who] indicated that he was going to be making the delivery." Other testimony elicited from Zamora and another agent concerned the attempted delivery of a sample of Silva's wares and conversations between Silva and the informant, plus the informant's observations.

The district judge overruled hearsay objections and instructed the jury that the evidence was "not being offered for the truth of the matter."....

So to what issue other than truth might the testimony have been relevant? The prosecutor contends that most of the statements were admissible to show "the actions taken by [each] witness." Allowing agents to narrate the course of their investigations, and thus spread before juries damning information that is not subject to cross-examination, would go far toward abrogating the defendant's rights under the sixth amendment and the hearsay rule. This court has warned against the potential for abuse when police testify to the out-of-court statements of a confidential informant. There are no doubt times when the testimony regarding a tip from an informant is relevant. If a jury would not otherwise understand why an investigation targeted a particular defendant, the testimony could dispel an accusation that the officers were officious intermeddlers staking out Silva for nefarious purposes. No such argument was made in this case, however, and no other explanation was given why the testimony would be relevant. Under the prosecution's theory, every time a person says to the police "X committed the crime," the statement (including all corroborating details) would be admissible to show why the police investigated X....

Here's another illustration. Police officer Jocson testified about a traffic stop of Luis Madrid for speeding. Silva was a passenger in this car. Jocson, who was unaware when he stopped Madrid's car that both Silva and Madrid were the targets of a federal investigation, testified that a search of the car turned up a few bundles of cash totaling $16,000 and "some plant-like materials consistent with cannabis." He continued: "At that time I called a crime scene technician to do a vacuum sweep of the trunk area to try to retrieve some of this plant like material, which we later tested as positive for cannabis." The court overruled Silva's objections and instructed the jury that the positive test—of which Jocson had no first-hand knowledge—was "not being offered for the truth of the matter, but for the actions taken by this officer only."

In what way could test results have explained Jocson's actions, let alone been relevant to the charges for which Silva was on trial? Jocson did not find methamphetamine. He was not aware of the federal investigation, and the lab tests, which post-dated the traffic stop, could not have "explained" any of Jocson's actions on the scene. Silva was not charged with any offense related to marijuana, …. So the evidence about events during and after the traffic stop either was irrelevant or was being used to show that Silva had a propensity for drug dealing. The latter explanation seems superior: when the prosecutor asked Jocson what he thought the cash revealed, Jocson replied that he thought it "was the result of drug smuggling acts, which would essentially be proceeds from narcotics transactions."

Perhaps all of this could be dismissed as harmless. The record has plenty of admissible evidence, and the judge did tell the jury that the contested evidence had not been admitted for a substantive use. Come the closing argument, however, the prosecutor explicitly used some of the hearsay as evidence of Silva's guilt. Defense counsel objected to the violation of the court's rulings that the evidence was not to be used to show Silva's culpability. Instead of sustaining the objection and giving a curative instruction, the judge told the jury:

> The jury will determine what the evidence shows and why it was admitted. If it was admitted for a different purpose, they will make that decision. I ruled on all of that. They heard the evidence. And if the evidence was not admitted for that purpose, they will so take it into account.

What was the jury to make of this? It left the prosecutor's transgressions without correction. Inviting a jury to decide for itself what evidence to use and how to use it amounts to abdication by the district judge. The subject before the court was not merely "what the evidence shows" (a perfectly acceptable question for the jury) but also whether the evidence was admissible for the purpose for which the prosecutor was using it. When the prosecutor violated the limitations on the evidence's use, the judge had to set things straight. This he failed to do; instead of enforcing his rulings, he abandoned them and deferred to the prosecutor and the jurors....

Far too much use was made of hearsay in this trial. Silva is entitled to another.

Reversed and Remanded

***

One way to view the *Silva* case is that the out of court statements were not relevant for anything other than their truth. Another way is to think of the statements' non-hearsay relevance as extremely minimal leading to exclusion under Rule 403.

IMPEACHMENT

A statement offered as impeachment need not be offered for the truth of the matter asserted. A statement is relevant to a witness' credibility if it shows that the witness said something that is inconsistent with their present testimony. This theory of relevance does not depend on the truth of the out-of-court statement. The factfinder need not decide that the out-of-court statement is true to conclude that a witness who says different things on different occasions regarding the same point is less worthy of belief on that point than would otherwise be the case. Or, as explained by one court with algebraic precision: "If a witness says 'X' on the stand, his out-of-court statement 'not-X' impeaches him, whether X is true or not."[1]

Importantly, this non-hearsay theory of relevance only works when the out-of-court statement being offered was made by the testifying witness. An effort to impeach a witness with an out-of-court statement made by another person

---

[1] U.S. v. Arteaga, 117 F.3d 388 (9th Cir. 1997).

necessarily relies on the truth of the out-of-court statement and, consequently, requires a hearsay exception for admission.

UNITED STATES v. INCE
21 F.3d 576 (4th Cir. 1994)

MURNAGHAN, Circuit Judge:

…. [After a shooting during] a rap concert and dance at the Sosa Recreation Center at Fort Belvoir, Virginia … Defendant-appellant Nigel Ince, Angela Neumann, and two of their friends hopped in their van and headed for Pence Gate, Fort Belvoir's nearest exit. The military police pulled the van, as well as other vehicles leaving the parking lot, over to the side of the road and asked the drivers and passengers to stand on the curb…. As part of the investigation that followed, Military Policeman Roger Stevens interviewed and took a signed, unsworn statement from Neumann. She recounted that Ince had admitted to firing the shots, but said he no longer had the gun.

The United States indicted Ince for assault with a dangerous weapon, with intent to do bodily harm. At Ince's trial the Government called Neumann to the stand. When her memory supposedly failed her, the prosecution attempted to refresh her recollection with a copy of the signed statement that she had given Stevens on the night of the shooting. Even with her recollection refreshed, she testified that she could no longer recall the details of her conversation with Ince. Following Neumann's testimony, the Government excused her and called Stevens, who testified (over the objection of defense counsel) as to what Neumann had told him shortly after the shooting. The trial ended with a deadlocked jury.

At the second trial, the Government again called Neumann. She again acknowledged that she had given the military police a signed statement describing what Ince had told her immediately after the shooting. But she repeatedly testified that she could no longer recall the details of Ince's remarks, despite the prosecution's effort to refresh her recollection with a copy of the statement….

Over defense counsel's repeated objections, the Government again called MP Stevens to the stand, supposedly to impeach Neumann as to her memory loss.

He testified that, within hours of the shooting, Neumann had told him that Ince had confessed to firing the gun. The Government also called two eyewitnesses who identified Ince as the gunman.

The defense's theory of the case was mistaken identity: Frank Kelly, not Nigel Ince, had fired the shots.... In an attempt to undermine the defense's theory of the case, the prosecution, in its closing argument, reminded the jurors that they had "heard testimony that Ms. Neumann made a statement to an MP [immediately following the shooting]. And she told [him] at that time that the defendant said, 'Frank didn't shoot the gun; I shot the gun.'"

The second time around, the jury convicted Ince. The district judge sentenced him to forty-one months in prison, plus two years of supervised release. Ince now appeals, requesting a reversal of his conviction and a new trial.

II

Appellant Ince argues that the testimony of MP Stevens was inadmissible hearsay because the Government offered it to prove the truth of the matter asserted in Neumann's out-of-court statement (i.e., that Ince confessed to the crime). The United States counters that Stevens's testimony was admissible because the Government offered it only to impeach Neumann's credibility. Ince responds that the prosecution, having already seen Neumann's performance on the stand at the first trial, was fully aware that she would not testify as to Ince's alleged confession at the second trial either. Nevertheless, the prosecution put her on the stand a second time to elicit testimony inconsistent with her prior statement to Stevens, so as to provide a foundation to offer Stevens's so-called "impeaching" evidence and thereby to get Ince's confession before the jury. Thus, the sole question presented on appeal is whether the admission of Stevens's testimony constituted reversible error.

A

Rule 607 of the Federal Rules of Evidence provides that "[t]he credibility of a witness may be attacked by any party, including the party calling the witness." One method of attacking the credibility of (i.e., impeaching) a witness is to show that he has previously made a statement that is inconsistent with his present testimony. Even if that prior inconsistent statement would otherwise be inadmissible as hearsay, it may be admissible for the limited purpose of impeaching the witness....

Federal evidence law does not ask the judge, either at trial or upon appellate review, to crawl inside the prosecutor's head to divine his or her true motivation. Rather, in determining whether a Government witness' testimony offered as impeachment is admissible, or on the contrary is a "mere subterfuge" to get before the jury substantive evidence which is otherwise inadmissible as hearsay, a trial court must apply Federal Rule of Evidence 403 and weigh the testimony's impeachment value against its tendency to prejudice the defendant unfairly or to confuse the jury.

When the prosecution attempts to introduce a prior inconsistent statement to impeach its own witness, the statement's likely prejudicial impact often substantially outweighs its probative value for impeachment purposes because the jury may ignore the judge's limiting instructions and consider the "impeachment" testimony for substantive purposes. That risk is multiplied when the statement offered as impeachment testimony contains the defendant's alleged admission of guilt....

B

In the case at bar, MP Stevens testified that Ince had admitted to firing the gun—the critical element of the crime for which he was being tried. It is hard to imagine any piece of evidence that could have had a greater prejudicial impact than such a supposed naked confession of guilt. Even if the other evidence which was properly admitted at trial had provided overwhelming proof of Ince's guilt—which it did not—and even if the judge had given the jury a clear limiting instruction—which he did not—Stevens's presentation of additional unsworn hearsay testimony going directly to the issue of Ince's guilt was extremely prejudicial.

Given the likely prejudicial impact of Stevens's testimony, the trial judge should have excluded it absent some extraordinary probative value. Because evidence of Neumann's prior inconsistent statement was admitted solely for purposes of impeachment, its probative value must be assessed solely in terms of its impeaching effect upon Neumann's testimony or overall credibility. Our review of the record below, however, shows that the probative value of Stevens's testimony for impeachment purposes was nil. Unlike the classic "turncoat" witness, Neumann certainly had not shocked the Government with her "loss of memory" at the second trial, as she had made it plain during the first trial that she would not readily testify to the alleged confession of her friend, Nigel Ince.

Furthermore, Neumann's actual in-court testimony did not affirmatively damage the Government's case; she merely refused to give testimony that the Government had hoped she would give. Thus, the prosecution had no need to attack her credibility. She testified that, immediately after the shooting, as they left the scene of the crime but before the military police pulled them over, (1) Ince stated that Frank Kelly—the person whom Ince's lawyer identified at trial as the likely perpetrator of the crime—was not the person who had fired the gun, (2) Ince stated that "he didn't have [the gun] with him," and (3) Ince instructed Neumann to tell the military police that she knew nothing about the events of the evening. She presented no evidence affirming or denying Ince's alleged confession. Taken as a whole, then, Neumann's testimony probably strengthened the Government's case. Therefore, evidence attacking her credibility had no probative value for impeachment purposes.

Because Stevens's so-called "impeachment" testimony was both highly prejudicial and devoid of probative value as impeachment evidence, the trial judge should have recognized the Government's tactic for what it was—an attempt to circumvent the hearsay rule and to infect the jury with otherwise inadmissible evidence of Ince's alleged confession....

Accordingly, we reverse the conviction of Nigel D. Ince and remand the case for a new trial.

***

As *Ince* demonstrates, introducing an out-of-court for something other than the truth of the matter asserted has consequences for the statement's admissibility under other rules, most obviously Rule 403. When an out-of-court statement is introduced as something other than substantive evidence, its probative value is often lessened (sometimes dramatically) and a danger of unfair prejudice arises -- that the jury will consider the statement as evidence of the truth of the matter asserted.

***

The best way to master hearsay is to practice. Here is a series of challenging hearsay problems that you can work through to test your understanding of the hearsay definition.

HEARSAY PROBLEMS

1. During a road-rage incident, a driver yells, "I am going to kill you" at another driver, while waving a gun. Is that statement hearsay if offered as evidence that the driver made a criminal threat?

2. The prosecution alleges that an accountant was involved in a criminal conspiracy with members of an organized crime family. To support its allegation, the prosecution seeks to introduce a screenshot of the contacts from the accountant's cell phone, which includes the names and phone numbers of people who other evidence shows are members of the crime family. Is the following screenshot hearsay?

   > Jimmy Two Guns 757-555-5551
   > Freddy Five Knives 757-555-5552
   > Barbara Brass Knuckles 757-555-5559

3. On direct examination at trial, a witness states that the defendant was holding a gun during a robbery. The defense now seeks to have a police detective testify that during the initial interview, the witness told the detective that the witness "did not see any weapons" during the robbery. Is the detective's testimony about what the witness said hearsay?

4. The police go to Brandon's house to arrest him for committing a recent arson. When they knock on the door, the suspect's brother answers. The police ask, "Is Brandon here?" The brother says, "No, I haven't seen him in weeks." The officers then see Brandon sneaking out a window. Is the brother's statement hearsay if offered in a later prosecution to suggest Brandon's involvement in wrongdoing?

5. Police find a diary that details a number of terrible crimes. The first page of the diary contains the following inscription: "property of Jesse James." Can the prosecutor offer the inscription as proof that Jesse James owns the diary?

6. A teenager sits down on a couch with a large bowl of spaghetti and red sauce. The teenager's parent exclaims: "Do you know how much that couch costs? Get off it with that spaghetti!" Hearsay if offered to prove that the couch was expensive?

7. A bank robber presents a note to a teller, "I have a gun. Give me the money in the register. No dye packs, no silent alarms, and no one will get hurt. Do it quickly." Is the note hearsay if offered to prove that the robber was armed? What if the note is only offered to prove that the bank was robbed?

8. A police dog smells drugs in a piece of luggage circling around an airport carousel. The luggage, an expensive electric pink rolling suitcase, has a label on its handle that states, "Freddie Langle," and a large purple sticker on the front that says, "Minnesota Vikings" - a professional sports team. As a police officer pulls the luggage off the carousel, an onlooker, Freddie Langle turns to the person next to him, Allison, and says, "I didn't tell anyone! How did they catch us so fast!?"

Analyze the following for hearsay if offered at a later trial:

- The luggage label, if offered to prove that the suitcase belonged to Freddie.
- The Minnesota Vikings sticker if offered to prove that the luggage belonged to Freddie (along with testimony from Freddie's mother that Freddie is an avid Vikings fan).
- Freddie's statement to Allison to support the government's claim that Allison was involved in the transportation of drugs in the luggage.

9. An entry in a hotel guestbook that states the name, "Gwyneth Paltrow" if offered as evidence that Gwyneth Paltrow stayed at the hotel?

10. Accomplice A texts Suspect S the following message, "Cops on the scene, lay low!" Hearsay if offered to prove that A and S are working together?

11. After Laci Peterson disappeared, police suspected her husband, Scott Peterson, of the crime. In an interview with ABC news, Scott stated that he did not believe Laci was dead and was looking forward to her safe return. Later, he was asked to describe his spouse. He stated, "She **was** amazing, is amazing." In a later trial proceeding, would that statement be hearsay if offered to prove that Scott knew that his wife was dead, and therefore was more likely the murderer?

12. This book has "Made in the USA" stamped on it. Is there a hearsay problem with introducing the stamped page as evidence of where the book was manufactured?

13. A murder is committed with a crossbow in a small retirement community. Police Officer Vinnie questions the victim's neighbors. One of the neighbors tells Vinnie, "Jimmy owns a crossbow." In a later trial of Jimmy for the murder, Officer Vinnie seeks to testify about what the neighbor told him. The defense objects that it is hearsay. The prosecutor responds, "The neighbor's statement is not being offered to prove that Jimmy had a crossbow. We are offering it as evidence that Jimmy killed the victim." How should the trial court rule?

14. Jill sends a tweet that says the following: "Don't worry about me ever running out of food, I live near Allie's apple orchard!" In a later case about theft of some apples found in Jill's home that were taken from Allie's orchard, would Jill's tweet be hearsay if offered to prove that Jill knew about the orchard?

15. In a kidnapping case, a young victim tells a police detective all about the home in which she was held. For example, the victim states, "The room was blue and had a large picture of an elephant." The defendant, however, contends that he has been wrongfully accused and he "has never met, much less had the victim over to his house." The victim is unable to testify at trial. The prosecution seeks to introduce the victim's statement along with a video of the room where the police alleged the victim was held. The video shows a large picture of an elephant on a blue wall. The defense seeks to offer the defendant's statement quoted above. Is any of this evidence hearsay?

16. Kansas police raided a house in Wichita after receiving a tip that the house's owner was growing marijuana on the extensive wooded property. At a trial of the person who lived at the home, Roger Emmons, the prosecution introduced "a hand-drawn map found in [the] kitchen, which [an officer] testified at trial corresponded to the configuration of the marijuana patches" found on the property. The prosecution argues that the map was offered to show Emmons' knowledge of the marijuana on his property. Hearsay?

RULE 801 HEARSAY EXEMPTIONS

Rule 802 states that hearsay is prohibited unless its admission is authorized by statute or rule. As we will see, there are many rules that authorize the admission of hearsay. This section covers those rules.

First, an aside on terminology. The Federal Rules include two kinds of exemptions from the hearsay prohibition. Sometimes, as in Rule 801(d), the rules carve out certain categories of out-of-court statements as **"not hearsay."** Other categories of hearsay statements are allowed into evidence through an **"exception"** to the hearsay prohibition in Rules 803, 804, and 807. While a few judges are sticklers for this "not hearsay" versus "hearsay exception" terminology, it is analytically irrelevant. As the Advisory Committee acknowledges, statements admitted under Rule 801(d) "literally fall within the definition" of hearsay. Declaring them "not hearsay" is a product of tradition not logic. It is also unfortunate. Under the federal rules, litigators and judges must distinguish between: (i) statements that are not hearsay because they do not satisfy the definition of hearsay in Rule 801(c); and (ii) statements that, while satisfying that definition, are nonetheless admissible because they are deemed "not hearsay" by fiat in Rule 801(d). Giving these two distinct categories the same "not hearsay" label is a recipe for confusion.

Analytically, it is cleaner to consider statements admitted through Rule 801(d) as "hearsay" that is nonetheless admissible through an exception to the hearsay prohibition delineated by either Rule 801(d)(1) (certain witness's prior statements) or Rule 801(d)(2) (certain opposing party's statements). Nothing is lost by approaching the hearsay problem this way and needless confusion can be avoided.

STATEMENTS OF TESTIFYING WITNESSES

RULE 801(d)(1)

The Advisory Committee Note to Rule 801(d)(1) reveals the Committee's ambivalence about including a testifying witness' own prior statements within the hearsay definition. To support the decision, the drafters cited a state court opinion that provides an argument for restricting out-of-court statements of testifying witnesses:

> The chief merit of cross examination is not that at some future time it gives the party opponent the right to dissect adverse testimony. Its principal virtue is in its immediate application of the testing process. Its strokes fall while the iron is hot.[1]

But as the Note reveals, the Advisory Committee seemed unconvinced, acknowledging the logic of the positions of Judge Learned Hand and Edmund Morgan that, if the witness is testifying in court, cross-examination regarding even previously expressed sentiments is adequate to the task of assessing reliability. The ambivalence comes through in the rule. The Advisory Committee rejected Hand and Morgan in crafting the hearsay definition, but nevertheless created exemptions for the admission of certain categories of testifying witness' prior *inconsistent* statements, Rule 801(d)(1)(A), and *consistent* statements, Rule 801(d)(1)(B).

Subject to Cross-Examination

For each of its exceptions, Rule 801(d)(1) ensures the opponent of any out-of-court statements an opportunity to cross-examine the declarant at the current trial. Thus, it is a necessary but not sufficient prerequisite to admission under Rule 801(d)(1) that the declarant testify at the current proceeding. Rule 801(d)(1) also requires that the declarant be subject to cross-examination about the prior statement. Since testimony and cross-examination are invariably intertwined, satisfaction of this requirement is rarely controversial. In the typical case, the declarant of a statement offered under Rule 801(d) testifies at trial and engages with cross-examination questions about the out-of-court statement. Nevertheless, there are times when satisfaction of the "subject to cross-examination" requirement is in doubt.

The primary questions in the "subject to cross-examination" context arise when a witness is present at trial but is either unwilling or unable to answer questions on cross-examination. One of the primary reasons a witness will

---

[1] State v. Saporen, 205 Minn. 358 (1939).

decline to answer is an inability to recollect the topic of the question. Prior to the next case, the evidentiary analysis of that scenario was unsettled.

UNITED STATES v. OWENS
484 U.S. 554 (1988)

Justice SCALIA delivered the opinion of the Court.

…. On April 12, 1982, John Foster, a correctional counselor at the federal prison in Lompoc, California, was attacked and brutally beaten with a metal pipe. His skull was fractured, and he remained hospitalized for almost a month. As a result of his injuries, Foster's memory was severely impaired. When Thomas Mansfield, an FBI agent investigating the assault, first attempted to interview Foster, on April 19, he found Foster lethargic and unable to remember his attacker's name. On May 5, Mansfield again spoke to Foster, who was much improved and able to describe the attack. Foster named respondent as his attacker and identified respondent from an array of photographs.

Respondent was tried in Federal District Court for assault with intent to commit murder. At trial, Foster recounted his activities just before the attack, and described feeling the blows to his head and seeing blood on the floor. He testified that he clearly remembered identifying respondent as his assailant during his May 5th interview with Mansfield. On cross-examination, he admitted that he could not remember seeing his assailant. He also admitted that, although there was evidence that he had received numerous visitors in the hospital, he was unable to remember any of them except Mansfield, and could not remember whether any of these visitors had suggested that respondent was the assailant. Defense counsel unsuccessfully sought to refresh his recollection with hospital records, including one indicating that Foster had attributed the assault to someone other than respondent. Respondent was convicted and sentenced to 20 years' imprisonment to be served consecutively to a previous sentence.

On appeal, the United States Court of Appeals for the Ninth Circuit considered challenges based on the Confrontation Clause and Rule 802 of the Federal Rules of Evidence. By divided vote it upheld both challenges … and reversed the judgment of the District Court.

[The Supreme Court first rejected the argument that the admission of the identification violated the Sixth Amendment Confrontation Clause: "[W]e agree with the answer suggested 18 years ago by Justice Harlan. '[T]he Confrontation Clause guarantees only 'an opportunity for effective cross-examination, not cross-examination that is effective in whatever way, and to whatever extent, the defense might wish.'"]

…. Respondent urges as an alternative basis for affirmance a violation of Federal Rule of Evidence 802, which generally excludes hearsay. Rule 801(d)(1)(C) defines as not hearsay a prior statement "of identification of a person made after perceiving the person," if the declarant "testifies at the trial or hearing and is subject to cross-examination concerning the statement." The Court of Appeals found that Foster's identification statement did not come within this exclusion because his memory loss prevented his being "subject to cross-examination concerning the statement."…

It seems to us that the more natural reading of "subject to cross-examination concerning the statement" includes what was available here. Ordinarily a witness is regarded as "subject to cross-examination" when he is placed on the stand, under oath, and responds willingly to questions. Just as with the constitutional prohibition, limitations on the scope of examination by the trial court or assertions of privilege by the witness may undermine the process to such a degree that meaningful cross-examination within the intent of the Rule no longer exists. But that effect is not produced by the witness' assertion of memory loss—which, as discussed earlier, is often the very result sought to be produced by cross-examination, and can be effective in destroying the force of the prior statement. Rule 801(d)(1)(C), which specifies that the cross-examination need only "concer[n] the statement," does not on its face require more.

…. For the reasons stated, we hold that neither the Confrontation Clause nor Federal Rule of Evidence 802 is violated by admission of an identification statement of a witness who is unable, because of a memory loss, to testify concerning the basis for the identification. The decision of the Court of Appeals is reversed.

***

Notice that the Court's language in *Owens* sweeps more broadly than the facts of that case. Justice Scalia's majority opinion does not simply state that a witness with significant, but not complete, memory gaps is still "subject to cross-examination." Rather, the opinion states that: "Ordinarily a witness is regarded as 'subject to cross-examination' when he is placed on the stand, under oath, and responds willingly to questions." This statement of a broad general principle appears to cover everything from the partial memory failings in *Owens* to complete and total memory loss.

To date, the federal courts largely follow *Owens'* lead. The only circumstances in federal case law where a testifying witness is deemed not subject to cross-examination are those suggested in *Owens*: a witness' refusal to answer questions citing privilege (even if the privilege claim is invalid); or a trial court's broad prohibition on pertinent cross-examination.

PRIOR INCONSISTENT STATEMENTS

RULE 801(d)(1)(A)

As explained in detail in a prior section, prior inconsistent statements of a testifying witness are routinely introduced to undermine the witness' credibility. Such statements need not be introduced for the truth of the matter asserted. A witness' prior inconsistent statements can be introduced solely as impeachment with any limits on admission left to Rules 401 and 403.

Prior statements of testifying witnesses can also be introduced as substantive evidence (for the truth of the matter asserted) if they qualify for admission under a hearsay exemption or exception. Rule 801(d)(1)(A) provides a hearsay exemption for certain inconsistent statements of a testifying witness.

The seemingly technical question of the hearsay treatment of prior inconsistent statements of testifying witnesses is an important one. Congress, a legislative body populated by former attorneys, recognized this fact. Indeed, the majority view prior to the enactment of Rule 801(d)(1)(A) was that witness' prior inconsistent statements were admissible only as impeachment and not as substantive evidence. Rule 801(d)(1)(A) represented a significant change to the law of evidence.

The change was almost more radical. The version of Rule 801(d)(1)(A) originally proposed by the Advisory Committee allowed all inconsistent statements of testifying witnesses to be introduced as substantive evidence. This fit the Advisory Committee's generally dim view of including testifying witness' prior statements within the hearsay definition. Congress saw things differently, consistent with its general reluctance to weaken the hearsay prohibition, and sporadically expressed desire to protect criminal defendants from prosecutorial overreach. The House of Representatives sought to severely limit the proposed rule, exempting only inconsistent statements made under oath and subject to cross-examination. The set of such statement is very small, consisting essentially of testimony at former trials and pretrial hearings. The Senate rejected the House limitations, intending to preserve a "realistic method ... for dealing with the turncoat witness who changes his story on the stand." The ultimately enacted rule reflects a compromise between the two chambers.

Under Rule 801(d)(1)(A), a statement by a testifying witness is exempted from the hearsay prohibition if it is inconsistent with the witness' testimony "and was given under penalty of perjury at a trial, hearing, or other proceeding, or in a deposition." By requiring that the prior statement be made under oath at a prior proceeding, the compromise vindicated the House's concern that there should "be no dispute as to whether the prior statement was made." By eliminating the House's proposed requirement that the prior statement itself have been subject to cross-examination, the compromise respected the Senate's desire to preserve a viable method for dealing with turncoat witnesses. The Conference Committee emphasized that the rule as adopted "covers statements before a grand jury," granting prosecutors a mechanism to "lock in" wavering witnesses. As the Seventh Circuit would later counsel: "Government officials dealing with witnesses who may later become uncooperative would be wise to secure their grand jury testimony while they are still cooperating."[1] This tactic works because, under Rule 801(d)(1)(A), a witness' statements to a grand jury can typically be introduced as substantive evidence if that same witness provides inconsistent testimony at a later trial.

---

[1] U.S. v. Schmitt, 770 F.3d 524 (7th Cir. 2014).

UNITED STATES v. CISNEROS-GUTIERREZ
517 F.3d 751 (5th Cir. 2008)

PATRICK E. HIGGINBOTHAM, Circuit Judge:

…. Edgardo Gutierrez (Edgardo), Defendant's brother, lived in DeSoto, Texas. He came to the attention of the Tarrant County Narcotics Task Force and the Drug Enforcement Agency (DEA) for his drug dealing….

[T]he Task Force and DEA executed [a] search warrant on Edgardo's house. Agents discovered several guns, some $47,000 in cash, and the interior shell of an ice chest containing thirteen pounds of methamphetamine in Edgardo's bedroom closet….

Defendant was charged in a superseding indictment with one count of conspiracy to possess with intent to distribute 500 grams or more of methamphetamine.

During post-arrest interviews with DEA Agent Ric Smith, Edgardo implicated Defendant in the drug conspiracy. In June 2005, Edgardo pled guilty to drug conspiracy and possession of a firearm during, and in connection with, a drug offense. Edgardo signed a factual resume that read in part, "[h]e agrees that he possessed the methamphetamine found in his master bedroom closet with the intent to distribute, that the Glock pistol belonged to him, and that his brother and co-defendant, Osvaldo Cisneros–Gutierrez delivered the methamphetamine to him from California prior to the execution of the search warrant on April 27, 2005." During his plea hearing, Edgardo admitted that the contents of the factual resume were true….

The week before Defendant's trial, Edgardo told the Government that he did not want to testify and that he was having problems remembering things….

At trial, the Government first called a number of law enforcement officers to testify regarding their investigation, and the surveillance and search of Edgardo's home. The Government then called Edgardo, initially treating him as a non-adverse witness. Edgardo exhibited extensive memory problems from the beginning of his testimony, and the district court allowed the Government to treat him as an adverse witness and to use leading questions. [See Fed. R. Ev. 611(c)]

Edgardo's testimony contradicted statements made during his interviews with Agent Smith. As the Government began to impeach Edgardo, Defendant requested that the court give the jury a limiting instruction on the use of prior statements admitted to impeach the witness…. The Government's questioning turned to Defendant's participation in Edgardo's drug dealing. Edgardo testified that Defendant had not agreed to bring the methamphetamine from California to him. The Government impeached Edgardo's testimony with his prior statements to Agent Smith; Edgardo generally stated that he could not recall making any of the statements to Agent Smith, and specifically said that he could not recall telling Agent Smith that Defendant and his cousin brought the methamphetamine from California. The Government then focused on Edgardo's factual resume, which the court admitted as impeachment evidence….

At the end of Edgardo's testimony, the Government moved to admit Edgardo's factual resume as substantive evidence under Rule 801(d)(1)(A)…. Defendant persisted in his objection that the factual resume was not admissible as substantive evidence. However, the court overruled his objection, and allowed a redacted version of the factual resume to be admitted as substantive evidence. Edgardo was recalled as a witness. After Defendant cross-examined Edgardo, the Government questioned him about the factual resume on re-direct. Edgardo specifically denied that Defendant brought the drugs from California, testifying that the drugs were already at his house when Defendant arrived for a visit.

The jury found Defendant guilty….

We begin with Defendant's contention that the district erred by admitting the redacted version of Edgardo's factual resume, which stated that Defendant delivered the methamphetamine, as substantive evidence under Rule 801(d)(1). Neither party cites to any precedent that is on point.

Rule 801(d)(1)(A) provides that "[a] statement is not hearsay if … [t]he declarant testifies at the trial or hearing and is subject to cross-examination concerning the statement, and the statement is inconsistent with the declarant's testimony, and was given under oath subject to the penalty of perjury at a trial, hearing, or other proceeding, or in a deposition." Edgardo testified at Defendant's trial and was subject to cross-examination.

We have previously concluded that a witness's "feigned" memory loss can be considered inconsistent under the Rule, for "'the unwilling witness often takes refuge in a failure to remember.'" The breadth and depth of Edgardo's claimed memory loss is facially suspect to say the least, and "[t]he district court reasonably could have concluded that this selective memory loss was more convenient than actual." Moreover, Edgardo denied that Defendant agreed to deliver methamphetamine to him during direct examination. While not a per se repudiation of the factual resume, "we do not read the word 'inconsistent' in Rule 801(d)(1)(A) to include only statements diametrically opposed or logically incompatible." Once the court indicated that the factual resume was substantively admissible, Defendant objected that Edgardo had not made an inconsistent statement; Edgardo was recalled as a witness and testified on re-redirect that the drugs were already at his home. We will not disturb the district court's finding of inconsistency on this record.

We are unaware of any decisions of this court, save one unpublished decision, addressing whether plea hearings fall within Rule 801(d)(1)(A)'s ambit. A number of our sister circuits have determined that plea hearings do. We are persuaded by this authority, and join them in so holding.

The difficulty is whether the factual resume constitutes a statement of Edgardo's given during the hearing under oath. The Government urges that Edgardo "adopted" the statement in the factual resume by testifying to its truth during his plea hearing, and we agree, while mindful that using the term "adoption" in these circumstances creates some awkwardness.

Although the factual resume was drafted by the Government, Edgardo inculpated Defendant in interviews with the Government, and the relevant wording in the resume indicates that it was based on Edgardo's admissions—the critical paragraph says that Edgardo cooperated with law enforcement and that he "agrees" that Defendant delivered the drugs. Prior to the plea hearing, Edgardo and his lawyer reviewed and signed the resume, and thereby, according to the resume, "agreed" to its content. At the hearing, Edgardo declined the opportunity to change or revise the factual resume, and stated that he understood its contents. Critical for our purposes, Edgardo admitted under oath that the factual resume was "true and correct in every respect." This was a sufficient adoption. Put more directly, Edgardo's testimony at the plea hearing is a sworn statement that the facts in the factual resume are true; thus, he made a sworn statement that it is true that he agrees Defendant delivered the drugs.

This is not, then, a case where the statements to be admitted under Rule 801(d)(1)(A) are only found in the notes, reports, or affidavits prepared by law enforcement officers, a situation, as Defendant notes, that a number of courts have held falls outside the Rule.

While it would have been an easier question if Edgardo had admitted under oath during the plea hearing that he made the inculpatory statement and that it was true—or to have otherwise testified that Defendant delivered the drugs—under these circumstances, his failure to do so is not fatal to finding that he adopted the statement. We need not, and do not, address whether facts in the factual resume of which Edgardo had no personal knowledge became part of his testimony at the plea hearing. The district court did not abuse its discretion by admitting the redacted factual resume as substantive evidence....

Defendant argues that the Government's "primary purpose" in calling Edgardo was to put otherwise inadmissible evidence before the jury under the guise of impeachment....

Federal Rule of Evidence 607 provides that "[t]he credibility of a witness may be attacked by any party, including the party calling the witness." The Government concedes that it "may not call a witness it knows to be hostile for the primary purpose of eliciting otherwise inadmissible impeachment testimony, for such a scheme merely serves as a subterfuge to avoid the hearsay rule." But, the Government continues, that was not its purpose in calling Edgardo.

We note initially that the admission of the redacted factual resume as substantive evidence saps this argument of much of its force, for the critical information that Defendant delivered the drugs was properly before the jury as substantive evidence. In any event, we conclude that there was no error....

PRIOR CONSISTENT STATEMENTS

RULE 801(d)(1)(B)(i)

Rule 801(d)(1)(B)(i) is a narrow pathway to admission. As explained by the Supreme Court in Tome v. United States (1995):

> The Rule permits the introduction of a declarant's consistent out-of-court statements to rebut a charge of recent fabrication or improper influence or motive only when those statements were made before the charged recent fabrication or improper influence or motive.

The Court reached this interpretive conclusion by parsing the rule's ambiguous text and the common law history. Only statements that predate an alleged motive to lie, the Court concluded, truly rebut a charge of "improper influence or motive" as the rule demands.

The "premotive" requirement for Rule 801(d)(1)(B)(i) is best illustrated by the facts of the *Tome* case itself. In *Tome*, the defense attempted at trial to impugn the motives of a child-witness who testified that her father sexually abused her. The defense suggested that the child's trial allegations were motivated by an ongoing custody dispute between her parents. The prosecution responded to the defense contention of improper motive by introducing a series of prior out-of-court statements made by the child to a babysitter and others; the statements were consistent with her trial testimony alleging sexual abuse. Critically, all the prior out-of-court consistent statements occurred in 1990. The custody dispute arose after a 1988 divorce and an unsuccessful 1989 petition by the mother for primary custody. The Supreme Court applied the "premotive" requirement to conclude that the out-of-court statements, which all arose *after the child's alleged motive to prevaricate first surfaced*, were not admissible under Rule 801(d)(1)(B)(i).

The premotive requirement serves to prevent the introduction of the bulk of consistent statements, such as those offered in *Tome* itself, under Rule 801(d)(1)(B)(i). As in *Tome*, prior consistent statements will frequently be tainted by the same alleged motive to lie that is claimed to taint the witness' trial testimony. If so, Rule 801(d)(1)(B)(i) does not permit their introduction. This result has favorable policy implications. As *Tome* stresses, the general exclusion of prior consistent statements ensures that "the whole emphasis of the trial" does not "shift to the out-of-court statements" as opposed to "the in-court ones." The narrow premotive rule described in *Tome* also serves to assuage the Advisory Committee's fear of the "general use of prior prepared statements as substantive evidence."

RULE 801(d)(1)(B)(ii)

Prior to a 2014 amendment, this rule consisted solely of what is now labeled, Rule 801(d)(1)(B)(i). The 2014 amendment added the language contained in Rule 801(d)(1)(B)(ii). This language states that a testifying witness' prior consistent statement is "not hearsay" if it is offered "to rehabilitate the declarant's credibility as a witness when attacked on another ground," i.e., any ground other than the narrow ground recognized in Rule 801(d)(1)(B)(i). The Advisory Committee Note downplays the significance of this change, explaining that: "The amendment does not make any consistent statement admissible that was not admissible previously—the only difference is that prior consistent statements otherwise admissible for rehabilitation are now admissible substantively as well." In other words, the 2014 amendment purports to make no change to the admissibility of prior consistent statements. It only expands the permissible use of such statements once admitted.

The tricky question is identifying the prior consistent statements that were admissible (because they were not hearsay) prior to 2014 but did not qualify for admission under Rule 801(d)(1)(B)(i). Even before the federal rules, savvy attorneys seeking to introduce prior consistent statements of testifying witnesses recognized that they could avoid the hearsay prohibition altogether by offering the statements for a purpose other than proving the truth of the matter asserted.

The non-hearsay purpose typically invoked when offering consistent prior statements—rehabilitating the witness' credibility—represents an intuitive non-hearsay analogue to prior inconsistent statements offered for the non-hearsay purpose of impeachment. If a witness who says different things on a specific topic is less credible with respect to that topic, it follows that a witness who remains consistent over time on a particular point is more credible. It was never clear, however, how this non-hearsay use of prior consistent statements interfaced with Rule 801(d)(1)(B). And *Tome* simply mirrored this ambiguity in interpreting the rule.

The question is further muddled by the infinitesimal distance between substantive and non-substantive use of a testifying witness' prior *consistent* statement. The ever-present challenge of restricting juror use of out-of-court statements to a non-hearsay purpose is especially problematic in the context of prior consistent statements. Where the distinction is enforced, the jury will hear the same sentiment expressed twice, once in the out-of-court statement and a second time in in-court testimony. Only the latter will be offered as substantive evidence. The court will then, upon request, instruct jurors that the prior consistent statement is not offered for its truth but only to support the credibility (i.e., truth) of the witness's in-court testimony to the same effect. It is hard to imagine this instruction altering the calculus of a typical juror. Indeed, the futility of such a limiting instruction appears to be the primary motivation for the 2014 amendment to Rule 801(d)(1)(B).

Prior to the 2014 amendment, prior consistent statements were being admitted, over hearsay objections, to support witness credibility in the manner described above. There was a familiar pattern in the case law. Parties could not simply offer prior consistent statements to bolster a testifying witness' credibility. The witness' credibility had to first be attacked, and the statements had to have some significant force in rebutting the credibility attack.

By far the most common scenario in the case law arises when a party first impeaches a testifying witness with prior inconsistent statements drawn from an out-of-court interview, witness statement, or conversation. The adverse party will then be permitted to introduce, as rehabilitation, the witness' prior consistent statements to the extent they come from *the same source* (i.e., the same interview, witness statement, or conversation). There is one other common example of the non-hearsay use of prior consistent statements...

PROBLEM 6.11: VERY OLD STATEMENTS

A cold-case unit at a local prosecutor's office gets a new lead on a murder of a beloved neighborhood character, Grover, 20 years ago. A detective investigates and finds a now-elderly witness, Mr. Rogers, who states that the defendant (A Large Yellow Bird) said, "yeah maybe I killed Grover, so what" shortly after the crime. At trial Mr. Rogers testifies about the 20-year-old confession. The defense attorney cross-examines Rogers, harping on the witness' age, the lengthy passage of time, and his inability to remember other events from the same time period with any specificity.

> "How is it you expect us to believe that you remember this one comment from 20 years ago and yet you don't remember anything else anyone said that day or even where you were when you heard it?!"

After the cross-examination, the prosecution seeks to introduce Ms. Rogers testimony that Mr. Rogers told her about the defendant's confession one week after the 20-year-old confession. *How should the trial court rule? Is the statement admissible as substantive evidence?*

***

Diving any deeper into the unsettled depths of Rule 801(d)(1)(B)(ii) is likely more trouble than it is worth. In the end, it appears that the 2014 amendment may live up to the Advisory Committee's humble claims. The key insight is this: Before the amendment, courts allowed prior consistent statements to be used in limited circumstances to rehabilitate a challenged witness. After the amendment, these out-of-court statements that would otherwise be admissible only for the non-hearsay purpose of corroboration or rehabilitation are now admissible as substantive evidence.

IDENTIFICATION STATEMENTS

RULE 801(d)(1)(C)

In every criminal case, the prosecution must offer evidence that identifies the defendant as the person who committed the charged crime. Civil litigation also often requires analogous evidence of identification. One way of providing this evidence is to ask testifying witnesses to point out the alleged perpetrator during their trial testimony. While the resulting courtroom identification offers a moment of drama, it is terribly suggestive. A testifying witness would be expected to pick the defendant out in most courtroom settings even if unable to make an identification in less suggestive circumstances. Rule 801(d)(1)(C) is intended to allow the introduction of out-of-court statements of identification that can supplement or replace the "generally unsatisfactory and inconclusive nature of courtroom identifications."

Specifically, the rule exempts from the hearsay prohibition a statement that "identifies a person as someone the declarant perceived earlier." The rule permits the jury to hear about pretrial procedures that more strenuously test the witness' ability to identify the defendant, such as pretrial lineups, photographic arrays and analogous identification procedures. Under the rule, these prior identifications are admissible even if the witness does not confirm the identification in court.

The rule contemplates a particular scenario: a witness testifies about a prior identification of the defendant during a lineup, show-up, photo array or other structured identification procedure. As a result, application of the rule is most straightforward and uncontroversial when it is invoked in the intended context. In each circumstance, the rule demands that the witness testify and be subject to cross examination at trial, reducing many of the traditional hearsay concerns. Courts commonly allow another person to testify about an eyewitness's out-of-court identification, so long as the eyewitness also testifies at the trial and is subject to cross-examination about the identification. The most common scenario involves a police officer who testifies about an identification procedure and resulting out-of-court identification made by a civilian eyewitness.

PROBLEM 6-12: STATEMENT OF IDENTIFICATION?

The following problem is drawn from U.S. v. Kaquatosh (E.D. Wis. 2003):

"The prosecution alleges that on December 31, 2001, defendant struck Marvin Wayka on the head with a wooden object, causing Wayka to lose consciousness and sustain an open skull fracture. The government moved in limine for an order that law enforcement officers be permitted, pursuant to Fed.R.Evid. 801(d)(1)(C), to testify that two witnesses told them that defendant assaulted Wayka.... The government indicated that the officers would testify to statements made by Connie Freeman and Virginia Waupoose regarding the incident alleged in count one of the indictment. On January 7, 2002,

Freeman informed one of the officers that on December 31 she observed defendant strike Wayka on the head and face with a piece of wood. Waupoose apparently told a second officer that she also observed defendant hit Wayka on the head with a piece of wood.

Neither Freeman nor Waupoose observed defendant in a line-up, show-up, or photo array and then identified him. Rather, they simply advised the officers that they observed defendant assault Wayka."

How should the court rule?

STATE VARIATION: PRIOR WITNESS STATEMENTS

North Carolina's evidence code does not provide hearsay exceptions for prior statements of a testifying witness. Here is the North Carolina rule drafting committee's note recognizing this divergence from the federal rules:

Subdivision (d)(1) of Fed.R.Evid. 801 departs markedly from the common law in North Carolina by excluding from the hearsay ban several statements that come within the common law definition of hearsay. Accordingly, the language of Fed.R.Evid. 801(d), which provides that in certain circumstances prior inconsistent statements, prior consistent statements, and out-of-court identifications are not hearsay, was deleted.

How might a prosecutor introduce an out-of-court identification in North Carolina? Virginia's version of Rule 801 similarly does not permit substantive use of prior witness statements, but does include an exception, Rule 2:803(22), for statements of identification.

Another interesting variation comes from Connecticut, where Evidence § 8-5 adds a subtle but important qualifier to the hearsay exception for statements of identification: "The identification of a person made by a declarant prior to trial where the identification is reliable."

STATEMENTS OF PARTY OPPONENTS

RULE 801(d)(2)(A)

Federal Rule of Evidence 801(d)(2) exempts five variants of opposing party statements from the hearsay prohibition. The Advisory Committee urges "generous treatment of this avenue to admissibility." Before addressing each variant, two preliminary points are worth highlighting.

First, litigants, judges and commentators sometimes describe the rule as applying to party "admissions." Indeed, the drafters originally titled the rule, "Admission by a party opponent"—a misleading moniker that the style revisers wisely changed in 2011. There is no requirement that statements admitted through Rule 801(d)(2) constitute "admissions." As the Seventh Circuit explains:

> [Qualifying] statements need neither be incriminating, inculpatory, against interest, nor otherwise inherently damaging to the declarant's case. Rule 801(d)(2)(A) simply admits those statements made by one party, but offered as evidence by the opposing party.[1]

Second, a party cannot introduce its own statements, or those of its own employee, conspirator, agent, and so on, under Rule 801(d)(2). Qualifying statements can only be "offered against" the party who uttered them. This prevents, among other things, criminal defendants from introducing their own exculpatory statements under the rule in lieu of live testimony to the same effect. As the Sixth Circuit explains:

> Rule 801(d)(2), …, does not extend to a party's attempt to introduce his or her own statements through the testimony of other witnesses. Indeed, if such statements were deemed admissible under Rule 801(d)(2), parties could effectuate an end-run around the adversarial process by, in effect, testifying without swearing an oath, facing cross-examination, or being subjected to first-hand scrutiny by the jury.[2]

---

[1] U.S. v. Reed, 227 F.3d 763 (7th Cir. 2000).
[2] U.S. v. McDaniel, 398 F.3d 540 (6th Cir. 2005).

The most straightforward and common application of Rule 801(d)(2) is found in subpart (A). Rule 801(d)(2)(A) covers statements "made by the party in an individual or representative capacity." This language is meant to cover every type of statement a party might make. All statements are made in either an individual or representative capacity; there is no other possibility.

In light of its overarching simplicity, Rule 801(d)(2)(A) rarely calls for significant legal analysis. The rule does not purport to be limited to reliable statements, damaging statements, or any other subset of party statements. The only question is: Were the statements authored by a party? If the answer is yes, and the statements are offered by the opposing party, the statements qualify for admission under Rule 801(d)(2)(A).

As the foregoing suggests, the justification for this hearsay exemption is a sense of fair play rather than any notion of reliability. As the Seventh Circuit explains, "Treating party admissions as nonhearsay is rooted in the nature of the adversarial system, and trustworthiness is not a requirement for admission."[1]

RULE 801(d)(2)(B)

Rule 801(d)(2) admits more than just statements directly uttered by an opposing party. Rule 801(d)(2)(B) extends the hearsay exemption for opposing party statements to statements the opposing party makes indirectly "by adopting or acquiescing in the statement of another." This makes intuitive sense. If a party adopts the statement of another, the other person's statement can fairly be treated as if it were the party's own. Rule 801(d)(2)(B) identifies two categories of adoption. The first category can be read to cover explicit adoptions; the second covers implicit adoptions. The same analysis applies in both circumstances. The trial judge must assess, in light of typical human behavior, whether a statement uttered by another person can, in context, fairly be characterized as a statement of the opposing party.

Statements can be adopted through any form of human activity. Speech is the most obvious mechanism. When a party explicitly agrees with the factual statement of another, the party typically can be characterized as adopting the other person's statement. Words that implicitly indicate agreement represent

---

[1] Jordan v. Binns, 712 F.3d 1123 (7th Cir. 2013).

another fairly easy case. For example, one common scenario where an adoption occurs is when a person's accusation is immediately responded to with an apology and a promise by the party that the conduct would not happen again. Non-verbal gestures such as nodding affirmatively also may manifest adoption of a preceding statement for purposes of the rule.

UNITED STATES v. JINADU
98 F.3d 239 (6th Cir. 1996)

[Customs agents in the San Francisco area intercepted a large quantity of heroin bound for Ohio. They then allowed the package to be delivered as intended to co-defendant Moruf Lawal and shortly after he took possession, arrested him. A jury convicted Lawal (and his co-defendant) for conspiracy to import and distribute heroin.]

Defendant Lawal argues that the testimony of Agent Sullivan about his alleged confession to Agent Hein was hearsay and was erroneously admitted at trial. Agent Sullivan was one of the agents present after Lawal was arrested after the controlled delivery of heroin on November 5, 1994. Agent Sullivan questioned defendant initially. After Agent Hein arrived, he interviewed Lawal. Agent Sullivan remained in the room and listened to the interview. Agent Hein died shortly thereafter. Although he took notes during the interview, the United States was not able to find them. Agent Sullivan testified at trial about the statements of Hein in the questioning of Lawal and Lawal's responses, which he had overheard on November 5, 1994.

In particular, defendant Lawal objects to the following colloquy which took place at trial between the prosecution and Agent Sullivan, who testified as follows:

> Q. And do you recall anything that Mr. Lawal was asked concerning the package itself, the content of the package?
>
> A. Yes sir. Agent Hein asked Mr. Lawal if—something to the effect if he knew how much the package weighed, and Mr. Lawal—
>
> MR. PEREZ: Objection, Your Honor. This is hearsay.
>
> THE COURT: He may answer. Proceed.

A. I heard Mr. Lawal answer Agent Hein that he did not know the weight of the package. I think Agent Hein at this time mentioned an amount somewhere over two—

THE COURT: I'll sustain the objection at this point.

MR. BRICHLER: Okay.

Q. Now, did you hear any conversation concerning what was actually in the package?

A. Yes sir. I heard Agent Hein ask—

MR. PEREZ: Same objection.

THE COURT: He may answer.

A. He said something to the effect, you know what's in the package, don't you. And I observed Mr. Lawal nod his head in a manner indicating yes. Immediately following this indication, Agent Hein stated, you know that's China White heroin, to which Mr. Lawal replied, "yes."

The United States argues that the statements of Agent Hein, about which Agent Sullivan testified, are not hearsay because defendant Lawal adopted the statements of Agent Hein as his own....

.... When a statement is offered as an adoptive admission, the primary inquiry is whether the statement was such that, under the circumstances, an innocent defendant would normally be induced to respond, and whether there are sufficient foundational facts from which the jury could infer that the defendant heard, understood, and acquiesced in the statement. The first criterion, which is of particular relevance in cases involving silent acquiescence, is not at issue here because defendant Lawal is alleged to have responded to Hein's questions by answering, "yes."

In regard to the second criterion, we believe that in the present case, there were sufficient foundational facts for the jury reasonably to conclude that defendant did actually hear, understand, and accede to the statements of Agent Hein at issue. Both Agents Sullivan and another agent present, Agent Sheard, and numerous other witnesses at trial testified that Lawal exhibited an understanding of English. Agent Sullivan stated that initially he questioned Lawal about his identity and that when Agent Hein arrived, Hein conducted a more specific interview. Sullivan testified that he was in the room throughout the interview, either sitting on a corner of the bed very close to Lawal and right next to Agent Hein or standing by the door.... The evidence, thus, indicates that there is sufficient indicia of reliability that Hein's statements were made in defendant's presence, that defendant understood the statements, and that he had an opportunity to deny them, but instead answered, "yes," indicating his acquiescence in the truth of the questions he was being asked....

***

A large portion of the Rule 801(d)(2)(B) case law concerns circumstances where a party's silence in response to a statement is offered as evidence of adoption. The central question when silence is offered as evidence of an adoption is whether, under the circumstances, a person who heard and understood the statement would have indicated disagreement had the person believed it to be untrue. Relevant circumstances include the precise content of the statement, the relationship between the speaker and the potentially adopting party, the party's mental state at the time, and the potential audience for any disagreement. A court that delves into these circumstances will often find sufficient ambiguity to deny admission when silence is the only evidence of adoption. After all, silence is most typically a means of signaling indifference, confusion, or disagreement. Social norms discourage voicing disagreement in many scenarios ("If you don't have anything nice to say....") In the cases where silence is properly relied on as an adoption, the party's silence is almost always buttressed by actions, such as non-verbal cues, that more clearly manifest agreement.

PROBLEM 6-13: ADOPTION BY SILENCE

John Forbes was convicted of aggravated sexual assault.[1] At his trial, the judge let in the following exchange that occurred after a grand jury indicted Forbes for sexual assault of a minor, K.S.:

---

[1] State v. Forbes, 157 N.H. 570 (2008).

[Wanda] Roberts, [the defendant's daughter] testified that ... she and the defendant's sister, Hazel Kelley, had a discussion about KS' allegations while the defendant was "sitting there." During that conversation, Kelley told Roberts that the defendant was "not going to plead guilty to something he didn't do." Roberts responded by stating: "I can't say for sure that it happened. I wasn't there. I don't know. But from my point of view, I do believe [KS]...." Roberts testified that, when she said that, the defendant "just sat there" and remained silent.

On appeal to the New Hampshire Supreme Court, "[t]he defendant contends that the trial court erred in concluding that his silence amounted to an adoptive admission of Roberts' statement." *How should the appellate court rule?*

PROBLEM 6-14: ADOPTION BY RETWEET

A male plaintiff sues his employer for gender discrimination after being denied a promotion. The plaintiff seeks to introduce a Twitter retweet by the company owner who made the promotion decision. On a personal account, the owner retweeted and liked the following tweet by a celebrity endorsing Hillary Clinton's candidacy for President:

> "I support Hillary because I believe a woman can do any job better than a man! ☺"

The company owner's Twitter bio includes the following language: "Retweets ≠ endorsements."

How should a trial court rule on the admissibility of the celebrity's tweet along with the owner's "like" and "retweet"?

RULE 801(d)(2)(C)

If a party authorizes another person to speak on the party's behalf, the resulting statement can be introduced against the party under Rule 801(d)(2)(C). The key limiting factor in the rule is that the party must have authorized the speaker to make a statement on the subject. The most obvious statements that come in under Rule 801(d)(2)(C) are those involving designated spokespersons. The rule also reaches statements by a party's lawyers, brokers, and others whose relationships "imply an authority to speak on certain occasions."[1]

RULE 801(d)(2)(D)

Rule 801(d)(2)(D) exempts from the hearsay prohibition statements made by the "party's agent or employee on a matter within the scope of that relationship and while" the relationship existed. The exemption does not require adoption or ratification of the statements by the party.

The question of who counts as an employee is typically straightforward. The inclusion of the term "agent" broadens the rule's coverage. As a general matter, an agent is someone who acts on a principal's behalf, subject to the principal's control.

With respect to subject matter, Rule 801(d)(2)(D) abandons strict common law requirements that the employee have specific authority to speak on a certain topic. Instead, Rule 801(d)(2)(D) allows statements to be admitted whenever an employee or agent speaks on a matter within the scope of the employment relationship, while it existed. This means that every employee can potentially generate admissible statements, not just supervisors or managers.

By liberalizing the scope of the employee-agent hearsay exemption to include any matters related to the employment or agency relationship, Rule 801(d)(2)(D) can create difficult questions of interpretation. These questions become particularly acute when employees make statements that are antagonistic to their employer, rather than, as befitting the traditional route of admissibility, speak on their employer's behalf.

PROBLEM 6-15: STATEMENTS AGAINST AN EMPLOYER

Consider the following scenario from Carter v. Univ. of Toledo (6th Cir. 2003):

> "Dr. Carolyn Carter, who is African–American, brought suit against her former employer, the University of Toledo, alleging that the

---

[1] U.S. v. Bonds, 608 F.3d 495 (9th Cir. 2010).

University failed to renew her contract as a visiting professor because of her race."

In the litigation that followed, Carter offered statements made by Dr. Earl Murry, the University's Vice Provost.

According to Carter, Murry told her that the School's Dean Dr. Czerniak: "'is trying to whitewash the college of education.' Carter also asserts that Murry 'told me that [Czerniak] was trying to get rid of the black professors and that he was in a struggle with her involving the appointment of an additional black professor.' When she contacted him a third time to find out whether her appointment would be renewed, Carter claims that Murry said 'I don't know what's going on, they're a bunch of racists over there.' Murry denies making any of these statements."

Can Carter testify about Murry's statements in the litigation against University of Toledo? It may help to know that:

"Murry's duties as Vice Provost included acting as chief negotiator for the faculty's collective bargaining agreements, coordinating faculty recruiting, hiring, training, and orientation, advising the Provost on tenure and promotions, reviewing salary matters, and ensuring compliance with affirmative action requirements."

RULE 801(d)(2)(E)

The most controversial part of Rule 801(d)(2) comes in subpart (E). The Advisory Committee Note itself offers little support for this section. The Note states that "the agency theory of conspiracy" that underlies the rule "is at best a fiction." This tepid endorsement (at best!) and the rule's "in furtherance" requirement, are properly viewed as an effort to limit the admission of co-conspirator statements.

The appeal of co-conspirator statements as evidence is powerful to both prosecutors and judges alike. As the Supreme Court stated, in rejecting a Confrontation Clause challenge to a co-conspirator statement in United States v. Inadi (1986):

Because they are made while the conspiracy is in progress, such statements provide evidence of the conspiracy's context that cannot be replicated, even if the declarant testifies to the same matters in court. ... Conspirators are likely to speak differently when talking to each other in furtherance of their illegal aims than when testifying on the witness stand. Even when the declarant takes the stand, his in-court testimony seldom will reproduce a significant portion of the evidentiary value of his statements during the course of the conspiracy.

For a statement to qualify for admission under Rule 801(d)(2)(E), the proffering party must be able to show the existence of a conspiracy involving the declarant and the party opponent, and that the statement was made "during and in furtherance of the conspiracy." As a result of a 1997 amendment, the rule contains specific guidance on the mechanics of its application: "The statement must be considered but does not by itself establish ... the existence of the conspiracy or participation in it under (E)."

BOURJAILY v. UNITED STATES
483 U.S. 171 (1987)

Chief Justice REHNQUIST delivered the opinion of the Court.

.... In May 1984, Clarence Greathouse, an informant working for the Federal Bureau of Investigation (FBI), arranged to sell a kilogram of cocaine to Angelo Lonardo. Lonardo agreed that he would find individuals to distribute the drug. When the sale became imminent, Lonardo stated in a tape-recorded telephone conversation that he had a "gentleman friend" who had some questions to ask about the cocaine. In a subsequent telephone call, Greathouse spoke to the "friend" about the quality of the drug and the price. Greathouse then spoke again with Lonardo, and the two arranged the details of the purchase. They agreed that the sale would take place in a designated hotel parking lot, and Lonardo would transfer the drug from Greathouse's car to the "friend," who would be waiting in the parking lot in his own car. Greathouse proceeded with the transaction as planned, and FBI agents arrested Lonardo and petitioner immediately after Lonardo placed a kilogram of cocaine into petitioner's car in the hotel parking lot. In petitioner's car, the agents found over $20,000 in cash.

Petitioner was charged with conspiring to distribute cocaine, and possession of cocaine with intent to distribute. The Government introduced, over petitioner's objection, Angelo Lonardo's telephone statements regarding the participation of the "friend" in the transaction. The District Court found that, considering the events in the parking lot and Lonardo's statements over the telephone, the Government had established by a preponderance of the evidence that a conspiracy involving Lonardo and petitioner existed, and that Lonardo's statements over the telephone had been made in the course of and in furtherance of the conspiracy. Accordingly, the trial court held that Lonardo's out-of-court statements satisfied Rule 801(d)(2)(E) and were not hearsay. Petitioner was convicted on both counts and sentenced to 15 years.... We affirm.

Before admitting a co-conspirator's statement over an objection that it does not qualify under Rule 801(d)(2)(E), a court must be satisfied that the statement actually falls within the definition of the Rule. There must be evidence that there was a conspiracy involving the declarant and the nonoffering party, and that the statement was made "during the course and in furtherance of the conspiracy." Federal Rule of Evidence 104(a) provides: "Preliminary questions concerning ... the admissibility of evidence shall be determined by the court." Petitioner and the Government agree that the existence of a conspiracy and petitioner's involvement in it are preliminary questions of fact that, under Rule 104, must be resolved by the court. The Federal Rules, however, nowhere define the standard of proof the court must observe in resolving these questions.

We are therefore guided by our prior decisions regarding admissibility determinations that hinge on preliminary factual questions. We have traditionally required that these matters be established by a preponderance of proof. Evidence is placed before the jury when it satisfies the technical requirements of the evidentiary Rules, which embody certain legal and policy determinations. The inquiry made by a court concerned with these matters is not whether the proponent of the evidence wins or loses his case on the merits, but whether the evidentiary Rules have been satisfied. Thus, the evidentiary standard is unrelated to the burden of proof on the substantive issues, be it a criminal case or a civil case. The preponderance standard ensures that before admitting evidence, the court will have found it more likely than not that the technical issues and policy concerns addressed by the Federal Rules of Evidence have been afforded due consideration. Therefore, we hold that when the preliminary facts relevant to Rule 801(d)(2)(E) are disputed, the offering party must prove them by a preponderance of the evidence.

Even though petitioner agrees that the courts below applied the proper standard of proof with regard to the preliminary facts relevant to Rule 801(d)(2)(E), he nevertheless challenges the admission of Lonardo's statements....

The out-of-court statements of Lonardo indicated that Lonardo was involved in a conspiracy with a "friend." The statements indicated that the friend had agreed with Lonardo to buy a kilogram of cocaine and to distribute it. The statements also revealed that the friend would be at the hotel parking lot, in his car, and would accept the cocaine from Greathouse's car after Greathouse gave Lonardo the keys. Each one of Lonardo's statements may itself be unreliable, but taken as a whole, the entire conversation between Lonardo and Greathouse was corroborated by independent evidence. The friend, who turned out to be petitioner, showed up at the prearranged spot at the prearranged time. He picked up the cocaine, and a significant sum of money was found in his car. On these facts, the trial court concluded, in our view correctly, that the Government had established the existence of a conspiracy and petitioner's participation in it....

The judgment of the Court of Appeals is Affirmed.

PROBLEM 6-16: LOST IN TRANSLATION[1]

Customs agents arrested Claudio Romo–Chavez after he drove a 1999 Buick Centry through an Arizona border checkpoint. The car had packages of methamphetamine concealed in its gas tank. Officer Hernandez and Agent Simboli questioned Romo-Chavez. Simboli, who does not speak Spanish, testified about the exchange at trial as follows:

> Officer Hernandez ... translated as Romo–Chavez explained that he came to the United States to return two shirts to a Dillard's in Phoenix.

---

[1] United States v. Romo-Chavez, 681 F.3d 955 (9th Cir. 2012).

When Agent Simboli asked why he was not going to the Dillard's in Tucson, Romo–Chavez changed his answer to say that he was indeed going to that store. Romo–Chavez also told the agent that the previous Saturday he had received an offer to sell the Buick in exchange for a small truck and $2,000 and that he was going to meet the buyer at an Auto–Zone in Nogales to complete the transaction. After Romo–Chavez told Simboli that he had recently had an engine sensor replaced in his car, Simboli asked him about the methamphetamine that had by this time been discovered in his car. Romo–Chavez denied knowledge, and the interview ended.

Later at trial, Romo-Chavez offered a different explanation for his trip to the United States and "attempted to explain away any apparent inconsistencies in his story as a result of Officer Hernandez's allegedly poor translation."

After his conviction, Romo-Chavez argued that Simboli's testimony about Hernandez's translation of Romo-Chavez's statements was inadmissible hearsay. *How should the appellate court rule?*

RULE 803 HEARSAY EXCEPTIONS

Hearsay statements can be admitted under the 23 exceptions listed in Rule 803, "regardless of whether the declarant is available as a witness." This means that the exceptions in Rule 803 can be invoked if the declarant testifies; or is unavailable due to death, privilege or any reason; or is available, but never called to the witness stand. In short, Rule 803 exceptions are simply unconcerned with the status of the declarant as a potential or actual live witness. The Advisory Committee Notes explain that Rule 803 "proceeds upon the theory that under appropriate circumstances a hearsay statement may possess circumstantial guarantees of trustworthiness sufficient to justify nonproduction of the declarant in person at the trial even though he may be available."

PRESENT SENSE IMPRESSIONS & EXCITED UTTERANCES

RULE 803(1) & (2)

UNITED STATES v. BOYCE
742 F.3d 792 (7th Cir. 2014)

WILLIAMS, Circuit Judge.

After a foot chase during which an officer said he saw Darnell Boyce throw a gun into a yard, officers recovered the gun from the area and also found ammunition for the gun in Boyce's pocket. A jury convicted Boyce of being a felon in possession of a firearm and ammunition…. Boyce … challenges the admission at trial of statements of Sarah Portis, the mother of four of his children, made during a 911 call, including that Boyce had a gun. We find no abuse of discretion in the district court's admission of the statements under the excited utterance exception to the hearsay rule because they were made while under the stress of a domestic battery and related to it.

I. BACKGROUND

Sarah Portis called 911 at around 7:45 p.m. on March 27, 2010, asking that police come to her residence because her child's father had just hit her and was "going crazy for no reason." The 911 operator asked, "Any weapons involved?" to which Portis responded, "Yes." The operator asked what kind, and Portis said, "A gun." The operator said, "He has a gun?", then "Hello?", and Portis responded, "I, I think so. 'Cause he just, he just." After the operator said, "Come on," Portis responded, "Yes!" twice. The operator again inquired, "Did you see one?" and Portis replied, "Yes!" The operator then cautioned Portis that if she wasn't telling the truth, she could be taken to jail. Portis responded, "I'm positive." After giving a description of what Boyce was wearing, the operator asked where he was at the moment. Portis responded that she "just ran upstairs to [her] neighbor's house" and didn't know whether Boyce had left her house yet.

Within minutes, Officers Robert Cummings and Eugene Solomon responded to the 911 call. After determining Boyce was no longer in the apartment, they interviewed Portis for about five to ten minutes. Officer Solomon described Portis as "appear[ing] emotional as if she just had an argument, perhaps a fight, someone who was just running." The officers then went to their car to complete a case report for domestic battery. While they were sitting in their squad car, the officers saw that Boyce had returned to the outside of Portis's residence and was calling out her name. Officer Solomon asked Boyce to come over, but Boyce ran away instead, and Officer Cummings ran after him. During the chase, Officer Cummings saw Boyce reach toward the midsection of his body, retrieve a nickel-plated handgun, and toss it over a garage into a yard. The officer caught up with Boyce soon afterward and detained him. Officers found a silver .357 Magnum handgun in the area where Officer Cummings saw Boyce throw a gun. Officers also found three .357 bullets in Boyce's right front pants pocket after they arrested him.

Boyce was charged with one count of being a felon in possession of a firearm and one count of being a felon in possession of ammunition. While he was in jail awaiting trial, Boyce sent Portis a letter requesting that she recant her statement that he had a gun. He even provided the language he wanted her to use in a letter he wanted her to write to him:

> It seems like my whole life is going down since I called the police and I lied on you. I didn't know that those police was going to actually put

a gun on you. Like I said before, I am so sorry for calling them and lying about you had a gun and hit me, but you just misunderstand how I felt when I saw you and the other girl hugging and kissing.... So the only way I thought of paying you back was to call the police and get you locked up once again. I'm so sorry.

Boyce and Portis also spoke by telephone while he was in jail, and Boyce said "our story" to which they would stick was that Portis made the whole thing up because she was mad he had been talking to another woman.

Portis did not testify at trial, but the government played a recording of her 911 call for the jury. In arguing that Boyce possessed a firearm on March 27, 2010, the government pointed to Officer Cummings's testimony that he saw Portis throw a gun, other officers' testimony recounting the recovery of the gun in the area and ammunition matching the gun in Boyce's pocket, and Portis's statement on the 911 call that Boyce had a gun. A jury found Boyce guilty on both charged counts. The district court concluded that Boyce had three prior violent felonies or serious drug offenses that mandated a minimum term of fifteen years' imprisonment.... The court sentenced him to 210 months' imprisonment, two and a half years over the mandatory minimum sentence. Boyce appeals.

II. ANALYSIS

...We next turn to Boyce's argument that the government should not have been allowed to introduce Portis's 911 call at trial. Portis did not testify at trial. The jury still heard her voice, though, as the government played the audio recording of her 911 call during the trial. (The jury received a transcript of the call as well.) The district court admitted Portis's 911 call on the basis that it was a present sense impression under Federal Rule of Evidence 803(1) and an excited utterance under Federal Rule of Evidence 803(2). Boyce maintains that the call does not fall within either of these hearsay exceptions. We review the district court's evidentiary rulings for an abuse of discretion.

Rule 803(1), the present sense impression exception, provides that "[a] statement describing or explaining an event or condition, made while or immediately after the declarant perceived it" is not excluded by the rule against hearsay. Rule 803(2) sets forth the exception for an "excited utterance," defined by the rule as "[a] statement relating to a startling event or condition, made while the declarant was under the stress of the excitement that it caused."

The theory underlying the present sense impression exception "is that substantial contemporaneity of event and statement negate the likelihood of deliberate or conscious misrepresentation." Fed.R.Evid. 803 advisory committee's note. Along similar lines, the idea behind the excited utterance exception is that "circumstances may produce a condition of excitement which temporarily stills the capacity of reflection and produces utterances free of conscious fabrication." In other words, the statement must have been a spontaneous reaction to the startling event and not the result of reflective thought.

But that is not to say the spontaneity exceptions in the Federal Rules of Evidence necessarily rest on a sound foundation. We have said before regarding the reasoning behind the present sense impression that "[a]s with much of the folk psychology of evidence, it is difficult to take this rationale entirely seriously, since people are entirely capable of spontaneous lies in emotional circumstances." As for the excited utterance exception, "The entire basis for the exception may ... be questioned. While psychologists would probably concede that excitement minimizes the reflective self-interest influencing the declarant's statements, they have questioned whether this might be outweighed by the distorting effect of shock and excitement upon the declarant's observation and judgement."

Nonetheless, we have recognized that despite these issues, the exceptions are well-established. Boyce, while pointing to some of this criticism, does not ask us to find the exceptions utterly invalid, and so we proceed to consider his arguments that the exceptions do not apply in the circumstances of his case.

To take the Rule 803(1) present sense impression exception first, we have said that to be admissible under this rule, "(1) the statement must describe an event or condition without calculated narration; (2) the speaker must have personally perceived the event or condition described; and (3) the statement must have been made while the speaker was perceiving the event or condition, or immediately thereafter." Here, Portis was personally present during the domestic battery she recounted during the 911 call. The questions here are whether Portis's statements were made without calculated narration and whether her 911 call was sufficiently contemporaneous to constitute a present sense impression.

To take the timing issue first, while Portis did not call 911 as Boyce was hitting her, nor would that have been feasible or wise to do, the Advisory Committee's Note to Federal Rule of Evidence 803 "recognizes that in many, if not most, instances precise contemporaneity is not possible and hence a slight lapse is allowable." Portis's statements to the 911 operator that Boyce had "just" hit her and that she had "just" run upstairs to her neighbor's house indicate that she called 911 nearly immediately after her observations. That timing is consistent with other circuits' interpretation of the present sense impression exception. See, e.g., United States v. Davis (6th Cir. 2009) (admitting 911 call where caller reported seeing defendant with a gun as present sense impression and excited utterance in § 922(g)(1) case and stating it did not matter whether statements were made thirty seconds or five minutes after witnessing event); United States v. Shoup (1st Cir. 2007) (finding that statements in 911 call made about one to two minutes after leaving dangerous situation and going into apartment constituted present sense impression and excited utterance).

A statement must also be made without calculated narration to qualify under the present sense impression exception, and Boyce points out that Portis did not mention a gun until questioned by the dispatcher as to whether Boyce had any weapons. One can still make statements without calculated narration even if made in responses to questions. Here, notably, when the operator asked what kind of weapon, Portis told the operator "a gun." The operator did not ask whether Boyce had a gun; it was Portis who first brought up the gun's presence.

But answering questions rather than giving a spontaneous narration could increase the chances that the statements were made with calculated narration, and, as we discussed, Portis ran to another residence between the battery and her 911 call. We need not definitively decide whether these concerns mean Portis's statements fail to qualify under the present sense impression exception because even if they did, they would still be admissible as an excited utterance. The excited utterance exception "allows for a broader scope of subject matter coverage" than the present sense impression. This is because the Federal Rules of Evidence provide that an excited utterance includes a statement "relating to" a startling event, Fed.R.Evid. 803(2), while the present sense impression exception is limited to "describing or explaining" the event, Fed.R.Evid. 803(1).

For the excited utterance exception to apply, we have said that the proponent must demonstrate that: "(1) a startling event occurred; (2) the declarant makes the statement under the stress of the excitement caused by the startling event; and (3) the declarant's statement relates to the startling event." The statement "need not be contemporaneous with the startling event to be admissible under rule 803(2) ... [r]ather, the utterance must be contemporaneous with the excitement engendered by the startling event."

Here, the startling event of a domestic battery occurred. Portis called 911 and reported that Boyce had just hit her and was "going crazy for no reason" and that he had a gun. Next, Portis made her 911 call while under the stress of the excitement caused by the domestic battery. She made the call right after the battery, telling the operator that she had "just" run upstairs to her neighbor's house. Officer Solomon's testimony that Portis appeared emotional, as though she had just been in an argument or fight, further supports the district court's conclusion that Portis made the call while under the stress or excitement of the startling event.

Boyce principally takes issue with the district's court finding that her statements related to the startling event. In particular, he argues that the gun Portis described in the call was not related to the domestic battery she was reporting. Instead, he says, her reference to a gun in the call referred to a separate, earlier time when Boyce possessed a gun.

We do not find an abuse of discretion in the district court's determination that Boyce's statement in the call that she had seen Boyce with a gun was related to the domestic battery. During her call to 911 requesting help from the police, Portis told the operator that Boyce had a gun and responded "Yes!" several times when the operator asked if she had seen it. Upon further questioning she replied that she was "positive." When the dispatcher asked Portis whether any weapons were involved, the dispatcher was trying to obtain information regarding the battery and the level of danger posed by her assailant. And Portis said a weapon, in particular a gun, was involved. In doing so, Portis provided the dispatcher with information about her assailant and the danger she experienced just minutes before the call. This description of the threat posed by the man who battered her relates to the incident which produced her agitated state....

Even if Boyce is correct that his gun was not at arms' length while he struck her, if a domestic battery victim in Portis's circumstances knows her assailant has access to a gun nearby, the potential for more lethal force to be used against her would be a subject likely to be evoked in the description of her assault. Under the facts of this case, we find no abuse of discretion in the district court's decision to admit Portis's statements during the 911 call as excited utterances under Rule 803(2).....

The judgment of the district court is AFFIRMED.

POSNER, Circuit Judge, concurring.

I agree that the district court should be affirmed—and indeed I disagree with nothing in the court's opinion. I write separately only to express concern with Federal Rules of Evidence 803(1) and (2), which figure in this case. That concern is expressed in a paragraph of the majority opinion; I seek merely to amplify it.

Portis's conversation with the 911 operator was a major piece of evidence of the defendant's guilt. What she said in the conversation, though recorded, was hearsay, because it was an out-of-court statement offered "to prove the truth of the matter asserted," Fed.R.Evid. 801(c)(2)—namely that the defendant (Boyce) had a gun.... But the government argued and the district court agreed that Portis's recorded statement was admissible as a "present sense impression" and an "excited utterance." No doubt it was both those things, but there is profound doubt whether either should be an exception to the rule against the admission of hearsay evidence.

One reason that hearsay normally is inadmissible (though the bar to it is riddled with exceptions) is that it often is no better than rumor or gossip, and another, which is closely related, is that it can't be tested by cross-examination of its author. But in this case either party could have called Portis to testify, and her testimony would not have been hearsay. Neither party called her—the government, doubtless because Portis recanted her story that Boyce had had a gun after he wrote her several letters from prison asking her to lie for him and giving her detailed instructions on what story she should make up; Boyce, because her testimony would have been likely to reinforce the evidence of the letters that he had attempted to suborn perjury, and also because his sexual relationship with Portis began when she was only 15. Boyce's counsel said "the concern is that if Ms. Portis were to testify, she does look somewhat young and so the jury could infer ... that this relationship could have started when she was underage."

To get her recorded statement admitted into evidence, the government invoked two exceptions to the hearsay rule....

The rationale for the exception for a "present sense impression" is that if the event described and the statement describing it are near to each other in time, this "negate[s] the likelihood of deliberate or conscious misrepresentation." Advisory Committee Notes to 1972 Proposed Rules. I don't get it, especially when "immediacy" is interpreted to encompass periods as long as 23 minutes, as in United States v. Blakey (7th Cir. 1979), 16 minutes in United States v. Mejia–Velez (E.D.N.Y. 1994), and 10 minutes in State v. Odom (N.C. 1986). Even real immediacy is not a guarantor of truthfulness. It's not true that people can't make up a lie in a short period of time. Most lies in fact are spontaneous. Suppose I run into an acquaintance on the street and he has a new dog with him—a little yappy thing—and he asks me, "Isn't he beautiful"? I answer yes, though I'm a cat person and consider his dog hideous.

.... It is time the law awakened from its dogmatic slumber. The "present sense impression" exception never had any grounding in psychology. It entered American law in the nineteenth century, long before there was a field of cognitive psychology; it has neither a theoretical nor an empirical basis; and it's not even common sense—it's not even good folk psychology.

The Advisory Committee Notes provide an even less convincing justification for the second hearsay exception at issue in this case, the "excited utterance" rule. The proffered justification is "simply that circumstances may produce a condition of excitement which temporarily stills the capacity of reflection and produces utterances free of conscious fabrication." The two words I've italicized drain the attempted justification of any content. And even if a person is so excited by something that he loses the capacity for reflection (which doubtless does happen), how can there be any confidence that his unreflective utterance, provoked by excitement, is reliable? "One need not be a psychologist to distrust an observation made under emotional stress; everybody accepts such statements with mental reservation." (This is more evidence that these exceptions to the hearsay rule don't even have support in folk psychology.)

…. The Advisory Committee Notes go on to say that while the excited utterance exception has been criticized, "it finds support in cases without number." I find that less than reassuring. Like the exception for present sense impressions, the exception for excited utterances rests on no firmer ground than judicial habit, in turn reflecting judicial incuriosity and reluctance to reconsider ancient dogmas….

***

The *Boyce* opinion says that to qualify as a present sense impression, a statement must be made "without calculated narration." *Where is that requirement in the rule? And how well did the court explain how to apply the requirement?*

NOTE: SOCIAL MEDIA AND TEXTS

The following excerpt from a law review article cited in Judge Posner's concurring opinion in *Boyce*[1] highlights new frontiers for the rarely used present sense impression exception:

> B. The Emerging Salience of Electronic Present Sense Impressions
>
> Advances in technology and changes in social norms foreshadow a greater role for present sense impressions in American litigation. This increased role arises most directly out of two simultaneous technological advances. First, scientists have miniaturized massive computing power, leading to the widespread availability of handheld mobile devices with breathtaking capabilities…. Given this functionality, more and more people carry handheld communication devices at all times--at home, at work, and at play. Second, advances in wireless technology have enabled these devices to be perpetually connected both to voice and data networks. As a consequence, at any

---

[1] Jeffrey Bellin, *Facebook, Twitter, and the Uncertain Future of Present Sense Impressions*, 160 U. Pa. L. Rev. 331 (2012).

given time, a substantial (and growing) percentage of the population can access a device, such as an iPhone, that allows instant broadcast and receipt of electronic communications.

The ability to electronically communicate contemporaneous observations would be of little significance if people were not inclined to use it. The changes described above, however, coincide with changing social norms. This is likely no coincidence. As technology enabling instantaneous communication evolved, entrepreneurs created social networking sites to harness and encourage such communication....

These recent technological and social changes eliminate many of the once-daunting obstacles to the widespread availability of present sense impression evidence. First, these changes encourage people to constantly express contemporaneous observations about nonstartling events. This changing norm is most evident among people born within the last twenty years--the "Look at Me Generation"--described by social commentators as a group that has "been documented like no group before them, most especially by themselves." This generation employs text messaging, Twitter, and Facebook, as well as other social media tools, to communicate their activities and observations (from the exciting to the banal) to the rest of the world. Furthermore, real-time communication devices ensure that no one is ever alone.

[For example,] If a tree falls in the forest with no one around, its voice can now be heard so long as it possesses an iPhone:

> **Cedar29** 2 minutes ago
> Just fell in the forest ☹ Any1 around?

No matter how remote the declarant's location or what time of day, there is an audience for her perceptions and thus greater reason to express them. Electronic updates of peoples' observations ("the number seven bus is late"), activities ("I'm watching a movie with Cathy"), and locations ("I'm at a diner in Kalamazoo") increasingly populate cyberspace.

Second, modern communication devices make it more likely that present sense impressions, once uttered, will be preserved for trial. A stray oral comment to an acquaintance will easily be forgotten. Even if remembered, it may be lost to future litigants when the declarant or acquaintance becomes unavailable through death, inconvenience, lack of diligence, or the absence of common cause. An electronic observation, on the other hand--say, a "tweet" to dozens of friends-- is more likely to be available to litigants due to the increased number of people who might potentially recall it and have an interest in presenting it at trial. Even more significantly, these communications can now be uncovered by savvy litigators reviewing electronic files. Electronic communications, unlike [traditional] present sense impressions, will often be preserved on the numerous computers involved in their transmission and receipt.

The increased quantity of present sense impressions available to litigants is only one facet of the dramatic changes currently unfolding in the evidentiary landscape. A potentially more significant development is the change in the quality (i.e., reliability) of statements now encompassed by the present sense impression exception.

Unlike its oral counterpart, a typical e-PSI is not likely to be accompanied by the powerful form of corroboration once inherent in all present sense impressions--a percipient witness who can testify about the event described. As an initial matter, it is unlikely that an e-PSI will be communicated to someone who is physically present at the location where it is uttered. There is usually no need to tweet or text your observations to someone who is standing next to you. An e-PSI's author will most naturally be alone or in the presence of people who either are not part of the statement's intended audience, or whose identities are unknown at the time of trial.

More importantly, litigants will not be forced by the absence of alternatives to introduce e-PSIs through the testimony of a percipient witness. Unlike oral present sense impressions, e-PSIs will be preserved in electronic records or, failing that, can be introduced through the testimony of text message recipients, Facebook "friends," or Twitter "followers" who, like the bare documentary record, cannot speak to the veracity of the statements' contents. Thus, particularly where the substance of an e-PSI might be contradicted by a percipient witness, litigants will be able to introduce the statement at trial by alternate means.

In sum, the new breed of present sense impression evidence--typified by text messages, tweets, and Facebook status updates--is distinct from its historical analogue in both quantity and quality. Electronic present sense impressions will be more readily available to modern litigators and, most significantly, can be presented at trial--for tactical reasons or out of necessity or sloth-- without any corroborating witness testimony.

STATE OF MIND

RULE 803(3)

MUTUAL LIFE INSURANCE v. HILLMON
145 U.S. 285 (1892)

Justice GRAY delivered the opinion of the Court.

On July 13, 1880, Sallie E. Hillmon, a citizen of Kansas, brought an action against the Mutual Life Insurance Company, a corporation of New York, on a policy of insurance, dated December 10, 1878, on the life of her husband, John W. Hillmon, in the sum of $10,000, payable to her within 60 days after notice and proof of his death. On the same day the plaintiff brought two other actions,—the one against the New York Life Insurance Company, a corporation of New York, on two similar policies of life insurance, dated, respectively, November 30, 1878, and December 10, 1878, for the sum of $5,000 each; and the other against the Connecticut Mutual Life Insurance Company, a corporation of Connecticut, on a similar policy, dated March 4, 1879, for the sum of $5,000.

In each case the declaration alleged that Hillmon died on March 17, 1879, during the continuance of the policy, but that the defendant, though duly notified of the fact, had refused to pay the amount of the policy, or any part thereof; and the answer denied the death of Hillmon, and alleged that he, together with John H. Brown and divers other persons, on or before November 30, 1878, conspiring to defraud the defendant, procured the issue of all the policies, and afterwards, in March and April, 1879, falsely pretended and represented that Hillmon was dead, and that a dead body which they had procured was his, whereas in reality he was alive and in hiding....

At the trial plaintiff introduced evidence tending to show that on or about March 5, 1879, Hillmon and Brown left Wichita, in the state of Kansas, and traveled together through southern Kansas in search of a site for a cattle ranch; that on the night of March 18th, while they were in camp at a place called 'Crooked Creek,' Hillmon was killed by the accidental discharge of a gun; that Brown at once notified persons living in the neighborhood, and that the body was thereupon taken to a neighboring town, where, after an inquest, it was buried. The defendants introduced evidence tending to show that the body found in the camp at Crooked creek on the night of March 18th was not the body of Hillmon, but was the body of one Frederick Adolph Walters. Upon the question whose body this was there was much conflicting evidence, including photographs and descriptions of the corpse, and of the marks and scars upon it, and testimony to its likeness to Hillmon and to Walters.

The defendants introduced testimony that Walters left his home at Ft. Madison, in the state of Iowa, in March, 1878, and was afterwards in Kansas in 1878, and in January and February, 1879; that during that time his family frequently received letters from him, the last of which was written from Wichita; and that he had not been heard from since March, 1879. The defendants also offered the following evidence:

Elizabeth Rieffenach testified that she was a sister of Frederick Adolph Walters, and lived at Ft. Madison; and thereupon, as shown by the bill of exceptions, the following proceedings took place:

'Witness further testified that she had received a letter written from Wichita, Kansas, about the 4th or 5th day of March, 1879, by her brother Frederick Adolph; that the letter was dated at Wichita, and was in the handwriting of her brother; that she had searched for the letter, but could not find the same, it being lost; that she remembered and could state the contents of the letter.

'Thereupon the defendants' counsel asked the question, 'State the contents of that letter;' to which the plaintiff objected, on the ground that the same is incompetent, irrelevant, and hearsay. The objection was sustained, and the defendants duly excepted. The following is the letter as stated by witness:

Wichita, Kansas, March 4th or 5th or 3d or 4th,—I don't know,— 1879. Dear Sister and All: I now in my usual style drop you a few lines to let you know that I expect to leave Wichita on or about March the 5th with a certain Mr. Hillmon, a sheep trader, for Colorado, or parts unknown to me. I expect to see the country now. News are of no interest to you, as you are not acquainted here. I will close with compliments to all inquiring friends. Love to all. I am truly your brother, FRED. ADOLPH WALTERS.'

Alvina D. Kasten testified that she was 21 years of age, and resided in Ft. Madison; that she was engaged to be married to Frederick Adolph Walters; that she last saw him on March 24, 1878, at Ft. Madison; that he left there at that time, and had not returned; that she corresponded regularly with him, and received a letter about every two weeks until March 3, 1879, which was the last time she received a letter from him; that this letter was dated at Wichita, March 1, 1879, and was addressed to her at Ft. Madison, and the envelope was postmarked 'Wichita, Kansas, March 2, 1879;' and that she had never heard from or seen him since that time.

The defendants put in evidence the envelope with the postmark and address, and thereupon offered to read the letter in evidence. The plaintiff objected to the reading of the letter. The court sustained the objection, and the defendants excepted.

This letter was dated 'Wichita, March 1, 1879,' was signed by Walters, and began as follows:

'Dearest Alvina: Your kind and ever welcome letter was received yesterday afternoon about an hour before I left Emporia. I will stay here until the fore part of next week, and then will leavo here to see a part of the country that I never expected to see when I left home, as I am going with a man by the name of Hillmon, who intends, to start a sheep ranch, and, as he promised me more wager than I could make at anything else, I concluded to take it, for a while at least, until I strike something better. There is so many folks in this country that have got the Leadville fever, and if I could not of got the situation that I have now I would have went there myself; but as it is at present I get to see the best portion of Kansas, Indian Territory, Colorado, and Mexico. The route that we intend to take would cost a man to travel from $150 to $200, but it will not cost me a cent; besides, I get good wages. I will drop you a letter occasionally until I get settled down. Then I want you to answer it.'

The court, after recapitulating some of the testimony introduced, instructed the jury as follows: 'You have perceived from the very beginning of the trial that the conclusion to be reached must practically turn upon one question of fact, and all the large volume of evidence, with its graphic and varied details, has no actual significance, save as the facts established thereby may throw light upon and aid you in answering the question, whose body was it that on the evening of March 18, 1879, lay dead by the camp fire on Crooked creek? The decision of that question decides the verdict you should render.'

The jury … returned verdicts for the plaintiff against the three defendants respectively for the amounts of their policies and interest, upon which separate judgments were rendered.…

This question is of the admissibility of the letters written by Walters on the first days of March, 1879, which were offered in evidence by the defendants, and excluded by the court. In order to determine the competency of these letters it is important to consider the state of the case when they were offered to be read.

The matter chiefly contested at the trial was the death of John W. Hillmon, the insured; and that depended upon the question whether the body found at Crooked creek on the night of March 18, 1879, was his body or the body of one Walters.

Much conflicting evidence had been introduced as to the identity of the body. The plaintiff had also introduced evidence that Hillmon and one Brown left Wichita, in Kansas, on or about March 5, 1879, and traveled together through southern Kansas in search of a site for a cattle ranch; and that on the night of March 18th, while they were in camp at Crooked creek, Hillmon was accidentally killed, and that his body was taken thence and buried. The defendants had introduced evidence, without objection, that Walters left his home and his betrothed in Iowa in March, 1878, and was afterwards in Kansas until March, 1879; that during that time he corresponded regularly with his family and Lis betrothed; that the last letters received from him were one received by his betrothed on March 3d, and postmarked at 'Wichita, March 2,' and one received by his sister about March 4th or 5th, and dated at Wichita a day or two before; and that he had not been heard from since.

The evidence that Walters was at Wichita on or before March 5th, and had not been heard from since, together with the evidence to identify as his the body found at Crooked creek on March 18th, tended to show that he went from Wichita to Crooked creek between those dates. Evidence that just before March 5th he had the intention of leaving Wichita with Hillmon would tend to corroborate the evidence already admitted, and to show that he went from Wichita to Crooked creek with Hillmon. Letters from him to his family and his betrothed were the natural, if not the only attainable, evidence of his intention.

The position taken at the bar that the letters were competent evidence … as memoranda made in the ordinary course of business, cannot be maintained, for they were clearly not such.

But upon another ground suggested they should have been admitted…. The existence of a particular intention in a certain person at a certain time being a material fact to be proved, evidence that he expressed that intention at that time is as direct evidence of the fact as his own testimony that he then had that intention would be. After his death these can hardly be any other way of proving it, and while he is still alive his own memory of his state of mind at a former time is no more likely to be clear and true than a bystander's recollection of what he then said, and is less trustworthy than letters written by him at the very time and under circumstances precluding a suspicion of misrepresentation.

The letters in question were competent not as narratives of facts communicated to the writer by others, nor yet as proof that he actually went away from Wichita, but as evidence that, shortly before the time when other evidence tended to show that he went away, he had the intention of going, and of going with Hillmon, which made it more probable both that he did go and that he went with Hillmon than if there had been no proof of such intention. In view of the mass of conficting testimony introduced upon the question whether it was the body of Walters that was found in Hillmon's camp, this evidence might properly influence the jury in determining that question.

The rule applicable to this case has been thus stated by this court: 'Wherever the bodily or mental feelings of an individual are material to be proved, the usual expressions of such feelings are original and competent evidence. Those expressions are the natural reflexes of what it might be impossible to show by other testimony. If there be such other testimony, this may be necessary to set the facts thus developed in their true light, and to give them their proper effect. As independent, explanatory, or corroborative evidence it is often indispensable to the due administration of justice. Such declarations are regarded as verbal acts, and are as competent as any other testimony, when relevant to the issue. Their truth or falsity is an inquiry for the jury.'

[The Court then described various precedents, including the following case:]

Upon an indictment of one Hunter for the murder of one Armstrong at Camden, the court of errors and appeals of New Jersey unanimously held that Armstrong's oral declarations to his son at Philadelphia, on the afternoon before the night of the murder, as well as a letter written by him at the same time and place to his wife, each stating that he was going with Hunter to Camden on business, were rightly admitted in evidence. Chief Justice BEASLEY said: 'In the ordinary course of things, it was the usual information that a man about leaving home would communicate, for the convenience of his family, the information of his friends, or the regulation of his business. At the time it was given, such declarations could, in the nature of things, mean harm to no one. He who uttered them was bent on no expedition of mischief or wrong, and the attitude of affairs at the time entirely explodes the idea that such utterances were intended to serve any purpose but that for which they were obviously designed. If it be said that such notice of an intention of leaving home could have been given without introducing in it the name of Mr. Hunter, the obvious answer to the suggestion, I think, is that a reference to the companion who is to accompany the person leaving is as natural a part of the transaction as is any other incident or quality of it. If it is legitimate to show by a man's own declarations that he left his home to be gone a week, or for a certain destination, which seems incontestable, why may it not be proved in the same way that a designated person was to bear him company? At the time the words were uttered or written they imported no wrongdoing to any one,

281

and the reference to the companion who was to go with him was nothing more, as matters then stood, than an indication of an additional circumstance of his going. If it was in the ordinary train of events for this man to leave word or to state where he was going, it seems to me it was equally so for him to say with whom he was going.'

Upon principle and authority, therefore, we are of opinion that the two letters were competent evidence of the intention of Walters at the time of writing them, which was a material fact bearing upon the question in controversy; and that for the exclusion of these letters, as well as for the undue restriction of the defendants' challenges, the verdicts must be set aside, and a new trial had....

***

In *Shepard v. United States* (1933), the Supreme Court considered whether the dying victim's statement to a nurse accusing her husband of murder -- "Dr. Shepard poisoned me" -- might be admissible under the hearsay exception announced in *Hillmon*. The prosecution suggested that the statement reflected the victim's state of mind and specifically, a desire to live. The Supreme Court rejected this argument, announcing an important boundary on the state of mind exception that lives on in Rule 803(3). (The Court also considered the dying declaration exception, to be discussed later.)

> .... [T]he accusatory declaration must have been rejected as evidence of a state of mind, though the purpose thus to limit it had been brought to light upon the trial. The defendant had tried to show by Mrs. Shepard's declarations to her friends that she had exhibited a weariness of life and a readiness to end it, the testimony giving plausibility to the hypothesis of suicide. By the proof of these declarations evincing an unhappy state of mind, the defendant opened the door to the offer by the government of declarations evincing a different state of mind, declarations consistent with the persistence of a will to live. The defendant would have no grievance if the testimony in rebuttal had been narrowed to that point. What the government put in evidence, however, was something very different. It did not use the declarations by Mrs. Shepard to prove her present thoughts and feelings, or even her thoughts and feelings in times past. It used the declarations as proof of an act committed by some one else, as evidence that she was

dying of poison given by her husband. This fact, if fact it was, the government was free to prove, but not by hearsay declarations. It will not do to say that the jury might accept the declarations for any light that they cast upon the existence of a vital urge, and reject them to the extent that they charged the death to some one else. Discrimination so subtle is a feat beyond the compass of ordinary minds. The reverberating clang of those accusatory words would drown all weaker sounds. It is for ordinary minds, and not for psychoanalysts, that our rules of evidence are framed. They have their source very often in considerations of administrative convenience, of practical expediency, and not in rules of logic. When the risk of confusion is so great as to upset the balance of advantage, the evidence goes out.

These precepts of caution are a guide to judgment here. There are times when a state of mind, if relevant, may be proved by contemporaneous declarations of feeling or intent. Mutual Life Ins. Co. v. Hillmon. Thus, in proceedings for the probate of a will, where the issue is undue influence, the declarations of a testator are competent to prove his feelings for his relatives, but are incompetent as evidence of his conduct or of theirs. Throckmorton v. Holt. In suits for the alienation of affections, letters passing between the spouses are admissible in aid of a like purpose. In damage suits for personal injuries, declarations by the patient to bystanders or physicians are evidence of sufferings or symptoms, but are not received to prove the acts, the external circumstances, through which the injuries came about. Even statements of past sufferings or symptoms are generally excluded though an exception is at times allowed when they are made to a physician. So also in suits upon insurance policies, declarations by an insured that he intends to go upon a journey with another may be evidence of a state of mind lending probability to the conclusion that the purpose was fulfilled. Mutual Life Ins. Co. v. Hillmon. The ruling in that case marks the high-water line beyond which courts have been unwilling to go. It has developed a substantial body of criticism and commentary. Declarations of intention, casting light upon the future, have been sharply distinguished from declarations of memory, pointing backwards to the past. There would be an end, or nearly that, to the rule against hearsay if the distinction were ignored.

The testimony now questioned faced backward and not forward. This at least it did in its most obvious implications. What is even more important, it spoke to a past act, and, more than that, to an act by some one not the speaker. Other tendency, if it had any, was a filament too fine to be disentangled by a jury."

Rule 803(3) reflects the continuing influence of both *Hillmon* and *Shepard* in modern doctrine. In fact, the unique contributions of each case can be traced in the rule's text.

Shepard also references the origins of the last portion of Rule 803(3) "validity or terms of the declarant's will" with its citation to *Throckmorton v. Holt*. The modern Rule, in fact, reverses *Throckmorton*, but the main point to see here is that this is a very narrow carve out dealing solely with matters of probate.

STATEMENTS FOR TREATMENT AND DIAGNOSIS

RULE 803(4)

Rule 803(4) creates a hearsay exception for statements made for medical diagnosis or treatment. The exception relies on a person's self interest in being candid with medical treatment providers. "If you tell the doctor that your knife wound is a bug bite, you risk being treated with useless ointment instead of life-saving surgery."[1]

Under Rule 803(4)(A), qualifying statements must be made for the purposes of medical diagnosis or treatment. For this often-dispositive, subjective inquiry, the party offering the statement "must establish that the declarant's frame of mind when making the hearsay declaration 'was that of a patient seeking medical treatment.'"[2] Generally, this showing is made through context. The declarant becomes injured or ill, seeks out a medical professional, and provides information related to the injury or illness. Rule 803(4) sweeps beyond this prototypical scenario, however. For example, proper applications of the rule can be found where the declarant presented medical symptoms and their cause to a family member.

---

[1] Wright & Bellin § 6842.
[2] U.S. v. Gabe (8th Cir. 2001).

Rule 803(4)(A) further requires an objective inquiry into whether the proffered statements were "reasonably pertinent" to the medical provider's diagnosis and treatment tasks.

An active area of controversy in interpreting Rule 803(4) concerns statements that identify the perpetrator of an injury, or similar background information, only tangentially related to the medical inquiry. The Advisory Committee Note emphasizes that statements "as to fault would not ordinarily qualify" as having been made for purposes of diagnosis or treatment. "Thus a patient's statement that he was struck by an automobile would qualify but not his statement that the car was driven through a red light."

Courts applying this principle distinguish between statements that concern what happened and those that assign fault. "The former in most cases is pertinent to diagnosis and treatment while the latter would seldom, if ever, be sufficiently related."[1] Nevertheless, the evidentiary importance of who caused the injury—often the sole disputed issue in a criminal case—has placed great pressure on this distinction. In injury-related cases the litigated question is rarely whether the person seeking treatment was injured. Rather, litigated disputes typically concern the cause.

PROBLEM 6-17: IDENTIFYING A SUSPECT

Consider these facts from Oldman v. State (Wyo. 2000):

> [A] badly beaten woman … arrived at the police station. The woman told the dispatcher that she had just left [her] apartment…. One of the officers asked what had happened, and the victim replied, "My husband beat me up." She then was asked, "Who is your husband"? The victim replied that it was "Steven Oldman."

> After the officers obtained some additional details from the victim, they went to the apartment to look for Oldman. They did not find Oldman, and when they returned to the police station, the victim informed them she was pregnant. The officers called an ambulance which took the victim to the hospital. The attending physician, who saw the victim in the emergency room, noted a black and blue eye;

---

[1] U.S. v. Iron Shell (8th Cir. 1980).

facial bruising; and a "significant number of human bite marks" on her back, arm, thigh, hands, and feet. Although the physician did not ask, the victim told him that her husband had beaten her and bitten her.

[At Oldman's trial for aggravated assault,] the victim did not appear, but a police officer and the attending physician in the emergency room both testified about the statements she made to them identifying Oldman as her assailant. Oldman objected to the testimony of the attending physician as hearsay, but the trial court overruled the objection, invoking W.R.E. 803(4).

Why do you think Oldman did not object to the victim's statements to the police officers identifying Oldman as her assailant?

How should the court rule on the admissibility of the victim's statement to the emergency room physician identifying Oldman as the perpetrator?

Now consider another case, Colvard v. Com. (Ky. 2010), with different facts but a similar legal question:

On March 2, 2006, Appellant allegedly sexually assaulted two girls, D.J. and D.Y., in their bedroom. D.J. and D.Y. were six and seven years old, respectively, at the time of the events. Appellant knew the children because not only did he live in the same apartment complex as them, but just a few months before, he was engaged to marry their grandmother. The grandmother ended the engagement when she learned that Appellant was convicted of attempting to rape a ten-year-old girl in 1994.

When D.J. and D.Y. told their mother that they had just been sexually assaulted by Appellant, she immediately reported it to the authorities. The girls were then medically examined and interviewed by several medical professionals....

Jennifer Polk, an EMT who responded to the emergency call, was called by the Commonwealth to testify about the events of March 2, 2006. Over ... objection, Polk was allowed to testify that the first child to whom she spoke said that "Fred from number seven [Appellant] ... [sexually assaulted her]."

Appellant argues on appeal that [this and other] testimony from medical personnel was improperly admitted through the hearsay exception under KRE 803(4).

How should the court rule on the admissibility of Polk's testimony?

RECORDED RECOLLECTION

RULE 803(5)

The hearsay exception for recorded recollection is uncontroversial but important. Implicit in the operation of Rule 803(5) is the existence at some point of a physical record containing the hearsay statement. Generally, the record is a paper or electronic document, such as notes or a police report. Records need not be written; they can be captured in audio, video or electronic form. Once the record is deemed admissible under the exception, it can be read by the witness to the jury and relied on by the jury as proof of the truth of the matter asserted.

It is important to distinguish hearsay admitted under Rule 803(5) from the common trial practice of using a document or other item to refresh a testifying witness' memory. A witness who is shown a document before or during their testimony can review the document and then testify based on the witness' now-refreshed recollection. This practice is implicitly recognized in Rule 612. When the witness testifies based on a refreshed recollection, the witness is still testifying from memory, as in any other presentation of live witness testimony. Indeed, the adverse party should ensure that the refreshing document is taken away from the witness prior to the refreshed testimony. If this process is followed, there is no hearsay bar to testimony based on a refreshed memory, and a hearsay exception is not required.

Here is a humorous example used to illustrate the notion that *anything* can be used to refresh a witness' recollection:

> A young district attorney has called his first witness, Mrs. Rossilini, an elderly woman whose home had been burglarized. The attorney asks his witness what happened on the evening of October 25 of the previous year. The witness … responds, "I don['t] remember." The dialogue continues with the panicked attorney attempting to get his witness to testify about the burglary. Failing, he asks for a recess and runs to a nearby restaurant. He returns with a bowl of pasta fagoli, shows it to the witness, and then asks if she remembers what happened on the evening of October 25. The witness exclaims, "I was a cookin'

pasta fagoli, when that man (pointing to the defendant) broke into my house."[1]

The analysis changes when a witness reads from a document *while testifying*. In that circumstance, the witness is not testifying from memory, but is instead presenting an out-of-court statement to the jury. A hearsay exception such as Rule 803(5) is required if that out-of-court statement is to be admitted for the truth of the matter asserted.

The Rule drafters were concerned that a hearsay exception for recorded recollection could be used to introduce "statements carefully prepared for purposes of litigation under the supervision of attorneys, investigators, or claim adjusters." As a consequence, there is an important limitation in the rule. The witness must testify and be, at least partially, unable to recall the matter captured in the recorded statement. As the next case discusses, the rule also requires that the testifying witness vouch for the accuracy of the prior recording.

UNITED STATES v. PORTER
986 F.2d 1014 (6th Cir. 1993)

EDGAR, District Judge.

Todd Michael Porter ("Porter") was convicted [of a series of crimes involving selling cocaine and illegal explosives]. Porter was sentenced to a total of 252 months on all counts. Porter appeals his conviction and sentence. We AFFIRM.

The disposition of this case on appeal hinges upon two evidentiary rulings made by the district court. In one of these rulings, the district court allowed portions of a written statement made by Kim Niswonger ("Niswonger"), Porter's teenaged girlfriend, to be read into evidence as past recollection recorded under Federal Rules of Evidence 803(5). These statements had particular reference to an incident wherein Porter told Niswonger, if beeped by him, to go to his grandmother's house, flush some cocaine to be found there down the toilet, and hide about $30,000 in cash. This testimony was

---

[1] John J. Capowski, Evidence and the One-Liner, 35 Ariz. St. L.J. 877 (2003).

directed in particular at Count 3 of the indictment charging Porter with forcing and inducing a minor to assist in avoiding apprehension or detection.

On October 5, 1989, Niswonger had given a very detailed written statement to the Federal Bureau of Investigation. This statement related various personal experiences with Porter involving cocaine and explosives between July and September 1989. Niswonger was then 17 years old. The written statement makes it clear that Porter had threatened Niswonger, and that she was afraid of him. On the witness stand, Niswonger said that while she did recall giving the written statement and signing it, she now really did not remember much about what she had said in the statement because, she testified, she was confused and on drugs at the time the statement was made.

... A document may be read to a jury under [Rule 803(5)] if (1) the witness once had knowledge about the matters in the document; (2) the witness now has insufficient recollection to testify fully and accurately; and (3) the record was made at a time when the matter was fresh in the witness' memory and reflected the witness' knowledge correctly.

"The touchstone for admission of evidence as an exception to the hearsay rule has been the existence of circumstances which attest to its trustworthiness." The district court made a very careful analysis of Niswonger's statement and the circumstances of her trial testimony, and found sufficient indicia of trustworthiness to admit portions of the statement. Among the factors considered by the district court were: (1) Niswonger admitted making the statement; (2) the statement was made soon after the events related in the statement; (3) the statement was signed by Niswonger on each of its five pages; (4) the wording of the statement had been changed and initialed by Niswonger 11 times; (5) the statement was made under penalty of perjury; (6) the statement contained considerable detail which was internally consistent, as well as consistent with other uncontradicted evidence which had already been admitted; and (7) Niswonger gave the statement at a time when she was fearful of reprisal from the defendant. Finally, the district judge, who had full opportunity to view the witness' demeanor and evaluate her testimony, determined that Niswonger, in attempting to distance herself from the contents of the statement, was being "disingenuous" and "evasive," and was acting either out of her recently professed desire to marry the defendant or out of fear of the defendant.

The facts found by the district court are sufficient to meet the criteria of Rule 803(5). The detail in the statement and the care with which it was put together make it clear that Niswonger once had knowledge of the matters in the statement. Whether by virtue of mind-altering drugs or by intentional design, she had insufficient recollection to testify truthfully and accurately about the matters comprising the statement's contents. Finally, the statement was made shortly after events set out in the statement when those events were fresh in her mind, and the statement reflected her knowledge correctly.

Whether or not the statement correctly reflected Niswonger's knowledge is a matter which bears further discussion in view of the particular facts in this case. Niswonger never actually testified … that what she said in her statement was accurate. In fact, Niswonger testified that she was "screwed up" on drugs at about the time the statement was made, and although she tried to tell the truth in the statement, she was not sure she had done so. Rule 803(5) does not specify any particular method of establishing the knowledge of the declarant nor the accuracy of the statement. It is not a sine qua non of admissibility that the witness actually vouch for the accuracy of the written memorandum. Admissibility is, instead, to be determined on a case-by-case basis upon a consideration, as was done by the district court in this case, of factors indicating trustworthiness, or the lack thereof.

While Rule 803(5) treats recorded recollection as an exception to the hearsay rule, the hearsay is not of a particularly unreliable genre. This is because the out-of-court declarant is actually on the witness stand and subject to evaluation by the finder of fact, in this case the jury. If the jury chose to believe what Niswonger said in the recorded statement rather than what she said while testifying, that decision was at least made based upon what it observed and heard from her in court. We find that the district judge did not abuse his discretion in allowing portions of Niswonger's statement to be read to the jury under Rule 803(5).

***

Porter reveals a court struggling to affirm a trial court ruling despite the witness' failure to endorse the accuracy of the statement. Here is a treatise excerpt[1] discussing this portion of the rule with a reference to the *Porter* case.

> The text of Federal Rule of Evidence 803(5)(C) requires that a qualifying recorded recollection "accurately reflects the witness's knowledge." This text is somewhat misleading. Admission is premised on the witness not fully remembering the recorded subject. Consequently, the witness cannot be expected to verify the accuracy of the recorded recollection at trial. Instead, the rule seeks indirect assurances from the testifying witness as to the statement's accuracy. A witness might say, for example, that she remembers thinking the statement accurate when she recorded it. Or she might testify that "she did not and would not have lied" in giving the recorded statement.

> More difficult questions of adequate verification arise when the testifying witness is uncooperative. Courts in these circumstances sometimes stretch the Rule 803(5)(C) requirement, accepting half-hearted affirmations by the witness, such as that the recorded statement "was accurate 'in general,'" or merely that the witness "did not think he had lied" in making the statement. Even a witness' testimony that "although she tried to tell the truth in the statement, she was not sure she had done so" was deemed sufficient to satisfy the rule's requirement. On the other hand, a witness' hope that the statement was accurate—"I don't know that for certain, but I would hope so."—should not be sufficient. The testifying witness' flat out rejection of a recorded statement's reliability clearly precludes admission under Rule 803(5)(C).

***

Rule 803(5) states that a qualifying record, once admitted, may "be read into evidence" but cannot be "received as an exhibit" except if "offered by an adverse party." The purpose of this proviso is to prevent the factfinder from subconsciously assigning more weight to recorded statements than it does to live witness testimony on equivalent points.

---

[1] Wright & Bellin § 6856.

BUSINESS RECORDS

RULE 803(6)

Rule 803(6) contains a hearsay exception for the records of an organization. Although its origins can be traced to the need to admit records of commercial entities, Rule 803(6)'s scope is broader than just "business" records. The records of virtually any entity can qualify.

The primary difficulties in introducing business records are practical. The party seeking admission must procure either live testimony (from someone familiar with the business' recordkeeping) or a certification that records (1) were prepared and kept in the normal course of business; (2) made at or near the time of the events recorded; and (3) are based on the personal knowledge of the entrant or of a person with a business duty to transmit the information to the entrant.

Two legal issues regularly arise with respect to the admission of business records. The first is the treatment of statements captured in a business record that were made by someone who was not part of the business.

Rule 803(6) permits the admission of records made through a coordinated process, where one employee perceives information and transmits the information to another who records it. The initial observer must have knowledge of the event observed, but neither the ultimate recorder of the information nor those involved in passing that information along to the recorder are required to have firsthand knowledge of the recorded event. As the next case reflects, an important distinction arises, however, when a business record contains a hearsay statement of an "outsider" to the business.

UNITED STATES v. GWATHNEY
465 F.3d 1133 (10th Cir. 2006)

O'BRIEN, Circuit Judge.

…. On May 23, 2004, Charles Gwathney, a commercial truck driver, stopped at the Gallup, New Mexico Port of Entry along Interstate 40 near the Arizona–New Mexico state line to obtain a trip permit through New Mexico for his load of potatoes. The truck was owned by Solomon Shaw. Officer Smid asked Gwathney for his driver's license, medical card, tractor and trailer registration, log book and bill of lading, all of which were provided. The bill of lading listed the truck as carrying 833 boxes of red potato creamers, required the truck to be maintained at forty-two degrees and was signed by Gwathney. The log book indicated potatoes had been loaded on the truck in Phoenix on May 21, but that Gwathney did not leave Phoenix until May 23. Although the truck was refrigerated, Officer Smid thought it unusual Gwathney would load the potatoes prior to having his truck repaired because potatoes are perishable goods. Officer Smid asked Gwathney why he had taken over a day to leave Phoenix after his truck was loaded. Gwathney explained the delay was caused by repairs he had made to his truck. Gwathney provided Officer Smid an invoice for the repair work. The invoice showed the repair work to have been completed on May 21. It also indicated Gwathney paid almost $14,000 in cash for the repairs.

Officer Smid instructed Gwathney to pull the truck into a bay where he would conduct a level 2 inspection. After checking the outside of the truck, Officer Smid instructed Gwathney to unlock the doors to the trailer. Upon opening the doors, Officer Smid discovered one of the pallets had tipped against the wall of the truck during transit. Officer Smid used a ladder to climb over the potatoes to make sure the rest of the pallets were secure and in place. While climbing over the leaning pallet, Officer Smid detected shoe prints and crushed boxes indicating someone had walked on the pallets after they were loaded on the truck. Officer Smid followed the footprints and smashed boxes until he reached an open area in the truck. There, he discovered several large non-conforming brown boxes that had numbers spray-painted on them and were wrapped in brown packing tape. They did not have the word "Potato" on them, and Officer Smid believed them to contain contraband. At that point,

Officer Smid crawled out of the truck and handcuffed Gwathney for the officer's protection while he continued his search. Upon returning to the boxes, Officer Smid cut them open and discovered what eventually was determined to be 152.2 kilograms of marijuana. Officer Smid then arrested Gwathney....

Beginning December 15, 2004, Gwathney was tried before a jury. At trial, Gwathney claimed he had no knowledge of the drugs on his truck. He explained the payment of $14,000 in cash for the truck repairs came from money wired to him by Solomon Shaw, who sent the money via Western Union. In rebuttal, the government introduced Exhibit 55—an administrative subpoena directed toward Western Union requiring the provision of any wire transfer records for Gwathney, or Solomon Shaw from May 13, 2004 through May 23, 2004, coupled with Western Union's response that it could find no such records. Gwathney objected to the admission of the evidence based on the lack of an adequate foundation. The district court allowed admission of Western Union's response based on the business record exception of Rule 803(6) of the Federal Rules of Evidence.

.... On December 16, 2004, the jury convicted Gwathney.

On May 11, 2005, Gwathney filed a motion for a new trial based on newly discovered evidence. The new evidence was a Western Union wire transfer receipt showing a transfer of $921.00 from Solomon Shaw to Gwathney on May 14, 2004, which contradicted Western Union's report attached to Exhibit 55. On May 25, 2005, the district court denied the motion. On May 27, 2005, Gwathney was sentenced to 137 months' imprisonment. He filed a timely notice of appeal on June 1, 2005....

Rule 803(6) of the Federal Rules of Evidence provides an exception to the hearsay rule for business records if they are "kept in the course of a regularly conducted business activity, and if it was the regular practice of that business activity to make the memorandum [record]." "The rationale behind the business records exception is that such documents have a high degree of reliability because businesses have incentives to keep accurate records." To satisfy Rule 803(6), "a document must (1) have been prepared in the normal course of business; (2) have been made at or near the time of the events it records; ... (3) be based on the personal knowledge of the entrant or of an informant who had a business duty to transmit the information to the entrant;" and (4) not have involved sources, methods, or circumstances indicating a lack of trustworthiness. Of course, the proponent of the document must lay a proper foundation for its admission.

"Not every item of business correspondence constitutes a business record." "It is well-established that one who prepares a document in anticipation of litigation is not acting in the regular course of business." Moreover, business records are potentially fraught with double hearsay. "Double hearsay in the context of a business record exists when the record is prepared by an employee with information supplied by another person." Any information provided by another person, if an outsider to the business preparing the record, must itself fall within a hearsay exception to be admissible.

In this case, Exhibit 55 contained two documents: a subpoena issued by Special Agent Ivar Hella of the Drug Enforcement Agency, and Western Union's Response to the subpoena. The district court admitted Exhibit 55 during Special Agent Hella's testimony, reasoning:

> as the case agent and the one who conducted the investigation, he can testify as to the contents of the results of his investigation in terms of issuing the subpoena. If there's a foundation laid under 803(6) on these subpoenas that they are treated as business records of the DEA, then I'm going to allow—it's not a business record of Western Union because he can't lay that foundation. But the agent can lay a foundation about the way DEA records and keeps its documents, and since it's a response to a DEA subpoena and part of the investigation, I think it would be a business record of DEA.

Gwathney does not challenge the district court's determination as to the DEA subpoena, but rather argues Exhibit 55 as a whole was inadmissible on this record because it contained hearsay statements of Western Union. We agree.

Western Union's response to the DEA's subpoena is a separate document from the subpoena itself and constitutes hearsay. As such, the response must fall within its own exception to the hearsay rule to be admissible. Contrary to the district court's reasoning, the DEA cannot claim Western Union's response as one of its own business records for the simple reason the DEA did not prepare the document. The fact Western Union's response is likely trustworthy given that it was "required to comply with the terms of the subpoena" does not change this basic fact. [A]ccord United States v. McIntyre (10th Cir.1993) (holding hearsay imbedded in a business record may be admissible only where information is trustworthy, such as where the preparer of the document checked the accuracy of the information)....

If the Western Union document was to be admitted as a business record under Rule 803(6), it would have to be admitted as a business record of Western Union. As the district court correctly noted, Special Agent Hella could not lay a foundation for the Western Union's response. Absent a proper foundation and applicable hearsay exception, it was error to admit Western Union's response to the DEA subpoena.

***

The problem the *Gwathney* court identifies is as much about effort as law. Western Union's response may well have also qualified as a business record. But the government did not provide any foundation for the admission of Western Union's business records. Instead, the government offered the testimony necessary to admit the DEA's business records -- and those records included a statement from Western Union, an outsider to the DEA's "business." Rule 803(6) does not itself authorize admission of "outsider" statements, even when those statements are captured in a business record. This interpretation of the rule, "despite its language,"[1] is supported both by the rationale for the exception and the Advisory Committee's Notes. Oddly enough, the point is made most forcefully in the Note to Rule 803(11), which states that Rule 803(6) "require[s] that the person furnishing the information be one in the business or activity."

The second legal issue that regularly arises in this context concerns records prepared in anticipation of litigation.

---

[1] U.S. v. Vigneau (1st Cir. 1999).

297

PALMER v. HOFFMAN
318 U.S. 109 (1943)

Justice DOUGLAS delivered the opinion of the Court.

This case arose out of a grade crossing accident which occurred in Massachusetts....

The accident occurred on the night of December 25, 1940. On December 27, 1940, the engineer of the train, who died before the trial, made a statement at a freight office of petitioners where he was interviewed by an assistant superintendent of the road and by a representative of the Massachusetts Public Utilities Commission. This statement was offered in evidence by petitioners under the Act of June 20, 1936:

> 'In any court of the United States ..., any writing or record, whether in the form of an entry in a book or otherwise, made as a memorandum or record of any act, transaction, occurrence, or event, shall be admissible as evidence of said act, transaction, occurrence, or event, if it shall appear that it was made in the regular course of any business, and that it was the regular course of such business to make such memorandum or record at the time of such act, transaction, occurrence, or event or within a reasonable time thereafter. All other circumstances of the making of such writing or record, including lack of personal knowledge by the entrant or maker, may be shown to affect its weight, but they shall not affect its admissibility. The term 'business' shall include business, profession, occupation, and calling of every kind.'

They offered to prove (in the language of the Act) that the statement was signed in the regular course of business, it being the regular course of such business to make such a statement. Respondent's objection to its introduction was sustained.

We agree with the majority view below that it was properly excluded.

We may assume that if the statement was made 'in the regular course' of business, it would satisfy the other provisions of the Act. But we do not think that it was made 'in the regular course' of business within the meaning of the

Act. The business of the petitioners is the railroad business. That business like other enterprises entails the keeping of numerous books and records essential to its conduct or useful in its efficient operation. Though such books and records were considered reliable and trustworthy for major decisions in the industrial and business world, their use in litigation was greatly circumscribed or hedged about by the hearsay rule—restrictions which greatly increased the time and cost of making the proof where those who made the records were numerous. It was that problem which started the movement towards adoption of legislation embodying the principles of the present Act. And the legislative history of the Act indicates the same purpose.

The engineer's statement which was held inadmissible in this case falls into quite a different category. It is not a record made for the systematic conduct of the business as a business. An accident report may affect that business in the sense that it affords information on which the management may act. It is not, however, typical of entries made systematically or as a matter of routine to record events or occurrences, to reflect transactions with others, or to provide internal controls. The conduct of a business commonly entails the payment of tort claims incurred by the negligence of its employees. But the fact that a company makes a business out of recording its employees' versions of their accidents does not put those statements in the class of records made 'in the regular course' of the business within the meaning of the Act. If it did, then any law office in the land could follow the same course, since business as defined in the Act includes the professions. We would then have a real perversion of a rule designed to facilitate admission of records which experience has shown to be quite trustworthy. Any business by installing a regular system for recording and preserving its version of accidents for which it was potentially liable could qualify those reports under the Act. The result would be that the Act would cover any system of recording events or occurrences provided it was 'regular' and though it had little or nothing to do with the management or operation of the business as such. Preparation of cases for trial by virtue of being a 'business' or incidental thereto would obtain the benefits of this liberalized version of the early shop book rule. The probability of trustworthiness of records because they were routine reflections of the day to day operations of a business would be forgotten as the basis of the rule. Regularity of preparation would become the test rather than the character of the records and their earmarks of reliability acquired from their source and origin and the nature of their compilation. We cannot so completely empty the words of the Act of their historic meaning. If the Act is to be extended to apply not only to a 'regular course' of a business but also to any 'regular course' of conduct which may have some relationship to business, Congress not this Court must extend it. Such a major change which opens wide the door to avoidance of cross-examination should not be left to implication. Nor is it any answer to say that Congress has provided in the Act that the various circumstances of the making of the record should affect its weight not its admissibility. That provision comes into play only in case the other requirements of the Act are met.

In short, it is manifest that in this case those reports are not for the systematic conduct of the enterprise as a railroad business. Unlike payrolls, accounts receivable, accounts payable, bills of lading and the like these reports are calculated for use essentially in the court, not in the business. Their primary utility is in litigating, not in railroading....

***

Many courts read Rule 803(6)(B)'s "regularly conducted activity" requirement to disqualify records generated with an eye toward litigation, citing *Palmer v. Hoffman*. Of course, that 1943 decision was not an interpretation of Rule 803(6). And the line the Court drew is blurry in a modern context where the prospect of litigation is embedded in the business model of many organizations. Indeed, as *Palmer v. Hoffman* made its way through the lower courts, Second Circuit Judge Charles Clark noted the "illogical" nature of the anticipation-of-litigation disqualification. He pointed out that: "Since the first cave man made notches on a stick, ... both the purpose and the value of records were their use in future disputes—to prevent many, to settle others." This criticism is increasingly powerful in a modern (non-caveman) context.

Modern courts can exclude litigation-minded records without resorting to *Palmer*'s somewhat strained "business as a business" reasoning. As the Advisory Committee suggests, exclusion of litigation-minded records can more comfortably be grounded in Rule 803(6)(E). Rule 803(6)(E) provides that even if a record otherwise qualifies for admission as a business record, it can nevertheless be excluded by the trial court if the "method or circumstances of preparation" of the document "indicate a lack of trustworthiness." This catch-all reliability requirement provides trial courts with broad discretion.

The Rule 803(6)(E) inquiry is fact specific. In a typical scenario, a party first demonstrates the applicability of the other requirements of the business records exception. The party opposing the records can then point out trustworthiness problems. The dispute will follow a similar pattern. The party offering the records will point to myriad factors, such as the experience or expertise of the persons generating the records, the importance of the records to the business, verification and reliance on the records, and the lack of an incentive to falsify. Each of these factors has a flip side that can be highlighted, as applicable, by the opposing party.

RULE 803(7)

Rule 803(7) provides a hearsay exception for "[e]vidence that a matter is not included" in a business record. The exception is rarely a subject of controversy. The exception is most interesting because it seems unnecessary. The Advisory Committee includes the exception nonetheless because "decisions may be found which class the evidence not only as hearsay but also as not within any exception."

PUBLIC RECORDS

RULE 803(8)

Rule 803(8) provides a hearsay exception for public records. The exception parallels the business records exception. The rule is grounded on the "assumption that a public official will perform his duty properly and the unlikelihood that he will remember details independently of the record."[1] As explained by the Supreme Court in a case cited by the Advisory Committee:[2]

> "[T]heir character as public records required by law to be kept, the official character of their contents entered under the sanction of public duty, the obvious necessity for regular contemporaneous entries in

---

[1] Advisory Committee Note.
[2] Chesapeake & Delaware Canal Co. v. U.S. (1919).

them and the reduction to a minimum of motive on the part of public officials and employés to either make false entries or to omit proper ones, all unite to make these books admissible as unusually trustworthy sources of evidence."

Parties can rely on Rule 803(8) to introduce the public records of federal, state, and local government agencies, foreign or domestic.

The public records hearsay exception covers three types of records.

Federal Rule of Evidence 803(8)(A)(i)—formerly Rule 803(8)(A)—permits the introduction over a hearsay objection of a record of a public office that sets out the "office's activities." The pertinent Advisory Committee Note sparingly, but helpfully, singles out "[t]reasury records of miscellaneous receipts and disbursements." This example comes from the Supreme Court case referenced above that endorsed the admission of printed Treasury books that showed "all of the miscellaneous receipts and disbursements of the government from 1848 to 1914." Illustrative examples of official activities that qualify for admission under Rule 803(8)(A)(i) include, meeting minutes, or a report of a government agency on its completed tasks.

Most cases addressing the public records hearsay exception deal with Rule 803(8)(A)(ii)—formerly Rule 803(8)(B). This provision extends the exception to records or statements about a matter observed by a recording party "while under a legal duty to report."

The "while under a legal duty to report" language comes from a Congressional amendment to the initially proposed rule. Congress intended the amendment to prevent the introduction under the public records exception of "random observations by a Government employee." During remarks on the floor, the sponsor of the change explained:

> Supposing you had a divorce case and you tried to put in a report of a social worker, rather than putting the social worker on the stand; under the committee's language anything she said in the report which would be observed by her pursuant to her general duties would be admissible. Under the amendment, only those things as to which she had some duty to make a report would be admissible.

Importantly, courts do not interpret the "legal duty" provision to require that a statute or other legal rule explicitly impose a duty on the declarant or agency to report a particular observation. "Rather, it suffices if the nature of the responsibilities assigned to the public agency are such that the record is appropriate to the function of the agency."[1] This functional interpretation makes the rule significantly broader than it would be under a more literal reading. Given the explosive growth of public agencies to encompass many employees with complex, long-term responsibilities, recordkeeping is a natural outgrowth of many public officials' duties.

A second Congressional amendment to the Advisory' Committee's proposed rule placed another important restriction on records admitted under Federal Rule of Evidence 803(8)(A)(ii). The amendment added the text: "excluding, however, in criminal cases matters observed by police officers and other law enforcement personnel." The amendment's sponsor explained the rationale behind this limit:

> [I]n a criminal case, only, we should not be able to put in the police report to prove your case without calling the policeman. I think in a criminal case you ought to have to call the policeman on the beat and give the defendant the chance to cross examine him, rather than just reading the report into evidence,…..

Despite opposition that the effect of the amendment "is to make police officers and law enforcement officers second-class citizens and persons less trustworthy than social workers or garbage collectors," the amendment passed with enthusiastic support.

As a result of the amendment, documents memorializing "a matter observed by law-enforcement personnel" cannot be admitted under Rule 803(8)(A)(ii). As Congress intended, this carve out (sometimes called the "law enforcement exception") prevents a large body of otherwise relevant documentation generated by police agencies from coming into evidence.

The question of outsider statements arises infrequently under the public records exception. This is because the bulk of public records evidence comes under Rule 803(8)(A)(ii) and only public officials typically have the requisite

---

[1] United States v. Lopez (9th Cir. 2014).

"legal duty to report." There are instances, however, when civilians are legally obligated to report matters to the government, and those reports end up as a part of a government record. Thus far, courts have resisted the notion that a legal duty to file information with the government, such as the obligation to file a tax return, renders the filed document a public record admissible under Rule 803(8). One way to view the analysis is that such records do not constitute "records" or "statements" of a public office, despite their immediate location.

An interesting wrinkle on these examples involves increasingly popular "mandatory reporter" statutes.

PROBLEM 6-18: MANDATORY REPORTER

A teacher at a private elementary school in Virginia calls the local social services agency and informs the social worker who answers the phone: "one of my 2d graders, John Smith, has had bruises on his neck and arms the past three Mondays; he says he 'got them for punishment.'"

The social services employee writes down the entire teacher's statement in an official "Mandatory Report Form" and files it away in the state's records for follow up.

Virginia Code § 63.2-1509 states:

> A. The following persons who, in their professional or official capacity, have reason to suspect that a child is an abused or neglected child, shall report the matter immediately to the local department of the county or city wherein the child resides or wherein the abuse or neglect is believed to have occurred …:

> 5. Any teacher or other person employed in a public or private school, kindergarten or nursery school.

The state later prosecutes the parent who has custody of Smith on the weekends for child abuse. *Can the prosecution introduce the unredacted Mandatory Report Form as evidence of both the bruises and the child's statements about their source?*

***

304

Federal Rule of Evidence 803(8)(A)(iii)—formerly Rule 803(8)(C)—extends the public records hearsay exception to a record of a public office that sets out "factual findings from a legally authorized investigation." The text limits its application to the introduction of records "in a civil case or against the government in a criminal case."

The leading case on Rule 803(8)(A)(iii) is *Beech Aircraft Corp. v. Rainey* (1988). *Beech Aircraft* holds that if a public report satisfies the prerequisites of Rule 803(8)(A)(iii), the entirety of the report qualifies for admission, not merely its factual components. This includes narratives relating what others stated and portions of the report that explicitly state opinions as opposed to facts. Importantly, any portion of the report can still be excluded if found to be untrustworthy under Rule 803(8)(B). As the Supreme Court emphasized, "a trial judge has the discretion, and indeed the obligation, to exclude an entire report or portions thereof—whether narrow 'factual' statements or broader 'conclusions'—that she determines to be untrustworthy."

Supplementing the public records exception, Rule 803(9) allows admission of public records of certain "vital statistics." Rule 803(10) provides a hearsay exception for testimony or a self-authenticating certificate stating "that a diligent search failed to disclose a public record or statement." This exception complements the public records exception in Rule 803(8) the same way that Rule 803(7) complements the business records exception in Rule 803(6).

MISCELLANEOUS RULE 803 EXCEPTIONS

The balance of exceptions in Rule 803 are rarely used. Here is a short summary of the remaining exceptions. There are, as always, a variety of complications but they do not arise frequently enough to justify extended treatment.

FAMILY HISTORY AND PROPERTY

The exceptions in Rule 803(11), (12), (13) & (19) are designed to facilitate the admission of records of family history, and particularly solemn religious ceremonies. (Another exception in Rule 804(b)(4) covers similar ground.) The drafters imported these exceptions from the common law which, often by necessity, included creative mechanisms for proving things like "pedigree," "legitimacy," and kinship. Times have changed. First, these matters are less commonly the subject of legal disputes. Second, record keeping has vastly improved. Consequently, facts that could once only be proven by the testimony of, say, a great aunt under Rule 803(19), or through an inscription in the family bible under Rule 803(16), are now established more convincingly through official records.

Rule 803(14) & (15) effectuate state property recording regimes. To the extent someone properly files paperwork regarding a property interest with the local jurisdiction, that document will generally be admissible in later litigation regarding the property.

ANCIENT DOCUMENTS

Rule 803(16) is the "ancient documents" hearsay exception. Documents that live up to the "ancient" moniker contain statements relating to events that few will remember, much less be available to testify about. The Advisory Committee Note adds that "age affords assurance that the writing antedates the present controversy."

The "ancient" moniker is an overstatement as the exception applies to any "statement in a document that was prepared before January 1, 1998." The January 1, 1998, cutoff replaces a previous twenty-year requirement, which arose from the common law sentiment that the "ancient documents rule applies to documents a generation or more in age." As the Advisory Committee Note to the authentication rule for ancient documents acknowledges, "Any time period selected is bound to be arbitrary."

The January 1, 1998, cutoff date for ancient documents was implemented in the 2017 amendment because the Advisory Committee believed the rule does not provide sufficient guarantees of reliability in an age of electronically stored information. The Advisory Committee explained:

> Given the exponential development and growth of electronic information since 1998, the hearsay exception for ancient documents has now become a possible open door for large amounts of unreliable [electronically stored information], as no showing of reliability needs to be made to qualify under the exception.

The Advisory Committee's Note highlights the exception's broad application to "all sorts of documents, including letters, records, contracts, maps, and certificates, in addition to title documents." That said, as the Committee recognizes, the ancient documents exception "has not been a subject of frequent discussion in reported opinions."

MARKET REPORTS / COMMERCIAL PUBLICATIONS

Rule 803(17) provides a hearsay exception for "[m]arket quotations, lists, directories, or other compilations that are generally relied on by the public or by persons in particular occupations." The Advisory Committee Note specifically references compilations widely consumed by the public, such as "newspaper market reports, telephone directories, and city directories," and also indicates that the exception covers data compilations "prepared for the use of a trade or profession." The traditional example is stock prices established through a published list in a daily newspaper. There are two primary limits on admissibility incorporated into Rule 803(17): (1) broad reliance on the publication; and (2) a factual, list-type nature.

The exception's relatively infrequent appearances in the case law suggests a conservative approach by the courts. Rule 803(17) may become more visible in the future with the explosion of easily accessible on-line compendiums of information that "are generally relied on by the public."

LEARNED TREATISES

Rule 803(18) provides a hearsay exception for statements in learned treatises and analogous reference materials. The exception finds its roots in the commonsense notion that a party should be able to cross-examine the other party's trial experts with statements found in leading reference works of the expert's discipline. As the Supreme Court long ago explained:

> It certainly is illogical, if not actually unfair, to permit witnesses to give expert opinions based on book knowledge, and then deprive the party challenging such evidence of all opportunity to interrogate them about divergent opinions expressed in other reputable books.[1]

---

[1] Reilly v. Pinkus, 338 U.S. 269 (1949).

It is a short leap from the proposition that a party can reference statements from learned treatises during cross-examination, to allowing the party to admit such statements into evidence. This is the leap the Federal Rules take in Rule 803(18). "Materials admitted under" Rule 803(18) are "accorded substantive value, and are not merely impeachment evidence."[1]

Under Rule 803(18)(A), a qualifying statement must be "called to the attention of an expert witness on cross-examination or relied on by the expert on direct examination." The Advisory Committee explains that this requirement mitigates the "danger of misunderstanding and misapplication" of the treatise by limiting its use as substantive evidence to "situations in which an expert is on the stand and available to explain and assist in the application of the treatise." Rule 803(18)(B) adds that statements can only be admitted if the source material in which they are found is "established as a reliable authority." The proponent of evidence can satisfy this requirement either through the testifying expert witness' own acknowledgement, or by "another expert's testimony, or by judicial notice."

CERTAIN CATEGORIES OF REPUTATION AND JUDGMENTS

Rule 803(19) (personal or family history), (20) (land boundaries) & (21) (character) permit a witness to testify about certain narrow forms of reputation. While Rule 803(22) and (23) concern the admission of court judgments.

---

[1] Maggipinto v. Reichman, 607 F.2d 621 (3d Cir. 1979).

RULE 804 HEARSAY EXCEPTIONS

Federal Rule of Evidence 804, like Rule 803, contains a series of hearsay exceptions. The key difference is that Rule 804 exceptions can only be invoked when the declarant is "unavailable." As the Advisory Committee explains, this requirement reflects that Rule 804 "proceeds upon a different theory" than Rule 803: "[H]earsay which admittedly is not equal in quality to testimony of the declarant on the stand may nevertheless be admitted" under Rule 804 "if the declarant is unavailable and if his statement meets a specified standard."

The five hearsay exceptions in Rule 804 are each premised on the unavailability of the declarant. Unavailability is defined in Rule 804(a) through a series of straightforward examples. The theme of the examples is that merely showing the difficulty of obtaining a live witness, or the witness' desire to avoid testifying is insufficient. Instead, the proponent of hearsay offered under Rule 804 must show that it is not possible through reasonable efforts, including formal judicial process, to obtain the declarant's live testimony (or in some circumstances, deposition testimony).

PRIOR TESTIMONY

RULE 804(b)(1)

The first requirement for hearsay offered under Rule 804(b)(1) is that it consist of testimony that was given by the declarant as a witness at a prior proceeding, specifically a trial, hearing, or deposition. This prior proceeding requirement indicates a desire for formality, typically including an oath or affirmation, some form of questioning, and an official record of the witness' statements. This flows naturally from the notion that the hearsay at issue constitutes former "testimony." The most obvious qualifying examples consist of testimony at a former trial, or trial proceeding, such as a preliminary hearing. The rule's use of the broad term "hearing" ensures that its coverage also extends to testimony provided in formal, but non-judicial proceedings, such as grand jury hearings as well as administrative hearings conducted by executive agencies.

Rule 804(b)(1)'s second requirement, encapsulated in Rule 804(b)(1)(B), generates the bulk of the legal analysis in this context. Former testimony only qualifies for admission if the party against whom the testimony is now offered had "an opportunity and similar motive to develop" the earlier testimony. This requirement speaks to the key inquiry underlying Rule 804(b)(1): whether, in the words of the Advisory Committee, "fairness allows imposing, upon the party against whom" the testimony is "now offered, the handling of the witness on the earlier occasion." Given the right circumstances, the rule deems the adverse party's prior opportunity to question the witness to be an adequate substitute for a present inability to cross-examine. This substitute is only adequate, however, when the party against whom the former testimony is offered had an "opportunity and similar motive to develop" that testimony at the prior proceeding.

PROBLEM 6-19: GRAND JURY TESTIMONY

Grand juries screen cases to determine whether an indictment should issue. An indictment functions as a formal charge, permitting a criminal matter to proceed in the courts. For an indictment to issue, the grand jury must vote (typically by a majority) that there is "probable cause" to believe that the defendant committed the offense. Apart from the witnesses, the only people present for grand jury proceedings are the grand jurors, the prosecutor and a court reporter who transcribes the proceedings.

Consider this scenario: After a bank robbery in which a bank guard was killed, the alleged getaway driver, Arthur Getaway, testified under oath before a grand jury that his high school friends, Jim Neighbors and Ann McCulloch committed the robbery. Getaway also testified that McCulloch bragged about having shot the guard as they fled the scene.

Later at Neighbors' trial, Getaway asserts a Fifth Amendment privilege. The judge rules that the witness is properly asserting the privilege.

(1) *Can the prosecutor introduce Getaway's testimony in the bank robbery trial against Neighbors?* (opportunity)

(2) Assume the prosecutor has charged Neighbors with shooting the bank guard. *Can Neighbors introduce Getaway's testimony to prove that Neighbors did not shoot the bank guard?* (similar motive)

DYING DECLARATIONS

RULE 804(b)(2)

SHEPARD v. UNITED STATES
290 U.S. 96 (1933)

Justice CARDOZO delivered the opinion of the Court.

The petitioner, Charles A. Shepard, a major in the medical corps of the United States Army, has been convicted of the murder of his wife, Zenana Shepard, at Fort Riley, Kan., a United States military reservation....

The crime is charged to have been committed by poisoning the victim with bichloride of mercury. The defendant was in love with another woman, and wished to make her his wife. There is circumstantial evidence to sustain a finding by the jury that to win himself his freedom he turned to poison and murder. Even so, guilt was contested, and conflicting inferences are possible. The defendant asks us to hold that by the acceptance of incompetent evidence the scales were weighted to his prejudice and in the end to his undoing.

The evidence complained of was offered by the government in rebuttal when the trial was nearly over. On May 22, 1929, there was a conversation in the absence of the defendant between Mrs. Shepard, then ill in bed, and Clara Brown, her nurse. The patient asked the nurse to go to the closet in the defendant's room and bring a bottle of whisky that would be found upon a shelf. When the bottle was produced, she said that this was the liquor she had taken just before collapsing. She asked whether enough was left to make a test for the presence of poison, insisting that the smell and taste were strange. And then she added the words, 'Dr. Shepard has poisoned me.'

The conversation was proved twice. After the first proof of it, the government asked to strike it out, being doubtful of its competence, and this request was granted. A little later, however, the offer was renewed; the nurse having then testified to statements by Mrs. Shepard as to the prospect of recovery. 'She said she was not going to get well; she was going to die.' With the aid of this new evidence, the conversation already summarized was proved a second time. There was a timely challenge of the ruling.

She said, 'Dr. Shepard has poisoned me.' The admission of this declaration, if erroneous, was more than unsubstantial error. As to that the parties are agreed. The voice of the dead wife was heard in accusation of her husband, and the accusation was accepted as evidence of guilt. If the evidence was incompetent, the verdict may not stand.

Upon the hearing in this court the government finds its main prop in the position that what was said by Mrs. Shepard was admissible as a dying declaration. This is manifestly the theory upon which it was offered and received. The prop, however, is a broken reed. To make out a dying declaration, the declarant must have spoken without hope of recovery and in the shadow of impending death. The record furnishes no proof of that indispensable condition....

We have said that the declarant was not shown to have spoken without hope of recovery and in the shadow of impending death. Her illness began on May 20. She was found in a state of collapse, delirious, in pain, the pupils of her eyes dilated, and the retina suffused with blood. The conversation with the nurse occurred two days later. At that time her mind had cleared up, and her speech was rational and orderly. There was as yet no thought by any of her physicians that she was dangerously ill, still less that her case was hopeless. To all seeming she had greatly improved, and was moving forward to recovery. There had been no diagnosis of poison as the cause of her distress. Not till about a week afterwards was there a relapse, accompanied by an infection of the mouth, renewed congestion of the eyes, and later hemorrhages of the bowels. Death followed on June 15.

Nothing in the condition of the patient on May 22 gives fair support to the conclusion that hope had then been lost. She may have thought she was going to die and have said so to her nurse, but this was consistent with hope, which could not have been put aside without more to quench it. Indeed, a fortnight later, she said to one of her physicians, though her condition was then grave, 'You will get me well, won't you?' Fear or even belief that illness will end in death will not avail of itself to make a dying declaration. There must be 'a settled hopeless expectation' that death is near at hand, and what is said must have been spoken in the hush of its impending presence. Despair of recovery may indeed be gathered from the circumstances if the facts support the inference. There is no unyielding ritual of words to be spoken by the dying.

Despair may even be gathered, though the period of survival outruns the bounds of expectation. What is decisive is the state of mind. Even so, the state of mind must be exhibited in the evidence, and not left to conjecture. The patient must have spoken with the consciousness of a swift and certain doom.

What was said by this patient was not spoken in that mood. There was no warning to her in the circumstances that her words would be repeated and accepted as those of a dying wife, charging murder to her husband, and charging it deliberately and solemnly as a fact within her knowledge. To the focus of that responsibility her mind was never brought. She spoke as one ill, giving voice to the beliefs and perhaps the conjectures of the moment. The liquor was to be tested, to see whether her beliefs were sound. She did not speak as one dying, announcing to the survivors a definitive conviction, a legacy of knowledge on which the world might act when she had gone.

…. The judgment should be reversed and the cause remanded to the District Court for further proceedings in accordance with this opinion.

PROBLEM 6-20: THE CHANCES ARE AGAINST YOU

Consider the circumstances in Mattox v. United States (1892), where the defendant Clyde Mattox was charged with the murder of John Mullen:

> The evidence tended to show that Mullen was shot in the evening between 8 and 9 o'clock, and that he died about 1 or 2 o'clock in the afternoon of the next day; that three shots were fired and three wounds inflicted; that neither of the wounds was necessarily fatal, but that the deceased died of pneumonia produced by one of them described as 'in the upper lobe of the right lung, entering about two or three inches above the right nipple, passing through the upper lobe of the right lung, fracturing one end of the fourth rib, passing through and lodging beneath the skin on the right side beneath the shoulder blade.' The attending physician, who was called a little after 9 o'clock and remained with the wounded man until about 9 o'clock in the morning, and visited him again between 8 and 9 o'clock, testified that Mrs. Hatch, the mother of Clyde Mattox, was present at that visit; that he regarded Mullen's recovery as hopeless; that Mullen, being 'perfectly conscious' and 'in a normal condition as regards his mind,' asked his opinion, and

the doctor said to him: 'The chances are all against you; I do not think there is any show for you at all.' The physician further testified, without objection, that, after he had informed Mullen as to his physical condition, he asked him as to who shot him, and he replied 'he didn't have any knowledge of who shot him. I interrogated him about three times in regard to that,-who did the shooting,-and he didn't know.' Counsel for defendant, after a colloquy with the court, propounded the following question: 'Did or did not John Mullen, in your presence and at that time, say, in reply to a question of Mrs. Hatch, 'I know your son, Clyde Mattox, and he did not shoot me; I saw the parties who shot me, and Clyde was not one of them?'' This question was objected to as incompetent, the objection sustained, and defendant excepted. Counsel also propounded to Mrs. Hatch this question: 'Did or did not John Mullen say to you, on the morning you visited him, and after Dr. Graham had told him that all the chances for life were against him, 'I know Clyde Mattox, your son, and he was not one of the parties who shot me?'' This was objected to on the ground of incompetency, the objection sustained, and defendant excepted.

Should the trial court have allowed the evidence?

PROBLEM 6-21: SUICIDE NOTE

Consider the following facts from a Louisiana case, Garza v. Delta Tau Delta Fraternity (La. 2006).

A civil lawsuit was filed by the family members (the plaintiffs) of a college student, Courtney, who committed suicide (the suit is against the student's college and others). In the suit:

> Motions in limine were filed by the college . . . challenging the plaintiffs' right to admit into evidence a suicide note left by Courtney some time before her death by hanging. The note is handwritten on letter-sized, lined paper-three pages, front and back, plus seven lines. It can be broken down into three parts. 1) At the beginning of the note Courtney states she had been thinking about suicide for months, having been constantly depressed [after being raped earlier in the semester]; she also talks about seeking counseling and deciding not to

seek further counseling. 2) Then, Courtney writes, "I guess I'll begin & explain what happened to me this semester." She relates her account of drinking at a local lounge until closing time, 2:00 a.m. According to the note, she and a sorority sister accepted a ride with a DTD member, and they willingly went to an off-campus house occupied by several fraternity members, where Courtney ended up in the bedroom of Paul Upshaw. She writes, "I was raped." . . . 3) The final portion of the note consists of goodbyes to family, instructions for getting in touch with friends, and instructions for her funeral. The note was dated "April 8, 2001, at 12:30," and Courtney died [from hanging] April 9, 2001.

If you were counsel for the defense, how would you argue that the suicide note is not a dying declaration? Should the trial court have admitted the note (or portions of it) as a dying declaration?

STATEMENTS AGAINST INTEREST

RULE 804(b)(3)

Rule 804(b)(3) provides a hearsay exception for statements that were uttered against the interest of the declarant. Due to its ability to generate powerful evidence, this exception generates abundant case law in the federal and state courts.

Rule 804(b)(3) assumes that people are unlikely to lie to hurt their own interests and so if a statement is sufficiently against the speaker's interest, it is likely to be true. The rule is unusual in that the rationale for the exception is embedded in the rule's text. A statement only qualifies for admission if it is so against the declarant's interest that "a reasonable person in the declarant's position would have made [it] only if the person believed it to be true."

Rule 804(b)(3)'s corroboration requirement demonstrates a distrust on the part of the rules' drafters of certain hearsay statements that satisfy the rule's terms. Precisely how much corroboration is required is left unclear. A typical expression of the requirement comes from the First Circuit, which explains that the "requirement for corroboration is not unrealistically severe but does go 'beyond minimal corroboration.'"[1]

WILLIAMSON v. UNITED STATES
512 U.S. 594 (1994)

Justice O'CONNOR delivered the Court's opinion, except as to Part II–C.

In this case we clarify the scope of the hearsay exception for statements against penal interest.

I

A deputy sheriff stopped the rental car driven by Reginald Harris for weaving on the highway. Harris consented to a search of the car, which revealed 19 kilograms of cocaine in two suitcases in the trunk. Harris was promptly arrested.

Shortly after Harris' arrest, Special Agent Donald Walton of the Drug Enforcement Administration (DEA) interviewed him by telephone. During that conversation, Harris said that he got the cocaine from an unidentified Cuban in Fort Lauderdale; that the cocaine belonged to petitioner Williamson; and that it was to be delivered that night to a particular dumpster....

Several hours later, Agent Walton spoke to Harris in person. Harris said ... he was transporting the cocaine to Atlanta for Williamson, and that Williamson was traveling in front of him in another rental car. Harris added that after his car was stopped, Williamson turned around and drove past the location of the stop, where he could see Harris' car with its trunk open. Because Williamson had apparently seen the police searching the car, Harris explained that it would be impossible to make a controlled delivery.

Harris told Walton that he had [initially] lied about the source of the drugs because he was afraid of Williamson. Though Harris freely implicated himself, he did not want his story to be recorded, and he refused to sign a written version of the statement. Walton testified that he had promised to report any

---

[1] U.S. v. Mackey, 117 F.3d 24 (1st Cir. 1997).

cooperation by Harris to the Assistant United States Attorney. Walton said Harris was not promised any reward or other benefit for cooperating.

Williamson was eventually convicted of possessing cocaine with intent to distribute, conspiring to possess cocaine with intent to distribute, and traveling interstate to promote the distribution of cocaine. When called to testify at Williamson's trial, Harris refused, even though the prosecution gave him … immunity and the court ordered him to testify and eventually held him in contempt. The District Court then ruled that, under Rule 804(b)(3), Agent Walton could relate what Harris had said to him….

Williamson appealed his conviction, claiming that the admission of Harris' statements violated Rule 804(b)(3)…. The Court of Appeals for the Eleventh Circuit affirmed without opinion, and we granted certiorari.

II

A

The hearsay rule is premised on the theory that out-of-court statements are subject to particular hazards. The declarant might be lying; he might have misperceived the events which he relates; he might have faulty memory; his words might be misunderstood or taken out of context by the listener. And the ways in which these dangers are minimized for in-court statements—the oath, the witness' awareness of the gravity of the proceedings, the jury's ability to observe the witness' demeanor, and, most importantly, the right of the opponent to cross-examine—are generally absent for things said out of court.

Nonetheless, the Federal Rules of Evidence also recognize that some kinds of out-of-court statements are less subject to these hearsay dangers, and therefore except them from the general rule that hearsay is inadmissible. One such category covers statements that are against the declarant's interest….

To decide whether Harris' confession is made admissible by Rule 804(b)(3), we must first determine what the Rule means by "statement," which Federal Rule of Evidence 801(a)(1) defines as "an oral or written assertion." One possible meaning, "a report or narrative," Webster's Third New International Dictionary, connotes an extended declaration. Under this reading, Harris' entire confession—even if it contains both self-inculpatory and non-self-inculpatory parts—would be admissible so long as in the aggregate the confession sufficiently inculpates him. Another meaning of "statement," "a single declaration or remark," would make Rule 804(b)(3) cover only those declarations or remarks within the confession that are individually self-inculpatory.

Although the text of the Rule does not directly resolve the matter, the principle behind the Rule, so far as it is discernible from the text, points clearly to the narrower reading. Rule 804(b)(3) is founded on the commonsense notion that reasonable people, even reasonable people who are not especially honest, tend not to make self-inculpatory statements unless they believe them to be true. This notion simply does not extend to the broader definition of "statement." The fact that a person is making a broadly self-inculpatory confession does not make more credible the confession's non-self-inculpatory parts. One of the most effective ways to lie is to mix falsehood with truth, especially truth that seems particularly persuasive because of its self-inculpatory nature.

In this respect, it is telling that the non-self-inculpatory things Harris said in his first statement actually proved to be false, as Harris himself admitted during the second interrogation. And when part of the confession is actually self-exculpatory, the generalization on which Rule 804(b)(3) is founded becomes even less applicable. Self-exculpatory statements are exactly the ones which people are most likely to make even when they are false; and mere proximity to other, self-inculpatory, statements does not increase the plausibility of the self-exculpatory statements.

…. In our view, the most faithful reading of Rule 804(b)(3) is that it does not allow admission of non-self-inculpatory statements, even if they are made within a broader narrative that is generally self-inculpatory. The district court may not just assume for purposes of Rule 804(b)(3) that a statement is self-inculpatory because it is part of a fuller confession, and this is especially true when the statement implicates someone else. "[T]he arrest statements of a codefendant have traditionally been viewed with special suspicion. Due to his strong motivation to implicate the defendant and to exonerate himself, a codefendant's statements about what the defendant said or did are less credible than ordinary hearsay evidence."…

B

We also do not share Justice Kennedy's fears that our reading of the Rule "eviscerate[s] the against penal interest exception," or makes it lack "meaningful effect." There are many circumstances in which Rule 804(b)(3) does allow the admission of statements that inculpate a criminal defendant. Even the confessions of arrested accomplices may be admissible if they are truly self-inculpatory, rather than merely attempts to shift blame or curry favor.

For instance, a declarant's squarely self-inculpatory confession—"yes, I killed X"—will likely be admissible under Rule 804(b)(3) against accomplices of his who are being tried under a co-conspirator liability theory. Likewise, by showing that the declarant knew something, a self-inculpatory statement can in some situations help the jury infer that his confederates knew it as well. And when seen with other evidence, an accomplice's self-inculpatory statement can inculpate the defendant directly: "I was robbing the bank on Friday morning," coupled with someone's testimony that the declarant and the defendant drove off together Friday morning, is evidence that the defendant also participated in the robbery.

Moreover, whether a statement is self-inculpatory or not can only be determined by viewing it in context. Even statements that are on their face neutral may actually be against the declarant's interest. "I hid the gun in Joe's apartment" may not be a confession of a crime; but if it is likely to help the police find the murder weapon, then it is certainly self-inculpatory. "Sam and I went to Joe's house" might be against the declarant's interest if a reasonable person in the declarant's shoes would realize that being linked to Joe and Sam would implicate the declarant in Joe and Sam's conspiracy. And other statements that give the police significant details about the crime may also, depending on the situation, be against the declarant's interest. The question under Rule 804(b)(3) is always whether the statement was sufficiently against the declarant's penal interest "that a reasonable person in the declarant's position would not have made the statement unless believing it to be true," and this question can only be answered in light of all the surrounding circumstances.

C

[Editor's Note: Only Justice Scalia joined Justice O'Connor's Section C]

319

In this case, however, we cannot conclude that all that Harris said was properly admitted. Some of Harris' confession would clearly have been admissible under Rule 804(b)(3); for instance, when he said he knew there was cocaine in the suitcase, he essentially forfeited his only possible defense to a charge of cocaine possession, lack of knowledge. But other parts of his confession, especially the parts that implicated Williamson, did little to subject Harris himself to criminal liability. A reasonable person in Harris' position might even think that implicating someone else would decrease his practical exposure to criminal liability, at least so far as sentencing goes. Small fish in a big conspiracy often get shorter sentences than people who are running the whole show, especially if the small fish are willing to help the authorities catch the big ones.

Nothing in the record shows that the District Court or the Court of Appeals inquired whether each of the statements in Harris' confession was truly self-inculpatory. As we explained above, this can be a fact-intensive inquiry, which would require careful examination of all the circumstances surrounding the criminal activity involved; we therefore remand to the Court of Appeals to conduct this inquiry in the first instance.

Justice GINSBURG Concurring (joined by JJ. Blackmun, Stevens and Souter)

… Unlike Justice O'Connor, … I conclude that Reginald Harris' statements, as recounted by Drug Enforcement Administration (DEA) Special Agent Donald E. Walton, do not fit, even in part, within the exception described in Rule 804(b)(3), for Harris' arguably inculpatory statements are too closely intertwined with his self-serving declarations to be ranked as trustworthy. Harris was caught redhanded with 19 kilos of cocaine—enough to subject even a first-time offender to a minimum of 12 ½ years' imprisonment. He could have denied knowing the drugs were in the car's trunk, but that strategy would have brought little prospect of thwarting a criminal prosecution. He therefore admitted involvement, but did so in a way that minimized his own role and shifted blame to petitioner Fredel Williamson (and a Cuban man named Shawn)….

***

The 804(b)(3) case law divides fairly evenly between against-interest statements made to police (like in *Williamson*) and against-interest statements made to confidantes (friends, family, accomplices). Each scenario raises related, but distinct concerns.

PROBLEM 6-22: STATEMENTS TO A SPOUSE

Consider this example from United States v. Katsougrakis, 715 F.2d 769 (2d Cir. 1983):

In an arson trial of John Katsougrakis, the prosecutor offered testimony from the wife of one of Katsougrakis alleged accomplices, Charlie Chrisanthou that, prior to the arson:

> Chrisanthou stated that he and Katsougraki had been hired for $6,000 to "torch" a diner and (in a later conversation) that he had received $800 as a down payment for the arson.

How do you think a judge should rule on these statements' admissibility (assuming sufficient corroboration)?

On appeal of the ruling, the Second Circuit highlighted the following points:

- "with each statement, Chrisanthou provided more evidence of his complicity in the arson scheme"
- "Chrisanthou had no motive to lie to his wife"

Are these the right considerations? Are there counterbalancing factors?

PROBLEM 6-23: MORE STATEMENTS TO A SPOUSE

Imagine that after Alvin Presley died suddenly in his sleep, the government prosecuted his fiancé Priscilla for poisoning him. Priscilla claims that the real killer is Paul McCartner. At trial, Priscilla seeks to introduce Alvin' admission to her, shortly before his death, that Alvis slept with Paul's wife and his heartfelt request for forgiveness of the transgression against their relationship. Can Priscilla introduce Alvin' statement under Rule 804(b)(3)?

FORFEITURE BY WRONGDOING

RULE 804(b)(6)

UNITED STATES v. GRAY
405 F.3d 227 (4th Cir. 2005)

SHEDD, Circuit Judge:

A grand jury indicted Josephine Gray on five counts of mail fraud and three counts of wire fraud relating to her receipt of insurance proceeds following the deaths of her second husband and a former paramour. Gray was convicted on all counts, and the district court sentenced her to 40 years' imprisonment....

I.

Wilma Jean Wilson met Gray in the late summer of 2000, and the two became friends. They spoke over the telephone, and Wilson sometimes visited Gray's house. During one of those visits, Gray was busy cleaning a cluttered room and Wilson offered to help. As they were talking, Gray stopped cleaning and left the room briefly; when she returned, she brought newspaper articles describing her prior arrests. In fact, those articles reported that Gray had killed her former husbands. Wilson asked if the reports were true, and Gray replied that she was going to tell Wilson something she had never told anyone before and she did not want Wilson to say anything about it. In an emotionless, matter-of-fact manner, Gray then told Wilson that "she had killed both her husbands and another gentleman."

Gray told Wilson that she had killed her first husband, Norman Stribbling, because she was tired of being abused by him. According to Wilson, "[s]he told me that they had gone out for a ride and that she had shot him.... [S]he left the body over on River Road, and it was set up to look like it was a robbery." Gray then confessed to Wilson that she had also killed her second husband, William "Robert" Gray. Although Gray said she was alone with Stribbling when she killed him, "she had help" killing Robert Gray. The help came from Clarence Goode, Gray's cousin and boyfriend. Gray explained to Wilson that Goode "had tried to blackmail her," demanding money in exchange for his silence about the murder of Robert Gray, so "she had to get rid of him too."

A.

Gray's first husband, Stribbling, maintained a life insurance policy through John Hancock Mutual Life Insurance Company and named Gray as the beneficiary. In the early morning of March 3, 1974, Stribbling was found dead in his parked car on River Road, near his home in Montgomery County, Maryland. An autopsy revealed that Stribbling died from a single gunshot wound to the head. Shortly after Stribbling's death, Gray made a claim for insurance benefits and later received a check in the amount of $16,000.

B.

Gray had been having an affair with Robert Gray while she was still married to Stribbling. In August 1975, the couple bought a house in Gaithersburg, Maryland—using most of the proceeds from Stribbling's insurance policy as a down payment—and three months later they married. Robert Gray maintained an insurance policy through Minnesota Mutual Life Insurance Company ("Minnesota Mutual") that provided for payment of the mortgage on the Grays' house in Gaithersburg in the event of his death, with any excess going to his spouse. Robert Gray also maintained an accidental death insurance policy through Life Insurance Company of North America ("LINA") and designated Gray as his beneficiary.

Robert Gray left the Gaithersburg house in August 1990, telling family members that his wife was trying to kill him and that she was having an affair with Goode, who had been living with the Grays. So convinced was Robert Gray that his wife intended him harm that he removed her as his beneficiary under two other insurance policies. He asked relatives and friends for help in avoiding a possible assault by Gray or Goode.

In late August 1990, Robert Gray brought criminal charges against Gray, alleging that Gray had assaulted him at his workplace by swinging at him with a club and lunging at him with a knife. Robert Gray also brought charges against Goode, alleging that Goode had threatened him with a 9–millimeter handgun. Robert Gray appeared in court on October 5, 1990, but the case against Gray and Goode was continued. Later that same day, Robert Gray was driving home when he noticed his wife's car behind him. She was flashing her lights and signaling her husband to pull over. When Robert Gray did not pull over, Gray drove her car alongside her husband's car. As Robert Gray turned to look toward his wife, Goode sat up (from a reclined position) in the front passenger seat and pointed a gun at him. Robert Gray reported this incident to police, and a warrant was issued for the arrests of Gray and Goode. One week before the November 16, 1990 trial date, Robert Gray was discovered dead in his new apartment, shot once in the chest and once in the neck with a .45 caliber handgun.

.... As a result of Robert Gray's death, Minnesota Mutual paid approximately $51,625 to Perpetual Savings Bank—the named beneficiary—to cover the mortgage on the Gaithersburg house. Once the mortgage was satisfied, Gray sold the house for a significant profit.....

C.

Gray told Wilson that she "had to get rid of" Goode because he was blackmailing her. Goode had conspired with Gray in Robert Gray's murder, and he was demanding "part of the insurance money that she received" from Robert Gray's death in return for his silence. On June 21, 1996, Baltimore City Police officers found Goode's body in the trunk of his car; he had been shot in the back with a 9–millimeter handgun....

2.

The district court ... admitted into evidence several out-of-court statements made by Robert Gray during the three months preceding his murder:

> Robert Gray's criminal complaint alleging that Goode had tossed a 9–millimeter handgun on the table at his house to provoke an argument;

> Robert Gray's criminal complaint alleging that Gray had tried to stab him with a knife and attack him with a club;

> Statements made by Robert Gray to Darnell Gray and a police detective, claiming that Gray and Goode had assaulted him in October 1990; and

> Statements made by Robert Gray to Rodney Gray claiming that Goode had pulled a gun on him outside a restaurant in September or October 1990.

Although out-of-court statements ordinarily may not be admitted to prove the truth of the matters asserted, the doctrine of forfeiture by wrongdoing allows such statements to be admitted where the defendant's own misconduct rendered the declarant unavailable as a witness at trial. The Supreme Court applied this doctrine in Reynolds v. United States (1878), stating that "[t]he Constitution gives the accused the right to a trial at which he should be confronted with the witnesses against him; but if a witness is absent by [the accused's] own wrongful procurement, he cannot complain if competent evidence is admitted to supply the place of that which he has kept away." By 1996, every circuit to address the issue had recognized this doctrine.

Fed.R.Evid. 804(b)(6), which took effect in 1997, codifies the common-law doctrine of forfeiture by wrongdoing as an exception to the general rule barring admission of hearsay evidence. Under Rule 804(b)(6), "[a] statement offered against a party that has engaged or acquiesced in wrong-doing that was intended to, and did procure the unavailability of the declarant as a witness" is admissible at trial. In order to apply the forfeiture-by-wrongdoing exception, the district court must find, by the preponderance of the evidence, that (1) the defendant engaged or acquiesced in wrongdoing (2) that was intended to render the declarant unavailable as a witness and (3) that did, in fact, render the declarant unavailable as a witness. The district court need not hold an independent evidentiary hearing if the requisite findings may be made based upon evidence presented in the course of the trial.

Gray contends that Rule 804(b)(6) should not apply in this case because she did not intend to procure Robert Gray's unavailability as a witness at this trial. "Because the Federal Rules of Evidence are a legislative enactment, we turn to the traditional tools of statutory construction in order to construe their provisions. We begin with the language itself." The text of Rule 804(b)(6) requires only that the defendant intend to render the declarant unavailable "as a witness." The text does not require that the declarant would otherwise be a witness at any particular trial, nor does it limit the subject matter of admissible statements to events distinct from the events at issue in the trial in which the statements are offered. Thus, we conclude that Rule 804(b)(6) applies whenever the defendant's wrongdoing was intended to, and did, render the declarant unavailable as a witness against the defendant, without regard to the nature of the charges at the trial in which the declarant's statements are offered.

Our interpretation of Rule 804(b)(6) advances the clear purpose of the forfeiture-by-wrongdoing exception. The advisory committee noted its specific goal to implement a "prophylactic rule to deal with abhorrent behavior which strikes at the heart of the system of justice itself." Fed.R.Evid. 804(b)(6) advisory committee note. More generally, federal courts have recognized that the forfeiture-by-wrongdoing exception is necessary to prevent wrongdoers from profiting by their misconduct.

Federal courts have sought to effect the purpose of the forfeiture-by-wrongdoing exception by construing broadly the elements required for its application. Although the Rule requires that the wrongdoing was intended to render the declarant unavailable as a witness, we have held that a defendant need only intend "in part" to procure the declarant's unavailability.

Like these applications of the forfeiture-by-wrongdoing exception, our interpretation of Rule 804(b)(6) ensures that a defendant will not be permitted to avoid the evidentiary impact of statements made by his victim, whether or not he suspected that the victim would be a witness at the trial in which the evidence is offered against him. A defendant who wrongfully and intentionally renders a declarant unavailable as a witness in any proceeding forfeits the right to exclude, on hearsay grounds, the declarant's statements at that proceeding and any subsequent proceeding.

Having rejected Gray's interpretation of Rule 804(b)(6), we need only determine whether the district court properly applied the Rule in admitting Robert Gray's out-of-court statements. Those statements were admissible only if the district court properly found, by a preponderance of the evidence, that (1) Gray engaged in some wrongdoing (2) that was intended to procure Robert Gray's unavailability as a witness and (3) that did, in fact, procure his unavailability as a witness. The district court in this case found that Robert Gray "was killed prior to the court date on November 15 and 16, and after the defendant was well aware of his status as a witness, justifies the inference that ... the killing was motivated ... to prevent [Robert Gray] from being available ... at court proceedings." These findings are supported by the evidence and are sufficient to warrant application of the Rule 804(b)(6). Accordingly, the district court did not abuse its discretion in admitting testimony concerning out-of-court statements made by Robert Gray.

PROBLEM 6-24: ASSERT YOUR RIGHTS

Consider the following facts drawn from a sex trafficking of minors and witness tampering prosecution, United States v. Doss (9th Cir. 2011):

The government alleged that defendant, Juan Rico Doss, "did things that were substantial steps toward intimidating, threatening and corruptly persuading [his wife] Jacquay Quinn Ford," not to testify in an upcoming criminal trial. Specifically, the government alleged that:

> (1) in a letter dated May 16, 2006, defendant Juan Rico Doss encouraged Jacquay Quinn Ford to refuse to testify against him at trial by stating "Believe me if I got to go back to trial which is most likely I will if I don't get a 5 year deal, they are going to try you again to come testify which they made clear against me and if and when that time comes, I would expect you to hold strong and say NO that you won't even get on the stand period"; and (2) in letters dated May 16, 18, 21, 2006, defendant Juan Rico Doss encouraged Jacquay Quinn Ford to refuse to testify against him based on their marital status.

If the government can show the facts specified above by a preponderance of the evidence and Ford later asserts marital privilege to not testify against Doss, *can the government now introduce Ford's hearsay statements under Rule 804(b)(6)?*

THE RESIDUAL EXCEPTION

RULE 807

Rule 807 contains a "residual" or "catch-all" hearsay exception intended to cover "new and presently unanticipated situations" when trustworthy hearsay evidence is offered but does not fall within an existing hearsay exception.[1]

The Advisory Committee first proposed the residual exception as two separate exceptions, Rule 803(24) and Rule 804(b)(5), each coming at the end of the list of exceptions in Rule 803 and Rule 804 respectively. The initially proposed residual exception took a simpler form than the ultimately enacted version. For both Rule 803 and Rule 804, the original residual rule would have excepted from the hearsay prohibition a "statement not specifically covered by any of the foregoing exceptions but having comparable circumstantial guarantees of trustworthiness." The House of Representatives rejected both rules. The House Judiciary Committee criticized the rules for "injecting too much uncertainty into the law of evidence and impairing the ability of practitioners to prepare for trial." "[I]f additional hearsay exceptions are to be created," the Committee explained, "they should be by amendments to the Rules, not on a case-by-case basis."

The Senate resurrected the residual exception with some modifications. The Senate Judiciary Committee explained its reasoning as follows:

> [W]ithout a separate residual provision, the specifically enumerated exceptions could become tortured beyond any reasonable circumstances which they were intended to include (even if broadly construed). Moreover, these exceptions, while they reflect the most typical and well recognized exceptions to the hearsay rule, may not encompass every situation in which the reliability and appropriateness of a particular piece of hearsay evidence make clear that it should be heard and considered by the trier of fact.
>
> The committee believes that there are certain exceptional circumstances where evidence which is found by a court to have

---

[1] The following background is drawn from Wright & Bellin § 7061.

guarantees of trustworthiness equivalent to or exceeding the guarantees reflected by the presently listed exceptions, and to have a high degree of probativeness and necessity could properly be admissible.

To support its point, the Senate Judiciary Committee primarily relied on the well-known case of Dallas County v. Commercial Union Assurance Company.[1] In *Dallas County*, the Fifth Circuit upheld the admission over a hearsay objection of a 50-year-old local newspaper story chronicling a fire in a courthouse tower. In an opinion by Judge Wisdom, the court emphasized that it did "not characterize this newspaper as a 'business record', nor as an 'ancient document,' nor as any other readily identifiable and happily tagged species of hearsay exception. It is admissible because it is necessary and trustworthy, relevant and material."

The Senate Judiciary Committee thought "exceptional cases" like *Dallas County* would continue to arise, and believed such cases supported its decision to "reinstate a residual exception." Nevertheless, the Committee attempted to accommodate their House colleagues "who felt that an overly broad residual hearsay exception could emasculate the hearsay rule and the recognized exceptions or vitiate the rationale behind codification of the rules." The Senate modified the residual exception to give it a "much narrower scope and applicability than the Supreme Court version."

Perhaps even more significant than the textual additions to the residual exception, the Senate added the following comments to clarify its intent:

> It is intended that the residual hearsay exceptions will be used very rarely, and only in exceptional circumstances. The committee does not intend to establish a broad license for trial judges to admit hearsay statements that do not fall within one of the other exceptions contained in rules 803 and 804(b). ... It is intended that in any case in which evidence is sought to be admitted under these subsections, the trial judge will exercise no less care, reflection and caution than the

---

[1] 286 F.2d 388 (5th Cir. 1961).

courts did under the common law in establishing the now-recognized exceptions to the hearsay rule.

The critical point here is the Senate's intent that the residual exception "will be used very rarely, and only in exceptional circumstances." Coupled with the House's desire to excise the residual exception entirely, Congressional intent for judicial restraint in this context is unmistakable. This legislative history indicating a diminutive role for the residual hearsay exception is probably the rule's most helpful interpretive guideline. Courts quote it regularly and, for the most part, internalize its spirit.

HARRIS v. CITY OF CHICAGO
327 F.R.D. 199 (N.D. Ill. 2018)

Gary Feinerman, United States District Judge

Andre Lepinay brought this 42 U.S.C. § 1983 suit against the City of Chicago and nine Chicago police officers, alleging that they violated the Fourth Amendment by using excessive force against him when executing a search warrant at his apartment. After Lepinay died, the court appointed his niece, Sharon Harris, as the special administrator of his estate for the purpose of continuing the suit. Although Lepinay was not deposed before he died, he did give a sworn interview to an investigator with the City's Independent Police Review Authority ("IPRA"). Harris moves for a pretrial determination that an electronic recording of the interview is admissible in evidence. The motion is granted.

The alleged excessive force took place on October 21, 2016. One week later, on October 28, Lepinay gave his sworn interview to the IPRA investigator. Lepinay told the investigator that he was sitting in the living room when the officers entered, that three officers immediately "bum rushed" him, with one jabbing him in the stomach with a rifle, and that the officers then took him to the floor, with one kneeing him in the back. Lepinay also stated that he had recently been diagnosed with advanced liver cancer and had "c[o]me home to die." After the interview, Lepinay signed an affidavit in which he "sw[ore] or affirm[ed], under penalties provided by law, that the information contained in ... [his] electronically recorded statement, [was] true and accurate." He filed this suit some three weeks later, on November 17, 2016, and died in April 2017.

Harris contends that the recording of Lepinay's IPRA interview is admissible under Federal Rule of Evidence 807, the residual exception to the hearsay rule. "A proponent of hearsay evidence must establish five elements in order to satisfy Rule 807: (1) circumstantial guarantees of trustworthiness; (2) materiality; (3) probative value; (4) the interests of justice; and (5) notice." Defendants do not contest the second and fifth elements, materiality and notice. And they make no argument regarding the fourth element, the interests of justice, which they describe as "not ... an element at all, but instead a statement of the policy underlying the residual exception." Defendants contest only the first and third elements, trustworthiness and probative value.

Trustworthiness. A hearsay statement satisfies Rule 807's trustworthiness element if it has circumstantial guarantees of trustworthiness "equivalent to those inherent in the more specific [hearsay] exceptions" in Rules 803 and 804. The following factors, which "are neither exhaustive nor absolute," are pertinent to assessing trustworthiness under Rule 807:

> the character of the witness for truthfulness and honesty, and the availability of evidence on the issue; whether the testimony was given voluntarily, under oath, subject to cross-examination and a penalty for perjury; the witness' ... motivation to testify ...; the extent to which the witness' testimony reflects his personal knowledge; whether the witness ever recanted his testimony; the existence of corroborating evidence; and, the reasons for the witness' unavailability.

The first trustworthiness factor—Lepinay's reputation for truthfulness—is inconclusive. Lepinay admitted in the interview that he possessed illegal drugs the day of the incident. As Defendants recognize, however, any damage that fact does to Lepinay's credibility is counterbalanced by his unprompted, forthright admission to possession. Neither party has presented any other evidence of Lepinay's reputation for truthfulness.

The second trustworthiness factor—whether the statement was given voluntarily, under oath, subject to cross-examination and penalty for perjury— strongly favors Harris, for Lepinay's interview was given voluntarily, under oath, and subject to penalty for perjury. Although Lepinay was not cross-examined by counsel for an adverse party, the IPRA investigator drove most of the conversation by asking a lengthy series of clarifying questions after Lepinay gave a brief account of the incident.

Defendants are correct that the interview took place in a car outside Lepinay's residence, rather than a more formal setting like a courtroom. And it is true that, had Lepinay been formally cross-examined in a courtroom or at a deposition, his statements would be admissible under the Rule 804(b)(1) hearsay exception for the prior trial or deposition testimony of unavailable witnesses. But if Rule 807 required circumstantial guarantees of trustworthiness that were identical to those in Rule 804(b)(1), it would do no work; instead, the residual exception requires only "equivalent" circumstantial guarantees. That Lepinay gave a sworn statement under penalty of perjury and responded to many clarifying questions from someone whose job it was to investigate allegations of police misconduct helps to establish that the circumstances of his statement were equivalent to those contemplated in Rule 804(b)(1).

Defendants object that the prospect of a perjury prosecution was illusory, given that, at the time of Lepinay's interview, no one had ever been prosecuted for making false statements to IPRA. But Lepinay surely was unaware of the prosecution record for false statements made to IPRA. He swore in an affidavit, "under penalties provided by law," that the information in his statement was true and accurate, and there is no reason to think he took that oath less seriously than any other declarant. Defendants also argue that Lepinay had little reason to fear a perjury prosecution because he knew that he was suffering from a terminal illness. This is true, but on the whole, and as noted below, Lepinay's awareness of his dire medical condition weighs in favor of admitting his statements.

The third trustworthiness factor—Lepinay's motivation for testifying—also favors Harris. Lepinay may have been contemplating filing this suit at the time of the IPRA interview, but there is no indication that he had reason to think that the interview would assist him in his lawsuit. In any event, mercenary motives could not have played much of a role in his decision to speak to IPRA, or even his decision to file suit. Lepinay knew that he had terminal liver cancer, stating that he "came home to die." It is highly unlikely that, as a layperson, he realized that his interview could provide a basis for a family member to pursue his claim after his death. And while his interview is not admissible as a dying declaration under Rule 804(b)(2), both because his death was not sufficiently imminent when he gave the interview and his statements did not concern the cause or circumstances of his death, the fact that he knew he was likely to die before realizing any gain from his suit bolsters his credibility. See Mattox v. United States (1895) ("[T]he sense of impending death is presumed to remove all temptation to falsehood.").

Defendants do not dispute that the fourth and fifth trustworthiness factors—whether the statements reflect Lepinay's personal knowledge and whether he ever recanted his testimony—weigh in Harris's favor. The sixth factor weighs against Harris, as there is no corroborating evidence of the truth of Lepinay's statements. (But this works in Harris's favor on the probative value element, as explained below.) The last factor, the reason for Lepinay's unavailability (his death), casts no doubt on the trustworthiness of his testimony.

Having considered the relevant factors, the court concludes that Lepinay's statements to the IPRA investigator have circumstantial guarantees of trustworthiness equivalent to those contemplated in the enumerated Rules 803 and 804 hearsay exceptions. His statements were voluntary, sworn, made under penalty of perjury, and subject to extensive questioning, and the knowledge that he had an advanced terminal illness diminished any motivation he might have had to distort the truth. See United States v. Doerr (7th Cir. 1989) (holding that grand jury testimony, which was not subject to cross-examination, was admissible under the residual exception because it had circumstantial guarantees of trustworthiness equivalent to those under the enumerated Rule 804(b) hearsay exceptions); United States v. Clarke (4th Cir. 1993) (same, reasoning that although "[t]he guarantees [of trustworthiness] are not identical to 804(b)(1), ... they are in their totality equivalent").

Probative Value. Rule 807's probative value element is satisfied where the hearsay statement is "more probative on the point for which it is offered than any other evidence that the proponent can obtain through reasonable efforts." Fed. R. Evid. 807(a)(3). According to Lepinay, three other people were present in the apartment's other rooms when the police arrived. Upon entering, some of the officers searched the other rooms and brought those individuals into the living room, where they witnessed at least some of the force used against Lepinay. However, as Harris observes, those individuals were not in the living room when the officers first entered, and thus could not have seen whether

Lepinay did anything to provoke the use of force or whether the officers simply "bum rushed" Lepinay, as he maintained. That is significant, as important considerations in the Fourth Amendment excessive force cases include whether the plaintiff "pose[d] an immediate threat to the safety of the officers or others, and whether he or she [was] actively resisting arrest or attempting to flee or evade arrest." Additionally, Harris's counsel has been unable to locate any of the three potential witnesses. Given these circumstances, Lepinay's statements are more probative than other evidence Harris could obtain through reasonable efforts.

Defendants object that Harris has not "met her burden" to show that the three other witnesses are truly unavailable. But based on Lepinay's interview, it would appear that the apartment was "like a boarding home" in which residents rented rooms on a short-term basis. Harris notes that one of the witnesses moved out of the apartment the next day without leaving a forwarding address. It therefore stands to reason that Harris has been unable to locate those witnesses "through reasonable efforts." Fed. R. Evid. 807(a)(3). In any event, even if Harris could locate those witnesses through reasonable efforts, their testimony would not be probative on the key question of what happened between Lepinay and the officers before those witnesses were brought into the room.

Defendants also argue that Harris cannot show that Lepinay's statements are more probative than other available evidence because the officers will be available to testify about what occurred when they entered the apartment and how they restrained Lepinay. That argument cannot be right. While Lepinay maintained he was jabbed in the stomach with a rifle, taken to the ground, and kneed in the back, the officers "deny that Plaintiff was struck at any time." A live adverse party's ability to show up and deny a deceased party's statement does not, standing alone, bar the admission of statements that would otherwise satisfy the requirements of Rule 807. In these kind of "he said, she said" cases, a jury should determine whose account is more credible....

In sum, Harris has met all of the required elements for admissibility under Rule 807. Her motion to admit the recording of Lepinay's sworn IPRA interview accordingly is granted.

***

In 2020, Congress approved an amendment to the residual exception that simplified its four factors to two. As the *Harris* case illustrates, this is an approach the courts were already taking.

HEARSAY WITHIN HEARSAY

RULE 805

PROBLEM 6-25: REPORT OF FIRE

In an arson investigation, the prosecution wants to introduce a police report that recounts Witness X's statement about a suspicious fire. The Report states: "When I (Officer Y) arrived at the scene, Witness X was yelling that the fire started in the top floor and that someone had jumped out of a window right after it started and ran down the alley." Officer Y is not available to testify. The defense objects that the report is hearsay. The prosecution responds that Witness X's statement is admissible as an excited utterance. How should the trial court rule?

Consider the same example above, but now Officer Y does testify. When asked about whether any witnesses spoke to her at the scene, Officer Y states that she once knew but cannot currently remember what the witness said. Officer Y testifies that she wrote it down accurately in her police report. *Now can the prosecution introduce the police report?*

***

Multiple layers of hearsay are not necessarily fatal to the admission of evidence. Out-of-court statements that include other nested statements can be admitted over a hearsay objection so long as "each part of the combined statements conforms with an exception to the rule." Any combination of hearsay exceptions is permissible and there is no limit, as far as the hearsay rules are concerned, on the number of layers of out-of-court statements that can be contained in a combined statement.

The correct analysis for any combined out-of-court statement is to analyze each layer to determine if it is barred by the hearsay rules. If each out-of-court statement in a combined statement, analyzed independently, would be admissible over a Rule 802 objection, the nested out-of-court statement overcomes a hearsay objection as well. If any included statement is barred by Rule 802, however, the combined statement is inadmissible.

IMPEACHING HEARSAY DECLARANTS

RULE 806

The Advisory Committee Note to Rule 806 acknowledges the reality that the "declarant of a hearsay statement which is admitted in evidence is in effect a witness." It would be odd, then, not to treat hearsay declarants in the same manner that they would have been treated had they appeared at trial and testified to the same effect as their hearsay declaration. Thus, Rule 806 provides that whenever an out-of-court statement is admitted for the truth of the matter asserted, "the declarant's credibility may be attacked, and then supported" to the same degree as would be permissible for a testifying witness.

The legal test is straightforward and intuitive. If the impeaching evidence would have been admissible had the hearsay declarant testified, it becomes admissible under Rule 806. Thus, a hearsay declarant's credibility can be attacked through the introduction of inconsistent statements or other forms of credibility impeachment, such as character attacks. Note that the rule does not permit a party to introduce an opposing party's statement and then attack the party's character, etc., under Rule 806.

PERSONAL KNOWLEDGE

RULE 602

Out-of-court statements admitted for the truth of the matter asserted through a hearsay exception must generally satisfy the same requirements as live witness testimony, including the requirement in Rule 602 that a testifying witness possess "personal knowledge of the matter."

Thus, personal knowledge constitutes an additional, unenumerated requirement for admissibility of hearsay offered under Rules 803, 804 and 807. The Advisory Committee Note to Rule 803 makes this point explicit: "In a hearsay situation, the declarant is, of course, a witness, and neither this rule

[Rule 803] nor Rule 804 dispenses with the requirement of firsthand knowledge."

The principle underlying the personal knowledge requirement received attention in the pre-Rules case of Shepard v. United States (1933). There, the Supreme Court questioned the admissibility of a purported dying declaration -- "Dr. Shepard poisoned me." -- that appeared to be based not on "known facts" but on "suspicion or conjecture." Absent qualification as an expert, a live witness cannot testify to conjecture; the hearsay declarant, the Court implied, should be similarly restricted. Here is the Court's language:

> "Homicide may not be imputed to a defendant on the basis of mere suspicions, though they are the suspicions of the dying. To let the declaration in, the inference must be permissible that there was knowledge or the opportunity for knowledge as to the acts that are declared. The argument is pressed upon us that knowledge and opportunity are excluded when the declaration in question is read in the setting of the circumstances. The form is not decisive, though it be that of a conclusion, a statement of the result with the antecedent steps omitted. 'He murdered me,' does not cease to be competent as a dying declaration because in the statement of the act there is also an appraisal of the crime. One does not hold the dying to the observance of all the niceties of speech to which conformity is exacted from a witness on the stand. What is decisive is something deeper and more fundamental than any difference of form. The declaration is kept out if the setting of the occasion satisfies the judge, or in reason ought to satisfy him, that the speaker is giving expression to suspicion or conjecture, and not to known facts. The difficulty is not so much in respect of the governing principle as in its application to varying and equivocal conditions.

As a general matter, the low threshold for establishing personal knowledge for a testifying witness under Rule 602 also governs the requisite personal knowledge of hearsay declarants. Thus, a declarant's firsthand or personal knowledge should be broadly conceived. A hearsay declarant, like any trial witness, can speak through admissible hearsay to anything that "hath fallen under his senses."[1] Or in a more modern variant: "Personal knowledge is that which comes to the witness through the use of his senses—that which is heard, felt, seen, smelled, or tasted."[2] Just as a testifying witness who claimed to have personal knowledge will be permitted to testify so long as the claim is plausible, a hearsay statement that professes, explicitly or implicitly, to be based on personal knowledge will generally pass the requisite threshold.

Some of the benefit of the doubt given to hearsay declarants in this context results from practicality; there will be little basis to refute the absent declarant's claim. The Advisory Committee states, the declarant's personal knowledge "may appear from [the] statement or be inferable from circumstances."

BEMIS v. EDWARDS
45 F.3d 1369 (9th Cir. 1995)

[Ronald Bemis brought a civil rights action against Oregon police officers for using excessive force in arresting him after Bemis apparently broke into his own house and then emerged with a gun prompting a neighbor, Gary Estep, to call 911 and report what appeared to be an armed burglary.]

In an evidentiary hearing, the judge had considered admission of a 911 tape from the night in question. In one part of the tape, ... Estep reported, "Now there's a cop beating the shit out of the guy now," and then:

> "There's five units—I got a scanner here in my house, so—but it's kind of getting ridiculous guys. I mean, the cop's beating the shit out of the guy right now. The guy's got a gun, though. I guess it's legal."

.... Bemis ... argues that even if the Estep Statement is hearsay, it should have been admitted under exceptions to the hearsay rule....

Hearsay statements on a 911 tape can be admitted into evidence as either a "public record," Fed.R.Evid. 803(8)(B), or a "business record," Fed.R.Evid. 803(6). However, because citizens who call 911 are not under any "duty to report," Fed.R.Evid. 803(8)(B), a recorded statement by a citizen must satisfy a separate hearsay exception. Fed.R.Evid. 805. Under certain circumstances,

---

[1] Bushel's Trial, 6 How. St. Tr. 999 (1670).
[2] Layno v. Brown, 6 Vet. App. 465 (1994).

such a statement may qualify as either a "present sense impression," Fed.R.Evid. 803(1), or an "excited utterance," Fed.R.Evid. 803(2). Certainly, a statement by a 911 caller who is witnessing the violent arrest of a suspect by the police could qualify under either exception.

The district court, however, properly refused to admit the Estep Statement [because it] does not meet the ... requirement of personal knowledge of the events described. Generally, a witness must have "personal knowledge of the matter" to which she testifies. Fed.R.Evid. 602. In the context of hearsay, the declarant must also have personal knowledge of what she describes. Fed.R.Evid. 803 advisory committee's note ("In a hearsay situation, the declarant is, of course, a witness, and neither this rule nor Rule 804 dispenses with the requirement of firsthand knowledge.")

.... As the proponent of the evidence, Bemis had the burden of establishing personal perception by a preponderance of the evidence. Estep's proximity to the scene at the time of the incident provided some circumstantial evidence of firsthand knowledge, which ordinarily may be sufficient to satisfy the foundational requirement in the context of a statement by a phone caller.

The district court, however, correctly noted that the record in this case gives an articulable basis to suspect that Estep did not witness the events he described, but instead had relayed to the 911 operator descriptions by other people who had been observing from the windows of Estep's house. Not only did Estep admit at one point that he could not describe what was happening outside, but he also could be heard repeating the words of an unidentified voice in the background. Although Estep was available to testify as to the circumstances surrounding his statements, Bemis declined to offer his testimony. Because there are affirmative indications that the declarant lacked firsthand knowledge of the events he described, we hold that the district court did not abuse its discretion in refusing to admit the Estep Statement....

***

Personal knowledge is not required for hearsay statements offered under Rule 801(d)(2). The Advisory Committee Note to Rule 801 emphasizes the traditional "freedom which [party] admissions have enjoyed from ... the rule requiring firsthand knowledge." As a consequence, statements of a party offered under Rule 801(d) can be admitted even when the party did not have personal knowledge of the matter related in the statement. The rationale is that statements of a party are not admitted because they are reliable. Rather, the Advisory Committee explains, their admission is "the result of the adversary system."

HEARSAY POLICY

This section presents the policy controversy surrounding the American hearsay prohibition. It begins with the Advisory Committee Note justifying the treatment of hearsay adopted by the Federal Rules of Evidence. After that comes two brief excerpts from law review articles that summarize past and present reform proposals. The section concludes with evidentiary schemes that do not include hearsay prohibitions, and a problem that explores the "why" of hearsay policy.

Introductory Note: The Hearsay Problem

The Advisory Committee drafted the following note to introduce the proposed hearsay rules.

"The factors to be considered in evaluating the testimony of a witness are perception, memory, and narration. Sometimes a fourth is added, sincerity, but in fact it seems merely to be an aspect of the three already mentioned.

In order to encourage the witness to do his best with respect to each of these factors, and to expose any inaccuracies which may enter in, the Anglo-American tradition has evolved three conditions under which witnesses will ideally be required to testify: (1) under oath, (2) in the personal presence of the trier of fact, (3) subject to cross-examination.

(1) Standard procedure calls for the swearing of witnesses. While the practice is perhaps less effective than in an earlier time, no disposition to relax the requirement is apparent, other than to allow affirmation by persons with scruples against taking oaths.

(2) The demeanor of the witness traditionally has been believed to furnish trier and opponent with valuable clues. The witness himself will probably be impressed with the solemnity of the occasion and the possibility of public disgrace. Willingness to falsify may reasonably become more difficult in the presence of the person against whom directed....

(3) Emphasis on the basis of the hearsay rule today tends to center upon the condition of cross-examination. All may not agree with Wigmore that cross-examination is "beyond doubt the greatest legal engine ever invented for the discovery of truth," but all will agree with his statement that it has become a

"vital feature" of the Anglo-American system. The belief, or perhaps hope, that cross-examination is effective in exposing imperfections of perception, memory, and narration is fundamental.

The logic of the preceding discussion might suggest that no testimony be received unless in full compliance with the three ideal conditions. No one advocates this position. Common sense tells that much evidence which is not given under the three conditions may be inherently superior to much that is. Moreover, when the choice is between evidence which is less than best and no evidence at all, only clear folly would dictate an across-the-board policy of doing without. The problem thus resolves itself into effecting a sensible accommodation between these considerations and the desirability of giving testimony under the ideal conditions.

The solution evolved by the common law has been a general rule excluding hearsay but subject to numerous exceptions under circumstances supposed to furnish guarantees of trustworthiness. Criticisms of this scheme are that it is bulky and complex, fails to screen good from bad hearsay realistically, and inhibits the growth of the law of evidence.

Since no one advocates excluding all hearsay, three possible solutions may be considered: (1) abolish the rule against hearsay and admit all hearsay; (2) admit hearsay possessing sufficient probative force, but with procedural safeguards; (3) revise the present system of class exceptions.

(1) Abolition of the hearsay rule would be the simplest solution. The effect would not be automatically to abolish the giving of testimony under ideal conditions. If the declarant were available, compliance with the ideal conditions would be optional with either party. Thus the proponent could call the declarant as a witness as a form of presentation more impressive than his hearsay statement. Or the opponent could call the declarant to be cross-examined upon his statement.... In criminal cases, the Sixth Amendment requirement of confrontation would no doubt move into a large part of the area presently occupied by the hearsay rule in the event of the abolition of the latter. The resultant split between civil and criminal evidence is regarded as an undesirable development.

(2) Abandonment of the system of class exceptions in favor of individual treatment in the setting of the particular case, accompanied by procedural

safeguards, has been impressively advocated. Admissibility would be determined by weighing the probative force of the evidence against the possibility of prejudice, waste of time, and the availability of more satisfactory evidence. The bases of the traditional hearsay exceptions would be helpful in assessing probative force. Procedural safeguards would consist of notice of intention to use hearsay, free comment by the judge on the weight of the evidence, and a greater measure of authority in both trial and appellate judges to deal with evidence on the basis of weight. The Advisory Committee has rejected this approach to hearsay as involving too great a measure of judicial discretion, minimizing the predictability of rulings, enhancing the difficulties of preparation for trial, adding a further element to the already over-complicated congeries of pre-trial procedures, and requiring substantially different rules for civil and criminal cases....

(3) The approach to hearsay in these rules is that of the common law, i.e., a general rule excluding hearsay, with exceptions under which evidence is not required to be excluded even though hearsay. The traditional hearsay exceptions are drawn upon for the exceptions, collected under two rules, one dealing with situations where availability of the declarant is regarded as immaterial and the other with those where unavailability is made a condition to the admission of the hearsay statement. Each of the two rules concludes with a provision for hearsay statements not within one of the specified exceptions "but having comparable circumstantial guarantees of trustworthiness." This plan is submitted as calculated to encourage growth and development in this area of the law, while conserving the values and experience of the past as a guide to the future...."

"EHEARSAY"[1]

...The now-codified [hearsay] prohibition, with its many discrete exceptions, is the most distinctive feature of American evidence law....

A. The Hearsay Prohibition

...Modern hearsay law traces its roots to the early 1700s. The English common law exclusion of out-of-court statements began to emerge about that time,

---

[1] Jeffrey Bellin, *eHearsay*, 98 Minn. L. Rev. 7 (2013).

grounded in the notion that "statements used as testimony must be made where the maker can be subjected to cross-examination." This justification still resonates with the modern conception that an adversary system requires live testimony, not out-of-court statements, as its inputs....

The necessary corollary to the sentiments expressed above is that an adversary process is not so well equipped to ferret out spurious out-of-court statements. Out-of-court speakers rarely speak under oath and need not fear perjury prosecution or even particularly severe moral condemnation for lying. More significantly, cross-examination, the critical adversarial tool for unearthing hidden flaws, is blunted when the real subject of the examination is absent from court. The American hearsay prohibition thus stands on firm theoretical ground. Yet skeptics persist. As will quickly become apparent, reformers traditionally focus on the prohibition's two most dubious facets. First, why does the prohibition apply to the out-of-court statements of testifying witnesses who can, in fact, be cross-examined? Second, encouraging parties to bring live witnesses to trial may be a worthy goal, but the prohibition extends to out-of-court statements of declarants who are deceased or otherwise unavailable to testify. Applying the hearsay prohibition to statements by unavailable witnesses deprives juries of evidence that, while imperfect, is often the best the circumstances allow.

B. The Model Code of Evidence

In recent history, the most direct assault on the hearsay prohibition came in the 1942 "Model Code of Evidence" promulgated by the American Law Institute (ALI). The Model Code represented the studied efforts of the era's evidence luminaries to codify the unruly, judge-made evidence law of the time. The Model Code's drafters had a second objective as well--to work a "radical change[]" in the common law hearsay prohibition. The drafters derided "the law governing hearsay" as a "conglomeration of inconsistencies" with little thematic purpose, adding that "[t]he courts by multiplying exceptions [to the prohibition] reveal their conviction that relevant hearsay evidence normally has real probative value, and is capable of valuation by a jury."

The Model Code's drafters attempted to transform the hearsay prohibition into a rule of necessity. Section 503 of the Model Code made hearsay admissible whenever the declarant is "unavailable as a witness." The Code also made hearsay admissible whenever the declarant was "present and subject to cross-examination." As a result, under the Model Code, hearsay would almost always be admissible, save for circumstances where the proponent of a statement could procure the declarant's live testimony, but declined to do so. In part because of this "radical attitude toward hearsay reform," no state adopted the Model Code....

C. The Uniform Rules of Evidence

In 1953, evidence scholars again tried to dilute the American hearsay prohibition. Building from the wreckage of the Model Code, and in consultation with the Code's drafters, a reconstituted committee of prominent jurists and scholars drafted the "Uniform Rules of Evidence." Designed in part to soften aspects of the Model Code that were "too far-reaching and drastic for present day acceptance," the Uniform Rules left the traditional hearsay prohibition intact, but proposed a novel and potentially expansive new hearsay exception. Awkwardly titled "Statements Admissible on Grounds of Necessity Generally," Uniform Rule 63(4)(c) excepted from the hearsay prohibition:

> [A] statement [of an unavailable witness] narrating, describing or explaining an event or condition which the judge finds was made by the declarant at a time when the matter had been recently perceived by him and while his recollection was clear, and was made in good faith prior to the commencement of the action.

The Commentary to the rule acknowledged that the exception was "new" but justified it as meeting a "vital need" to "prevent miscarriage of justice resulting from the arbitrary exclusion of evidence which is worthy of consideration, when it is the best evidence available." In concert with the Uniform Rules' treatment of out-of-court statements of testifying witnesses as non-hearsay, Rule 63(4)(c) again promised to substantially unravel the American hearsay prohibition. The Uniform Rules, however, "were only slightly more successful than the Model Code," achieving lasting acceptance only in Kansas, the home state of the chairman of the Committee that drafted the rules.

D. The Federal Rules of Evidence

Evidence reformers tried one last time to liberalize the hearsay prohibition in the next, and most successful, effort to create a uniform system of American evidence law: the Federal Rules of Evidence adopted by Congress in 1975 and shortly thereafter in most state jurisdictions. While purporting to adopt "the approach to hearsay . . . of the common law," the Federal Rules' drafters included an exception unknown to the common law, Rule 804(b)(2), "Statement of Recent Perception." [SRP] This rule, which borrowed heavily from Uniform Rule 63(4)(c), excepted from the hearsay prohibition:

> A statement, not in response to the instigation of a person engaged in investigating, litigating, or settling a claim, which narrates, describes, or explains an event or condition recently perceived by the declarant, made in good faith, not in contemplation of pending or anticipated litigation in which he was interested, and while his recollection was clear.

The proposed rule was approved by the Supreme Court, but rejected by Congress. The House Judiciary Committee explained that it could not endorse this "new and unwarranted hearsay exception of great potential breadth" because it "did not believe that statements of the type referred to bore sufficient guarantees of trustworthiness." Congress, being the final word on the matter, prevailed. Consequently, the Federal Rules and, with four exceptions, the evidence codes governing state jurisdictions (which largely mirror the enacted federal rules) contain no provision analogous to the SRP exception. Although these evidence codes contain numerous hearsay exceptions distilled from the common law, including, in many cases, an ill-defined "residual" exception intended for use in "rare" and "exceptional" circumstances, adherents to the status quo have largely turned back modern efforts to liberalize hearsay doctrine.

"THE CASE FOR EHEARSAY"[1]

... C. Judge Posner's Proposal: The Residual Exception As a Replacement for the Hearsay Exceptions

.... Judge Richard Posner [recently proposed] to replace the hearsay exceptions with a discretionary regime modeled on the residual rule. Judge Posner succinctly states his proposal in United States v. Boyce:

---

[1] Jeffrey Bellin, *The Case for eHearsay*, 83 Fordham L. Rev. 1317.

> .... What I would like to see is Rule 807 ("Residual Exception") swallow much of Rules 801 through 806 and thus many of the exclusions from evidence, exceptions to the exclusions, and notes of the Advisory Committee. The "hearsay rule" is too complex, as well as being archaic. Trials would go better with a simpler rule, the core of which would be the proposition (essentially a simplification of Rule 807) that hearsay evidence should be admissible when it is reliable, when the jury can understand its strengths and limitations, and when it will materially enhance the likelihood of a correct outcome.

Judge Posner's suggestion resonates with a venerable tradition dating back well before the drafting of the Federal Rules of Evidence. In the modern era, Judge Jack Weinstein crafted perhaps the classic formulation of this argument. Judge Weinstein argued that the class-based system of hearsay exceptions championed by John Henry Wigmore should be replaced with a rule permitting trial courts to determine the admission of hearsay by weighing its "probative force" against "the possibility of prejudice, unnecessary use of court time, and availability of more satisfactory evidence" --roughly the sentiment now captured in Rule 403. In the process, he referenced similar proposals by other leading evidence scholars and implicitly endorsed a generous "residual exception" that could achieve much of his stated goal. In crafting the Federal Rules of Evidence, the Advisory Committee considered and rejected Judge Weinstein's approach. It explained:

> The Advisory Committee has rejected this approach to hearsay as involving too great a measure of judicial discretion, minimizing the predictability of rulings, enhancing the difficulties of preparation for trial, adding a further element to the already over-complicated congeries of pretrial procedures, and requiring substantially different rules for civil and criminal cases.

[A]ll of the objections the Advisory Committee brandished against Judge Weinstein can similarly be brought to bear against Judge Posner. If anything, given ever-expanding dockets and increasing reliance on settlements and guilty pleas, the criticisms have gained strength since 1969. Further, the passage of time has likely made it more difficult as a practical matter to abolish a classbased hearsay framework, given litigators' long experience with the framework and its adoption in every American jurisdiction. There is, in fact, no guarantee that if the Advisory Committee made such a drastic change, the states would follow suit. The result could be an even more convoluted system of American evidence law, where federal and state practitioners would need to learn two vastly different systems of hearsay rules....

OTHER APPROACHES

AMERICAN ARBITRATION ASSOCIATION
Rules for Arbitration and Mediation (Employment)

... At the Arbitration Management Conference the matters to be considered shall include, ...

the law, standards, rules of evidence and burdens of proof that are to apply to the proceeding;...

30. Evidence The parties may offer such evidence as is relevant and material to the dispute and shall produce such evidence as the arbitrator deems necessary to an understanding and determination of the dispute. All evidence shall be taken in the presence of all of the arbitrators and all of the parties, ...

...The arbitrator shall be the judge of the relevance and materiality of the evidence offered, and conformity to legal rules of evidence shall not be necessary....

***

INTERIM STUDENT SEXUAL HARASSMENT AND MISCONDUCT GRIEVANCE/COMPLAINT PROCEDURE

...J. Rules of Evidence and "Second Hand" Information. University proceedings are not judicial or policy procedures designed to enforce laws. They are internal, administrative processes designed to address reported violations of university policy. Universities do not conduct judicial proceedings and do not follow the rules of evidence employed by courts of law. Information that does not come from a first-hand source (hearsay) may be considered. Lie detector/polygraph evidence is not permissible. Except as specifically provided in this procedure, the university is not required to consider evidence and may decide which evidence to exclude or consider. It is in the investigator's discretion to determine what evidence is relevant and material to the case....

Fed. R. Ev. 1101

(d) **Exceptions**. These rules — except for those on privilege — do not apply to the following:...

(2) grand-jury proceedings; and

(3) miscellaneous proceedings such as:

- extradition or rendition;

- issuing an arrest warrant, criminal summons, or search warrant;

- a preliminary examination in a criminal case;

- sentencing;

- granting or revoking probation or supervised release; and

- considering whether to release on bail or otherwise.

PROBLEM 6-26: HEARSAY POLICY

Imagine you are a legislator in a jurisdiction considering a revision of its evidence rules. Would you recommend adoption of the hearsay framework of the federal rules, broad exceptions like those proposed for the Model Rules or Uniform Code, Judge Posner and Weinstein's suggestions, or something else entirely? Why?

Does your reasoning extend to non-trial dispute resolution systems (arbitration, campus misconduct hearings, sentencings)? Those proceedings also need guidelines regarding what evidence will be considered. Is it sufficient to simply allow a judge or investigator to determine what evidence to consider? Or should there be external constraints that limit what the judge or investigators are permitted to rely on in reaching a conclusion.

Chapter 7

CONSTITUTIONAL EVIDENCE RULES

This Chapter explore the complex relationship between the Constitution and federal and state rules of evidence. Just like other legislative statutes and judicial rules, rules of evidence must give way to Constitutional commands.

THE CONFRONTATION CLAUSE

Sixth Amendment, U.S. Constitution

"In all criminal prosecutions, the accused shall enjoy the right . . . to be confronted with the witnesses against him."

CROSS-EXAMINATION OF LIVE WITNESSES

The most important constitutional rule of evidence is the criminal defendant's Sixth Amendment right to confront prosecution witnesses. The obvious implication of this right is that witnesses offered by the prosecution must testify in person before the jury that determines the accused's guilt.

> "Confrontation: (1) insures that the witness will give his statements under oath—thus impressing him with the seriousness of the matter and guarding against the lie by the possibility of a penalty for perjury; (2) forces the witness to submit to cross-examination, the 'greatest legal engine ever invented for the discovery of truth'; (3) permits the jury that is to decide the defendant's fate to observe the demeanor of the witness in making his statement, thus aiding the jury in assessing his credibility."[1]

(Consistent with these requirements, Rule 603 requires any witness before testifying to "give an oath or affirmation to testify truthfully.")

A clear violation of the confrontation right arises if a witness testifies on direct examination for the prosecution, but then refuses to submit to cross-examination. In such a circumstance, the trial court would, at a minimum, instruct the jury to disregard the direct examination testimony.

---

[1] California v. Green, 399 U.S. 149 (1970).

Sometimes the potential violation is less obvious, for example when the defense's inability to cross-examine a witness is only partial, arising from the witness' memory loss. The Supreme Court addressed that circumstance in *Delaware v. Fensterer* (1985), where it ruled that there was no Confrontation Clause violation when an expert witness testified as to the opinion he formed, but "was unable to recall the basis for his opinion." The Court explained:

> The Confrontation Clause includes no guarantee that every witness called by the prosecution will refrain from giving testimony that is marred by forgetfulness, confusion, or evasion. To the contrary, the Confrontation Clause is generally satisfied when the defense is given a full and fair opportunity to probe and expose these infirmities through cross-examination, thereby calling to the attention of the factfinder the reasons for giving scant weight to the witness' testimony.

In *United States v. Owens*, the Court extended this reasoning to a scenario where the prosecution introduced an out-of-court statement from a testifying witness, who was suffering from memory loss, that identified the defendant as his assailant. The Court's constitutional analysis paralleled the hearsay analysis excerpted in Chapter 7 (discussing *Owens*): As long as the witness answers cross-examination questions, even if those answers consist of the bland repetition that the witness does not remember, the confrontation right is satisfied.

Obstacles to cross-examination also arise from court rulings. As we have already seen, when witnesses testify, judges often make rulings that restrict cross-examination. Conscious of this dimension of the problem, the *Owens* Court noted that "limitations on the scope of examination by the trial court or assertions of privilege by the witness may undermine the process to such a degree that meaningful cross-examination ... no longer exists." The next case illustrates this point.

DAVIS v. ALASKA
415 U.S. 308 (1974)

Chief Justice BURGER delivered the opinion of the Court.

(1)

[The State of Alaska prosecuted Joshaway Davis for burglary and grand larceny for stealing a safe from "the Polar Bar" in Anchorage.]

Richard Green was a crucial witness for the prosecution.... Before testimony was taken at the trial of petitioner, the prosecutor moved for a protective order to prevent any reference to Green's juvenile record by the defense in the course of cross-examination. At the time of the trial and at the time of the events Green testified to, Green was on probation by order of a juvenile court after having been adjudicated a delinquent for burglarizing two cabins....

In opposing the protective order, petitioner's counsel made it clear that he would not introduce Green's juvenile adjudication as a general impeachment of Green's character as a truthful person but, rather, to show specifically that at the same time Green was assisting the police in identifying petitioner he was on probation for burglary. From this petitioner would seek to show—or at least argue—that Green acted out of fear or concern of possible jeopardy to his probation. Not only might Green have made a hasty and faulty identification of petitioner to shift suspicion away from himself as one who robbed the Polar Bar, but Green might have been subject to undue pressure from the police and made his identifications under fear of possible probation revocation....

The trial court granted the motion for a protective order, relying on Alaska [state law].

Although prevented from revealing that Green had been on probation for the juvenile delinquency adjudication for burglary at the same time that he originally identified petitioner, counsel for petitioner did his best to expose Green's state of mind at the time Green discovered that a stolen safe had been discovered near his home....

Defense counsel cross-examined Green in part as follows:

'Q. Were you upset at all by the fact that this safe was found on your property?

'A. No, sir.

'Q. Did you feel that they might in some way suspect you of this?

'A. No.

'Q. Did you feel uncomfortable about this though?

'A. No, not really.

'Q. The fact that a safe was found on your property?

'A. No.

'Q. Did you suspect for a moment that the police might somehow think that you were involved in this?

'A. I thought they might ask a few questions is all.

'Q. Did that thought ever enter your mind that you—that the police might think that you were somehow connected with this?

'A. No, it didn't really bother me, no....

'Q. Had you ever been questioned like that before by any law enforcement officers?

'A. No....

Since defense counsel was prohibited from making inquiry as to the witness' being on probation under a juvenile court adjudication, Green's protestations of unconcern over possible police suspicion that he might have had a part in the Polar Bar burglary and his categorical denial of ever having been the subject of any similar law-enforcement interrogation went unchallenged.....

(2)

The Sixth Amendment to the Constitution guarantees the right of an accused in a criminal prosecution 'to be confronted with the witnesses against him.' This right is secured for defendants in state as well as federal criminal proceedings. Confrontation means more than being allowed to confront the witness physically. 'Our cases construing the (confrontation) clause hold that a primary interest secured by it is the right of cross-examination.' Professor Wigmore stated:

> 'The main and essential purpose of confrontation is to secure for the opponent the opportunity of cross-examination. The opponent demands confrontation, not for the idle purpose of gazing upon the witness, or of being gazed upon by him, but for the purpose of cross-examination, which cannot be had except by the direct and personal putting of questions and obtaining immediate answers.'

Cross-examination is the principal means by which the believability of a witness and the truth of his testimony are tested. Subject always to the broad discretion of a trial judge to preclude repetitive and unduly harassing interrogation, the cross-examiner is not only permitted to delve into the witness' story to test the witness' perceptions and memory, but the cross-examiner has traditionally been allowed to impeach, i.e., discredit, the witness. One way of discrediting the witness is to introduce evidence of a prior criminal conviction of that witness. By so doing the cross-examiner intends to afford the jury a basis to infer that the witness' character is such that he would be less likely than the average trustworthy citizen to be truthful in his testimony. The introduction of evidence of a prior crime is thus a general attack on the credibility of the witness. A more particular attack on the witness' credibility is effected by means of cross-examination directed toward revealing possible biases, prejudices, or ulterior motives of the witness as they may relate directly to issues or personalities in the case at hand. The partiality of a witness is subject to exploration at trial, and is 'always relevant as discrediting the witness and affecting the weight of his testimony.' We have recognized that the exposure of a witness' motivation in testifying is a proper and important function of the constitutionally protected right of cross-examination.

…. The accuracy and truthfulness of Green's testimony were key elements in the State's case against petitioner. The claim of bias which the defense sought to develop was admissible to afford a basis for an inference of undue pressure because of Green's vulnerable status as a probationer, as well as of Green's possible concern that he might be a suspect in the investigation.

…. Petitioner was thus denied the right of effective cross-examination….

(3)

The claim is made that the State has an important interest in protecting the anonymity of juvenile offenders and that this interest outweighs any competing interest this petitioner might have in cross-examining Green about his being on probation. The State argues that exposure of a juvenile's record of delinquency would likely cause impairment of rehabilitative goals of the juvenile correctional procedures. This exposure, it is argued, might encourage the juvenile offender to commit further acts of delinquency, or cause the juvenile offender to lose employment opportunities or otherwise suffer unnecessarily for his youthful transgression.

…. The State's policy interest in protecting the confidentiality of a juvenile offender's record cannot require yielding of so vital a constitutional right as the effective cross-examination for bias of an adverse witness. The State could have protected Green from exposure of his juvenile adjudication in these circumstances by refraining from using him to make out its case; the State cannot, consistent with the right of confrontation, require the petitioner to bear the full burden of vindicating the State's interest in the secrecy of juvenile criminal records. The judgment affirming petitioner's convictions of burglary and grand larceny is reversed and the case is remanded for further proceedings not inconsistent with this opinion.

LIMITS ON PROSECUTION HEARSAY EVIDENCE

The most common Confrontation Clause questions arise when the prosecution introduces hearsay against a criminal defendant. The considerations in this context parallel the hearsay rules covered in the previous Chapter. In fact, in many circumstances, defense attorneys will raise both a hearsay and a Confrontation Clause objection to the same evidence. That said, it is important to keep the doctrines separate. While often overlapping in their policy implications, the hearsay rules and the Confrontation Clause are distinct authorities. Consequently, courts have crafted a distinct body of Confrontation Clause doctrine to govern out-of-court statements. The following excerpt from a law review article sketches the broad contours of the Supreme Court's path.

CONFRONTATION CLAUSE JURISPRUDENCE[1]

The Sixth Amendment guarantee of an accused's right to "be confronted with the witnesses against him" spawns an array of possible interpretations. At a minimum, the right guarantees a defendant's opportunity to cross-examine any witness called by the prosecution at trial. After a prosecution witness testifies, the defense must be permitted to test the witness's credibility before the jury through cross-examination, the "greatest legal engine ever invented for the discovery of truth." The difficult interpretive question is how this right applies when the prosecution offers out-of-court statements of absent declarants - hearsay - as substantive evidence against the accused.

Over a century ago, Dean Wigmore took a famously narrow view, contending that the Confrontation Clause provides a right to cross-examine any live

---

[1] Jeffrey Bellin, *The Incredible Shrinking Confrontation Clause*, 92 B.U. L. Rev. 1865 (2012).

witness who testifies for the prosecution at trial, and nothing more. Limits on the introduction of the statements of out-of-court declarants, Wigmore argued, were the province of the hearsay rules, not the Constitution. At the other extreme, the Confrontation Clause could be interpreted to bar any unconfronted statement .... That interpretation would override "virtually every hearsay exception" the prosecution might invoke in a criminal trial.

The Supreme Court has consistently rejected the two extreme positions described above, claiming throughout its history to be charting "a middle course."

MATTOX v. UNITED STATES
156 U.S. 237 (1895)

Justice BROWN, ..., delivered the opinion of the court.

[A jury convicted Clyde Mattox of murder. The Supreme Court reversed his conviction and remanded the case for a new trial. The new trial also resulted in a conviction. Mattox appealed. On appeal, Mattox claimed that at the second trial, he was denied his Sixth Amendment right to confront the witnesses against him when the trial court admitted "to the jury the reporter's notes of the testimony of two witnesses at the former trial, who had since died." The Supreme Court rejected the claim as explained below:]

.... The primary object of the constitutional provision in question was to prevent depositions or ex parte affidavits, such as were sometimes admitted in civil cases, being used against the prisoner in lieu of a personal examination and cross-examination of the witness, in which the accused has an opportunity, not only of testing the recollection and sifting the conscience of the witness, but of compelling him to stand face to face with the jury in order that they may look at him, and judge by his demeanor upon the stand and the manner in which he gives his testimony whether he is worthy of belief. There is doubtless reason for saying that the accused should never lose the benefit of any of these safeguards even by the death of the witness; and that, if notes of his testimony are permitted to be read, he is deprived of the advantage of that personal presence of the witness before the jury which the law has designed for his protection. But general rules of law of this kind, however beneficent in their operation and valuable to the accused, must occasionally give way to considerations of public policy and the necessities of the case. To say that a criminal, after having once been convicted by the testimony of a certain witness, should go scot free simply because death has closed the mouth of that witness, would be carrying his constitutional protection to an unwarrantable extent. The law, in its wisdom, declares that the rights of the public shall not be wholly sacrificed in order that an incidental benefit may be preserved to the accused.

.... We are bound to interpret the constitution in the light of the law as it existed at the time it was adopted, not as reaching out for new guaranties of the rights of the citizen, but as securing to every individual such as he already possessed as a British subject,—such as his ancestors had inherited and defended since the days of Magna Charta. Many of its provisions in the nature of a bill of rights are subject to exceptions, recognized long before the adoption of the constitution, and not interfering at all with its spirit. Such exceptions were obviously intended to be respected. ... For instance, there could be nothing more directly contrary to the letter of the provision in question than the admission of dying declarations. They are rarely made in the presence of the accused; they are made without any opportunity for examination or cross-examination, nor is the witness brought face to face with the jury; yet from time immemorial they have been treated as competent testimony, and no one would have the hardihood at this day to question their admissibility.....

[In this case,] [t]he substance of the constitutional protection is preserved to the prisoner in the advantage he has once had of seeing the witness face to face, and of subjecting him to the ordeal of a cross-examination....

***

Incremental Supreme Court decisions like *Mattox* gave way to a generally applicable rule in *Ohio v. Roberts* (1980). As *Roberts* was later overruled, the excerpt below consists solely of the test that applied between 1980-2004.

OHIO v. ROBERTS
448 U.S. 56 (1980)

...In sum, when a hearsay declarant is not present for cross-examination at trial, the Confrontation Clause normally requires a showing that he is unavailable. Even then, his statement is admissible only if it bears adequate "indicia of reliability." Reliability can be inferred without more in a case where the evidence falls within a firmly rooted hearsay exception. In other cases, the evidence must be excluded, at least absent a showing of particularized guarantees of trustworthiness.

CRAWFORD v. WASHINGTON
541 U.S. 36 (2004)

Justice SCALIA delivered the (7-2) opinion of the Court.

… On August 5, 1999, Kenneth Lee was stabbed at his apartment. Police arrested petitioner [Michael Crawford] later that night. After giving petitioner and his wife *Miranda* warnings, detectives interrogated each of them twice. Petitioner eventually confessed that he and Sylvia had gone in search of Lee because he was upset over an earlier incident in which Lee had tried to rape her. The two had found Lee at his apartment, and a fight ensued in which Lee was stabbed in the torso and petitioner's hand was cut.…

Sylvia generally corroborated petitioner's story about the events leading up to the fight, but her account of the fight itself was arguably different—particularly with respect to whether Lee had drawn a weapon before petitioner assaulted him…[:]

> A. [Lee] lifted his hand over his head maybe to strike Michael's hand down or something and then he put his hands in his … put his right hand in his right pocket … took a step back … Michael proceeded to stab him … then his hands were like … how do you explain this … open arms … with his hands open and he fell down … and we ran (describing subject holding hands open, palms toward assailant).

…. The State charged petitioner with assault and attempted murder. At trial, he claimed self-defense. Sylvia did not testify because of the state marital privilege, which generally bars a spouse from testifying without the other spouse's consent. In Washington, this privilege does not extend to a spouse's out-of-court statements admissible under a hearsay exception, so the State sought to introduce Sylvia's tape-recorded statements to the police as evidence that the stabbing was not in self-defense. Noting that Sylvia had admitted she led petitioner to Lee's apartment and thus had facilitated the assault, the State invoked the hearsay exception for statements against penal interest. [The trial court admitted Sylvia's tape recorded statement and the] jury convicted petitioner of assault.

The Washington Court of Appeals reversed. It applied a nine-factor test to determine whether Sylvia's statement bore particularized guarantees of trustworthiness [under *Ohio v. Roberts*], and noted several reasons why it did not: .... The Washington Supreme Court reinstated the conviction, unanimously concluding that, although Sylvia's statement did not fall under a firmly rooted hearsay exception, it bore guarantees of trustworthiness ....

> [Footnote 1] The court rejected the State's argument that ... petitioner waived his confrontation rights by invoking the marital privilege.... We express no opinion on th[is] matter[].

II

The Sixth Amendment's Confrontation Clause provides that, "[i]n all criminal prosecutions, the accused shall enjoy the right ... to be confronted with the witnesses against him." We have held that this bedrock procedural guarantee applies to both federal and state prosecutions. *Pointer v. Texas* (1965). ... *Roberts* says that an unavailable witness's out-of-court statement may be admitted so long as it has adequate indicia of reliability—*i.e.*, falls within a "firmly rooted hearsay exception" or bears "particularized guarantees of trustworthiness." Petitioner argues that this test strays from the original meaning of the Confrontation Clause and urges us to reconsider it.

A

The Constitution's text does not alone resolve this case. One could plausibly read "witnesses against" a defendant to mean those who actually testify at trial, those whose statements are offered at trial, or something in-between. We must therefore turn to the historical background of the Clause to understand its meaning.

The right to confront one's accusers is a concept that dates back to Roman times. The founding generation's immediate source of the concept, however, was the common law. English common law has long differed from continental civil law in regard to the manner in which witnesses give testimony in criminal trials. The common-law tradition is one of live testimony in court subject to adversarial testing, while the civil law condones examination in private by judicial officers.

Nonetheless, England at times adopted elements of the civil-law practice.

Justices of the peace or other officials examined suspects and witnesses before trial. These examinations were sometimes read in court in lieu of live testimony, a practice that "occasioned frequent demands by the prisoner to have his 'accusers,' *i.e.* the witnesses against him, brought before him face to face." In some cases, these demands were refused. ...

The most notorious instances of civil-law examination occurred in the great political trials of the 16th and 17th centuries. One such was the 1603 trial of Sir Walter Raleigh for treason. Lord Cobham, Raleigh's alleged accomplice, had implicated him in an examination before the Privy Council and in a letter. At Raleigh's trial, these were read to the jury. Raleigh argued that Cobham had lied to save himself: "Cobham is absolutely in the King's mercy; to excuse me cannot avail him; by accusing me he may hope for favour." Suspecting that Cobham would recant, Raleigh demanded that the judges call him to appear, arguing that "[t]he Proof of the Common Law is by witness and jury: let Cobham be here, let him speak it. Call my accuser before my face ...." The judges refused, and, despite Raleigh's protestations that he was being tried "by the Spanish Inquisition," the jury convicted, and Raleigh was sentenced to death.

One of Raleigh's trial judges later lamented that "'the justice of England has never been so degraded and injured as by the condemnation of Sir Walter Raleigh.'" Through a series of statutory and judicial reforms, English law developed a right of confrontation that limited these abuses....

B

Controversial examination practices were also used in the Colonies. ... Many [State] declarations of rights adopted around the time of the Revolution guaranteed a right of confrontation. The proposed Federal Constitution, however, did not. At the Massachusetts ratifying convention, Abraham Holmes objected to this omission precisely on the ground that it would lead to civil-law practices: "The mode of trial is altogether indetermined; ... whether [the defendant] is to be allowed to confront the witnesses, and have the advantage of cross-examination, we are not yet told .... [W]e shall find Congress possessed of powers enabling them to institute judicatories little less inauspicious than a certain tribunal in Spain, ... the *Inquisition*." Similarly, a prominent Antifederalist writing under the pseudonym Federal Farmer criticized the use of "written evidence" while objecting to the omission of a vicinage right: "Nothing can be more essential than the cross examining [of] witnesses, and generally before the triers of the facts in question .... [W]ritten evidence ... [is] almost useless; it must be frequently taken ex parte, and but very seldom leads to the proper discovery of truth." The First Congress responded by including the Confrontation Clause in the proposal that became the Sixth Amendment....

III

This history supports two inferences about the meaning of the Sixth Amendment.

A

First, the principal evil at which the Confrontation Clause was directed was the civil-law mode of criminal procedure, and particularly its use of *ex parte* examinations as evidence against the accused. It was these practices that the Crown deployed in notorious treason cases like Raleigh's; ... that English law's assertion of a right to confrontation was meant to prohibit; and that the founding-era rhetoric decried. The Sixth Amendment must be interpreted with this focus in mind.

... This focus also suggests that not all hearsay implicates the Sixth Amendment's core concerns. An off-hand, overheard remark might be unreliable evidence and thus a good candidate for exclusion under hearsay rules, but it bears little resemblance to the civil-law abuses the Confrontation Clause targeted. On the other hand, *ex parte* examinations might sometimes be admissible under modern hearsay rules, but the Framers certainly would not have condoned them.

The text of the Confrontation Clause reflects this focus. It applies to "witnesses" against the accused—in other words, those who "bear testimony." 2 N. Webster, An American Dictionary of the English Language (1828). "Testimony," in turn, is typically "[a] solemn declaration or affirmation made for the purpose of establishing or proving some fact." *Ibid.* An accuser who makes a formal statement to government officers bears testimony in a sense that a person who makes a casual remark to an acquaintance does not. The constitutional text, like the history underlying the common-law right of confrontation, thus reflects an especially acute concern with a specific type of out-of-court statement....

In sum, even if the Sixth Amendment is not solely concerned with testimonial hearsay, that is its primary object, and interrogations by law enforcement officers fall squarely within that class.

B

The historical record also supports a second proposition: that the Framers would not have allowed admission of testimonial statements of a witness who did not appear at trial unless he was unavailable to testify, and the defendant had had a prior opportunity for cross-examination. The text of the Sixth Amendment does not suggest any open-ended exceptions from the confrontation requirement to be developed by the courts. Rather, the "right ... to be confronted with the witnesses against him," is most naturally read as a reference to the right of confrontation at common law, admitting only those exceptions established at the time of the founding. As the English authorities above reveal, the common law in 1791 conditioned admissibility of an absent witness's examination on unavailability and a prior opportunity to cross-examine. The Sixth Amendment therefore incorporates those limitations....

> [Footnote 6]... The existence of [the dying declaration] exception as a general rule of criminal hearsay law cannot be disputed. Although many dying declarations may not be testimonial, there is authority for admitting even those that clearly are. We need not decide in this case whether the Sixth Amendment incorporates an exception for testimonial dying declarations. If this exception must be accepted on historical grounds, it is sui generis.

> [Footnote 9]... we reiterate that, when the declarant appears for cross-examination at trial, the Confrontation Clause places no constraints at all on the use of his prior testimonial statements. California v. Green (1970).... (The Clause also does not bar the use of testimonial statements for purposes other than establishing the truth of the matter asserted.)

V

Although the results of our decisions have generally been faithful to the original meaning of the Confrontation Clause, the same cannot be said of our rationales. *Roberts* conditions the admissibility of all hearsay evidence on whether it falls under a "firmly rooted hearsay exception" or bears "particularized guarantees of trustworthiness." This test departs from the historical principles identified above in two respects. First, it is too broad: It applies the same mode of analysis whether or not the hearsay consists of *ex parte* testimony. This often results in close constitutional scrutiny in cases that are far removed from the core concerns of the Clause. At the same time, however, the test is too narrow: It admits statements that *do* consist of *ex parte* testimony upon a mere finding of reliability. This malleable standard often fails to protect against paradigmatic confrontation violations.....

A

Where testimonial statements are involved, we do not think the Framers meant to leave the Sixth Amendment's protection to the vagaries of the rules of evidence, much less to amorphous notions of "reliability." Certainly none of the authorities discussed above acknowledges any general reliability exception to the common-law rule. Admitting statements deemed reliable by a judge is fundamentally at odds with the right of confrontation. To be sure, the Clause's ultimate goal is to ensure reliability of evidence, but it is a procedural rather than a substantive guarantee. It commands, not that evidence be reliable, but that reliability be assessed in a particular manner: by testing in the crucible of cross-examination. The Clause thus reflects a judgment, not only about the desirability of reliable evidence (a point on which there could be little dissent), but about how reliability can best be determined.

The *Roberts* test allows a jury to hear evidence, untested by the adversary process, based on a mere judicial determination of reliability. It thus replaces the constitutionally prescribed method of assessing reliability with a wholly foreign one.... Dispensing with confrontation because testimony is obviously reliable is akin to dispensing with jury trial because a defendant is obviously guilty. This is not what the Sixth Amendment prescribes.

B

The legacy of *Roberts* in other courts vindicates the Framers' wisdom in rejecting a general reliability exception. The framework is so unpredictable that it fails to provide meaningful protection from even core confrontation violations.

Reliability is an amorphous, if not entirely subjective, concept. There are countless factors bearing on whether a statement is reliable; the nine-factor

363

balancing test applied by the Court of Appeals below is representative. Whether a statement is deemed reliable depends heavily on which factors the judge considers and how much weight he accords each of them. Some courts wind up attaching the same significance to opposite facts. ....

The unpardonable vice of the *Roberts* test, however, is not its unpredictability, but its demonstrated capacity to admit core testimonial statements that the Confrontation Clause plainly meant to exclude....

C

.... We readily concede that we could resolve this case by simply reweighing the "reliability factors" under *Roberts* and finding that Sylvia Crawford's statement falls short. But we view this as one of those rare cases in which the result below is so improbable that it reveals a fundamental failure on our part to interpret the Constitution in a way that secures its intended constraint on judicial discretion. Moreover, to reverse the Washington Supreme Court's decision after conducting our own reliability analysis would perpetuate, not avoid, what the Sixth Amendment condemns. The Constitution prescribes a procedure for determining the reliability of testimony in criminal trials, and we, no less than the state courts, lack authority to replace it with one of our own devising.

We have no doubt that the courts below were acting in utmost good faith when they found reliability. The Framers, however, would not have been content to indulge this assumption. They knew that judges, like other government officers, could not always be trusted to safeguard the rights of the people; the likes of the dread Lord Jeffreys were not yet too distant a memory. They were loath to leave too much discretion in judicial hands. By replacing categorical constitutional guarantees with open-ended balancing tests, we do violence to their design. Vague standards are manipulable, and, while that might be a small concern in run-of-the-mill assault prosecutions like this one, the Framers had an eye toward politically charged cases like Raleigh's—great state trials where the impartiality of even those at the highest levels of the judiciary might not be so clear. It is difficult to imagine *Roberts'* providing any meaningful protection in those circumstances.

Where nontestimonial hearsay is at issue, it is wholly consistent with the Framers' design to afford the States flexibility in their development of hearsay law—as does *Roberts,* and as would an approach that exempted such statements from Confrontation Clause scrutiny altogether. Where testimonial evidence is at issue, however, the Sixth Amendment demands what the common law required: unavailability and a prior opportunity for cross-examination. We leave for another day any effort to spell out a comprehensive definition of "testimonial." Whatever else the term covers, it applies at a minimum to prior testimony at a preliminary hearing, before a grand jury, or at a former trial; and to police interrogations. These are the modern practices with closest kinship to the abuses at which the Confrontation Clause was directed.

In this case, the State admitted Sylvia's testimonial statement against petitioner, despite the fact that he had no opportunity to cross-examine her. That alone is sufficient to make out a violation of the Sixth Amendment. *Roberts* notwithstanding, we decline to mine the record in search of indicia of reliability. Where testimonial statements are at issue, the only indicium of reliability sufficient to satisfy constitutional demands is the one the Constitution actually prescribes: confrontation.

PROBLEM 7.1: ROBERTS v. CRAWFORD

Recall the evidence from US v. Boyce (7th Cir. 2014) - a recorded 911 call that captured the following statements:

> **S. Portis:** "I need the police, my boyfriend [Boyce] just hit me and is going crazy."
>
> **911:** "Any weapons involved?"
>
> **Portis:** "Yes."
>
> **911:** "What kind?"
>
> **Portis:** "A gun."
>
> **911:** "He has a gun?"
>
> **Portis:** "I, I think so … Yes! Yes!"
>
> **911:** "Did you see one?"
>
> **Portis:** "Yes!"
>
> **911:** "Are you sure? If you aren't telling the truth, you could go to jail."
>
> **Portis:** "I'm positive."

If Boyce made a Confrontation Clause challenge to the admission of this evidence, what would the analysis have looked like under Roberts v. Ohio?

365

How does that analysis change under Crawford?

***

Crawford set forth a clear rule limiting the admissibility of "testimonial" hearsay. It also left two important questions unanswered.

(1) What is the definition of the "testimonial"?

(2) What about "nontestimonial" hearsay?

The Court clarified its answer to the second question in a later case (excerpted briefly immediately below). The first question receives a lengthier treatment in the excerpts that follow.

WHORTON v. BOCKTING
549 U.S. 406, 420 (2007)

…. Under Roberts, an out-of-court nontestimonial statement not subject to prior cross-examination could not be admitted without a judicial determination regarding reliability. Under Crawford, on the other hand, the Confrontation Clause has no application to such statements and therefore permits their admission even if they lack indicia of reliability….

MICHIGAN v. BRYANT
562 U.S. 344 (2011)

Justice SOTOMAYOR delivered the opinion of the Court.

…I

Around 3:25 a.m. on April 29, 2001, in Detroit, Michigan, police officers responded to a radio dispatch indicating that a man had been shot. At the scene, they found the victim, Anthony Covington, lying on the ground next to his car in a gas station parking lot. Covington had a gunshot wound to his abdomen, appeared to be in great pain, and spoke with difficulty.

The police asked him "what had happened, who had shot him, and where the shooting had occurred." Covington stated that "Rick" shot him at around 3 a.m. He also indicated that he had a conversation with [respondent Richard] Bryant, whom he recognized based on his voice, through the back door of Bryant's house. Covington explained that when he turned to leave, he was shot

366

through the door and then drove to the gas station, where police found him.

Covington's conversation with the police ended within 5 to 10 minutes when emergency medical services arrived. Covington was transported to a hospital and died within hours. The police left the gas station after speaking with Covington, called for backup, and traveled to Bryant's house. They did not find Bryant there but did find blood and a bullet on the back porch and an apparent bullet hole in the back door. Police also found Covington's wallet and identification outside the house.

At trial, which occurred prior to our decisions in *Crawford* and *Davis*, the police officers who spoke with Covington at the gas station testified about what Covington had told them. The jury returned a guilty verdict on charges of second-degree murder....

II

.... In 2006, the Court in *Davis v. Washington* and *Hammon v. Indiana* [two consolidated cases], ... made clear ... that not all those questioned by the police are witnesses and not all "interrogations by law enforcement officers," are subject to the Confrontation Clause.

Davis and *Hammon* were both domestic violence cases. In *Davis*, Michelle McCottry made the statements at issue to a 911 operator during a domestic disturbance with Adrian Davis, her former boyfriend. McCottry told the operator, "'He's here jumpin' on me again,'" and, "'He's usin' his fists.'" The operator then asked McCottry for Davis' first and last names and middle initial, and at that point in the conversation McCottry reported that Davis had fled in a car. McCottry did not appear at Davis' trial, and the State introduced the recording of her conversation with the 911 operator.

In *Hammon*, decided along with *Davis*, police responded to a domestic disturbance call at the home of Amy and Hershel Hammon, where they found Amy alone on the front porch. She appeared "'somewhat frightened,'" but told them "'nothing was the matter.'" She gave the police permission to enter the house, where they saw a gas heating unit with the glass front shattered on the floor. One officer remained in the kitchen with Hershel, while another officer talked to Amy in the living room about what had happened. Hershel tried several times to participate in Amy's conversation with the police and became angry when the police required him to stay separated from Amy. The police asked Amy to fill out and sign a battery affidavit. She wrote: "'Broke our Furnace & shoved me down on the floor into the broken glass. Hit me in the chest and threw me down. Broke our lamps & phone. Tore up my van where I couldn't leave the house. Attacked my daughter.'" Amy did not appear at Hershel's trial, so the police officers who spoke with her testified as to her statements and authenticated the affidavit. The trial court admitted the affidavit as a present sense impression and admitted the oral statements as excited utterances under state hearsay rules.

To address the facts of both cases, we expanded upon the meaning of "testimonial" that we first employed in *Crawford* and discussed the concept of an ongoing emergency. We explained:

> "Statements are nontestimonial when made in the course of police interrogation under circumstances objectively indicating that the primary purpose of the interrogation is to enable police assistance to meet an ongoing emergency. They are testimonial when the circumstances objectively indicate that there is no such ongoing emergency, and that the primary purpose of the interrogation is to establish or prove past events potentially relevant to later criminal prosecution."

Examining the *Davis* and *Hammon* statements in light of those definitions, we held that the statements at issue in *Davis* were nontestimonial and the statements in *Hammon* were testimonial....

Davis did not "attemp[t] to produce an exhaustive classification of all conceivable statements—or even all conceivable statements in response to police interrogation—as either testimonial or nontestimonial." The basic purpose of the Confrontation Clause was to "targe[t]" the sort of "abuses" exemplified at the notorious treason trial of Sir Walter Raleigh. Thus, the most important instances in which the Clause restricts the introduction of out-of-court statements are those in which state actors are involved in a formal, out-of-court interrogation of a witness to obtain evidence for trial. Even where such an interrogation is conducted with all good faith, introduction of the resulting statements at trial can be unfair to the accused if they are untested by cross-examination. Whether formal or informal, out-of-court statements can evade the basic objective of the Confrontation Clause, which is to prevent the accused from being deprived of the opportunity to cross-examine the declarant about statements taken for use at trial. When, as in *Davis*, the primary purpose of an interrogation is to respond to an "ongoing emergency," its purpose is not to create a record for trial and thus is not within the scope of the Clause. But there may be other circumstances, aside from ongoing emergencies, when a statement is not procured with a primary purpose of creating an out-of-court substitute for trial testimony. In making the primary purpose determination, standard rules of hearsay, designed to identify some statements as reliable, will be relevant. Where no such primary purpose exists, the admissibility of a statement is the concern of state and federal rules of evidence, not the Confrontation Clause....

IV

As we suggested in *Davis*, when a court must determine whether the Confrontation Clause bars the admission of a statement at trial, it should determine the "primary purpose of the interrogation" by objectively evaluating the statements and actions of the parties to the encounter, in light of the circumstances in which the interrogation occurs. The existence of an emergency or the parties' perception that an emergency is ongoing is among the most important circumstances that courts must take into account in determining whether an interrogation is testimonial because statements made to assist police in addressing an ongoing emergency presumably lack the testimonial purpose that would subject them to the requirement of confrontation. As the context of this case brings into sharp relief, the existence and duration of an emergency depend on the type and scope of danger posed to the victim, the police, and the public....

As explained above, the scope of an emergency in terms of its threat to individuals other than the initial assailant and victim will often depend on the type of dispute involved. Nothing Covington said to the police indicated that the cause of the shooting was a purely private dispute or that the threat from the shooter had ended.... The police did not know, and Covington did not tell them, whether the threat was limited to him. The potential scope of the dispute and therefore the emergency in this case thus stretches more broadly than those at issue in *Davis* and *Hammon* and encompasses a threat potentially to the police and the public....

At no point during the questioning did either Covington or the police know the location of the shooter.... This is not to suggest that the emergency continued until Bryant was arrested in California a year after the shooting. We need not decide precisely when the emergency ended because Covington's encounter with the police and all of the statements he made during that interaction occurred within the first few minutes of the police officers' arrival and well before they secured the scene of the shooting—the shooter's last known location.

We reiterate, moreover, that the existence *vel non* of an ongoing emergency is not the touchstone of the testimonial inquiry; rather, the ultimate inquiry is whether the "primary purpose of the interrogation [was] to enable police assistance to meet [the] ongoing emergency." We turn now to that inquiry, as informed by the circumstances of the ongoing emergency just described. The circumstances of the encounter provide important context for understanding Covington's statements to the police. When the police arrived at Covington's side, their first question to him was "What happened?" Covington's response was either "Rick shot me" or "I was shot," followed very quickly by an identification of "Rick" as the shooter. In response to further questions, Covington explained that the shooting occurred through the back door of Bryant's house and provided a physical description of the shooter. When he made the statements, Covington was lying in a gas station parking lot bleeding from a mortal gunshot wound to his abdomen. His answers to the police officers' questions were punctuated with questions about when emergency medical services would arrive. He was obviously in considerable pain and had difficulty breathing and talking. From this description of his condition and report of his statements, we cannot say that a person in Covington's situation would have had a "primary purpose" "to establish or prove past events potentially relevant to later criminal prosecution."

For their part, the police responded to a call that a man had been shot. As discussed above, they did not know why, where, or when the shooting had occurred. Nor did they know the location of the shooter or anything else about the circumstances in which the crime occurred. The questions they asked—"what had happened, who had shot him, and where the shooting had occurred," —were the exact type of questions necessary to allow the police to "'assess the situation, the threat to their own safety, and possible danger to the potential victim'" and to the public, including to allow them to ascertain "whether they would be encountering a violent felon." In other words, they solicited the information necessary to enable them "to meet an ongoing emergency." …

Finally, we consider the informality of the situation and the interrogation…. The informality suggests that the interrogators' primary purpose was simply to address what they perceived to be an ongoing emergency, and the circumstances lacked any formality that would have alerted Covington to or focused him on the possible future prosecutorial use of his statements.

Because the circumstances of the encounter as well as the statements and actions of Covington and the police objectively indicate that the "primary purpose of the interrogation" was "to enable police assistance to meet an ongoing emergency," Covington's identification and description of the shooter and the location of the shooting were not testimonial hearsay. The Confrontation Clause did not bar their admission at Bryant's trial….

Justice SCALIA, dissenting.

Today's tale—a story of five officers conducting successive examinations of a dying man with the primary purpose, not of obtaining and preserving his testimony regarding his killer, but of protecting him, them, and others from a murderer somewhere on the loose—is so transparently false that professing to believe it demeans this institution. But reaching a patently incorrect conclusion on the facts is a relatively benign judicial mischief; it affects, after all, only the case at hand. In its vain attempt to make the incredible plausible, however— or perhaps as an intended second goal—today's opinion distorts our Confrontation Clause jurisprudence and leaves it in a shambles. Instead of clarifying the law, the Court makes itself the obfuscator of last resort. Because I continue to adhere to the Confrontation Clause that the People adopted, as described in *Crawford v. Washington*, I dissent….

Justice GINSBURG, dissenting.

I agree with Justice Scalia that Covington's statements were testimonial and that "[t]he declarant's intent is what counts." Even if the interrogators' intent were what counts, I further agree, Covington's statements would still be testimonial. It is most likely that "the officers viewed their encounter with Covington [as] an investigation into a past crime with no ongoing or immediate consequences." Today's decision, Justice SCALIA rightly notes, "creates an expansive exception to the Confrontation Clause for violent crimes." In so doing, the decision confounds our recent Confrontation Clause jurisprudence, which made it plain that "[r]eliability tells us nothing about whether a statement is testimonial."

I would add, however, this observation. In *Crawford v. Washington*, this Court noted that, in the law we inherited from England, there was a well-established exception to the confrontation requirement: The cloak protecting the accused against admission of out-of-court testimonial statements was removed for dying declarations. This historic exception applied to statements made by a person about to die and aware that death was imminent. Were the issue properly tendered here, I would take up the question whether the exception for dying declarations survives our recent Confrontation Clause decisions. The Michigan Supreme Court, however, held, as a matter of state law, that the prosecutor had abandoned the issue. The matter, therefore, is not one the Court can address in this case.

PROBLEM 7.2: 911 CALL

The following is a transcript of a 911 call

[caller's address redacted]

911 Operator: Is that a business residence or an apartment?

Brooke: It's a residence and it's domestic abuse.

911 Operator: OK, what's the phone number that you're calling me from?

Brooke: 970, I don't even know (audio muffles at source).

911 Operator: OK and you have a domestic disturbance? OK, tell me exactly what happened.

Brooke: My husband had me with a knife and I'm scared for my life and he threatened me.

911 Operator: OK, are you guys separated right now?

Brooke: Yes, right now we have people who are separating us, but I have to file the report.

911 Operator: Are there other people there? Does he still have the knife?

Brooke: Yes, he's still got it, but there are other people with him.

911 Operator: Who are the other people who are there?

Brooke: Um, I have people here, my family's here, but right now, if I don't file this, I need to file it right now.

911 Operator: OK, where is he with the knife?

Brooke: He's in the other room.

911 Operator: Who is he with?

Brooke: He's with somebody talking to him, but if I don't file the report...

911 Operator: OK, I understand, I'm sending officers to help you. I just need some information. Does he have any other weapons?

Brooke: No.

911 Operator: OK, which room is he in? When the officers enter the house, which room will he be in?

Brooke: In the bathroom.

911 Operator: And which room are you in?

Brooke: In the kitchen. And I thought I was gonna die for one hour.

911 Operator: OK, what's your name?

Brooke: Brooke.

911 Operator: And what's your husband's name?

Brooke: It's Charlie Sheen.

Consider whether admission of the 911 transcript responses as excited utterances in a trial of Charlie for threatening Brooke with a knife would violate the Confrontation Clause in the following scenarios:

> *(1) Brooke testifies as a prosecution witness that Charlie threatened her with a knife.*

> *(2) Brooke testifies as a prosecution witness, but states that Charlie did not threaten her and it was all a misunderstanding.*

> *(3) The prosecution does not call Brooke as a witness.*

PROBLEM 7.3: ARE THERE "TESTIMONIAL" HEARSAY EXCEPTIONS?

In *Bryant*, Justice Sotomayor, writing for the majority, stated that: "In making the primary purpose determination, standard rules of hearsay, designed to identify some statements as reliable, will be relevant." In a footnote, the majority then listed a series of hearsay exceptions that "rest on the belief that certain statements are, by their nature, made for a purpose other than use in a prosecution and therefore should not be barred by hearsay prohibitions." One of the exceptions listed was "804(b)(3) (statement against interest)" – the exception relied on by the prosecution in *Crawford*.

Reflect on the hearsay exceptions we covered earlier in the course. *After Bryant, are any of those exceptions likely to allow in unconfronted "testimonial" hearsay? Which ones?*

OHIO v. CLARK
135 S. Ct. 2173 (2015)

Justice ALITO delivered the opinion of the Court.

....I

Darius Clark, who went by the nickname "Dee," lived in Cleveland, Ohio, with his girlfriend, T.T., and her two children: L.P., a 3–year–old boy, and A.T., an 18–month–old girl.... In March 2010, T.T. went on [a] trip, and she left the children in Clark's care.

The next day, Clark took L.P. to preschool. In the lunchroom, one of L.P.'s teachers, Ramona Whitley, observed that L.P.'s left eye appeared bloodshot. She asked him "'[w]hat happened,'" and he initially said nothing. Eventually, however, he told the teacher that he "'fell.'" When they moved into the brighter lights of a classroom, Whitley noticed "'[r]ed marks, like whips of some sort,'" on L.P.'s face. She notified the lead teacher, Debra Jones, who asked L.P., "'Who did this? What happened to you?'" According to Jones, L.P. "'seemed kind of bewildered'" and "'said something like, Dee, Dee.'" Jones asked L.P. whether Dee is "big or little," to which L.P. responded that "Dee is big." Jones then brought L.P. to her supervisor, who lifted the boy's shirt, revealing more injuries. Whitley called a child abuse hotline to alert authorities about the suspected abuse.

When Clark later arrived at the school, he denied responsibility for the injuries and quickly left with L.P. The next day, a social worker found the children at Clark's mother's house and took them to a hospital, where a physician discovered additional injuries suggesting child abuse....

A grand jury indicted Clark on five counts of felonious assault (four related to

A.T. and one related to L.P.), two counts of endangering children (one for each child), and two counts of domestic violence (one for each child). At trial, the State introduced L.P.'s statements to his teachers as evidence of Clark's guilt, but L.P. did not testify. Under Ohio law, children younger than 10 years old are incompetent to testify if they "appear incapable of receiving just impressions of the facts and transactions respecting which they are examined, or of relating them truly." Ohio Rule Evid. 601(A). After conducting a hearing, the trial court concluded that L.P. was not competent to testify. But under Ohio Rule of Evidence 807, which allows the admission of reliable hearsay by child abuse victims, the court ruled that L.P.'s statements to his teachers bore sufficient guarantees of trustworthiness to be admitted as evidence.

Clark moved to exclude testimony about L.P.'s out-of-court statements under the Confrontation Clause. The trial court denied the motion, ruling that L.P.'s responses were not testimonial statements covered by the Sixth Amendment. The jury found Clark guilty on all counts except for one assault count related to A.T., and it sentenced him to 28 years' imprisonment. Clark appealed his conviction, and a state appellate court reversed on the ground that the introduction of L.P.'s out-of-court statements violated the Confrontation Clause…. We … reverse.

II

B

In this case, we consider statements made to preschool teachers, not the police. We are therefore presented with the question we have repeatedly reserved: whether statements to persons other than law enforcement officers are subject to the Confrontation Clause. Because at least some statements to individuals who are not law enforcement officers could conceivably raise confrontation concerns, we decline to adopt a categorical rule excluding them from the Sixth Amendment's reach. Nevertheless, such statements are much less likely to be testimonial than statements to law enforcement officers. And considering all the relevant circumstances here, L.P.'s statements clearly were not made with the primary purpose of creating evidence for Clark's prosecution. Thus, their introduction at trial did not violate the Confrontation Clause.

L.P.'s statements occurred in the context of an ongoing emergency involving suspected child abuse. When L.P.'s teachers noticed his injuries, they rightly became worried that the 3–year–old was the victim of serious violence.

Because the teachers needed to know whether it was safe to release L.P. to his guardian at the end of the day, they needed to determine who might be abusing the child. Thus, the immediate concern was to protect a vulnerable child who needed help....

There is no indication that the primary purpose of the conversation was to gather evidence for Clark's prosecution. On the contrary, it is clear that the first objective was to protect L.P....

L.P.'s age fortifies our conclusion that the statements in question were not testimonial. Statements by very young children will rarely, if ever, implicate the Confrontation Clause. Few preschool students understand the details of our criminal justice system. Rather, "[r]esearch on children's understanding of the legal system finds that" young children "have little understanding of prosecution." And Clark does not dispute those findings. Thus, it is extremely unlikely that a 3–year–old child in L.P.'s position would intend his statements to be a substitute for trial testimony. On the contrary, a young child in these circumstances would simply want the abuse to end, would want to protect other victims, or would have no discernible purpose at all....

Finally, although we decline to adopt a rule that statements to individuals who are not law enforcement officers are categorically outside the Sixth Amendment, the fact that L.P. was speaking to his teachers remains highly relevant. Courts must evaluate challenged statements in context, and part of that context is the questioner's identity. Statements made to someone who is not principally charged with uncovering and prosecuting criminal behavior are significantly less likely to be testimonial than statements given to law enforcement officers....

III

Clark's efforts to avoid this conclusion are all off-base. He emphasizes Ohio's mandatory reporting obligations, in an attempt to equate L.P.'s teachers with the police and their caring questions with official interrogations. But the comparison is inapt. The teachers' pressing concern was to protect L.P. and remove him from harm's way. Like all good teachers, they undoubtedly would have acted with the same purpose whether or not they had a state-law duty to report abuse. And mandatory reporting statutes alone cannot convert a conversation between a concerned teacher and her student into a law enforcement mission aimed primarily at gathering evidence for a prosecution.

It is irrelevant that the teachers' questions and their duty to report the matter had the natural tendency to result in Clark's prosecution. The statements at issue in *Davis* and *Bryant* supported the defendants' convictions, and the police always have an obligation to ask questions to resolve ongoing emergencies. Yet, we held in those cases that the Confrontation Clause did not prohibit introduction of the statements because they were not primarily intended to be testimonial. … We have never suggested, …, that the Confrontation Clause bars the introduction of all out-of-court statements that support the prosecution's case. Instead, we ask whether a statement was given with the "primary purpose of creating an out-of-court substitute for trial testimony." Here, the answer is clear: L.P.'s statements to his teachers were not testimonial….

COMMENTARY ON CRAWFORD: PART I[1]

Commentators cheered when the Supreme Court decided Crawford v. Washington in 2004. The decision finally put "some teeth in the Confrontation Clause," repudiating the wishy-washy and widely-reviled Ohio v. Roberts framework that governed the Court's jurisprudence over the preceding two decades….

Crawford was a victory not just for criminal defendants, but for the Constitution as well. The Crawford Court reversed a conviction because the prosecution had introduced unconfronted, "testimonial" hearsay - the type of evidence most analogous to the sworn statements of absent witnesses that the Sixth Amendment's drafters abhorred. Such hearsay is inadmissible against a criminal defendant, Crawford announced, because the Sixth Amendment demands face-to-face confrontation, not the "malleable" tests of reliability set forth in Roberts.

… As ambitious as the case was, Crawford only mapped out the rough contours of the long-awaited Confrontation Clause revolution, leaving a number of important questions "for another day." As the Supreme Court began to answer those questions in later cases, the new jurisprudence took a dramatic and surprising turn. Three years after Crawford, the Court strictly cabined the category of hearsay to which the reinvigorated confrontation right applied…. [W]hile "testimonial" hearsay was inadmissible absent

---

[1] Jeffrey Bellin, *The Incredible Shrinking Confrontation Clause*, 92 B.U. L. Rev. 1865 (2012).

confrontation, "nontestimonial" hearsay - a broad category of admissible hearsay - was "not subject to the Confrontation Clause" at all. The next blow to the celebrated reinvigoration of the Confrontation Clause came in the 2011 case of Michigan v. Bryant. In Bryant, a new majority of the Supreme Court…, while claiming fidelity to Crawford, constricted the definition of "testimonial" statements to its minimalist core: statements "procured with a primary purpose of creating an out-of-court substitute for trial testimony." In addition, the Bryant Court erected a framework for analyzing "primary purpose" that appears just as malleable as the Roberts test - a flexibility that, if Roberts is any guide, is more likely to favor the prosecution (by admitting hearsay) than the defense (by excluding it)….

COMMENTARY ON CRAWFORD: PART II[1]

A large and increasing portion of our social discourse takes place electronically, through email and texting, as well as on social media Internet sites such as Facebook and Twitter. These communications are particularly susceptible to use in litigation. Unlike oral communication, and even much of traditional written discourse, electronic communications are difficult to keep private because (1) they are often broadcast to multiple recipients; (2) they reside (or pass through) computer servers owned and operated by third parties; and (3) they are generally preserved, sometimes indefinitely, on the computers involved in their creation and transmission. As a consequence, this form of evidence can be discovered long after its creation by savvy investigators and presented to a jury in its original, and thus uniquely compelling, form.

Interestingly, the expanding category of electronic out-of-court statements seems to be left, after Crawford and Michigan v. Bryant, largely unrestricted by the Confrontation Clause…. [A]s far as the modern Confrontation Clause is concerned, and assuming a compliant hearsay exception, electronic communications-the bulk of out-of-court communication in an increasingly digital age-can be introduced by the prosecution in criminal cases without confrontation.

---

[1] Jeffrey Bellin, *Applying Crawford's Confrontation Right in A Digital Age*, 45 Tex. Tech L. Rev. 33 (2012).

NOTE ON THE "WITNESSES AGAINST"

The Sixth Amendment guarantees the accused's right to confront the "witnesses against him." Recall that *Crawford* introduced the testimonial/non-testimonial distinction to identify the "witnesses against" an accused. How well did the test perform in achieving that function in *Davis* and *Bryant*, where the Supreme Court found strongly incriminating out-of-court statements to be non-testimonial?[1]

Here is some additional context for thinking about that question:

During a pretrial hearing in *Bryant* on the admissibility of the deceased victim's statement "Rick shot me," the prosecutor warned that if the trial court excluded the statement, "we won't have a trial." In his opening remarks, the prosecutor told the jury that the statement was "[t]he most important piece of evidence you'll hear during this trial" and urged the jurors to view the statement as the victim "speaking to you from the grave and telling you what happened . . . and telling you who's responsible."

In *Davis*, defense counsel stressed a critical weakness in the domestic violence case: no one present during the assault testified. In response, the prosecutor relied on the victim's out-of-court statements to fill the void:

> "[T]here was a person present [during the assault] . . . and although she is not here today to talk to you[,] she left you something better. She left you her testimony on the day that this happened[;] . . . this shows that the defendant, Adrian Davis was at her home and assaulted her. It is right here in her voice."

Were the out-of-court declarants in Davis and Crawford "witnesses against" the defendants?

Scientific Analysis and Confrontation

Prohibitions of illegal substances like cocaine often require precise statutory prohibitions. Here is an example of a prohibited substance from the United States Code, 21 U.S.C.A. § 841

---

[1] This Note is drawn from Jeffrey Bellin, *The Incredible Shrinking Confrontation Clause*, 92 B.U. L. REV. 1865 (2012).

"400 grams or more of a mixture or substance containing a detectable amount of N-phenyl-N-[1-(2-phenylethyl)-4-piperidinyl] propanamide or 100 grams or more of a mixture or substance containing a detectable amount of any analogue of N-phenyl-N-[1-(2-phenylethyl)-4-piperidinyl] propenamide"

Determining whether a white powdery substance is the substance specified above, cocaine or baking soda, typically requires expert chemical analysis. The next case answers the question whether the government chemist who conducts that analysis can submit a certificate attesting to such a finding (typically the weight and nature of a tested substance) or must testify in court.

MELENDEZ-DIAZ v. MASSACHUSETTS
557 U.S. 305 (2009)

Justice SCALIA delivered the opinion of the Court.

…I

… [Luis] Melendez–Diaz was charged with distributing cocaine and with trafficking in cocaine in an amount between 14 and 28 grams. At trial, the prosecution placed into evidence the bags seized [during investigation into drug activity involving Melendez-Diaz]. It also submitted three "certificates of analysis" showing the results of the forensic analysis performed on the seized substances. The certificates reported the weight of the seized bags and stated that the bags "[h]a[ve] been examined with the following results: The substance was found to contain: Cocaine." The certificates were sworn to before a notary public by analysts at the State Laboratory Institute of the Massachusetts Department of Public Health, as required under Massachusetts law.

Petitioner objected to the admission of the certificates, asserting that our Confrontation Clause decision in *Crawford v. Washington* (2004), required the analysts to testify in person. The objection was overruled, and the certificates were admitted pursuant to state law as "prima facie evidence of the composition, quality, and the net weight of the narcotic … analyzed."

II

…There is little doubt that the documents at issue in this case fall within the "core class of testimonial statements" …. The documents at issue here, while denominated by Massachusetts law "certificates," are quite plainly affidavits:

380

"declaration [s] of facts written down and sworn to by the declarant before an officer authorized to administer oaths." They are incontrovertibly a "'solemn declaration or affirmation made for the purpose of establishing or proving some fact." *Crawford* (quoting 2 N. Webster, An American Dictionary of the English Language (1828)). The fact in question is that the substance found in the possession of Melendez–Diaz and his codefendants was, as the prosecution claimed, cocaine—the precise testimony the analysts would be expected to provide if called at trial. The "certificates" are functionally identical to live, in-court testimony, doing "precisely what a witness does on direct examination."

Here, moreover, not only were the affidavits "'made under circumstances which would lead an objective witness reasonably to believe that the statement would be available for use at a later trial,'" but under Massachusetts law the sole purpose of the affidavits was to provide "prima facie evidence of the composition, quality, and the net weight" of the analyzed substance, Mass. Gen. Laws, ch. 111, § 13. We can safely assume that the analysts were aware of the affidavits' evidentiary purpose, since that purpose—as stated in the relevant state-law provision—was reprinted on the affidavits themselves.

In short, under our decision in *Crawford* the analysts' affidavits were testimonial statements, and the analysts were "witnesses" for purposes of the Sixth Amendment. Absent a showing that the analysts were unavailable to testify at trial and that petitioner had a prior opportunity to cross-examine them, petitioner was entitled to "'be confronted with'" the analysts at trial.…

C

Respondent asserts that we should find no Confrontation Clause violation in this case because petitioner had the ability to subpoena the analysts. But that power—whether pursuant to state law or the Compulsory Process Clause—is no substitute for the right of confrontation. Unlike the Confrontation Clause, those provisions are of no use to the defendant when the witness is unavailable or simply refuses to appear. Converting the prosecution's duty under the Confrontation Clause into the defendant's privilege under state law or the Compulsory Process Clause shifts the consequences of adverse-witness no-shows from the State to the accused. More fundamentally, the Confrontation Clause imposes a burden on the prosecution to present its witnesses, not on the defendant to bring those adverse witnesses into court. Its value to the defendant is not replaced by a system in which the prosecution presents its evidence via ex parte affidavits and waits for the defendant to subpoena the affiants if he chooses....

Finally, respondent asks us to relax the requirements of the Confrontation Clause to accommodate the "'necessities of trial and the adversary process.'" It is not clear whence we would derive the authority to do so. The Confrontation Clause may make the prosecution of criminals more burdensome, but that is equally true of the right to trial by jury and the privilege against self-incrimination. The Confrontation Clause—like those other constitutional provisions—is binding, and we may not disregard it at our convenience.

We also doubt the accuracy of respondent's and the dissent's dire predictions. The dissent, respondent, and its amici highlight the substantial total number of controlled-substance analyses performed by state and federal laboratories in recent years. But only some of those tests are implicated in prosecutions, and only a small fraction of those cases actually proceed to trial.

Perhaps the best indication that the sky will not fall after today's decision is that it has not done so already. Many States have already adopted the constitutional rule we announce today, while many others permit the defendant to assert (or forfeit by silence) his Confrontation Clause right after receiving notice of the prosecution's intent to use a forensic analyst's report. Despite these widespread practices, there is no evidence that the criminal justice system has ground to a halt in the States that, one way or another, empower a defendant to insist upon the analyst's appearance at trial....

The dissent finds this evidence "far less reassuring than promised." But its doubts rest on two flawed premises. First, the dissent believes that those state statutes "requiring the defendant to give early notice of his intent to confront the analyst," are "burden-shifting statutes [that] may be invalidated by the Court's reasoning." That is not so. In their simplest form, notice-and-demand statutes require the prosecution to provide notice to the defendant of its intent to use an analyst's report as evidence at trial, after which the defendant is given a period of time in which he may object to the admission of the evidence absent the analyst's appearance live at trial. Contrary to the dissent's perception, these statutes shift no burden whatever. The defendant always has the burden of raising his Confrontation Clause objection; notice-and-demand statutes simply govern the time within which he must do so. States are free to adopt procedural rules governing objections....

This case involves little more than the application of our holding in *Crawford v. Washington*. The Sixth Amendment does not permit the prosecution to prove its case via ex parte out-of-court affidavits, and the admission of such evidence against Melendez–Diaz was error. We therefore reverse the judgment of the Appeals Court of Massachusetts ....

NOTE: "NOTICE AND DEMAND"

D.C. Code § 48-905.06 (1981). Chemist reports.

> In a proceeding for a violation of [narcotics laws], the official report of chain of custody and of analysis of a controlled substance performed by a chemist charged with an official duty to perform such analysis, when attested to by that chemist ... shall be admissible in evidence as evidence of the facts stated therein and the results of that analysis. A copy ... must be furnished upon demand by the defendant ... or, if no demand is made, no later than 5 days prior to trial. In the event that the defendant or his or her attorney subpoenas the chemist for examination, the subpoena shall be without fee or cost and the examination shall be as on cross-examination.

Is a chemist's affidavit asserting that a substance seized from the defendant was cocaine admissible if offered in compliance with this section?

Here is what the D.C. Court of Appeals ruled after *Crawford*:[1]

> Although we do not hold D.C.Code § 48–905.06 unconstitutional in light of *Crawford*, we are obliged to re-interpret the statute so as to preserve its constitutionality. As we now construe § 48–905.06, it still authorizes the government to introduce a chemist's report without calling the chemist in its case-in-chief, but only so long as the record shows a valid waiver by the defendant of his confrontation right. Absent a valid waiver, which usually must be express but under some circumstances may be inferable from a defendant's failure to request the government to produce the author of the report, the defendant

---

[1] Thomas v. United States, 914 A.2d 1 (D.C. 2006).

enjoys a Sixth Amendment right to be confronted with the chemist in person.

The Supreme Court in *Melendez-Diaz* listed the D.C. court ruling (quoted above) in a footnote after stating: "Many States have already adopted the constitutional rule we announce today"; the Court went on to say "while many others permit the defendant to assert (or forfeit by silence) his Confrontation Clause right after receiving notice of the prosecution's intent to use a forensic analyst's report." The *Melendez-Diaz* Court suggested this weaker form of waiver is also permissible.

Melendez-Diaz offered, as an example of a permissible notice statue, this Georgia statute:

Ga. Code Ann., § 35-3-154.1

...

(c) The prosecuting attorney shall serve a copy on the defendant's attorney of record, or on the defendant if pro se, prior to the first proceeding in which the report is to be used against the defendant.

(d) Any report under this Code section shall contain notice of the right to demand the testimony of the person signing the report.

(e) The defendant may object in writing any time after service of the report, but at least ten days prior to trial, to the introduction of the report. If objection is made, the judge shall require the [chemist] to be present to testify.

The Supreme Court again blessed these "notice and demand" regimes in Bullcoming v. New Mexico (2011), a case that tracked *Melendez-Diaz* in holding that New Mexico could not introduce a report on the alcohol content of a DWI suspect's blood sample without presenting the testimony of an analyst who participated in the testing. Here is the language from *Bullcoming*:

> Furthermore, notice-and-demand procedures, long in effect in many jurisdictions, can reduce burdens on forensic laboratories. Statutes governing these procedures typically "render ... otherwise hearsay forensic reports admissible[,] while specifically preserving a defendant's right to demand that the prosecution call the author/analyst of [the] report."

The Court has repeatedly rejected the suggestion that the defense right to confrontation is satisfied by its independent right to subpoena the analyst. *How is a notice and demand regime different?*

PROBLEM 7.4: DOCKET ENTRIES

Washington D.C. abolished its cash bail system in 1992. But to ensure that defendants appear in court, the District enacted criminal penalties for a defendant who "having been released under this title ... willfully fails to appear before any court or judicial officer." To prove this offense, the government typically must rely on court documents.

Here is how the prosecution sought to do that in one case:[1]

> Superior Court employee Alonzo Wiggins, who was qualified without objection as an expert in Superior Court courtroom procedure, was called to the stand to lay a foundation for the admission of the government exhibits which are challenged on this appeal. For both exhibits, Mr. Wiggins identified the documents as certified copies of Superior Court records and testified that the records appeared to have been made in conformity with normal courtroom procedures.

> The first of these exhibits, marked Government Exhibit Number 1, consisted of certified photocopies of three pages from the Superior Court case file in criminal case number M–841–05, the second page of which included two relevant docket entries dated February 17, 2005, and February 24, 2005. The February 17th entry contained checked boxes indicating that the defendant "is present" and that the "Defendant [was] Advised of Penalties for Failure to Appear" and showed the "continued date" of 2–24–05. The February 24th entry contained a checked box indicating that the defendant "is not present" and included a handwritten note indicating that the defendant had failed to appear. Each of the entries was signed with the initials of the courtroom clerk who made the entry.

> The second exhibit, marked Government Exhibit Number 2, consisted of, inter alia, a certified photocopy of a one-page document from the court records entitled "Notice to Return to Court," dated February 17,

---

[1] Jackson v. United States, 924 A.2d 1016 (D.C. 2007).

2005. This standard printed form included blanks that were completed with handwritten case-specific details, including the date and time of the next scheduled court appearance (February 24, 2005, at 9:30 a.m.), the name of the presiding judge (Johnson), and the courtroom number and location (Courtroom 211 on the second level of the Superior Court). The document stated that "failure to appear promptly may result in the issuance of a warrant for your arrest" and noted the penalties for failure to appear as "5 years or $5,000 fine" for a pending felony charge or "180 days or $1,000 fine" for a pending misdemeanor or traffic charge. The document also contained signatures on the lines reserved for the Deputy Clerk (signed "Barbie")[1] and the Defendant (containing an illegible signature and indicating "No Fix[ed] Address, 425 2nd Street N.W.").

Defense counsel objected to the admission of the exhibits, invoking Crawford and the Sixth Amendment Confrontation Clause.

Did the admission of these records violate the Confrontation Clause?

GILES v. CALIFORNIA
554 U.S. 353 (2008)

Justice SCALIA delivered the opinion of the Court.

...On September 29, 2002, petitioner Dwayne Giles shot his ex-girlfriend, Brenda Avie, outside the garage of his grandmother's house.... At trial, Giles testified that he had acted in self-defense.

.... Prosecutors sought to introduce statements that Avie had made to a police officer responding to a domestic-violence report about three weeks before the shooting....

... The [Sixth] Amendment contemplates that a witness who makes testimonial statements admitted against a defendant will ordinarily be present at trial for cross-examination.... The State does not dispute here, and we accept without deciding, that Avie's statements accusing Giles of assault were testimonial. But it maintains (as did the California Supreme Court) that the Sixth Amendment did not prohibit prosecutors from introducing the

---

[1] The signature was that of a court clerk, Russell Barbie.

statements because an exception to the confrontation guarantee permits the use of a witness's unconfronted testimony if a judge finds, as the judge did in this case, that the defendant committed a wrongful act that rendered the witness unavailable to testify at trial. We held in Crawford that the Confrontation Clause is "most naturally read as a reference to the right of confrontation at common law, admitting only those exceptions established at the time of the founding." We therefore ask whether the theory of forfeiture by wrongdoing accepted by the California Supreme Court is a founding-era exception to the confrontation right.

A

We have previously acknowledged that two forms of testimonial statements were admitted at common law even though they were unconfronted. The first of these were declarations made by a speaker who was both on the brink of death and aware that he was dying. Avie did not make the unconfronted statements admitted at Giles' trial when she was dying, so her statements do not fall within this historic exception.

A second common-law doctrine, which we will refer to as forfeiture by wrongdoing, permitted the introduction of statements of a witness who was "detained" or "kept away" by the "means or procurement" of the defendant....

The terms used to define the scope of the forfeiture rule suggest that the exception applied only when the defendant engaged in conduct designed to prevent the witness from testifying....

Cases and treatises of the time indicate that a purpose-based definition of these terms governed. A number of them said that prior testimony was admissible when a witness was kept away by the defendant's "means and contrivance." This phrase requires that the defendant have schemed to bring about the absence from trial that he "contrived."....

In 1997, this Court approved a Federal Rule of Evidence, entitled "Forfeiture by wrongdoing," which applies only when the defendant "engaged or acquiesced in wrongdoing that was intended to, and did, procure the unavailability of the declarant as a witness." Fed. Rule Evid. 804(b)(6). We have described this as a rule "which codifies the forfeiture doctrine." Every commentator we are aware of has concluded the requirement of intent "means that the exception applies only if the defendant has in mind the particular purpose of making the witness unavailable."...

In sum, our interpretation of the common-law forfeiture rule is supported by (1) the most natural reading of the language used at common law; (2) the absence of common-law cases admitting prior statements on a forfeiture theory when the defendant had not engaged in conduct designed to prevent a witness from testifying; (3) the common law's uniform exclusion of unconfronted inculpatory testimony by murder victims (except testimony given with awareness of impending death) in the innumerable cases in which the defendant was on trial for killing the victim, but was not shown to have done so for the purpose of preventing testimony; (4) a subsequent history in which the dissent's broad forfeiture theory has not been applied. The first two and the last are highly persuasive; the third is in our view conclusive....

***

Giles is most easily understood as holding that the intent requirement for forfeiture under the Confrontation Clause (conveniently) tracks the intent requirement included in Rule 804(b)(6) discussed in Chapter 6.

CONFRONTATION CLAUSE POSTSCRIPT

Trial of Sir Walter Raleigh (1603)

Justice Warburton: "I marvel, Sir Walter, that you being of such experience and wit, should stand on this point; for many horse-stealers should escape if they may not be condemned without witnesses."

Meanwhile in America:

State v. Webb (1794)
Superior Courts of Law and Equity of North Carolina.

PLEASANT WEBB was indicted for horse-stealing, and upon the trial the Attorney General offered to give in evidence the deposition of one Young, to whom he had sold the horse in South-Carolina, but a very short time after the horse was stolen.

But *per curiam,* Judge Ashe and Judge Williams:

.... [I]t is a rule of the common law, founded on natural justice, that no man shall be prejudiced by evidence which he had not the liberty to cross examine; and though it be insisted that the act intended to make an exception in this instance, to the rule of the common law, yet the act has not expressly said so, and we will not by implication derogate from the salutary rule established by the common law.-- So the deposition was rejected.

OTHER CONSTITUTIONAL EVIDENCE RULES

Criminal defendants have other constitutional rights that implicate trial evidence, including the textual right to "due process" and the constitutional right to a fair trial. These rights come into play in two scenarios: (1) a trial court allows the prosecution to introduce unfair or unreliable evidence, or (2) a trial court refuses to allow the defense to introduce favorable evidence.

UNFAIR OR UNRELIABLE PROSECUTION EVIDENCE

Outside the Confrontation Clause context, constitutional challenges to evidence allowed under state or federal evidence rules are rarely successful.

For example, in Spencer v. Texas (1967), the Supreme Court rejected a due process challenge to a Texas procedure that allowed the introduction of a defendant's past criminal convictions prior to the jury's determination of guilt, even though those convictions were relevant only at sentencing. (In Texas, the same jury that determines guilt typically sentences the defendant.) The Court explained its reasoning as follows:

> It is contended … that … the Due Process Clause of the Fourteenth Amendment requires the exclusion of prejudicial evidence of prior convictions even though limiting instructions are given and even though a valid state purpose—enforcement of the habitual-offender statute—is served. We recognize that the use of prior-crime evidence in a one-stage recidivist trial may be thought to represent a less cogent state interest than does its use for other purposes, in that other procedures for applying enhancement-of-sentence statutes may be available to the State that are not suited in the other situations in which such evidence is introduced. We do not think that this distinction should lead to a different constitutional result.
>
> Cases in this Court have long proceeded on the premise that the Due Process Clause guarantees the fundamental elements of fairness in a criminal trial. But it has never been thought that such cases establish this Court as a rule-making organ for the promulgation of state rules of criminal procedure. And none of the specific provisions of the Constitution ordains this Court with such authority. In the face of the legitimate state purpose and the long-standing and widespread use that attend the procedure under attack here, we find it impossible to say

that because of the possibility of some collateral prejudice the Texas procedure is rendered unconstitutional under the Due Process Clause as it has been interpreted and applied in our past cases. As Mr. Justice Cardozo had occasion to remark, a state rule of law 'does not run afoul of the Fourteenth Amendment because another method may seem to our thinking to be fairer or wiser or to give a surer promise of protection to the prisoner at bar.'

Relying on cases like *Spencer*, lower federal courts have rejected similar due process challenges to rules like Federal Rule of Evidence 413. As noted in Chapter 4, courts reach this result even though Rule 413 "runs counter to a centuries-old legal tradition that views propensity evidence with a particularly skeptical eye."[1]

PERRY v. NEW HAMPSHIRE
565 U.S. 228 (2012)

Justice GINSBURG delivered the opinion of the Court.

[Barion Perry was convicted of theft and criminal mischief. On appeal, he argued that testimony that an eyewitness identified him at the scene as the perpetrator of the offense should have been excluded because the identification was so unreliable that its admission constituted a violation of due process. The Supreme Court rejected the claim as explained below.]

...The Constitution, our decisions indicate, protects a defendant against a conviction based on evidence of questionable reliability, not by prohibiting introduction of the evidence, but by affording the defendant means to persuade the jury that the evidence should be discounted as unworthy of credit. Constitutional safeguards available to defendants to counter the State's evidence include the Sixth Amendment rights to counsel; compulsory process; and confrontation plus cross-examination of witnesses. Apart from these guarantees, we have recognized, state and federal statutes and rules ordinarily govern the admissibility of evidence, and juries are assigned the task of determining the reliability of the evidence presented at trial. Only when evidence "is so extremely unfair that its admission violates fundamental conceptions of justice," have we imposed a constraint tied to the Due Process

---

[1] U.S. v. Mound (8th Cir. 1998) (Morris Sheppard Arnold, J.) (dissenting).

Clause. See, e.g., *Napue v. Illinois* (1959) (Due process prohibits the State's "knowin[g] use [of] false evidence," because such use violates "any concept of ordered liberty.").

...We have concluded in other contexts ... that the potential unreliability of a type of evidence does not alone render its introduction at the defendant's trial fundamentally unfair. See, e.g., *Kansas v. Ventris* (2009) (declining to "craft a broa[d] exclusionary rule for uncorroborated statements obtained [from jailhouse snitches]," even though "rewarded informant testimony" may be inherently untrustworthy); *Dowling v. United States* (1990) (rejecting argument that the introduction of evidence concerning acquitted conduct is fundamentally unfair because such evidence is "inherently unreliable"). We reach a similar conclusion here: The fallibility of eyewitness evidence does not, without the taint of improper state conduct, warrant a due process rule requiring a trial court to screen such evidence for reliability before allowing the jury to assess its creditworthiness.

Our unwillingness to enlarge the domain of due process as Perry and the dissent urge rests, in large part, on our recognition that the jury, not the judge, traditionally determines the reliability of evidence. We also take account of other safeguards built into our adversary system that caution juries against placing undue weight on eyewitness testimony of questionable reliability. These protections include the defendant's Sixth Amendment right to confront the eyewitness. Another is the defendant's right to the effective assistance of an attorney, who can expose the flaws in the eyewitness' testimony during cross-examination and focus the jury's attention on the fallibility of such testimony during opening and closing arguments. Eyewitness-specific jury instructions, which many federal and state courts have adopted, likewise warn the jury to take care in appraising identification evidence. The constitutional requirement that the government prove the defendant's guilt beyond a reasonable doubt also impedes convictions based on dubious identification evidence.

State and federal rules of evidence, moreover, permit trial judges to exclude relevant evidence if its probative value is substantially outweighed by its prejudicial impact or potential for misleading the jury. In appropriate cases, some States also permit defendants to present expert testimony on the hazards of eyewitness identification evidence.

***

Defendants have been successful in excluding evidence on constitutional grounds in one common scenario.

Often multiple co-defendants are prosecuted in a single proceeding before the same jury. In such circumstances, some evidence may be admissible against one co-defendant but not another. The usual solution when evidence is admissible for one purpose but not another is to instruct the jury accordingly. In the next case, the Supreme Court considered whether that practice sufficed in a common scenario: when a co-defendant's confession is only admissible against the co-defendant who made it (as a statement of a party), but not the other co-defendant.

BRUTON v. UNITED STATES
391 U.S. 123 (1968)

BRENNAN, J. delivered the opinion of the Court.

...A joint trial of petitioner [George Bruton] and [William] Evans ... resulted in the conviction of both by a jury on a federal charge of armed postal robbery. [At the trial, a] postal inspector testified that Evans orally confessed to him that Evans and petitioner committed the armed robbery. [Evans did not testify. After the jury convicted, Bruton appealed on the grounds that Evans' confession was only admissible against Evans – not Bruton. The federal appeals court] affirmed petitioner's conviction because the trial judge instructed the jury that although Evans' confession was competent evidence against Evans it was inadmissible hearsay against petitioner and therefore had to be disregarded in determining petitioner's guilt or innocence.

... We hold that, because of the substantial risk that the jury, despite instructions to the contrary, looked to the incriminating extrajudicial statements in determining petitioner's guilt, admission of Evans' confession in this joint trial violated petitioner's right of cross-examination secured by the Confrontation Clause of the Sixth Amendment. We therefore ... reverse.

....'The fact of the matter is that too often such admonition against misuse is intrinsically ineffective in that the effect of such a nonadmissible declaration cannot be wiped from the brains of the jurors. The admonition therefore becomes a futile collocation of words and fails of its purpose as a legal protection to defendants against whom such a declaration should not tell.' ... 'The Government should not have the windfall of having the jury be influenced by evidence against a defendant which, as a matter of law, they should not consider but which they cannot put out of their minds.' To the same effect, ..., is the statement of Mr. Justice Jackson in his concurring opinion in *Krulewitch v. United States*: 'The naive assumption that prejudicial effects can be overcome by instructions to the jury * * * all practicing lawyers know to be unmitigated fiction. * * *'

.... [T]here are many circumstances in which [reliance on jury instructions] is justified. Not every admission of inadmissible hearsay or other evidence can be considered to be reversible error unavoidable through limiting instructions; instances occur in almost every trial where inadmissible evidence creeps in, usually inadvertently. 'A defendant is entitled to a fair trial but not a perfect one.' It is not unreasonable to conclude that in many such cases the jury can and will follow the trial judge's instructions to disregard such information. Nevertheless, ..., there are some contexts in which the risk that the jury will not, or cannot, follow instructions is so great, and the consequences of failure so vital to the defendant, that the practical and human limitations of the jury system cannot be ignored. Such a context is presented here, where the powerfully incriminating extrajudicial statements of a codefendant, who stands accused side-by-side with the defendant, are deliberately spread before the jury in a joint trial. Not only are the incriminations devastating to the defendant but their credibility is inevitably suspect, a fact recognized when accomplices do take the stand and the jury is instructed to weigh their testimony carefully given the recognized motivation to shift blame onto others. The unreliability of such evidence is intolerably compounded when the alleged accomplice, as here, does not testify and cannot be tested by cross-examination. It was against such threats to a fair trial that the Confrontation Clause was directed.

***

The Court in *Bruton* framed the error as a Confrontation Clause violation. But the problem in that case seems more closely tied to the jury's inability to follow its instructions, rather than the defendant's right to confront the confessing co-defendant. If so, *Bruton* can be viewed as enforcing a due process or fair trial right. See Dutton v. Evans (1970) (Harlan J. concurring) ("I would be prepared to hold as a matter of due process that a confession of an accomplice resulting from formal police interrogation cannot be introduced as evidence of the guilt of an accused, absent some circumstance indicating authorization or adoption.").

One potential response to *Bruton* is redaction. For example, Evans' confession could be introduced in a way that omits any reference to Bruton, such as: "[Redacted] and I committed the robbery." The Supreme Court has cautioned that this superficial remedy is not sufficient.

> "Redactions that simply replace a name with an obvious blank space or a word such as 'deleted' or a symbol or other similarly obvious indications of alteration, however, leave statements that, considered as a class, so closely resemble Bruton's unredacted statements that, in our view, the law must require the same result."[1]

Exactly where the line is between permissible and impermissible redactions, however, remains unclear.

EXCLUSION OF DEFENSE EVIDENCE

Defendants typically have more success arguing, not that the due process or fair trial rights require exclusion of prosecution evidence, but that these rights mandate admission of exculpatory defense evidence. The following excerpt from a treatise summarizes the case law.

DEFENSE EVIDENCE OF INNOCENCE[2]

....[In] the 1973 Supreme Court case of Chambers v. Mississippi..., the trial court prohibited testimony from witnesses offered by a defendant on trial for murder; the witnesses would have testified to a third party's confession to the charged murder. Although the trial court's ruling relied on a standard application of traditional hearsay rules, the Supreme Court held that the hearsay prohibition must give way in the circumstances of the case. Importantly, however, the Court's pronouncement recognized that the hearsay prohibition generally applies with full force to block inadmissible hearsay offered by the defense in a criminal case. The delicate dance between this critical caveat and the Court's ultimate reversal of the state court conviction requires quoting in full:

---

[1] Gray v. Maryland (1998).
[2] Wright & Bellin § 6795.

Few rights are more fundamental than that of an accused to present witnesses in his own defense. In the exercise of this right, the accused, as is required of the State, must comply with established rules of procedure and evidence designed to assure both fairness and reliability in the ascertainment of guilt and innocence. Although perhaps no rule of evidence has been more respected or more frequently applied in jury trials than that applicable to the exclusion of hearsay, exceptions tailored to allow the introduction of evidence which in fact is likely to be trustworthy have long existed. The testimony rejected by the trial court here bore persuasive assurances of trustworthiness and thus was well within the basic rationale of the exception for declarations against interest. That testimony also was critical to Chambers' defense. In these circumstances, where constitutional rights directly affecting the ascertainment of guilt are implicated, the hearsay rule may not be applied mechanistically to defeat the ends of justice.

This passage suggests that the constitutional override of state or federal hearsay prohibitions applied in Chambers has two touchstones. One, there must be a strong argument for the reliability of the hearsay at issue.... Two, the hearsay offered must significantly strengthen the defense case. When both of these ingredients are present, the defense can invoke the Chambers rule to argue that Rule 802's hearsay prohibition, as well as an analogous prohibition in any state evidence code, must give way to the defendant's constitutional right to "a meaningful opportunity to present a complete defense."

The Supreme Court later applied the Chambers rule to reverse a conviction in another case, Green v. Georgia, where Georgia's evidence law resulted in the exclusion of exculpatory evidence, again a third-party confession. The Court explained, "Regardless of whether the proffered testimony comes within Georgia's hearsay rule, under the facts of this case its exclusion constituted a violation of the Due Process Clause of the Fourteenth Amendment." Although the per curiam opinion provides only cursory analysis, it echoes the discussion above. The Court explained "The excluded testimony was highly relevant to a critical issue ... and substantial reasons existed to assume its reliability." ...

Predictably, the lower federal courts have not relied on Chambers to reflexively admit hearsay offered by defendants. The case does not, these courts correctly recognize, "open the gates to all hearsay" offered by the defense. Indeed, defense claims in the lower courts are typically rejected on one of the two grounds noted above.

First, "a defendant must demonstrate that the excluded evidence was important to his defense." The Seventh Circuit has suggested this is a high bar, identifying the touchstone of a successful claim as the trial court's rejection of "critical" evidence and explaining that "critical evidence is evidence which would make a material difference to the outcome." .... Hearsay evidence that, while relevant, is deemed relatively insignificant to the defense case will not meet this bar.

Second, weaknesses in the apparent reliability of the hearsay proffered by the defense undermine the applicability of the Chambers rule. Insightful guidance on this point again comes from the Seventh Circuit, which suggests a kind of reciprocity rule: "if a [third-party] confession is sturdy enough for the state to use in its own case—if it is the sort of evidence that prosecutors regularly use against defendants—then defendants are entitled to use it for their own purposes." Although application relies on hypothetical reasoning, courts are quite familiar with the types of statements prosecutors use to convict defendants. It seems only fair (fairness being a constitutional touchstone in this context) that courts permit defendants to use the same type of statements to seek exoneration.

Judge Posner ably summarizes the overall requirement as follows: "[I]f the defendant tenders vital evidence the judge cannot refuse to admit it without giving a better reason than that it is hearsay." After all, a mere nod to the hearsay prohibition is exactly what the Court in Chambers warned against: "the hearsay rule may not be applied mechanistically to defeat the ends of justice."

Outside of these broad contours, there is little benefit to making general pronouncements about the constitutional override of the hearsay prohibition applied in Chambers. The broad "meaningful opportunity to present a complete defense" principle is straightforward. Application comes down to the facts and circumstances in any particular case. It is a necessarily, "fact-intensive inquiry."....

Invocation of Chambers by defense attorneys is common. Success on this ground, at least in the published case law, appears increasingly rare. The lack of success on Chambers-like claims is likely due to multiple factors: (1) the Supreme Court's repeated emphasis of the narrow scope of the rule it applied in Chambers; (2) the increasing conformity of various jurisdictions' evidence codes; and (3) the presence of residual hearsay exceptions that perform a function that is similar to the constitutional override applied in Chambers...

***

As the next case illustrates, the constitutional principle described above can, in the right circumstances, override any exclusionary rule of evidence (not just hearsay rules).

HOLMES v. SOUTH CAROLINA
547 U.S. 319 (2006)

ALITO, J., delivered the opinion for a unanimous Court.

.... Petitioner was convicted by a South Carolina jury of murder, first-degree criminal sexual conduct, first-degree burglary, and robbery, and he was sentenced to death....

[T]he prosecution relied heavily on ... forensic evidence, [including a palm print match].... In addition, the prosecution introduced evidence that petitioner had been seen near [the victim, Mary Stewart's] home within an hour of the time when, according to the prosecution's evidence, the attack took place.

As a major part of his defense, petitioner attempted to undermine the State's forensic evidence by suggesting that it had been contaminated and that certain law enforcement officers had engaged in a plot to frame him. Petitioner's expert witnesses criticized the procedures used by the police in handling the fiber and DNA evidence and in collecting the fingerprint evidence. Another defense expert provided testimony that petitioner cited as supporting his claim that the palm print had been planted by the police.

Petitioner also sought to introduce proof that another man, Jimmy McCaw White, had attacked Stewart. At a pretrial hearing, petitioner proffered several witnesses who placed White in the victim's neighborhood on the morning of the assault, as well as four other witnesses who testified that White had either acknowledged that petitioner was "'innocent'" or had actually admitted to committing the crimes....

The trial court excluded petitioner's third-party guilt evidence citing *State v. Gregory,* 198 S.C. 98 (1941), which held that such evidence is admissible if it "'raise[s] a reasonable inference or presumption as to [the defendant's] own innocence'" but is not admissible if it merely "'cast[s] a bare suspicion upon another'" or "'raise[s] a conjectural inference as to the commission of the crime by another.'"...

II

"[S]tate and federal rulemakers have broad latitude under the Constitution to establish rules excluding evidence from criminal trials." This latitude, however, has limits. "Whether rooted directly in the Due Process Clause of the Fourteenth Amendment or in the Compulsory Process or Confrontation Clauses of the Sixth Amendment, the Constitution guarantees criminal defendants 'a meaningful opportunity to present a complete defense.'" This right is abridged by evidence rules that "infring[e] upon a weighty interest of the accused" and are "'arbitrary' or 'disproportionate to the purposes they are designed to serve.'"

This Court's cases contain several illustrations of "arbitrary" rules, *i.e.,* rules that excluded important defense evidence but that did not serve any legitimate interests....

While the Constitution thus prohibits the exclusion of defense evidence under rules that serve no legitimate purpose or that are disproportionate to the ends that they are asserted to promote, well-established rules of evidence permit trial judges to exclude evidence if its probative value is outweighed by certain other factors such as unfair prejudice, confusion of the issues, or potential to mislead the jury. See, *e.g.,* Fed. Rule Evid. 403. Plainly referring to rules of this type, we have stated that the Constitution permits judges "to exclude evidence that is 'repetitive ..., only marginally relevant' or poses an undue risk of 'harassment, prejudice, [or] confusion of the issues.'"

.... [I]n the present case, as noted, the State Supreme Court applied the rule that "where there is strong evidence of [a defendant's] guilt, especially where there is strong forensic evidence, the proffered evidence about a third party's alleged guilt" may (or perhaps must) be excluded.

Under this rule, the trial judge does not focus on the probative value or the potential adverse effects of admitting the defense evidence of third-party guilt. Instead, the critical inquiry concerns the strength of the prosecution's case: If the prosecution's case is strong enough, the evidence of third-party guilt is excluded even if that evidence, if viewed independently, would have great probative value and even if it would not pose an undue risk of harassment, prejudice, or confusion of the issues....

Interpreted in this way, the rule applied by the State Supreme Court does not rationally serve the end that the *Gregory* rule and its analogues in other jurisdictions were designed to promote, *i.e.,* to focus the trial on the central issues by excluding evidence that has only a very weak logical connection to the central issues. The rule applied in this case appears to be based on the following logic: Where (1) it is clear that only one person was involved in the commission of a particular crime and (2) there is strong evidence that the defendant was the perpetrator, it follows that evidence of third-party guilt must be weak. But this logic depends on an accurate evaluation of the prosecution's proof, and the true strength of the prosecution's proof cannot be assessed without considering challenges to the reliability of the prosecution's evidence. Just because the prosecution's evidence, *if credited,* would provide strong support for a guilty verdict, it does not follow that evidence of third-party guilt has only a weak logical connection to the central issues in the case. And where the credibility of the prosecution's witnesses or the reliability of its evidence is not conceded, the strength of the prosecution's case cannot be assessed without making the sort of factual findings that have traditionally been reserved for the trier of fact and that the South Carolina courts did not purport to make in this case.

The rule applied in this case is no more logical than its converse would be, rule barring the prosecution from introducing evidence of a defendant's guilt if the defendant is able to proffer, at a pretrial hearing, evidence that, if believed, strongly supports a verdict of not guilty. In the present case, for example, petitioner proffered evidence that, if believed, squarely proved that White, not petitioner, was the perpetrator. It would make no sense, however, to hold that this proffer precluded the prosecution from introducing its evidence, including the forensic evidence that, if credited, provided strong proof of petitioner's guilt.

The point is that, by evaluating the strength of only one party's evidence, no logical conclusion can be reached regarding the strength of contrary evidence offered by the other side to rebut or cast doubt. Because the rule applied by the State Supreme Court in this case did not heed this point, the rule is "arbitrary" in the sense that it does not rationally serve the end that the *Gregory* rule and other similar third-party guilt rules were designed to further. Nor has the State identified any other legitimate end that the rule serves. It follows that the rule applied in this case by the State Supreme Court violates a criminal defendant's right to have "'a meaningful opportunity to present a complete defense.'"

Chapter 8

AUTHENTICATION AND BEST EVIDENCE

AUTHENTICATION

RULE 901

A common issue at trial concerns the authenticity of a piece of evidence. For example, in a murder prosecution, the prosecutor may attempt to introduce a knife into evidence claiming that it was found next to the victim. An authentication objection essentially contends that the party introducing the evidence has not established that the evidence is what the party claims.

Notice that authentication is, as the Advisory Committee acknowledges, "a special aspect of relevancy." If the police found the knife at the crime scene, the knife is relevant. If, instead, the prosecutor got the knife from a kitchen drawer on the way into work, the knife is irrelevant to the case.

To overcome an authentication objection, the party offering evidence need only "produce evidence sufficient to support a finding that the item is what the proponent claims it is." That standard should look familiar. It is the same as the conditional relevance standard we saw in Rule 104(b). The Advisory Committee Note makes this connection explicit:

> "This requirement of showing authenticity or identity fails in the category of relevancy dependent upon fulfillment of a condition of fact and is governed by the procedure set forth in Rule 104(b)."

Authentication comes down to facts. (The missing, or conditional, fact is that the evidence is what the party claims it is.) The party offering evidence must introduce evidence, such as testimony from the police officer who found the knife, sufficient to allow the factfinder to conclude that the knife was indeed found at the murder scene.

Rule 901(a) is all that is needed to govern authentication. Rule 901(b) merely offers illustrations of the type of evidence that can serve as authentication.

Rule 902 provides examples of evidence that is self-authenticating, which means that no witness will be required to authenticate evidence that fits the requirements of Rule 902.

PROBLEM 8-1: "THE GUN JUST COMES IN"

Most handguns look about the same. They are often black and look like ... a gun. Imagine you are planning to introduce a gun connected to a murder into evidence. Just prior to trial, a police officer obtains the gun from an evidence locker at the police station. Assume the events in the case occurred 11 months prior to trial. *What type of evidence do you think you could offer to overcome an authentication objection to the admission of the gun into evidence? What else do you need to think about before attempting to introduce the gun?*

UNITED STATES v. VAYNER
769 F.3d 125 (2d Cir. 2014)

DEBRA ANN LIVINGSTON, Circuit Judge:

In Defendant–Appellant Aliaksandr Zhyltsou's criminal trial on a single charge of transfer of a false identification document, the government offered into evidence a printed copy of a web page, which it claimed was Zhyltsou's profile page from a Russian social networking site akin to Facebook. The district court admitted the printout over Zhyltsou's objection that the page had not been properly authenticated under Rule 901 of the Federal Rules of Evidence. We conclude that the district court erred in admitting the web page evidence because the government presented insufficient evidence that the page was what the government claimed it to be—that is, Zhyltsou's profile page, as opposed to a profile page on the Internet that Zhyltsou did not create or control. Because the district court abused its discretion in admitting the evidence, and because this error was not harmless, we vacate the conviction and remand for retrial.

BACKGROUND

.... At trial, the government's principal evidence against Zhyltsou was the testimony of Vladyslav Timku, a Ukrainian citizen residing in Brooklyn who testified pursuant to a cooperation agreement and who had earlier pled guilty to conspiracy to commit wire fraud, aggravated identity theft, and impersonating a diplomat. Timku testified that he was a friend of Zhyltsou's and was familiar with Zhyltsou's work as a forger because he had previously paid Zhyltsou to create false diplomatic identification documents... Timku said that in the summer of 2009 he asked Zhyltsou to create a forged birth certificate that would reflect that Timku was the father of an invented infant daughter. Timku sought the birth certificate in an attempt to avoid compulsory military service in his native Ukraine, which permits a deferment of service for the parents of children under three years of age. According to Timku, Zhyltsou agreed to forge the birth certificate without charge, as a "favor," and began creating the fake birth certificate on a computer while the pair chatted in a Brooklyn Internet café. Timku testified that Zhyltsou sent the completed forgery to Timku via e-mail on August 27, 2009 from azmadeuz@gmail.com (the "Gmail address"), an e-mail address that Timku had often used to correspond with Zhyltsou. After receiving the document, Timku thanked Zhyltsou and then went on to use the fake document to receive the deferment from military service that he sought. The government introduced a copy of the e-mail, with the forged birth certificate as an attachment, which reflected that it was sent to Timku's e-mail address, "timkuvlad@yahoo.com," from azmadeuz@gmail.com.

The government presented several other witnesses who corroborated certain aspects of Timku's testimony—regarding the falsity of the birth certificate, the Ukrainian military deferment for parents of young children, and the path of the e-mail in question through servers in California. There was expert testimony to the effect that the e-mail originated in New York, but no evidence as to what computer it was sent from, or what IP addresses were linked to it. Thus, near the conclusion of the prosecution's case, only Timku's testimony directly connected Zhyltsou with the Gmail address that was used to transmit the fake birth certificate to Timku. Before the prosecution rested, however, the government indicated to the district court that it planned to call an unexpected final witness: Robert Cline, a Special Agent with the State Department's Diplomatic Security Service ("DSS"). The government said that it intended to introduce a printout of a web page that the government claimed to be Zhyltsou's profile on VK.com ("VK"), which Special Agent Cline described as "the Russian equivalent of Facebook." Zhyltsou objected, contending that the page had not been properly authenticated and was thus inadmissible under Federal Rule of Evidence 901. The district court overruled the defense objection, concluding that the VK page was "[Zhyltsou's] Facebook page. The information on there, I think it's fair to assume, is information which was provided by him." Moreover, the court ruled, "There's no question about the authenticity of th[e] document so far as it's coming off the Internet now."

During his testimony, Special Agent Cline identified the printout as being from "the Russian equivalent of Facebook." He noted to the jury that the page purported to be the profile of "Alexander Zhiltsov" (an alternate spelling of Zhyltsou's name), and that it contained a photograph of Zhyltsou. Importantly for the government's case, Special Agent Cline next pointed out that under the heading, "Contact Information," the profile listed "Azmadeuz" as "Zhiltsov's" address on Skype (a service that Special Agent Cline described as a "voiceover IP provider").…. On cross-examination, Special Agent Cline admitted that he had only a "cursory familiarity" with VK, had never used the site except to view this single page, and did not know whether any identity verification was required in order for a user to create an account on the site. In its summation, the government argued that it had proven that Zhyltsou had produced the fake birth certificate and sent it to Timku using the Gmail address. In the final words of her summation, the Assistant United States Attorney ("AUSA") argued that proof of the connection between Zhyltsou and the Gmail address could be found on Zhyltsou's "own Russian Facebook page":

> It has the defendant's profile picture on it. You'll see that it confirms other facts that you've learned about the defendant. That he worked at Martex and at Cyber Heaven, for example. He told [a DSS agent] that he's from Belarus. This page says he's from Minsk, the capital of Belarus. And on that page, you'll see the name he uses on Skype which, like e-mail, is a way to correspond with people over the Internet.

> Azmadeuz. That [is] his online identity, ladies and gentlemen, for Skype and for [G]mail. That is [w]hat the defendant calls himself. Timku even told you that the defendant sometimes uses azmadeuz@yahoo.com. That [is] his own name on the Internet. Timku didn't make it up for him. The defendant made it up for himself.

Aliaksandr Zhyltsou made a fake birth certificate and he sent it through e-mail. Those are the facts. The defendant is guilty. Find him so. Thank you.

After deliberating for approximately a day and a half, the jury found Zhyltsou guilty on the single charge contained in the indictment. Subsequently, the district court sentenced Zhyltsou principally to time served and one year of post-release supervision....

DISCUSSION

.... "The requirement of authentication is ... a condition precedent to admitting evidence." Rule 901 of the Federal Rules of Evidence governs the authentication of evidence and provides, in pertinent part: "To satisfy the requirement of authenticating or identifying an item of evidence, the proponent must produce evidence sufficient to support a finding that the item is what the proponent claims it is." Fed.R.Evid. 901(a)....

Rule 901 "does not definitively establish the nature or quantum of proof that is required" preliminarily to authenticate an item of evidence. "The type and quantum of evidence" required is "related to the purpose for which the evidence is offered," and depends upon a context-specific determination whether the proof advanced is sufficient to support a finding that the item in question is what its proponent claims it to be. We have said that "[t]he bar for authentication of evidence is not particularly high." But even though "[t]he proponent need not rule out all possibilities inconsistent with authenticity, or ... prove beyond any doubt that the evidence is what it purports to be," there must nonetheless be at least "sufficient proof ... so that a reasonable juror could find in favor of authenticity or identification."

The "proof of authentication may be direct or circumstantial." The simplest (and likely most common) form of authentication is through "the testimony of a 'witness with knowledge' that 'a matter is what it is claimed to be.'" This is by no means exclusive, however: Rule 901 provides several examples of proper authentication techniques in different contexts, and the advisory committee's note states that these are "not intended as an exclusive enumeration of allowable methods but are meant to guide and suggest, leaving room for growth and development in this area of the law."

Some examples illustrate the point. For instance, we have said that a document can be authenticated by "distinctive characteristics of the document itself, such as its '[a]ppearance, contents, substance, internal patterns, or other distinctive characteristics, taken in conjunction with the circumstances.'" Or, where the evidence in question is a recorded call, we have said that "[w]hile a mere assertion of identity by a person talking on the telephone is not in itself sufficient to authenticate that person's identity, some additional evidence, which need not fall into any set pattern, may provide the necessary foundation." And in a case where credit card receipts purportedly signed by the defendant would have tended to support his alibi defense, we ruled that the defendant's copies had been sufficiently authenticated, despite some question as to when these copies had been signed, where the defendant offered testimony from store managers as to how the receipts were produced, testimony from the defendant's wife (a joint holder of the credit card) that she had not made the purchases in question, and testimony from a handwriting expert that the defendant's signature was genuine.

As we have said, "[a]uthentication of course merely renders [evidence] admissible, leaving the issue of [its] ultimate reliability to the jury." Thus, after the proponent of the evidence has adduced sufficient evidence to support a finding that the proffered evidence is what it is claimed to be, the opposing party "remains free to challenge the reliability of the evidence, to minimize its importance, or to argue alternative interpretations of its meaning, but these and similar other challenges go to the weight of the evidence—not to its admissibility."

II.

Based on these principles, we conclude that the district court abused its discretion in admitting the VK web page, as it did so without proper authentication under Rule 901. The government did not provide a sufficient basis on which to conclude that the proffered printout was what the government claimed it to be—Zhyltsou's profile page—and there was thus insufficient evidence to authenticate the VK page and to permit its consideration by the jury.

In the district court, the government initially advanced the argument that it offered the evidence simply as a web page that existed on the Internet at the time of trial, not as evidence of Zhyltsou's own statements. The prosecution first represented to the district court that it was presenting the VK page only as "what [Special Agent Cline] is observing today on the Internet, just today," conceded that "the agent does not know who created it," and averred that Special Agent Cline would testify only that "he saw [the VK page] and this is what it says." Consistent with these representations, Special Agent Cline testified only that the page containing information related to Zhyltsou was presently accessible on the Internet and provided no extrinsic information showing that Zhyltsou was the page's author or otherwise tying the page to Zhyltsou.

At other times, however, the government repeatedly made a contrary argument to both the trial court and the jury, and insisted that the page belonged to and was authored by Zhyltsou. Nor is this surprising. The VK profile page was helpful to the government's case only if it belonged to Zhyltsou—if it was his profile page, created by him or someone acting on his behalf—and thus tended to establish that Zhyltsou used the moniker "Azmadeuz" on Skype and was likely also to have used it for the Gmail address from which the forged birth certificate was sent, just as Timku claimed. Moreover, the district court overruled Zhyltsou's hearsay objection and admitted a printout of the profile page, which stated that "Zhiltsov's" Skype username was "Azmadeuz," because it found that the page was created by Zhyltsou, and the statement therefore constituted a party admission.

As noted above, Rule 901 requires "evidence sufficient to support a finding that the item is what the proponent claims it is." It is uncontroverted that information about Zhyltsou appeared on the VK page: his name, photograph, and some details about his life consistent with Timku's testimony about him. But there was no evidence that Zhyltsou himself had created the page or was responsible for its contents. Had the government sought to introduce, for instance, a flyer found on the street that contained Zhyltsou's Skype address and was purportedly written or authorized by him, the district court surely would have required some evidence that the flyer did, in fact, emanate from Zhyltsou. Otherwise, how could the statements in the flyer be attributed to him? And contrary to the government's argument, the mere fact that a page with Zhyltsou's name and photograph happened to exist on the Internet at the time of Special Agent Cline's testimony does not permit a reasonable conclusion that this page was created by the defendant or on his behalf.

It is true that the contents or "distinctive characteristics" of a document can sometimes alone provide circumstantial evidence sufficient for authentication. Fed. R. Evid. 901(b)(4). For example, a writing may be authenticated by evidence "that the contents of the writing were not a matter of common knowledge." Here, however, all the information contained on the VK page allegedly tying the page to Zhyltsou was also known by Timku and likely others, some of whom may have had reasons to create a profile page falsely attributed to the defendant. Other than the page itself, moreover, no evidence in the record suggested that Zhyltsou even had a VK profile page, much less that the page in question was that page. Nor was there any evidence that identity verification is necessary to create such a page with VK, which might also have helped render more than speculative the conclusion that the page in question belonged to Zhyltsou.

.... Rule 901 required that there be some basis ... on which a reasonable juror could conclude that the page in question was not just any Internet page, but in fact Zhyltsou's profile. No such showing was made and the evidence should therefore have been excluded....

PROBLEM 8-2: WHO'S THIS?

Consider the following text message introduced in a prosecution for threatening a person with a firearm in State v. Smith (La. Ct. App. 2016). The victim received the text message the day before the in-person threat and showed it to the investigating police officer afterwards. *What type of evidence would the prosecution need to offer to be able to introduce the text message into evidence?*

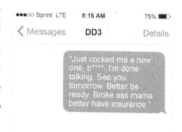

THE "BEST EVIDENCE" RULE

RULES 1001-1008

We begin our exploration of the so-called "Best Evidence Rule" with a classic case.

SEILER v. LUCASFILM
808 F.2d 1316 (9th Cir. 1986)

FARRIS, Circuit Judge:

…. [Graphic artist, Leo] Seiler contends that he created and published in 1976 and 1977 science fiction creatures called Garthian Striders. In 1980, George Lucas released The Empire Strikes Back, a motion picture that contains a battle sequence depicting giant machines called Imperial Walkers. In 1981 Seiler obtained a copyright on his Striders, depositing with the Copyright Office "reconstructions" of the originals as they had appeared in 1976 and 1977.

Seiler contends that Lucas' Walkers were copied from Seiler's Striders which were allegedly published in 1976 and 1977. Lucas responds that Seiler did not obtain his copyright until one year after the release of The Empire Strikes Back and that Seiler can produce no documents that antedate The Empire Strikes Back.

[T]he district judge held an evidentiary hearing on the admissibility of the "reconstructions" of Seiler's Striders. Applying the "best evidence rule," Fed.R.Evid. 1001–1008, the district court found at the end of a seven-day hearing that Seiler lost or destroyed the originals in bad faith under Rule 1004(1) and that consequently no secondary evidence, such as the post-Empire Strikes Back reconstructions, was admissible. In its opinion the court found specifically that Seiler testified falsely, purposefully destroyed or withheld in bad faith the originals, and fabricated and misrepresented the nature of his reconstructions. The district court granted summary judgment to Lucas after the evidentiary hearing….

DISCUSSION

The best evidence rule embodied in Rules 1001–1008 represented a codification of longstanding common law doctrine. Dating back to 1700, the rule requires not, as its common name implies, the best evidence in every case but rather the production of an original document instead of a copy. Many commentators refer to the rule not as the best evidence rule but as the original document rule.

Rule 1002 states: "To prove the content of a writing, recording, or photograph, the original writing, recording, or photograph is required, except as otherwise provided in these rules or by Act of Congress." Writings and recordings are defined in Rule 1001 as "letters, words, or numbers, or their equivalent, set down by handwriting, typewriting, printing, photostating, photographing, magnetic impulse, mechanical or electronic recording, or other form of data compilation."

.... The contents of Seiler's work are at issue. There can be no proof of "substantial similarity" and thus of copyright infringement unless Seiler's works are juxtaposed with Lucas' and their contents compared. Since the contents are material and must be proved, Seiler must either produce the original or show that it is unavailable through no fault of his own. Rule 1004(1). This he could not do.

.... Seiler argues that the best evidence rule does not apply to his work, in that it is artwork rather than "writings, recordings, or photographs." He contends that the rule both historically and currently embraces only words or numbers....

To recognize Seiler's works as writings does not, as Seiler argues, run counter to the rule's preoccupation with the centrality of the written word in the world of legal relations. Just as a contract objectively manifests the subjective intent of the makers, so Seiler's drawings are objective manifestations of the creative mind....

A creative literary work, which is artwork, and a photograph whose contents are sought to be proved, as in copyright, defamation, or invasion of privacy, are both covered by the best evidence rule. We would be inconsistent to apply the rule to artwork which is literary or photographic but not to artwork of other forms. Furthermore, blueprints, engineering drawings, architectural designs may all lack words or numbers yet still be capable of copyright and susceptible to fraudulent alteration. In short, Seiler's argument would have us restrict the definitions of Rule 1001(1) to "words" and "numbers" but ignore "or their equivalent." We will not do so in the circumstances of this case.

.... As we hold that the district court correctly concluded that the best evidence rule applies to Seiler's drawings, Seiler was required to produce his original drawings unless excused by the exceptions set forth in Rule 1004. The pertinent subsection is 1004(1), which provides:

> The original is not required, and other evidence of the contents of a writing, recording, or photograph is admissible if—
>
> (1) Originals lost or destroyed. All originals are lost or have been destroyed, unless the proponent lost or destroyed them in bad faith ...

In the instant case, ... [a]t the conclusion of [a seven day] hearing, the trial judge found that the reconstructions were inadmissible under the best evidence rule as the originals were lost or destroyed in bad faith. This finding is amply supported by the record.

Seiler argues on appeal that regardless of Rule 1004(1), Rule 1008 requires a trial because a key issue would be whether the reconstructions correctly reflect the content of the originals.... Seiler's position confuses admissibility of the reconstructions with the weight, if any, the trier of fact should give them, after the judge has ruled that they are admissible. Rule 1008 states, in essence, that when the admissibility of evidence other than the original depends upon the fulfillment of a condition of fact, the trial judge generally makes the determination of that condition of fact. The notes of the Advisory Committee are consistent with this interpretation in stating: "Most preliminary questions of fact in connection with applying the rule preferring the original as evidence of contents are for the judge ... [t]hus the question of ... fulfillment of other conditions specified in Rule 1004 ... is for the judge." In the instant case, the condition of fact which Seiler needed to prove was that the originals were not lost or destroyed in bad faith. Had he been able to prove this, his reconstructions would have been admissible and then their accuracy would have been a question for the jury. In sum, since admissibility of the reconstructions was dependent upon a finding that the originals were not lost or destroyed in bad faith, the trial judge properly held the hearing to determine their admissibility....

AFFIRMED.

***

Seiler illustrates how the various components of the "best evidence" rule work together to reach a sensible result. Leo Seiler claimed he created a series of sketches in 1976 that bore substantial similarity to the space-age vehicles made famous in the second Star Wars movie, entitling Seiler to compensation. To evaluate this claim, the jury needed to compare Seiler's sketches to footage from the 1980 movie. As the court stated: "There can be no proof of 'substantial similarity' and thus of copyright infringement unless Seiler's works are juxtaposed with Lucas' and their contents compared." The problem was that Seiler no longer had the 1976 sketches. Instead, he sought to demonstrate what those sketches looked like with the "reconstructions" he created in 1981.

Applying the evidence rules, Seiler needed to "prove the content" (Rule 1002) of the 1976 sketches to support his infringement claim. Under Rule 1001, those sketches were a "writing" or "photograph" or "their equivalent." Consequently, the rules required the "original" (Rule 1002) or a "duplicate" (Rule 1003). Seiler did not have the original. Rule 1001(e) defines "duplicate" in a way that excluded Seiler's reconstructions. Even after all that, Rule 1004 excuses the absence of the original if, among other things, the original was "lost or destroyed" through no fault of the party offering the evidence -- another hurdle Seiler could not overcome. Finally, Rule 1008, as the *Seiler* court explained, only applies after the judge determines admissibility as described above.

While the best evidence rule doomed Seiler's claim, Seiler's abundant chances to avoid the Rule's prohibition illustrate how rarely the modern Best Evidence Rule excludes evidence. As a practical matter, litigants will rarely offer such obviously second-best evidence since it is likely to be discounted by the jury. Second, the rule only applies to writings, recordings, and photographs. Third, it is a rare occasion when parties seek "to prove the content" of such items. Fourth, when they do, it is typically because the original has, in fact, been lost or destroyed and not through their own bad faith.

PROBLEM 8-3: PHOTOS OF TEXTS

In *United States v. Ramirez* (11th Cir. 2016), the defendant worked with Diana L. to fill forged Oxycodone prescriptions, often sending instructions to her via text message. Diana L. regularly sent screenshots of these text message to a DEA Agent. At trial, the prosecution introduced the screenshots of the text messages to show the defendant's involvement in illegal activities. As for Diana L.'s phone, "The government explained that, while the investigation was continuing, the original phone had dropped in water and was rendered inoperable."

On appeal, the defendant argued that admission of the screenshots of his text messages violated the Best Evidence rule. *What are the prosecution's best arguments to counter this claim?*

PROBLEM 8-4: CLOSED CIRCUIT TELEVISION

Consider the facts of *Cox v. State* (Tex. App. 2012):

> A Walmart employee, Daniel Flores observed appellant on a closed-circuit television monitor located in the store's Asset Protection office…. Flores watched appellant on the television monitor selecting two fishing reels and placing them inside his shirt, and then walking through the store, past the registers, and out a door into the patio area.

At a later theft trial, Flores testified about what he observed on the monitor. In addition,

> Flores testified that videotape footage automatically generated through the closed-circuit television system is maintained on the system for ninety days. Unless a manual request is made on the computer server to make a compact disc recording of the videotaped footage, the system server deletes the video recording after ninety days. The closed-circuit television monitor Flores watched showed what was occurring in real time as it happened.

Cox appealed the admission of this testimony on the ground that it violated Texas' Best Evidence rule which mirrors the federal rule. *How should the appellate court rule?*

STATE VARIATION: WRITINGS NOT PHOTOS

As the *Seiler* case notes, the common law tradition limited the scope of the Best Evidence rule to "writings." This history is still reflected in some state jurisdictions. Virginia Rule 2:1002 states:

> To prove the content of a writing, the original writing is required…

As a consequence, testimony about surveillance video would not trigger any Best Evidence problem in Virginia state courts. Virginia courts do interpret "writings" to include electronic variants, however, such as text messages. But this extension may not lead to the exclusion of much evidence. Echoing an emerging trend regarding the best evidence rule and electronic evidence, the Virginia Court of Appeals explained:

> In the present case, Warren [a confidential informant] testified that he could not produce the text messages because he did "not have that phone any longer," and therefore did not have the messages either. As such, Rule 2:1004(a) and (b) are applicable to the present context as the text messages were both lost and unattainable. Indeed the exceptions of Rule 2:1004 are particularly suited to electronic evidence given the myriad of ways that electronic records may be deleted, lost, or purged as a result of routine electronic records management. Additionally, there is no evidence which suggests that the absence of the text messages in the present case was a result of bad faith.[1]

Not all courts accept this line of argument, particularly when the party later offering a substitute for the original had access to the original and, without good reason, failed to preserve it despite a foreseeable likelihood that it would be important evidence. In *United States v. Bennett* (9th Cir. 2004), the prosecution offered an officer's testimony that a GPS device found on a ship intercepted at a United States port reflected that the ship had traveled across the border. The court ruled that the testimony violated the best evidence rule:

> "[O]ther evidence" of the contents of a writing, recording or photograph is admissible if the original is shown to be lost, destroyed

---

[1] Dalton v. Commonwealth, 64 Va. App. 512 (2015).

or otherwise unobtainable. Fed.R.Evid. 1004. But the government made no such showing. When asked on cross-examination to produce the GPS or its data, [Agent] Chandler simply stated that he was not the GPS's custodian. He further testified that "there was no need to" videotape or photograph the data and that he had nothing other than his testimony to support his assertions about the GPS's contents. Moreover, the government has not offered any record evidence that it would have been impossible or even difficult to download or print out the data on Bennett's GPS. On the record before us, the government is not excused from the best evidence rule's preference for the original.

Chapter 9

SPECIAL RELEVANCE RULES

This Chapter discusses a handful of evidence rules that arise less frequently, but can still significantly impact a case: Rules 406-411.

HABIT

RULE 406

BABCOCK v. GENERAL MOTORS
299 F.3d 60 (1st Cir. 2002)

BOWNES, Senior Circuit Judge.

This appeal is taken by defendant-appellant General Motors Corporation ("GM") from an adverse jury verdict in favor of plaintiff-appellee Frances A. Babcock as executrix of the estate of Paul A. Babcock, III, and individually. The case arose from an accident on February 21, 1998, when a General Motors pickup truck driven by Paul A. Babcock, III, went off the road and struck a tree.... Babcock died as a result of complications from his injuries.

Plaintiff brought suit alleging negligence and strict liability against the defendant. The jury returned a verdict finding GM liable on the negligence count and not liable on the strict liability count. It is undisputed that when Babcock was first seen after the accident his seat belt was not fastened around him. The complaint alleged that Babcock was wearing his seat belt prior to the accident, but that the belt unbuckled as soon as pressure was exerted on it and the buckle released due to a condition known as "false latching." The main focus of the trial was on this claim of false latching....

GM argues that there was an absence of evidence that Babcock was wearing his seat belt at the time of the accident. It points out that no one saw a seat belt on him immediately after the accident. GM also argues that although Babcock himself was covered with blood and blood was on the interior of the cab of the truck, no blood was on the seat belt straps.

Plaintiff did not challenge these facts, but claimed that she would prove by habit or custom evidence that Babcock always wore a seat belt when he drove a motor vehicle. The district court ruled that such evidence would be allowed and that the question of whether Babcock was wearing a seat belt at the time of the accident was for the jury.... It is well-established that habit evidence may be used to prove a person's conduct on a particular occasion. Fed.R.Evid. 406.

We recount testimony by three of the plaintiff's witnesses, all of whom described Babcock's habitual seat belt use. Ernest Babcock, brother of the decedent, testified that he drove with his brother, Paul Babcock, at least ten to twenty times a year from 1972 to 1998. George Clausen, Paul Babcock's neighbor, had known him for about a year and a half prior to the accident and had ridden with him about a dozen times. Judith Hobbs Jackson had known Babcock since the two were children. She had ridden with him eight to twelve times over the last several years, most of these times with Babcock as the driver. All three witnesses testified that Babcock always wore his seat belt, regardless of whether he was the driver or a passenger and regardless of the length of the trip. Jackson also testified that Babcock always put on his seat belt before the vehicle in which he was riding started.

We rule that the district court did not err in [allowing the evidence].... The judgment below is affirmed.

***

It would be a strange system of evidence that did not allow evidence of a person's habits. In fact, you might wonder why Rule 406 is even necessary. Evidence of a person's habit, as in the *Babcock* case, seems clearly relevant. Why not leave the admission and exclusion of this evidence to the other rules?

One clue comes in the Advisory Committee Note's effort in its initial paragraphs to distinguish habit from character evidence. The other comes at the end of the Note, where the Advisory Committee rejects corroboration requirements that some States imposed on habit evidence. Rule 406 is included in the federal rules for the purpose of eliminating, rather than creating, obstacles to admission.

Controversies regarding habit evidence center on how much evidence about repeated conduct is needed to establish a "habit." Here is a representative excerpt from the case law regarding the necessary showing:

> Habit evidence under Rule 406 may be probative of "'the regular practice of meeting a particular kind of situation with a specific type of conduct, such as the habit of going down a particular stairway two stairs at a time, or of giving the hand-signal for a left turn....'" Fed.R.Evid. 406, advisory committee's note. Although there are no "precise standards" for determining whether a behavior pattern has matured into a habit, two factors are considered controlling as a rule: "adequacy of sampling and uniformity of response." Fed.R.Evid. 406, advisory committee's notes. These factors focus on whether the behavior at issue "occurred with sufficient regularity making it more probable than not that it would be carried out in every instance or in most instances." The requisite regularity is tested by the "'ratio of reaction to situations.'" It is essential, therefore, that the regularity of the conduct alleged to be habitual rest on an analysis of instances "'numerous enough to [support] an inference of systematic conduct' and to establish 'one's regular response to a repeated specific situation.'"[1]

It is the invariable regularity and essentially "semi-automatic" nature of habits that distinguishes them from character. Thus, the Advisory Committee Note's examples, of "going down a particular stairway two stairs at a time, or of giving the hand-signal for a left turn, or of alighting from railway cars while they are moving."

PROBLEM 9-1: INTOXICATION[2]

"Shortly after midnight on June 17, 1974, appellant Reyes was run over by appellee-railroad's train as he lay on the railroad tracks near a crossing in Brownsville, Texas. Reyes brought this diversity suit against the railroad, alleging negligence on the part of the railroad's employees in failing to discover plaintiff as he lay on the tracks and stop the train

---

[1] United States v. Newman, 982 F.2d 665 (1st Cir. 1992).
[2] Reyes v. Missouri Pac. R. Co., 589 F.2d 791 (5th Cir. 1979).

in time to avoid the accident. The railroad answered by claiming that Reyes, dressed in dark clothing that night, was not visible from the approaching train until it was too late for its employees to avert the accident. Moreover, the railroad alleged that Reyes was contributorily negligent because he was intoxicated on the night of the accident and passed out on the tracks before the train arrived. Reyes explained his presence on the railroad tracks by claiming that he was knocked unconscious by an unknown assailant as he walked along the tracks.

Reyes made a motion In limine to exclude evidence of his "four prior convictions for public intoxication spanning a three and one-half year period." The railroad opposed this motion, arguing that the convictions were admissible to show that Reyes was intoxicated on the night of the accident. The district court agreed and refused to grant Reyes' motion."

The railroad prevailed at trial. Reyes' appealed, challenging the trial court's ruling. The railroad defended the admission of the prior convictions, citing Rule 406. *How should the appellate court rule?*

REMEDIAL MEASURES

RULE 407

Rule 407 restricts the admission of "subsequent remedial measures." More precisely, the rule provides for the exclusion of evidence of the actions someone takes to "make an earlier injury or harm less likely to occur," if those actions are offered to prove: "negligence, culpable conduct, a defect in a product or its design; or a need for a warning or instruction."

Although the rule's text is ambiguous on this point, the Advisory Committee Note to the 1997 Amendment clarifies that "the rule applies only to changes made after the occurrence that produced the damages giving rise to the action."

PROBLEM 9-2: DISNEY ALLIGATORS

In June 2016, an alligator killed a 2-year-old boy who was vacationing at Walt Disney World Resort in Orlando, Florida. The alligator swam up and grabbed the boy while he was playing at the edge of the man-made "Seven Seas Lagoon" on the property.

There were signs at the location that said, "No Swimming." After the incident, the resort installed new signs, stating "Stay Away from the Water, Alligators!" along with a picture of an alligator. It also installed ropes to keep people from playing at the water's edge.

Imagine the child's family sued the resort for the death. *Can the family introduce the resort's actions -- adding new signs and ropes -- as proof that the resort itself recognized that its previous safety measures were inadequate?*

Now imagine that after the new signs are installed, another child is killed by an alligator. *Can this child's family introduce evidence about the prior alligator attack and the subsequent installation of the ropes/signs?*

MAHNKE v. WASHINGTON METRO
821 F. Supp. 2d 125 (D.D.C. 2011)

BERYL HOWELL, District Judge.

On September 3, 2009, plaintiff Amanda Mahnke suffered serious injuries when she was hit by a Washington Metropolitan Area Transit Authority (hereinafter "WMATA") bus in Washington, D.C. The plaintiff filed a Complaint against WMATA, alleging, inter alia, that the bus driver, a WMATA employee, negligently operated the bus…. [T]he parties have … filed eleven additional motions in limine to preclude the admission of certain evidence at trial…. The parties' additional motions in limine, as well as their objections to proposed exhibits, are addressed seriatim below….

The defendant seeks to prevent the plaintiff from introducing evidence or commenting on the "conduct and results" of WMATA's internal investigation, including WMATA's Final Investigation Report which is plaintiff's proposed exhibit 44, as well as disciplinary and arbitration proceedings regarding Carla Proctor, the WMATA bus driver, and her termination....

.... In [a] supplemental filing, the defendant argued for the first time that evidence regarding its investigation, internal disciplinary proceedings, and its disciplinary action against the bus driver should be inadmissible under Federal Rule of Evidence 407, which states, in relevant part, that "evidence of the subsequent [remedial] measures is not admissible to prove negligence, culpable conduct."... Following review of the parties' additional briefs on this issue, the Court concludes that Federal Rule of Evidence 407 applies to evidence of WMATA's internal investigation and disciplinary proceedings, and the termination of the bus driver.

The grounds for exclusion of evidence of subsequent remedial measures under Federal Rule of Evidence rests in large part "on a social policy of encouraging people to take, or at least not discouraging them from taking, steps in furtherance of added safety." Advisory Committee Note. As the Advisory Committee explains, "courts have applied this principle to exclude evidence of ... changes in company rules, and discharge of employees, and the language of the present rule is broad enough to encompass all of them." Thus, pursuant to Rule 407, courts have excluded "evidence that an employer subsequently discharged an employee accused of causing a plaintiff's injury."

The plaintiff concedes "that under most circumstances the fact that WMATA terminated Ms. Proctor would be inadmissible as a subsequent remedial measure under Federal Rule of Evidence 407." The plaintiff contends, however, that after "terminating Ms. Proctor, Defendant WMATA made the decision as a governmental agency to file a Press Release." According to the plaintiff, the defendant's issuance of a press release containing an express public admission about the conclusions of the investigation and termination of the employee push these events outside of the protection of Rule 407.

The press release issued by the defendant does not alter the salient fact that the Final Report of the internal investigation, the discipline proceeding before the panel of arbitrators, and the termination of the bus driver were all steps taken internally by the defendant in response to the accident. Other courts confronting similar facts have concluded that Rule 407 applies to bar admissibility of remedial measures, even when these measures have been publicly touted…. In this case, the defendant similarly stated in its press release that it was taking remedial steps in response to the accident by terminating Ms. Proctor from her employment because she had violated WMATA's standard operating procedures. This press release, along with WMATA's internal investigation and arbitration proceedings, are within the purview of Federal Rule of Evidence 407 and are thus inadmissible to prove negligence and culpable conduct. The defendant's motion to exclude evidence and comment of its Final Report, internal disciplinary proceedings, labor-union arbitration proceedings, and termination of the bus driver is granted.

The Court cautions, however, that Rule 407 "does not require the exclusion of evidence of subsequent measures when offered for another purpose, such as … impeachment." The purpose of Rule 407 is to encourage remedial measures, but it is not to be used by a party to disavow its own findings or take positions inconsistent with its past representations. Thus, if at trial, a defense witness asserts a position in conflict with statements made by the defendant in its press release, or in its internal investigatory and arbitration proceedings, the plaintiff may use that evidence for impeachment purposes.

*****

One of the key takeaways from *Mahnke* is its illustration of the breadth of the "measures are taken" language in Rule 407. As the Advisory Committee Note to the rule states: "The courts have applied this principle to exclude evidence of subsequent repairs, installation of safety devices, changes in company rules, and discharge of employees, and the language of the present rules is broad enough to encompass all of them."

Note also Judge Howell's caution at the end of her opinion regarding other purposes for which the subsequent remedial measures may yet be admissible. The caution stems from the Rule itself. The prohibition in Rule 407 gives way when the defendant offers certain defenses, including disputing "the feasibility of precautionary measures." In addition, the evidence can become admissible as impeachment of inconsistent witness testimony.

This proviso creates a difficult line drawing problem. If the rule's language about disputing feasibility and impeachment is interpreted too broadly, virtually any defense to civil claims would trigger the admission of subsequent remedial measures, swallowing the rule. It cannot be, for example, that if the defendant simply claims (in testimony or more generally) to not have been negligent in doing (or not doing) an act that led to harm, then the defendant can be "impeached" with subsequent remedial measures, or that the remedial measures now become admissible because the defense has disputed feasibility.

Here is a discussion of this point from a Seventh Circuit case, Flaminio v. Honda Motor (7th Cir. 1984). Note: Prior to the 2011 restyling, Rule 407 used the phrase "if controverted" rather than "if disputed."

> .... The issue with respect to the allegation of defective design is whether the district court erred in excluding evidence (consisting of two blueprints) that, the plaintiffs say, shows that after the accident, Honda, in an effort to reduce wobble, made the struts ("front forks") that connect the Gold Wing's handlebars to its front wheel two millimeters thicker. Rule 407 of the Federal Rules of Evidence makes evidence of subsequent remedial measures "not admissible to prove negligence or culpable conduct in connection with the event," but adds: "This rule does not require the exclusion of evidence of subsequent measures when offered for another purpose, such as proving ownership, control, or feasibility of precautionary measures, if controverted, or impeachment." Flaminio [the plaintiff] argues that the blueprints were admissible under the exceptions for "proving ... feasibility of precautionary measures, if controverted," and for impeaching the defendants' evidence. But the first of these exceptions is inapplicable because the defendants did not deny the feasibility of precautionary measures against wobble. Their argument was that there is a tradeoff between wobble and "weave," and that in designing the model on which Flaminio was injured, Japanese Honda had decided that weave was the greater danger because it occurs at high speeds and because the Gold Wing model—what motorcycle buffs call a "hog"— was designed for high speeds. The feasibility, as distinct from the net advantages, of reducing the danger of wobble was not in issue. As for the second exception, if the defendants had testified that they would

never have thickened the struts on the Gold Wing the blueprints would have been impeaching. But the defendants offered no such testimony. Although any evidence of subsequent remedial measures might be thought to contradict and so in a sense impeach a defendant's testimony that he was using due care at the time of the accident, if this counted as "impeachment" the exception would swallow the rule.

The passage from *Flaminio* explains that defendants who merely contend that they made what they thought was the best decision at the time, do not trigger the admissibility of subsequent remedial measures. This is consistent with the Advisory Committee Notes' statement that Rule 407 "rejects the notion that 'because the world gets wiser as it gets older, therefore it was foolish before.'"

But defendants sometimes go further in their claims to have acted reasonably, or so courts rule. For example, in the next excerpt a plaintiff who was assaulted while staying in a hotel, sued the hotel operators for failing to provide reasonably safe lodging. The Eighth Circuit considered whether the plaintiff should have been able to introduce evidence that the hotel subsequently installed peepholes in its room doors.

ANDERSON v. MALLOY
700 F.2d 1208 (8th Cir. 1983)

.... The plaintiffs assert on appeal that the defendants controverted the feasibility of the use of peep holes and safety chains. Thus, the plaintiffs argue that the evidence comes within the exception of rule 407. Although the trial court held to the contrary, we find that the defendants did affirmatively controvert the feasibility of the chain locks and peep holes. We conclude that the trial court committed a prejudicial abuse of discretion when it excluded the evidence.

The first witness called by the plaintiffs was the defendant, Malloy, one of the owners of the motel. Malloy was asked by the plaintiffs' counsel about the security measures taken by the defendants since they purchased the motel in 1974, but he was not asked about the absence of peep holes or chain locks on the doors. On cross-examination defense counsel opened up the issue in the following exchange:

Q. We've already talked about the additional lighting that was installed. Did [the village police chief] indicate to you anything about putting these peepholes, as they are called, in the solid core doors?

A. He felt like we had six-foot picture windows right next to the door. If we'd put peepholes in, it would be false security.

Q. Did you follow the officer's recommendation in that regard?

A. Yes. We did not put the peepholes in at that time.

Q. Did he indicate to you anything about these chains you see on doors on occasion?

A. He felt like they were unnecessary, also. False security.

On redirect, in rebuttal, the plaintiffs' counsel then asked:

Do I understand, [the police chief] indicated to you that it wouldn't be feasible to put in peepholes and chain guards on the front doors?

Mr. Malloy replied:

A. At that time he felt like the picture windows were adequate for— that the peephole would be sort of a false security, because they could look out these picture windows and see the door, the step there.

Whether something is feasible relates not only to actual possibility of operation, and its cost and convenience, but also to its ultimate utility and success in its intended performance. That is to say, "feasible" means not only "possible," but also means "capable of being ... utilized, or dealt with successfully." Webster's Third New International Dictionary. See also American Airlines v. United States (5th Cir.1969) (defendant's witness had testified that an airplane altimeter in issue was "feasible and safe and that there was no reason to change it"; plaintiff allowed to show that defendant changed altimeter design after crash).

For the defendant to suggest that installation of peep holes and chain locks would provide only a false sense of security not only infers that the devices would not successfully provide security, it also infers that the devices would in fact create a lesser level of security if they were installed. With this testimony the defendants controverted the feasibility of the installation of these devices, because the defendant Malloy in effect testified that these devices were not "capable of being utilized or dealt with successfully."

PROBLEM 9-3: CHUTES

Litigation followed the death of a person operating an "Eeger Beever" wood chipper that was designed with an allegedly, dangerously-too-short infeed chute. At trial, the defendant, who was the President of the company that manufactured the machine, testified:

> "A: I've said it once and a thousand times, it's the safest length chute you could possibly put on the machine."

In fact, after the accident, the company extended the chute and now sold it at the longer length. The trial court had initially precluded the chute-lengthening evidence under Rule 407. *How should a court rule after the testimony quoted above?* See Wood v. Morbark Indus., 70 F.3d 1201 (11th Cir. 1995) ("After a careful review of the testimony, …, we are persuaded that the posture of the defense and the manner in which the evidence developed at trial required that, under Rule 407, evidence of the design change be permitted for purposes of impeachment.")

SETTLEMENT COMMUNICATIONS

Civil parties frequently try to settle litigation rather than incur the expense of trial. A potential obstacle to settlement arises if the parties cannot speak candidly about the potential for settlement due to the possibility that their comments will be introduced against them at a later trial.

RULE 408

ALPEX COMPUTER v. NINTENDO
770 F. Supp. 161 (S.D.N.Y. 1991)

KIMBA M. WOOD, District Judge.

Plaintiff Alpex Computer Corporation ("Alpex") moves for an order pursuant to Federal Rules of Evidence 408 precluding defendants Nintendo Company,

Ltd. and Nintendo of America ("Nintendo") from introducing any evidence concerning plaintiff's efforts to compromise disputed claims regarding the '555 patent and the amounts involved in those efforts to compromise. For the reasons set forth below, the court grants plaintiff's motion.

Background

This case arises from a dispute over the validity and alleged infringement of U.S. Patent No. 4,026,555 (the '555 patent), a patent that involves the earliest video games....

Although the parties disagree over exactly how to characterize the evidence Alpex seeks to preclude, the evidence falls roughly into three categories. The first category includes documents relating to Alpex's offers to license the '555 patent to a large number of companies in the video game industry. The second category includes exhibits relating to licenses granted by Alpex to seven companies "after extensive business negotiations and without any commencement of litigation." The third category includes licenses agreed to by four companies during litigation and certain documents relating to those licenses.

After receiving the right to sue for past infringement of the '555 patent from Fairchild Camera & Instrument Co., the original licensee of the patent, Alpex embarked on a program to combat what it viewed as widespread infringement of the patent. As part of this program, outside counsel for Alpex wrote letters to a number of companies in the video game industry in December 1979 notifying them of Alpex's view that they were infringing the '555 patent. The letter to Atari, one of the leaders in the video game industry at the time, is illustrative. Alpex's counsel informed Atari that "[a] number of the TV games which Atari is manufacturing and selling under the name PONG clearly infringe the '555 patent." The letter concluded with Alpex offering "to extend a non-exclusive license under its patents on a royalty basis." This notice led to "extended negotiations," and eventually a settlement between Alpex and Atari under which Atari paid for and received a non-exclusive license. Alpex's counsel sent similar letters to Mattel and Bally. As was the case with Atari, the notice to Mattel resulted in extended negotiations, a settlement, and a license. Nintendo seeks to designate as trial exhibits a variety of documents from these two negotiations, including letters between the parties describing the negotiations over the license price, news articles about the Atari settlement, Bankruptcy Court pleadings describing the Mattel settlement, and the actual license agreements.

In 1983, after the settlement with Atari and another with Magnavox, counsel for Alpex sent infringement letters to approximately 70 companies. These letters announced that Alpex had recently granted licenses under the patent to Atari and Magnavox, and stated that Alpex had "recently obtained information indicating that your company manufactures and/or sells video game cartridges and/or consoles which may infringe the subject patent." "We would prefer to resolve this matter without litigation," the letters continued, "and the purpose of this letter is to advise you that our client is prepared to extend a nonexclusive license under the '555 patent on a paid-up or royalty basis."

As a result of Alpex's efforts, as expressed in these and subsequent letters, six companies entered into license agreements with Alpex without litigation, including Mattel, Imagic, Sierra-on-Line, Texas Instrument, IBM, and Epyx. From the course of the negotiations leading to these licenses, defendants seek to designate as trial exhibits numerous documents that discuss the history of the negotiations, disputes over the size of the settlement offers, the license agreements themselves, and bankruptcy court documents describing and approving the agreements....

Discussion

I. Preclusion Under Rule 408

Alpex argues simply that the same considerations that led to the enactment of this rule, namely "the promotion of the public policy favoring the compromise and settlement of disputes," F.R.Evid. 408 advisory committee's note, compel the granting of this motion. Faced with widespread infringement of its patent over a long period of time, Alpex contends, the company followed a reasonable course of action in alerting companies it believed were infringing the patent and then attempting to negotiate a settlement or filing suit or both, as the circumstances warranted.

A. Evidence of Unsuccessful Offers to License the Patent

Nintendo counters with several different arguments. It argues first that, as to the documents relating to Alpex's licensing offers that did not result in a completed agreement, Rule 408 does not apply because no actual dispute existed at the time. Nintendo characterizes Alpex's offers to license the patent as merely the "opening gambit" in an expected negotiation and thus not protected by the privilege afforded offers to compromise. Because some of those licensing offers never received a response, Nintendo argues, no dispute could possibly have existed, and Rule 408 does not bar the admission of these offers.

Nintendo's reading of this requirement of Rule 408, however is too narrow.... Alpex's offers to license the patent were sent only to those it believed were infringing on the patent. Nintendo would read these letters, in essence, as part of an irreducible whole; without a response, the letters could not be evidence of a dispute, because two parties are necessary for a dispute to exist. But this logic assumes that communications in response to Alpex's infringement letters are required in order for this court to hold that a dispute existed between the parties. This is not the case. By infringing on the patent, or at least selling products that Alpex reasonably believed were infringing on the patent, the infringers signaled that they held an opinion at variance with Alpex's position. The dispute or difference of opinion begins with the act of infringement; Alpex's letters—those that provoked responses as well as those that did not— were offers to compromise that dispute and thus fall within the ambit of Rule 408....

***

The next case illustrates the limits of Rule 408. The case turned on whether there was a live controversy sufficient to establish jurisdiction for a suit seeking declaratory relief. The primary basis for the claim came from a letter sent during settlement negotiations.

DERMANEW v. AVON PROD.
504 F.3d 1151 (9th Cir. 2007)

.... Even discounting the allegations of oral threats, DermaNew's [complaint] establishes jurisdiction. It alleges that Avon's counsel threatened an infringement suit by letter, a copy of which we have reviewed. The letter, which promises that Avon will "initiate whatever additional proceedings or litigation is necessary to protect Avon's trademark rights," is sufficient in itself to leave DermaNew with a reasonable apprehension of an infringement suit. Avon argues that we should ignore the letter because "allegations based on settlement discussions ... are inadmissible for any purpose, including showing jurisdiction," and the letter specifically warned it was "written for settlement purposes only and shall not be admissible for any purpose in any legal proceeding." Quite simply, this argument is not an accurate statement of the law....

The text of [Rule 408] is clear: evidence from settlement negotiations may not be considered in court "when offered to prove liability for, invalidity of, or amount of a claim that was disputed as to validity or amount, or to impeach through a prior inconsistent statement or contradiction." Rule 408, however, does not bar such evidence when "offered for [other] purposes ... [such as] proving a witness's bias or prejudice." See, e.g., United States v. Technic Servs. (9th Cir.2002) (holding that evidence from settlement negotiations was admissible to prove "obstruction of the EPA's investigation"). Notwithstanding the letter's attempt to claim an absolute privilege, therefore, statements made in settlement negotiations are only excludable under the circumstances protected by the Rule.

Here, DermaNew does not rely on the threats in an attempt to prove whose trademark is valid, or to impeach Avon. Instead, it uses the threats to satisfy the jurisdictional requirements of an action for declaratory relief. This is perfectly acceptable under Rule 408. Avon's citation to Aspen Title & Escrow, Inc. v. Jeld–Wen (D.Or.1987), for the proposition that "settlement conferences in their entirety are covered under Rule 408, even when purported threats are made during those conferences," is misleading and taken out of context....

Avon makes much of the "policy behind" Rule 408, as if any recognition of statements made during settlement will ruin the "freedom of communication with respect to compromise" that the Rule protects. Yet the Rule, by its own terms, is one of limited applicability. In other words, Rule 408 is designed to ensure that parties may make offers during settlement negotiations without fear that those same offers will be used to establish liability should settlement efforts fail. When statements made during settlement are introduced for a purpose unrelated to liability, the policy underlying the Rule is not injured....

PROBLEM 9-4: MEMO TO FILE

AMI worked on a system to assist in making computer chips for another company, Alcoa.[1] During the project, AMI submitted two invoices totaling almost $500,000 for work it completed, but that had not been agreed upon as part of AMI and Alcoa's contract. An Alcoa manager, Thomas Pollak, conducted an internal investigation to evaluate the merits of AMI's request for payment of the invoices.

> "Pollak consulted with Alcoa employees Earle Lockwood and Phil Kasprzyk concerning the invoices, because both were closely involved with the project. In memoranda, Lockwood and Kasprzyk each evaluated one of the two invoices from AMI."

Here are a few portions of the memoranda:

> "AMI's claim of 6251 hours of programming time is [un]reasonable when you consider the additional 4100 hours that ALCOA personnel contributed.....
>
> Since the original purchase order for the line did not thoroughly specify the capability of the line, I feel that AMI has a legitimate claim to some software compensation. I feel that AMI should only be compensated for ⅓ of the requested amount since the line does not meet the 600 card per hour specification...."

The memoranda were only circulated internally at Alcoa. In later litigation over the invoices, the trial court applied Rule 408 to exclude the memoranda. *If you were AMI, how would you argue that this ruling was incorrect? Was the trial court right?*

---

[1] See Affiliated Mfrs. v. Aluminum Co. of Am., 56 F.3d 521 (3d Cir. 1995).

The World Before Rule 408

To fully understand Rule 408, it is helpful to understand what it replaced. Here is a brief excerpt from a book comparing the Federal Rule to a state rule based in the common-law.[1]

> The primary distinction between the two rules is that the federal rule … renders inadmissible any statement made during settlement discussions. Virginia, by contrast, provides no protection for an "express admission of liability, or an admission concerning an independent fact pertinent to a question in issue."
>
> …. The Virginia rule is best understood by tracing its origins to the general common-law rule that permitted the introduction at trial of "admissions of fact" even if made during settlement negotiations. This common-law rule is specifically disparaged in the federal advisory committee notes. See Advisory Committee Note to Fed. R. Evid. 408 (indicating departure from common-law rule's "inapplicability to admissions of fact, even though made in the course of compromise negotiations, unless hypothetical, stated to be 'without prejudice,' or so connected with the offer as to be inseparable from it"). Given this pedigree, it becomes clear that the "independent" facts referred to in the Virginia rule are simply facts stated without qualifying language (e.g., "without prejudice") and not otherwise directly tethered to the offer of compromise. Thus, a pertinent fact uttered during settlement discussions that is not carefully couched in qualifying language is potentially admissible under Rule 2:408.
>
> The Virginia rule also carves out "explicit admission[s] of liability" from its protection. The meaning here is more obscure, but best understood as simply a particularly damaging subset of "independent" fact admissions. Just as a statement of fact uttered during settlement negotiations will be admissible under the Virginia rule, so will an "explicit admission of liability" unless the admission is explicitly qualified or shown from the circumstances to be an integral part of the compromise offer itself.

---

[1] Bellin, The Virginia and Federal Rules of Evidence: A Concise Comparison (July 2015).

Virginia amended its rule in October 2015, after publication of the quoted excerpt. The amendment largely conforms the Virginia rule to the Federal Rule.

MEDICAL EXPENSES AND APOLOGIES

RULE 409

While the rationale for a rule like Rule 409 seems clear, the rule is rarely invoked in published case law. In fact, a recent search of the federal courts of appeals database for opinions invoking Rule 409 turned up only one case -- and that case merely references the rule as inapplicable in a footnote. *Why do you think that is?*

PROBLEM 9.5: PAYING FOR EXPENSES

A Business School professor bumps into a Law School professor in the hallway. The Law School professor falls to the ground in agony, yelling, "my teeth!" The B-School Professor apologizes profusely but is in a hurry. The B-School Prof later sends the L-School Prof the following email:

> "My apologies for bumping into you. I was late for a meeting. Please let me reimburse you if you should have to pay any dental bills as a result of your injuries. And I am also happy to reimburse you for lost wages should you have to take any leave as a result."

Is the note admissible in a later civil lawsuit?

STATE VARIATION: APOLOGIES

Many states have an additional restriction on the admissibility of apologies. The idea is to incentivize apologies as a means of short circuiting the litigation process. Here is a representative example from a Florida statute:

> "The portion of statements, writings, or benevolent gestures expressing sympathy or a general sense of benevolence relating to the pain, suffering, or death of a person involved in an accident and made to that person or to the family of that person shall be inadmissible as evidence in a civil action. A statement of fault, however, which is part

of, or in addition to, any of the above shall be admissible pursuant to this section."[1]

Do you think a statute like this has a significant impact on the willingness of people to offer apologies or the evidence about such apologies that would be introduced in court?

PLEA DISCUSSIONS

RULE 410

Rule 410 limits the admissibility of offers to plead guilty and statements made during plea negotiations "with an attorney for the prosecuting authority," when those plea negotiations fail and the defendant goes to trial. Rule 410 is cross-referenced in Rule 11 of the Federal Rules of Criminal Procedure. The Advisory Committee Notes to that rule apply equally to Rule 410. (Rule 11 sets forth the plea procedures for federal courts.)

Rule 410 can be viewed as the analogue to Rule 408, but for the criminal context, where there are plea negotiations rather than efforts to compromise civil claims. The rationale for Rule 408 is uncontroversial: to encourage settlement. Is it as easy to state the rationale for Rule 410? Why should the rules of evidence encourage plea bargains?

One way to understand the rule is to view it as targeting a particular subset of plea bargaining statements. While Rule 408 incentivizes both plaintiffs and civil defendants to engage in settlement talks, Rule 410's protections apply only to defendants. On its face, the rule places no limits on the use of the prosecutors' plea offers or accompanying statements, if offered by the defense. Consistent with this observation, the rule then need not be viewed as encouraging plea bargaining in the general sense. Rather, it seeks to make it possible for defendants to seek out plea bargains, and negotiate freely when the defense feels doing so is in its interest. This concern becomes particularly salient in the type of scenario where the rule most obviously comes into play. Imagine a defendant candidly admits guilt during negotiations, but then determines that the ultimately offered plea deal is unfavorable. Without Rule 410, the defendant would face great pressure to nonetheless plead guilty, since the

---

[1] Fla. Stat. Ann. § 90.4026 (2).

earlier admission of guilt would be admissible at a later trial. This narrative fits the Advisory Committee Note to Rule 410, which states:

> Limiting the exclusionary rule to use against the accused is consistent with the purpose of the rule, since the possibility of use for or against other persons will not impair the effectiveness of withdrawing pleas or the freedom of discussion which the rule is designed to foster.

If protecting *defense* efforts to engage in plea bargaining is the purpose of the rule, however, there is a complication. While the Rule prohibits only the use of plea evidence "against the defendant," some courts invoke the rule to reject defense efforts to introduce plea discussions *against the government*. Why? The rule itself bears some blame. The Advisory Committee Note to the 1980 Amendment to Fed. R. Crim Proc. 11(e)(6) -- which mirrors Rule 410 -- states:

> Unlike [the] ABA Standards Relating to Pleas of Guilty and ALI Model Code of Pre-Arraignment Procedure, rule 11(e) (6) does not also provide that the described evidence is inadmissible "in favor of" the defendant. This is not intended to suggest, however, that such evidence will inevitably be admissible in the defendant's favor. Specifically, no disapproval is intended of such decisions as United States v. Verdoorn (8th Cir. 1976), holding that the trial judge properly refused to permit the defendants to put into evidence at their trial the fact the prosecution had attempted to plea bargain with them, as "meaningful dialogue between the parties would, as a practical matter, be impossible if either party had to assume the risk that plea offers would be admissible in evidence."

One way to understand the seeming contradiction between the note and the text is to see the note quoted above as merely funneling the analysis to other rules. There is, after all, an imbalance between the relevance of a defendant's statements during plea negotiations and those of the prosecutor. The prosecutor's views on the defendants' guilt or innocence will likely be of questionable relevance, and even if relevant, constitute a type of hearsay that will be difficult to introduce into evidence. Consequently, Rule 410 may not be needed to restrict *defense* efforts to introduce a prosecutor's plea offers and statements. That evidence can readily be analyzed and excluded, if warranted, under other rules.

Rule 410 is distinct from the other rules in this Chapter in its structure. The rule excludes all evidence of a certain type -- offers to plead guilty, actual efforts to plead guilty, and accompanying statements -- with only two extremely narrow exceptions. This structure reflects the drafters' goal of eliminating any advantage that might otherwise accrue to the prosecution when defendants begin the plea bargaining process, but then change their mind and proceed to trial.

In one respect, the rule is not favorable to defendants. The rule goes out of its way to avoid being invoked by those who admit guilt to police officers, as opposed to prosecutors. As the Advisory Committee Note to the 1980 Amendment to Rule 11 states: "It thus fully protects the plea discussion process authorized by rule 11 *without attempting to deal with confrontations between suspects and law enforcement agents*, which involve problems of quite different dimensions" (emphasis added).

INSURANCE

RULE 411

Rule 411 may be the most peculiar of the policy-based relevance rules. After all, do we really need a separate evidence rule to keep out evidence of insurance offered to prove that a person acted negligently or otherwise wrongfully. *How would that kind of evidence be relevant in the first place?* In addition, the potential for unfair prejudice of such evidence is clear, suggesting that Rule 403 alone could handle the task given to Rule 411. Nevertheless, the preclusion of insurance coverage from litigation is a critical part of American law.

Rule 411 appears in the case law in a multitude of scenarios where litigants attempt to introduce the specter of insurance coverage for purposes ostensibly permitted by the rule, as in the next case.

VENTURA v. KYLE
825 F.3d 876 (8th Cir. 2016)

RILEY, Chief Judge.

…. The alleged altercation underlying this [defamation] action occurred at McP's, a bar in Coronado, California, where [Chris] Kyle and some friends were gathered in October 2006 after the funeral of a fellow [Navy] SEAL. According to Kyle,

> Scruff started running his mouth about the war and everything and anything he could connect to it. President Bush was an asshole. We were only over there [Iraq] because Bush wanted to show up his father. We were doing the wrong thing, killing men and women and children and murdering….
>
> Scruff said he hates America.

Kyle approached Scruff and asked him to "cool it." "You deserve to lose a few," Scruff replied. Kyle was "calm," but Scruff swung at him. Kyle "laid him out. Tables flew. Stuff happened. Scruff Face ended up on the floor. [Kyle] left."

On January 4, 2012, the day after his book [American Sniper] was released, Kyle was interviewed on a radio program and the television program "The O'Reilly Factor" to promote the book. During the radio interview, one of the hosts said there was a caller on the line who was saying Kyle was "in a bar fight with Jesse [Ventura]," a political commentator who formerly served as the Governor of Minnesota and in the Navy special forces. When asked if this was true, Kyle confirmed it was. During the television interview later that day, host Bill O'Reilly asked Kyle, "[Y]ou say you knocked Jesse Ventura to the floor with a punch. Now, you don't mention his name, but everybody knows who that is…. [T]hat happened?" Kyle again confirmed he "knocked him down."….

Kyle's editor described the publicity resulting from Kyle's radio interview as "priceless" in an email, and Kyle's publicist agreed the publicity response was "HOT, hot, hot!" The book was by all accounts a success. In 2014, Kyle's editor testified 1.5 million copies had been sold.

After the interviews, Ventura sued Kyle for defamation, misappropriation, and unjust enrichment on the grounds that Kyle fabricated the entire interaction with Ventura.....

The case was tried in summer 2014, almost eight years after the alleged altercation. Ventura testified he had a normal evening without any verbal or physical altercation. Three people who were with him that evening also testified they witnessed no altercation.... Ventura also introduced evidence Kyle told different versions of the story.

.... Kyle ... presented several witnesses who were at the bar that evening, who testified they either heard Ventura make the alleged comments, witnessed some type of physical altercation, or both. All of Kyle's witnesses were current or former SEALs or friends or family of SEALs....

Two witnesses from HarperCollins, American Sniper's publisher, also testified at trial. Sharyn Rosenblum, HarperCollins's publicist for Kyle's book, testified about the general process of preparing the book for publication and said she did not know who "Scruff Face" was when she read the manuscript of the book, and did not ask. She testified she did not see the "Scruff Face" subchapter as relevant to her publicity campaign for the book but she wanted to focus on "the themes of the war, military service, love of country, [and] the patriotism to serve one's country." She was "surprise[d]" when Ventura's name came up in Kyle's interview. When asked whether "the Ventura story ha[d] any impact on the success of the book," Rosenblum replied it was "a very insignificant part" and did not impact the book's success. Kyle's editor, Peter Hubbard, testified the "Scruff Face" story was not relevant to his decision to enter into a book contract with Kyle. Hubbard indicated he never suggested incorporating that subchapter into HarperCollins's marketing campaign for the book. He characterized the "mention of Jesse Ventura" as having a "negligible" effect on the success of the book.

Ventura's counsel sought to impeach the HarperCollins witnesses by questioning them about Kyle's and HarperCollins's insurance coverage to show HarperCollins had "a direct financial interest in the outcome of th[e] litigation" and the witnesses were biased in favor of Kyle. See Fed. R. Evid. 411 (permitting questioning about insurance coverage to show a witness's bias). Kyle's counsel objected to this testimony prior to its introduction, but the district court allowed it....

Ventura's counsel asked Rosenblum, "[A]re you aware that the legal fees for the estate's attorneys ... are being paid by the insurance company for HarperCollins?" and "Are you aware that HarperCollins has a direct financial interest in the outcome of this litigation because they are providing the insurance?" Rosenblum denied knowledge of HarperCollins's insurance policy. Ventura's counsel asked Hubbard if he knew about any insurance provisions in Kyle's contract with HarperCollins. He said he did not. Kyle's counsel moved for a mistrial after both inquiries. The district court denied both motions.

Then, during closing arguments, Ventura's counsel opined:

> Sharyn Rosenblum testified that she did not know her company's insurer is on the hook if you find that Jesse Ventura was defamed. Both her and Peter Hubbard also testified that they do not know that their company's insurer was paying for the defense of this lawsuit. But they are not the disinterested, unbiased witnesses they were put in front of you for you to believe. It's hard to believe that they didn't know about the insurance policy because it's right in Kyle's publishing contract. Paragraph 6.B.3. of Exhibit 82, Chris Kyle is an additional insured for defamation under the publisher's insurance policy.

.... The jury ultimately reached an 8–2 verdict on the fifth full day of deliberations. The jury found for Ventura on the defamation claim, made an advisory recommendation in Ventura's favor on the unjust-enrichment claim, and found for Kyle on the misappropriation claim. The jury awarded damages of $500,000 for defamation and recommended damages of approximately $1.35 million for unjust enrichment. The district court adopted the jury's recommendations as to the unjust-enrichment claim and accompanying damages award....

We vacate the ... award and remand ... for a new trial....

II. DISCUSSION

.... We [now] consider the insurance testimony elicited from the HarperCollins employees. At trial, Ventura's counsel asked Rosenblum whether she was aware Kyle's attorneys were "being paid by the insurance company for HarperCollins" and "HarperCollins has a direct financial interest in the outcome of this litigation because they are providing the insurance." Ventura's counsel asked Hubbard whether he was "aware of any insurance provision in [HarperCollins's] contract [with Kyle]" and inquired "you obtain insurance coverage in the case when an author may get sued for libel or defamation, correct?" These questions assumed facts never in evidence—an insurance policy purchased by HarperCollins that covered Kyle, and Kyle's attorneys were paid by the insurer. Both witnesses denied awareness of any insurance policy. Kyle's counsel objected to this questioning before Ventura's counsel's cross-examination, tried to object at the time, and moved for a mistrial after each witness testified. The district court permitted this cross-examination, by which Ventura's counsel ostensibly sought to show the HarperCollins witnesses were biased in favor of Kyle because HarperCollins and Kyle were covered by the same insurance policy.

Rule 411 of the Federal Rules of Evidence prohibits the introduction of insurance evidence to prove whether a person acted wrongfully but permits it for other purposes, such as proving a witness's bias. For example, we have permitted the use of evidence of insurance to show bias where a defense witness was employed by the defendant's insurance company.

A majority of jurisdictions addressing this issue have applied a "substantial connection" analysis in order to balance the probative value and potential prejudice.... The substantial connection analysis looks to whether a witness has "a sufficient degree of connection with the liability insurance carrier to justify allowing proof of this relationship as a means of attacking the credibility of the witness." These courts have rejected a mere "commonality of insurance" approach, holding that the likelihood of bias is so attenuated that the risk of prejudice substantially outweighs the probative value.

.... Here, there is no evidence Rosenblum and Hubbard had any economic tie or "substantial connection" to HarperCollins's insurance carrier. They were not currently or formerly employed by the insurance company, seeking employment with the insurance company, paid for their testimony by the insurance company, or holders of stock in the insurance company. There was

441

no risk Rosenblum and Hubbard might personally contribute to the payment of any judgment in favor of Ventura. Ventura even failed to show a judgment in his favor could adversely affect Rosenblum's and Hubbard's employment with HarperCollins....

[A]ny "connection" they had to the insurance carrier was far too remote to create a risk of bias strong enough to outweigh the substantial prejudice of Ventura's counsel's pointed and repeated references to unproven insurance. See Fed. R. Evid. 403....

We now consider Ventura's counsel's statement during closing argument that HarperCollins's "insurer is on the hook if you find that Jesse Ventura was defamed" and "Kyle is an additional insured for defamation under the publisher's insurance policy.".... Although relatively brief, Ventura's counsel's closing remarks about insurance "'were not minor aberrations made in passing.'" Given Ventura's repeated efforts to introduce evidence of HarperCollins's and Kyle's insurance at trial, it is difficult to see how Ventura's counsel's comments were anything other than "a deliberate strategic choice" to try to influence and enhance damages by referencing an impersonal deep-pocket insurer.

.... [T]he risk of prejudice is high. In Halladay v. Verschoor, we explained it was "utterly repugnant to a fair trial or ... a just verdict" for the jury to hear that "the damages sued for ... will be taken care of by an insurance ... company." We observed that "it has been almost universally held that the receipt of such evidence constitutes prejudicial error sufficient to require reversal."....

MISCELLANEOUS RULES

There are a series of miscellaneous evidence rules that deal with testifying witnesses and/or prior statements, but typically do not lead to the admission or exclusion of evidence. Rule 611 authorizes the trial judge to control the process of witness examinations; describes the scope of cross-examination (the "subject matter of the direct examination and matters affecting the witness's credibility"); and limits the use of "leading questions." Rules 612 and 613 include common sense disclosure requirements when a statement is used to refresh or impeach a witness. Rule 613 also suggests that the witness should generally be given a chance to explain an inconsistency. Rule 614 permits the trial judge to call witnesses to testify. Rule 615 authorizes the court to exclude witnesses from the courtroom "so that they cannot hear other witness' testimony." Finally, if one party introduces part of a "writing or recorded statement," Rule 106 permits the other party to offer other parts of that statement that "in fairness ought to be considered at the same time."

RULE 106

Consider the following excerpt from an appeal of convictions for terrorism related offenses.

UNITED STATES v. HASSAN
742 F.3d 104 (4th Cir. 2014)

[The government prosecuted Mohammad Hassan for "several offenses arising from terrorism activities." In the trial, among the evidence admitted into evidence at the prosecutor's request, and over Hassan's objections, was "a physical training video that [Hassan] posted on a website called RossTraining.com."]

.... Turning to the physical training video uploaded by Hassan to RossTraining.com, Hassan maintains that the trial court's refusal to admit his own related postings contravened the evidentiary "rule of completeness." The rule of completeness has its origins at common law, and is codified in Rule 106.... As we have explained, a trial court, in applying the rule of completeness, may allow into the record "relevant portions of [otherwise] excluded testimony which clarify or explain the part already received," in order to "prevent a party from misleading the jury" by failing to introduce the entirety of the statement or document. Nevertheless, the rule of completeness does not "render admissible ... evidence which is otherwise inadmissible under the hearsay rules." Nor does the rule of completeness "require the admission of self-serving, exculpatory statements made by a party which are being sought for admission by that same party."

The physical training video posted by Hassan on RossTraining.com depicted Hassan in a series of physical training workouts. It opened with a series of quotations on the video screen, such as "[t]here is no God but ALLAH and

Muhammad is his Messenger," the "strong Muslim is better than the weak Muslim," and "[l]et's please ALLAH and train hard." The training video concluded with the words "support our troops," which appeared on the screen above an Arabic phrase and an image of an assault rifle. After Hassan had uploaded the training video to RossTraining.com, other users of the website posted various comments and questions, some of which were critical of Hassan. Hassan responded to them with postings of his own, including an apology for any controversy his training video had caused. Hassan then posted additional statements about his beliefs and his support of those troops fighting "for the truth." In one of those subsequent postings, Hassan said that he "do[es] not support terrorists." Hassan's defense lawyer thus sought to introduce into evidence—under the rule of completeness—the follow-up statements posted by Hassan. The court, however, sustained the hearsay objection interposed by the prosecution and excluded those statements.

Hassan's excluded statements, though possibly exculpatory, do not fall within any hearsay exception that would authorize their admission into evidence. Nor was the jury likely to have been confused or misled by their exclusion. The court simply ruled that Hassan's follow-up postings on RossTraining.com could not be used to establish the truth of any matter asserted—specifically, to show that Hassan did not support terrorists. That ruling was not an abuse of the court's discretion.

***

The *Hassan* court's statement that the rule of completeness does not "render admissible ... evidence which is otherwise inadmissible under the hearsay rules" is not followed by all courts. Some courts, as in the following excerpt from United States v. Sutton (D.C. Cir. 1986), take the opposite approach:

> Rule 106 can adequately fulfill its function only by permitting the admission of some otherwise inadmissible evidence when the court finds in fairness that the proffered evidence should be considered contemporaneously. A contrary construction raises the specter of distorted and misleading trials, and creates difficulties for both litigants and the trial court.

Chapter 10

PRIVILEGES

The drafters of the Federal Rules of Evidence included a series of rules on privileges. Here is a list of the rules, with the drafter's labels:

- Attorney-Client Privilege: Rule 503
- Psychotherapist-Patient Privilege: Rule 504
- Husband-Wife Privilege: Rule 505
- Communications to Clergymen: Rule 506
- Political Vote: Rule 507
- Trade Secrets: Rule 508
- Secrets of State: Rule 509
- Identity of Informer: Rule 510

Congress rejected these rules. In their place, Congress adopted Rule 501, a generic privilege rule that leaves the complicated task of determining federal privilege rules to the courts.

RULE 501

TRAMMEL v. UNITED STATES
445 U.S. 40 (1980)

Chief Justice BURGER delivered the opinion of the Court.

…. On March 10, 1976, petitioner Otis Trammel was indicted with two others, Edwin Lee Roberts and Joseph Freeman, for importing heroin into the United States from Thailand and the Philippine Islands and for conspiracy to import heroin. The indictment also named six unindicted co-conspirators, including petitioner's wife Elizabeth Ann Trammel.

…. Prior to trial on this indictment, petitioner … advised the court that the Government intended to call his wife as an adverse witness and asserted his claim to a privilege to prevent her from testifying against him. At a hearing on the motion, Mrs. Trammel was called as a Government witness under a grant of use immunity. She testified that she and petitioner were married in May 1975 and that they remained married. She explained that her cooperation with the Government was based on assurances that she would be given lenient treatment. She then described, in considerable detail, her role and that of her husband in the heroin distribution conspiracy.

After hearing this testimony, the District Court ruled that Mrs. Trammel could testify in support of the Government's case to any act she observed during the marriage and to any communication "made in the presence of a third person"; however, confidential communications between petitioner and his wife were held to be privileged and inadmissible....

At trial, Elizabeth Trammel testified within the limits of the court's pretrial ruling; her testimony, as the Government concedes, constituted virtually its entire case against petitioner. He was found guilty on both the substantive and conspiracy charges and sentenced to an indeterminate term of years pursuant to the Federal Youth Corrections Act.

II

The privilege claimed by petitioner has ancient roots. Writing in 1628, Lord Coke observed that "it hath beene resolved by the Justices that a wife cannot be produced either against or for her husband."....

Despite its medieval origins, this rule of spousal disqualification remained intact in most common-law jurisdictions well into the 19th century....

The modern justification for this privilege against adverse spousal testimony is its perceived role in fostering the harmony and sanctity of the marriage relationship. Notwithstanding this benign purpose, the rule was sharply criticized.... In its place, Wigmore and others suggested a privilege protecting only private marital communications, modeled on the privilege between priest and penitent, attorney and client, and physician and patient....

In Hawkins v. United States (1958), this Court considered the continued vitality of the privilege against adverse spousal testimony in the federal courts. There the District Court had permitted petitioner's wife, over his objection, to testify against him. With one questioning concurring opinion, the Court held the wife's testimony inadmissible; it took note of the critical comments that the common-law rule had engendered, but chose not to abandon it....

Hawkins, then, left the federal privilege for adverse spousal testimony where it found it, continuing "a rule which bars the testimony of one spouse against the other unless both consent."....

III

A

The Federal Rules of Evidence acknowledge the authority of the federal courts to continue the evolutionary development of testimonial privileges in federal criminal trials "governed by the principles of the common law as they may be interpreted . . . in the light of reason and experience." Fed.Rule Evid. 501. The general mandate of Rule 501 was substituted by the Congress for a set of privilege rules drafted by the Judicial Conference Advisory Committee on Rules of Evidence and approved by the Judicial Conference of the United States and by this Court. That proposal defined nine specific privileges, including a husband-wife privilege which would have codified the Hawkins rule and eliminated the privilege for confidential marital communications. See proposed Fed.Rule Evid. 505. In rejecting the proposed Rules and enacting Rule 501, Congress manifested an affirmative intention not to freeze the law of privilege. Its purpose rather was to "provide the courts with the flexibility to develop rules of privilege on a case-by-case basis," and to leave the door open to change.

Although Rule 501 confirms the authority of the federal courts to reconsider the continued validity of the Hawkins rule, the long history of the privilege suggests that it ought not to be casually cast aside. That the privilege is one affecting marriage, home, and family relationships—already subject to much erosion in our day—also counsels caution. At the same time, we cannot escape the reality that the law on occasion adheres to doctrinal concepts long after the reasons which gave them birth have disappeared and after experience suggest the need for change....

B

Since 1958, when Hawkins was decided, support for the privilege against adverse spousal testimony has been eroded further. Thirty-one jurisdictions, including Alaska and Hawaii, then allowed an accused a privilege to prevent adverse spousal testimony. The number has now declined to 24.... The trend in state law toward divesting the accused of the privilege to bar adverse spousal testimony has special relevance because the laws of marriage and domestic relations are concerns traditionally reserved to the states....

C

Testimonial exclusionary rules and privileges contravene the fundamental principle that "'the public . . . has a right to every man's evidence.'" As such, they must be strictly construed and accepted "only to the very limited extent that permitting a refusal to testify or excluding relevant evidence has a public good transcending the normally predominant principle of utilizing all rational means for ascertaining truth." Here we must decide whether the privilege against adverse spousal testimony promotes sufficiently important interests to outweigh the need for probative evidence in the administration of criminal justice.

It is essential to remember that the Hawkins privilege is not needed to protect information privately disclosed between husband and wife in the confidence of the marital relationship—once described by this Court as "the best solace of human existence." Those confidences are privileged under the independent rule protecting confidential marital communications. The Hawkins privilege is invoked, not to exclude private marital communications, but rather to exclude evidence of criminal acts and of communications made in the presence of third persons.

No other testimonial privilege sweeps so broadly. The privileges between priest and penitent, attorney and client, and physician and patient limit protection to private communications. These privileges are rooted in the imperative need for confidence and trust. The priest-penitent privilege recognizes the human need to disclose to a spiritual counselor, in total and absolute confidence, what are believed to be flawed acts or thoughts and to receive priestly consolation and guidance in return. The lawyer-client privilege rests on the need for the advocate and counselor to know all that relates to the client's reasons for seeking representation if the professional mission is to be carried out. Similarly, the physician must know all that a patient can articulate in order to identify and to treat disease; barriers to full disclosure would impair diagnosis and treatment.

The Hawkins rule stands in marked contrast to these three privileges. Its protection is not limited to confidential communications; rather it permits an accused to exclude all adverse spousal testimony. As Jeremy Bentham observed more than a century and a half ago, such a privilege goes far beyond making "every man's house his castle," and permits a person to convert his house into "a den of thieves." It "secures, to every man, one safe and unquestionable and ever ready accomplice for every imaginable crime."…

IV

Our consideration of the foundations for the privilege and its history satisfy us that "reason and experience" no longer justify so sweeping a rule as that found acceptable by the Court in Hawkins. Accordingly, we conclude that the existing rule should be modified so that the witness-spouse alone has a privilege to refuse to testify adversely; the witness may be neither compelled to testify nor foreclosed from testifying. This modification—vesting the privilege in the witness-spouse—furthers the important public interest in marital harmony without unduly burdening legitimate law enforcement needs.

Here, petitioner's spouse chose to testify against him. That she did so after a grant of immunity and assurances of lenient treatment does not render her testimony involuntary. Accordingly, the District Court and the Court of Appeals were correct in rejecting petitioner's claim of privilege, and the judgment of the Court of Appeals is affirmed.

JAFFEE v. REDMOND
518 U.S. 1 (1996)

Justice STEVENS delivered the opinion of the Court.

After a traumatic incident in which she shot and killed a man, a police officer received extensive counseling from a licensed clinical social worker. The question we address is whether statements the officer made to her therapist during the counseling sessions are protected from compelled disclosure in a federal civil action brought by the family of the deceased. Stated otherwise, the question is whether it is appropriate for federal courts to recognize a "psychotherapist privilege" under Rule 501 of the Federal Rules of Evidence.

I

Petitioner is the administrator of the estate of Ricky Allen. Respondents are Mary Lu Redmond, a former police officer, and the Village of Hoffman Estates, Illinois, her employer during the time that she served on the police force. Petitioner commenced this action against respondents after Redmond shot and killed Allen while on patrol duty....

Petitioner filed suit in Federal District Court alleging that Redmond had violated Allen's constitutional rights by using excessive force .... The complaint sought damages under 42 U.S.C. § 1983, and the Illinois wrongful-death statute. At trial, petitioner presented testimony from members of Allen's family that conflicted with Redmond's version of the incident in several important respects....

During pretrial discovery petitioner learned that after the shooting Redmond had participated in about 50 counseling sessions with Karen Beyer, a clinical social worker licensed by the State of Illinois and employed at that time by the Village of Hoffman Estates. Petitioner sought access to Beyer's notes concerning the sessions for use in cross-examining Redmond. Respondents vigorously resisted the discovery. They asserted that the contents of the conversations between Beyer and Redmond were protected against involuntary disclosure by a psychotherapist-patient privilege. The district judge rejected this argument. Neither Beyer nor Redmond, however, complied with his order to disclose the contents of Beyer's notes. At depositions and on the witness stand both either refused to answer certain questions or professed an inability to recall details of their conversations.

In his instructions at the end of the trial, the judge advised the jury that the refusal to turn over Beyer's notes had no "legal justification" and that the jury could therefore presume that the contents of the notes would have been unfavorable to respondents. The jury awarded petitioner $45,000 on the federal claim and $500,000 on her state-law claim.....

II

Rule 501 of the Federal Rules of Evidence authorizes federal courts to define new privileges by interpreting "common law principles ... in the light of reason and experience."....

The common-law principles underlying the recognition of testimonial privileges can be stated simply. "'For more than three centuries it has now been recognized as a fundamental maxim that the public ... has a right to every man's evidence. When we come to examine the various claims of exemption, we start with the primary assumption that there is a general duty to give what testimony one is capable of giving, and that any exemptions which may exist are distinctly exceptional, being so many derogations from a positive general rule.'" Exceptions from the general rule disfavoring testimonial privileges may be justified, however, by a "'public good transcending the normally predominant principle of utilizing all rational means for ascertaining truth.'"

Guided by these principles, the question we address today is whether a privilege protecting confidential communications between a psychotherapist and her patient "promotes sufficiently important interests to outweigh the need for probative evidence...." Both "reason and experience" persuade us that it does.

III

Like the spousal and attorney-client privileges, the psychotherapist-patient privilege is "rooted in the imperative need for confidence and trust." Treatment by a physician for physical ailments can often proceed successfully on the basis of a physical examination, objective information supplied by the patient, and the results of diagnostic tests. Effective psychotherapy, by contrast, depends upon an atmosphere of confidence and trust in which the patient is willing to make a frank and complete disclosure of facts, emotions, memories, and fears. Because of the sensitive nature of the problems for which individuals consult psychotherapists, disclosure of confidential communications made during counseling sessions may cause embarrassment or disgrace. For this reason, the mere possibility of disclosure may impede development of the confidential relationship necessary for successful treatment..... By protecting confidential communications between a psychotherapist and her patient from involuntary disclosure, the proposed privilege thus serves important private interests.

Our cases make clear that an asserted privilege must also "serv[e] public ends."…. The psychotherapist privilege serves the public interest by facilitating the provision of appropriate treatment for individuals suffering the effects of a mental or emotional problem. The mental health of our citizenry, no less than its physical health, is a public good of transcendent importance.

In contrast to the significant public and private interests supporting recognition of the privilege, the likely evidentiary benefit that would result from the denial of the privilege is modest. If the privilege were rejected, confidential conversations between psychotherapists and their patients would surely be chilled, particularly when it is obvious that the circumstances that give rise to the need for treatment will probably result in litigation. Without a privilege, much of the desirable evidence to which litigants such as petitioner seek access—for example, admissions against interest by a party—is unlikely to come into being. This unspoken "evidence" will therefore serve no greater truth-seeking function than if it had been spoken and privileged.

That it is appropriate for the federal courts to recognize a psychotherapist privilege under Rule 501 is confirmed by the fact that all 50 States and the District of Columbia have enacted into law some form of psychotherapist privilege…. In addition, given the importance of the patient's understanding that her communications with her therapist will not be publicly disclosed, any State's promise of confidentiality would have little value if the patient were aware that the privilege would not be honored in a federal court. Denial of the federal privilege therefore would frustrate the purposes of the state legislation that was enacted to foster these confidential communications….

The uniform judgment of the States is reinforced by the fact that a psychotherapist privilege was among the nine specific privileges recommended by the Advisory Committee in its proposed privilege rules….

Because we agree with the judgment of the state legislatures and the Advisory Committee that a psychotherapist-patient privilege will serve a "public good transcending the normally predominant principle of utilizing all rational means for ascertaining truth," we hold that confidential communications between a licensed psychotherapist and her patients in the course of diagnosis or treatment are protected from compelled disclosure under Rule 501 of the Federal Rules of Evidence.

IV

All agree that a psychotherapist privilege covers confidential communications made to licensed psychiatrists and psychologists. We have no hesitation in concluding in this case that the federal privilege should also extend to confidential communications made to licensed social workers in the course of psychotherapy. The reasons for recognizing a privilege for treatment by psychiatrists and psychologists apply with equal force to treatment by a clinical social worker such as Karen Beyer. Today, social workers provide a significant amount of mental health treatment. Their clients often include the poor and those of modest means who could not afford the assistance of a psychiatrist or psychologist, but whose counseling sessions serve the same public goals. Perhaps in recognition of these circumstances, the vast majority of States explicitly extend a testimonial privilege to licensed social workers. We therefore agree with the Court of Appeals that "[d]rawing a distinction between the counseling provided by costly psychotherapists and the counseling provided by more readily accessible social workers serves no discernible public purpose."

We part company with the Court of Appeals on a separate point. We reject the balancing component of the privilege implemented by that court and a small number of States. Making the promise of confidentiality contingent upon a trial judge's later evaluation of the relative importance of the patient's interest in privacy and the evidentiary need for disclosure would eviscerate the effectiveness of the privilege. As we explained in Upjohn v. United States (1981), if the purpose of the privilege is to be served, the participants in the confidential conversation "must be able to predict with some degree of certainty whether particular discussions will be protected. An uncertain privilege, or one which purports to be certain but results in widely varying applications by the courts, is little better than no privilege at all."

These considerations are all that is necessary for decision of this case. A rule that authorizes the recognition of new privileges on a case-by-case basis makes it appropriate to define the details of new privileges in a like manner. Because this is the first case in which we have recognized a psychotherapist privilege, it is neither necessary nor feasible to delineate its full contours in a way that would "govern all conceivable future questions in this area."

V

The conversations between Officer Redmond and Karen Beyer and the notes taken during their counseling sessions are protected from compelled disclosure under Rule 501 of the Federal Rules of Evidence. The judgment of the Court of Appeals is affirmed.

***

The approach illustrated in the preceding cases applies to non-constitutional privilege determinations in the federal courts. One of the most commonly invoked privileges is constitutional: the Fifth Amendment privilege against compelled self-incrimination, typically covered in a Criminal Procedure course.

ATTORNEY-CLIENT PRIVILEGE

Although the rules do not specifically address attorney-client privilege, as the cases excerpted below discuss, it is well established in the federal and state case law. The federal rules also include Rule 502, which is intended to limit the impact of waivers of attorney-client and work product privileges. A caveat: the case law surrounding attorney-client privilege is vast, what follows is only an introduction to the topic.

As a general rule, a client has a privilege to prevent disclosure of any confidential communications that the client makes to an attorney for the purposes of obtaining legal advice. The precise borders of the privilege vary by jurisdiction and circumstances. The next two cases illustrate some of the Supreme Court's efforts to define those borders for the federal courts under Rule 501.

SWIDLER & BERLIN v. UNITED STATES
524 U.S. 399 (1998)

Chief Justice REHNQUIST delivered the opinion of the Court.

.... This dispute arises out of an investigation conducted by the Office of the Independent Counsel into whether various individuals made false statements, obstructed justice, or committed other crimes during investigations of the 1993 dismissal of employees from the White House Travel Office. Vincent W.

Foster, Jr., was Deputy White House Counsel when the firings occurred. In July 1993, Foster met with petitioner [James] Hamilton, an attorney at petitioner Swidler & Berlin, to seek legal representation concerning possible congressional or other investigations of the firings. During a 2–hour meeting, Hamilton took three pages of handwritten notes. One of the first entries in the notes is the word "Privileged." Nine days later, Foster committed suicide.

In December 1995, a federal grand jury, at the request of the Independent Counsel, issued subpoenas to petitioners Hamilton and Swidler & Berlin for, inter alia, Hamilton's handwritten notes of his meeting with Foster. Petitioners filed a motion to quash, arguing that the notes were protected by the attorney-client privilege and by the work-product privilege. The District Court, after examining the notes in camera, concluded they were protected from disclosure by both doctrines and denied enforcement of the subpoenas.

The Court of Appeals for the District of Columbia Circuit reversed[, ruling] that there is a posthumous exception to the privilege for communications whose relative importance to particular criminal litigation is substantial.... The Court of Appeals also held that the notes were not protected by the work-product privilege.... We granted certiorari and we now reverse.

The attorney-client privilege is one of the oldest recognized privileges for confidential communications. The privilege is intended to encourage "full and frank communication between attorneys and their clients and thereby promote broader public interests in the observance of law and the administration of justice." The issue presented here is the scope of that privilege; more particularly, the extent to which the privilege survives the death of the client. Our interpretation of the privilege's scope is guided by "the principles of the common law ... as interpreted by the courts ... in the light of reason and experience." Fed.Rule Evid. 501.

The Independent Counsel argues that the attorney-client privilege should not prevent disclosure of confidential communications where the client has died and the information is relevant to a criminal proceeding.

.... [W]e think there are weighty reasons that counsel in favor of posthumous application. Knowing that communications will remain confidential even after death encourages the client to communicate fully and frankly with counsel. While the fear of disclosure, and the consequent withholding of information from counsel, may be reduced if disclosure is limited to posthumous disclosure in a criminal context, it seems unreasonable to assume that it vanishes altogether. Clients may be concerned about reputation, civil liability, or possible harm to friends or family. Posthumous disclosure of such communications may be as feared as disclosure during the client's lifetime.

The Independent Counsel suggests, however, that his proposed exception would have little to no effect on the client's willingness to confide in his attorney. He reasons that only clients intending to perjure themselves will be chilled by a rule of disclosure after death, as opposed to truthful clients or those asserting their Fifth Amendment privilege. This is because for the latter group, communications disclosed by the attorney after the client's death purportedly will reveal only information that the client himself would have revealed if alive.

The Independent Counsel assumes, incorrectly we believe, that the privilege is analogous to the Fifth Amendment's protection against self-incrimination. But as suggested above, the privilege serves much broader purposes. Clients consult attorneys for a wide variety of reasons, only one of which involves possible criminal liability. Many attorneys act as counselors on personal and family matters, where, in the course of obtaining the desired advice, confidences about family members or financial problems must be revealed in order to assure sound legal advice. The same is true of owners of small businesses who may regularly consult their attorneys about a variety of problems arising in the course of the business. These confidences may not come close to any sort of admission of criminal wrongdoing, but nonetheless be matters which the client would not wish divulged.

The contention that the attorney is being required to disclose only what the client could have been required to disclose is at odds with the basis for the privilege even during the client's lifetime. In related cases, we have said that the loss of evidence admittedly caused by the privilege is justified in part by the fact that without the privilege, the client may not have made such communications in the first place. This is true of disclosure before and after the client's death. Without assurance of the privilege's posthumous application, the client may very well not have made disclosures to his attorney at all, so the loss of evidence is more apparent than real. In the case at hand, it seems quite plausible that Foster, perhaps already contemplating suicide, may not have sought legal advice from Hamilton if he had not been assured the conversation was privileged.

The Independent Counsel additionally suggests that his proposed exception would have minimal impact if confined to criminal cases, or, as the Court of Appeals suggests, if it is limited to information of substantial importance to a particular criminal case. However, there is no case authority for the proposition that the privilege applies differently in criminal and civil cases.... In any event, a client may not know at the time he discloses information to his attorney whether it will later be relevant to a civil or a criminal matter, let alone whether it will be of substantial importance. Balancing ex post the importance of the information against client interests, even limited to criminal cases, introduces substantial uncertainty into the privilege's application. For just that reason, we have rejected use of a balancing test in defining the contours of the privilege.

In a similar vein, the Independent Counsel argues that existing exceptions to the privilege, such as the crime-fraud exception and the testamentary exception, make the impact of one more exception marginal. However, these exceptions do not demonstrate that the impact of a posthumous exception would be insignificant, and there is little empirical evidence on this point. The established exceptions are consistent with the purposes of the privilege, while a posthumous exception in criminal cases appears at odds with the goals of encouraging full and frank communication and of protecting the client's interests. A "no harm in one more exception" rationale could contribute to the general erosion of the privilege, without reference to common-law principles or "reason and experience."

.... It has been generally, if not universally, accepted, for well over a century, that the attorney-client privilege survives the death of the client in a case such as this. While the arguments against the survival of the privilege are by no means frivolous, they are based in large part on speculation—thoughtful speculation, but speculation nonetheless—as to whether posthumous termination of the privilege would diminish a client's willingness to confide in an attorney. In an area where empirical information would be useful, it is scant and inconclusive.

Rule 501's direction to look to "the principles of the common law as they may be interpreted by the courts of the United States in the light of reason and experience" does not mandate that a rule, once established, should endure for all time. But here the Independent Counsel has simply not made a sufficient showing to overturn the common-law rule embodied in the prevailing caselaw. Interpreted in the light of reason and experience, that body of law requires that the attorney-client privilege prevent disclosure of the notes at issue in this case.

***

The next case discusses the well-established crime-fraud exception to the attorney-client privilege. Importantly, the crime-fraud exception only applies to a narrow subset of attorney-client communications, where "the communications with counsel were intended in some way to facilitate or to conceal … criminal activity."[1]

UNITED STATES v. ZOLIN
491 U.S. 554 (1989)

Justice BLACKMUN delivered the opinion of the Court.

This case arises out of the efforts of the Criminal Investigation Division of the Internal Revenue Service (IRS) to investigate the tax returns of L. Ron Hubbard, founder of the Church of Scientology (the Church), for the calendar years 1979 through 1983….

The second issue [in the case] concerns the testimonial privilege for attorney-client communications and, more particularly, the generally recognized exception to that privilege for communications in furtherance of future illegal conduct—the so-called "crime-fraud" exception. The specific question presented is whether the applicability of the crime-fraud exception must be established by "independent evidence" (i.e., without reference to the content of the contested communications themselves), or, alternatively, whether the applicability of that exception can be resolved by an in camera inspection of the allegedly privileged material. We reject the "independent evidence" approach and hold that the district court, under circumstances we explore

---

[1] In re Grand Jury Subpoenas Duces Tecum, 798 F.2d 32 (2d Cir. 1986).

below, and at the behest of the party opposing the claim of privilege, may conduct an in camera review of the materials in question. Because the Court of Appeals considered only "independent evidence," we vacate its judgment on this issue and remand the case for further proceedings....

III

Questions of privilege that arise in the course of the adjudication of federal rights are "governed by the principles of the common law as they may be interpreted by the courts of the United States in the light of reason and experience." Fed.Rule Evid. 501. We have recognized the attorney-client privilege under federal law, as "the oldest of the privileges for confidential communications known to the common law." Although the underlying rationale for the privilege has changed over time, courts long have viewed its central concern as one "to encourage full and frank communication between attorneys and their clients and thereby promote broader public interests in the observance of law and administration of justice." That purpose, of course, requires that clients be free to "make full disclosure to their attorneys" of past wrongdoings in order that the client may obtain "the aid of persons having knowledge of the law and skilled in its practice."

The attorney-client privilege is not without its costs. "[S]ince the privilege has the effect of withholding relevant information from the factfinder, it applies only where necessary to achieve its purpose." The attorney-client privilege must necessarily protect the confidences of wrongdoers, but the reason for that protection—the centrality of open client and attorney communication to the proper functioning of our adversary system of justice—"ceas[es] to operate at a certain point, namely, where the desired advice refers not to prior wrongdoing, but to future wrongdoing." It is the purpose of the crime-fraud exception to the attorney-client privilege to assure that the "seal of secrecy," between lawyer and client does not extend to communications "made for the purpose of getting advice for the commission of a fraud" or crime.

The District Court and the Court of Appeals found that the tapes at issue in this case recorded attorney-client communications and that the privilege had not been waived when the tapes were inadvertently given to [a member of the church, Gerald] Armstrong. 809 F.2d, at 1417 (noting that Armstrong had acquired the tapes from L. Ron Hubbard's personal secretary, who was under the mistaken impression that the tapes were blank). These findings are not at issue here. Thus, the remaining obstacle to respondents' successful assertion of the privilege is the Government's contention that the recorded attorney-client communications were made in furtherance of a future crime or fraud.

A variety of questions may arise when a party raises the crime-fraud exception. The parties to this case have not been in complete agreement as to which of these questions are presented here. In an effort to clarify the matter, we observe, first, that we need not decide the quantum of proof necessary ultimately to establish the applicability of the crime-fraud exception. Rather, we are concerned here with the type of evidence that may be used to make that ultimate showing. Within that general area of inquiry, the initial question in this case is whether a district court, at the request of the party opposing the privilege, may review the allegedly privileged communications in camera to determine whether the crime-fraud exception applies. If such in camera review is permitted, the second question we must consider is whether some threshold evidentiary showing is needed before the district court may undertake the requested review. Finally, if a threshold showing is required, we must consider the type of evidence the opposing party may use to meet it: i.e., in this case, whether the partial transcripts the IRS possessed may be used for that purpose.

A

We consider first the question whether a district court may ever honor the request of the party opposing the privilege to conduct an in camera review of allegedly privileged communications to determine whether those communications fall within the crime-fraud exception. We conclude that no express provision of the Federal Rules of Evidence bars such use of in camera review, and that it would be unwise to prohibit it in all instances as a matter of federal common law.

…. We begin our analysis by recognizing that disclosure of allegedly privileged materials to the district court for purposes of determining the merits of a claim of privilege does not have the legal effect of terminating the privilege. Indeed, this Court has approved the practice of requiring parties who seek to avoid disclosure of documents to make the documents available for in camera inspection, and the practice is well established in the federal courts. Respondents do not dispute this point: they acknowledge that they would have

460

been free to request in camera review to establish the fact that the tapes involved attorney-client communications, had they been unable to muster independent evidence to serve that purpose.

Once it is clear that in camera review does not destroy the privileged nature of the contested communications, the question of the propriety of that review turns on whether the policies underlying the privilege and its exceptions are better fostered by permitting such review or by prohibiting it. In our view, the costs of imposing an absolute bar to consideration of the communications in camera for purpose of establishing the crime-fraud exception are intolerably high.

"No matter how light the burden of proof which confronts the party claiming the exception, there are many blatant abuses of privilege which cannot be substantiated by extrinsic evidence. This is particularly true ... of ... situations in which an alleged illegal proposal is made in the context of a relationship which has an apparent legitimate end." A per se rule that the communications in question may never be considered creates, we feel, too great an impediment to the proper functioning of the adversary process. This view is consistent with current trends in the law....

B

We turn to the question whether in camera review at the behest of the party asserting the crime-fraud exception is always permissible, or, in contrast, whether the party seeking in camera review must make some threshold showing that such review is appropriate. In addressing this question, we attend to the detrimental effect, if any, of in camera review on the policies underlying the privilege and on the orderly administration of justice in our courts. We conclude that some such showing must be made.

.... A blanket rule allowing in camera review as a tool for determining the applicability of the crime-fraud exception, ..., would place the policy of protecting open and legitimate disclosure between attorneys and clients at undue risk. There is also reason to be concerned about the possible due process implications of routine use of in camera proceedings. Finally, we cannot ignore the burdens in camera review places upon the district courts, which may well be required to evaluate large evidentiary records without open adversarial guidance by the parties.

.... In fashioning a standard for determining when in camera review is appropriate, we begin with the observation that "in camera inspection ... is a smaller intrusion upon the confidentiality of the attorney-client relationship than is public disclosure." We therefore conclude that a lesser evidentiary showing is needed to trigger in camera review than is required ultimately to overcome the privilege. The threshold we set, in other words, need not be a stringent one.

We think that the following standard strikes the correct balance. Before engaging in in camera review to determine the applicability of the crime-fraud exception, "the judge should require a showing of a factual basis adequate to support a good faith belief by a reasonable person," that in camera review of the materials may reveal evidence to establish the claim that the crime-fraud exception applies.

.... D

In sum, ... [w]e hold that in camera review may be used to determine whether allegedly privileged attorney-client communications fall within the crime-fraud exception. We further hold, however, that before a district court may engage in in camera review at the request of the party opposing the privilege, that party must present evidence sufficient to support a reasonable belief that in camera review may yield evidence that establishes the exception's applicability. Finally, we hold that the threshold showing to obtain in camera review may be met by using any relevant evidence, lawfully obtained, that has not been adjudicated to be privileged....

Made in the USA
Middletown, DE
13 August 2020